PROLOG PROGRAMMING IN DEPTH

Michael A. Covington
The University of Georgia
Athens, Georgia

Donald Nute
The University of Georgia
Athens, Georgia

André Vellino
Nortel Technologies
Ottawa, Ontario, Canada

 Prentice Hall, Upper Saddle River, New Jersey 07458

Library of Congress Cataloging-in-Publication Data

Covington, Michael A.
   Prolog programming in depth/Michael A. Covington, Donald Nute,
Andre' Vellino.
      p.   cm.
   Includes bibliographical references and index.
   ISBN 0-13-138645-X
      1. Prolog (Computer program language). I. Nute, Donald, 1947-   .
II. Vellino, Andre'. III. Title.
QA76.73.P76C68 1997
005.13' 3--dc20   96-1642
                                                      CIP

Acquisitions editor: **Marcia Horton**
Production editor: **Sharyn Vitrano**
Managing editor: **Bayani Mendoza de Leon**
Cover designer: **Bruce Kenselaar**
Director of production and manufacturing: **David W. Riccardi**
Manufacturing buyer: **Donna Sullivan**
Editorial assistant: **Delores Mars**

© 1997 by Prentice-Hall, Inc.
Simon & Schuster/A Viacom Company
Upper Saddle River, NJ 07458

The author and publisher of this book have used their best efforts in preparing this book. These efforts include the development, research, and testing of the theories and programs to determine their effectiveness. The author and publisher make no warranty of any kind, expressed or implied, with regard to these programs or the documentation contained in this book. The author and publisher shall not be liable in any event for incidental or consequential damages in connection with, or arising out of, the furnishing, performance, or use of these programs.

Printed in the United States of America

10 9 8 7 6 5 4 3 2 1

ISBN 0-13-138645-X

Prentice-Hall International (UK) Limited, *London*
Prentice-Hall of Australia Pty. Limited, *Sydney*
Prentice-Hall Canada Inc., *Toronto*
Prentice-Hall Hispanoamericana, S.A., *Mexico*
Prentice-Hall of India Private Limited, *New Delhi*
Prentice-Hall of Japan, Inc., *Tokyo*
Simon & Schuster Asia Pte. Ltd., *Singapore*
Editora Prentice-Hall do Brasil, Ltda., *Rio de Janeiro*

Contents

II Artificial Intelligence Applications

Preface

Prolog is an up-and-coming computer language. It has taken its place alongside Lisp in artificial intelligence research, and industry has adopted it widely for knowledge-based systems.

In this book, we emphasize practical Prolog programming, not just theory. We present several ready-to-run expert system shells, as well as routines for sorting, searching, natural language processing, and even numerical equation solving.

We also emphasize interoperability with other software. For example, Chapter 5 presents techniques for reading Lotus spreadsheets and other special file formats from within a Prolog program.

There is now an official ISO standard for the Prolog language, and this book follows it while retaining compatibility with earlier implementations. We summarize the ISO Prolog standard in Appendix A. It is essentially what has been called "Edinburgh" Prolog. Our programs have been tested under Quintus Prolog, Arity Prolog, ALS Prolog, LPA Prolog, and a number of other commercial implementations, as well as freeware Prologs from ESL and SWI. (We do not cover Turbo [PDC] Prolog, nor Colmerauer's Prolog II and III, which are distinctly different languages.)

An earlier version of this book was published by Scott, Foresman in 1987. Since then, we have used the book in our own courses every year, and the present version reflects numerous refinements based on actual classroom experience. We want to thank all our students and colleagues who made suggestions, especially Don Potter, Harold Dale, Judy Guinan, Stephen McSweeney, Xun Shao, Joerg Zeppen, Joerg Grau, Jason Prickett, Ron Rouhani, Ningyu Chen, Feng Chen, Jon Hamlin, and Mario Nakazawa. We thank Melody Covington for her diligent work with the typesetting.

When necessary, Chapter 7 can be skipped since the remainder of the book does not rely on it. Those who are not preparing for work in the software industry may take Chapter 5 somewhat lightly or skip it altogether. A Prolog language course for experienced AI programmers should cover Chapters 1–7 and 12 but may place less emphasis on the basic AI topics in Chapters 8–11.

The programs and data files from this book are available by anonymous FTP from `ai.uga.edu`. From the same FTP site you can also obtain freeware Prolog compilers and demonstrations of commercial products.

We are always interested in hearing from readers who have questions or suggestions for improvement.

Michael A. Covington
Donald Nute
The University of Georgia

André Vellino
Nortel Technologies

Part I

The Prolog Language

Chapter 1

Introducing Prolog

1.1. THE IDEA OF PROLOG

Until recently, programming a computer meant giving it a list of things to do, step by step, in order to solve a problem. In Prolog, this is no longer the case. A Prolog program can consist of a set of facts together with a set of conditions that the solution must satisfy; the computer can figure out for itself how to deduce the solution from the facts given.

This is called LOGIC PROGRAMMING. Prolog is based on formal logic in the same way that FORTRAN, BASIC, and similar languages are based on arithmetic and simple algebra. Prolog solves problems by applying techniques originally developed to prove theorems in logic.

Prolog is a very versatile language. We want to emphasize throughout this book that *Prolog can implement all kinds of algorithms, not just those for which it was specially designed.* Using Prolog does not tie you to any specific algorithm, flow of control, or file format. That is, Prolog is no *less* powerful than Pascal, C, or C++; in many respects it is *more* powerful. Whether Prolog is the best language for your purposes will depend on the kind of job you want it to do, and we will do our best to equip you to judge for yourself.

Prolog was invented by Alain Colmerauer and his colleagues at the University of Aix-Marseille, in Marseilles, France, in 1972. The name stands for *programming in logic*. Today Prolog is used mainly for artificial intelligence applications, especially automated reasoning systems. Prolog was the language chosen for the Fifth Generation Project, the billion-dollar program initiated by the Japanese government

1

in 1982 to create a new generation of knowledge-based computers. Commercially, Prolog is often used in expert systems, automated helpdesks, intelligent databases, and natural language processing programs.

Prolog has much in common with Lisp, the language traditionally used for artificial intelligence research. Both languages make it easy to perform complex computations on complex data, and both have the power to express algorithms elegantly. Both Lisp and Prolog allocate memory dynamically, so that the programmer does not have to declare the size of data structures before creating them. Both languages allow the program to examine and modify itself; thus, a program can "learn" from information obtained at run time.

The main difference is that Prolog has an automated reasoning procedure — an INFERENCE ENGINE — built into it, while Lisp does not. As a result, programs that perform logical reasoning are much easier to write in Prolog than in Lisp. If the built-in inference engine is not suitable for a particular problem, the Prolog programmer can usually use part of the built-in mechanism while rewriting the rest. In Lisp, on the other hand, if an inference engine is needed, the programmer must supply it.

Is Prolog "object-oriented"? Not exactly. Prolog is a different, newer, and more versatile solution to the problem that object orientation was designed to solve. It is quite possible to organize a Prolog program in an object-oriented way, but in Prolog, that's not the only option available to you. Prolog lets you talk about properties and relations directly, rather than approaching them indirectly through an inheritance mechanism.

1.2. HOW PROLOG WORKS

Prolog derives its power from a PROCEDURAL INTERPRETATION OF LOGIC — that is, it represents knowledge in terms of procedure definitions, and reasoning becomes a simple process of calling the right procedures. To see how this works, consider the following two pieces of information:

[1]   For any **x**, if **x** is in Georgia, then **x** is in the United States.
[2]   Atlanta is in Georgia.

We will call a collection of information such as this a KNOWLEDGE BASE. We will call item [1] a RULE because it enables us to infer one piece of information from another, and we will call item [2] a FACT because it does not depend on any other information. Note that a rule contains an "if" and a fact does not. Facts and rules are the two types of CLAUSES.

A fact need not be a true statement about the real world; if you said Minneapolis was in Florida, Prolog would believe you. Facts are sometimes called GROUND CLAUSES because they are the basis from which other information is inferred.

Suppose we want to know whether Atlanta is in the United States. Clearly, [1] and [2] can be chained together to answer this question, but how should this chaining be implemented on a computer? The key is to express [1] and [2] as definitions of procedures:

[1']   To prove that X is in the United States, prove that X is in Georgia.

[2']   To prove that Atlanta is in Georgia, do nothing.

We ask our question by issuing the instruction:

Prove that Atlanta is in the United States.

This calls procedure [1'], which in turn calls procedure [2'], which returns the answer "yes."

Prolog has its own notation for representing knowledge. Our sample knowledge base can be represented in Prolog as follows:

```
in_united_states(X) :- in_georgia(X).

in_georgia(atlanta).
```

Here `in_georgia` and `in_united_states` are PREDICATES — that is, they say things about individuals. A predicate can take any fixed number of ARGUMENTS (parameters); for example,

```
female(sharon).
```

might mean "Sharon is female," and

```
mother(melody,sharon).
```

might mean "Melody is the mother of Sharon." A predicate that takes N arguments (for any number N) is called an N-PLACE PREDICATE; thus we say that `in_georgia`, `in_united_states`, and `female` are ONE-PLACE PREDICATES, while `mother` is a TWO-PLACE PREDICATE. A one-place predicate describes a PROPERTY of one individual; a two-place predicate describes a RELATION between two individuals.

The number of arguments that a predicate takes is called its ARITY (from terms like *unary, binary, ternary,* and the like). Two distinct predicates can have the same name if they have different arities; thus you might have both `mother(melody)`, meaning Melody is a mother, and `mother(melody,sharon)`, meaning Melody is the mother of Sharon. We will avoid this practice because it can lead to confusion.

In some contexts a predicate is identified by giving its name, a slash, and its arity; thus we can refer to the two predicates just mentioned as `mother/1` and `mother/2`.

Exercise 1.2.1

Give an example, in Prolog, of a fact, a rule, a clause, a one-place predicate, and a predicate of arity 2.

Exercise 1.2.2

In the previous example, we represented "in Georgia" as a property of Atlanta. Write a Prolog fact that represents "in" as a relation between Atlanta and Georgia.

Exercise 1.2.3

How would you represent, in Prolog, the fact "Atlanta is at latitude 34 north and longitude 84 west"? (Hint: More than one approach is possible. Second hint: It is OK to use numbers as constants in Prolog.)

1.3. VARIETIES OF PROLOG

An important goal of this book is to teach you how to write portable Prolog code. Accordingly, we will stick to features of the language that are the same in practically all implementations. The programs in this book were developed in Arity Prolog and ALS Prolog on IBM PCs and Quintus Prolog on Sun workstations. Most of them have also been tested in SWI Prolog, LPA Prolog, Cogent (Amzi) Prolog, and Expert Systems Limited's Public Domain Prolog-2.[1]

For many years, the de facto standard for Prolog was the language described by Clocksin and Mellish in their popular textbook, *Programming in Prolog* (1981, second edition 1984). This is essentially the language implemented on the DEC-10 by D. H. D. Warren and his colleagues in the late 1970s, and is often called "Edinburgh Prolog" or "DEC-10 Prolog." Most commercial implementations of Prolog aim to be compatible with it.

In 1995 the International Organization for Standardization (ISO) published an international standard for the Prolog language (Scowen 1995). ISO Prolog is very similar to Edinburgh Prolog but extends it in some ways. Our aim in this book is to be as compatible with the ISO standard as possible, but without using features of ISO Prolog that are not yet widely implemented. See Appendix A for more information about ISO Prolog.

Finally, we must warn you that this book is not about Turbo Prolog (PDC Prolog), nor about Colmerauer's Prolog II and Prolog III. Turbo Prolog is Prolog with data type declarations added. As a result, programs run faster but are largely unable to examine and modify themselves. Colmerauer's Prolog II and III are CONSTRAINT LOGIC PROGRAMMING languages, which means they let you put limits on the value of a variable before actually giving it a value; this makes many new techniques available. The concepts in this book are certainly relevant to Turbo (PDC) Prolog and Prolog II and III, but the details of the languages are different.

Exercise 1.3.1

If you have not done so already, familiarize yourself with the manuals for the version of Prolog that you will be using.

Exercise 1.3.2

In the Prolog that you are using, does the query '?- `help.`' do anything useful? Try it and see.

1.4. A PRACTICAL KNOWLEDGE BASE

Figure 1.1 shows a Prolog knowledge base that describes the locations of certain North American cities. It defines a single relation, called `located_in`, which relates a city to a larger geographical unit. The knowledge base consists of facts such as

---

[1]Users of ESL Public Domain Prolog-2 must select Edinburgh-compatible syntax by adding the line ':- `state(token_class,_,dec10).`' at the beginning of every program. Note that ESL Prolog-2 has nothing to do with Colmerauer's Prolog II.

```
% File GEO.PL
% Sample geographical knowledge base

/* Clause 1 */   located_in(atlanta,georgia).
/* Clause 2 */   located_in(houston,texas).
/* Clause 3 */   located_in(austin,texas).
/* Clause 4 */   located_in(toronto,ontario).
/* Clause 5 */   located_in(X,usa) :- located_in(X,georgia).
/* Clause 6 */   located_in(X,usa) :- located_in(X,texas).
/* Clause 7 */   located_in(X,canada) :- located_in(X,ontario).
/* Clause 8 */   located_in(X,north_america) :- located_in(X,usa).
/* Clause 9 */   located_in(X,north_america) :- located_in(X,canada).
```

Figure 1.1   A simple Prolog knowledge base.

"Atlanta is located in Georgia," "Houston is located in Texas," and the like, plus rules such as "X is located in the United States if X is located in Georgia."

Notice that names of individuals, as well as the predicate located_in, always begin with lowercase letters. Names that begin with capital letters are variables and can be given any value needed to carry out the computation. This knowledge base contains only one variable, called X. Any name can contain the underscore character (_).

Notice also that there are two ways to delimit comments. Anything bracketed by /* and */ is a comment; so is anything between % and the end of the line, like this:

```
/* This is a comment */
% So is this
```

Comments are ignored by the computer; we use them to add explanatory information and (in this case) to number the clauses so we can talk about them conveniently.

It is not clear whether to call this knowledge base a *program*; it contains nothing that will actually cause computation to start. Instead, the user loads the knowledge base into the computer and then starts computation by typing a QUERY, which is a question that you want the computer to answer. A query is also called a GOAL. It looks like a Prolog clause except that it is preceded by '?-' — although in most cases the Prolog implementation supplies the '?-' and you need only type the goal itself.

Unfortunately, we cannot tell you how to use Prolog on your computer because there is considerable variation from one implementation to another. In general, though, the procedure is as follows. First use a text editor to create a file of clauses such as GEO.PL in Figure 1. Then get into the Prolog interpreter and type the special query:

```
?- consult('geo.pl').
```

(Remember the period at the end — if you don't type it, Prolog will assume your query continues onto the next line.) Prolog replies yes

to indicate that it succeeded in loading the knowledge base.

Two important notes: First, if you want to load the same program again after escaping to an editor, use `reconsult` instead of `consult`. That way you won't get two copies of it in memory at the same time. Second, if you're using a PC, note that backslashes (\) in the file name may have to be written twice (e.g., `consult('c:\\myprog.pl')` to load C:\MYPROG.PL). This is required in the ISO standard but not in most of the MS-DOS Prologs that we have worked with.

As soon as `consult` has done its work, you can type your queries. Eventually, you'll be through using Prolog, and you can exit from the Prolog system by typing the special query

```
?- halt.
```

Most queries, however, retrieve information from the knowledge base. You can type

```
?- located_in(atlanta,georgia).
```

to ask whether Atlanta is in Georgia. Of course it is; this query matches Clause 1 exactly, so Prolog again replies "yes." Similarly, the query

```
?- located_in(atlanta,usa).
```

can be answered (or, in Prolog jargon, SOLVED or SATISFIED) by calling Clause 5 and then Clause 1, so it, too, gets a "yes." On the other hand, the query

```
?- located_in(atlanta,texas).
```

gets a "no" because the knowledge base contains no information from which the existence of an Atlanta in Texas can be deduced.

We say that a query SUCCEEDS if it gets a "yes" answer, or FAILS if it gets a "no" answer.

Besides answering yes or no to specific queries, Prolog can fill in the blanks in a query that contains variables. For example, the query

```
?- located_in(X,texas).
```

means "Give me a value of X such that `in(X,texas)` succeeds."

Here we run into another unique feature of Prolog — a single query can have multiple solutions. Both Houston and Austin are in Texas. What happens in this case is that Prolog finds one solution and then asks you whether to look for another. This continues until all alternatives are found or you stop asking for them. In some Prologs, the process looks like this:

```
?- located_in(X,texas).
X = houston
More (y/n)? y
X = austin
More (y/n)? y
no
```

The "no" at the end means there are no *more* solutions.

In Arity Prolog, the notation is more concise. After each solution, the computer displays an arrow (->). You respond by typing a semicolon (meaning look for more alternatives) or by hitting Return (meaning quit), like this:

```
?- located_in(X,texas).
X = houston -> ;
X = austin  -> ;
no
```

In Quintus Prolog and many others, there isn't even an arrow; the computer just pauses and waits for you to type a semicolon and then hit Return, or else hit Return by itself:

```
?- located_in(X,texas).
X = houston ;
X = austin  ;
no
```

Also, you'll find it hard to predict whether the computer pauses after the last solution; it depends partly on the way the user interface is written, and partly on exactly what you have queried. From here on, we will present interactions like these by printing only the solutions themselves and leaving out whatever the user had to type to get the alternatives.

Sometimes your Prolog system may not let you ask for alternatives (by typing semicolons, or whatever) even though alternative solutions do exist. There are two possible reasons. First, if your query has performed any output of its own, the Prolog system will assume that you've already printed out whatever you wanted to see, and thus that you're not going to want to search for alternatives interactively. So, for example, the query

```
?- located_in(X,texas), write(X).
```

displays only one answer even though, logically, there are alternatives. Second, if your query contains no variables, Prolog will only print "yes" once no matter how many ways of satisfying the query there actually are.

Regardless of how your Prolog system acts, here's a sure-fire way to get a list of all the cities in Texas that the knowledge base knows about:

```
?- located_in(X,texas), write(X), nl, fail.
```

The special predicate **write** causes each value of X to be written out; **nl** starts a new line after each value is written; and **fail** forces the computer to backtrack to find all solutions. We will explain how this works in Chapter 2. For now, take it on faith.

We say that the predicate **located_in** is NONDETERMINISTIC because the same question can yield more than one answer. The term "nondeterministic" does not mean that computers are unpredictable or that they have free will, but only that they can produce more than one solution to a single problem.

Another important characteristic of Prolog is that any of the arguments of a predicate can be queried. Prolog can either compute the state from the city or compute the city from the state. Thus, the query

```
?- located_in(austin,X).
```

retrieves the names of regions that contain Austin, and

```
?- located_in(X,texas).
```

retrieves the names of cities that are in Texas. We will call this feature REVERSIBILITY or INTERCHANGEABILITY OF UNKNOWNS. In many — but not all — situations, Prolog can fill in any argument of a predicate by searching the knowledge base. In Chapter 3 we will encounter some cases where this is not so.

We can even query all the arguments of a predicate at once. The query

```
?- located_in(X,Y).
```

means "What is in what?" and each answer contains values for both X and Y (Atlanta is in Georgia, Houston is in Texas, Austin is in Texas, Toronto is in Ontario, Atlanta is in the U.S.A., Houston is in the U.S.A., Austin is in the U.S.A., Toronto is in Canada, and so forth). On the other hand,

```
?- located_in(X,X).
```

means "What is in itself?" and fails — both occurrences of X have to have the same value, and there is no value of X that can successfully occur in both positions at the same time. If we were to add New York to the knowledge base, this query could succeed because the city has the same name as the state containing it.

Exercise 1.4.1

Load GEO.PL into your Prolog system and try it out. How does your Prolog system respond to each of the following queries? Give all responses if there is more than one.
```
?- located_in(austin,texas).
?- located_in(austin,georgia).
?- located_in(What,texas).
?- located_in(atlanta,What).
```

Exercise 1.4.2

Add your home town and state (or region) and country to GEO.PL and demonstrate that the modified version works correctly.

Exercise 1.4.3

How does GEO.PL respond to the query '?- located_in(texas,usa).'? Why?

Exercise 1.4.4   (for PC users only)

Does your Prolog require backslashes in file names to be written double? That is, to load C:\MYDIR\MYPROG.PL, do you have to type consult('c:\\mydir\\myprog.pl')? Try it and see.

1.5. UNIFICATION AND VARIABLE INSTANTIATION

The first step in solving any query is to match — or UNIFY — the query with a fact or with the left-hand side (the HEAD) of a rule. Unification can assign a value to a variable in order to achieve a match; we refer to this as INSTANTIATING the variable. For example, the query

```
?- located_in(austin,north_america).
```

unifies with the head of Clause 8 by instantiating X as austin. The right-hand side of Clause 8 then becomes the new goal. Thus:

```
Goal:           ?- located_in(austin,north_america).  ⊂ what are we asking here?
Clause 8:       located_in(X,north_america) :- located_in(X,usa).
Instantiation:  X = austin
New goal:       ?- located_in(austin,usa).
```

We can then unify the new query with Clause 6:

```
Goal:           ?- located_in(austin,usa).
Clause 6:       located_in(X,usa) :- located_in(X,texas).   why do we do two
Instantiation:  X = austin                                      queries?
New query:      ?- located_in(austin,texas).
```

This query matches Clause 3. Since Clause 3 does not contain an "if," no new query is generated and the process terminates successfully. If, at some point, we had had a query that would not unify with any clause, the process would terminate with failure.

   Notice that we have to instantiate X two times, once when we call Clause 8 and once again when we call Clause 6. Although called by the same name, the X in Clause 8 is not the same as the X in Clause 6. There is a general principle at work here:

Variable instantiated to NEW VALUE in each case

> *Like-named variables are not the same variable unless they occur in the same clause or the same query.*

In fact, if we were to use Clause 8 twice, the value given to X the first time would not affect the value of X the second time. Each instantiation applies only to one clause and only to one invocation of that clause. However, it does apply to all of the occurrences of that variable in that clause; when we instantiate X, all the X's in the clause take on the same value at once.

   If you've never used a language other than Prolog, you're probably thinking that this is obvious, and wondering why we made such a point of it; Prolog couldn't possibly work any other way. If you're accustomed to a conventional language, we want to make sure that you don't think of instantiation as *storing* a value in a variable. Instantiation is more like *passing a parameter*. Suppose you have a Pascal procedure such as this:

```
procedure p(x:integer);                    { This is Pascal, not Prolog! }
begin
  writeln('The answer is ',x)
end;
```

If you call this with the statement

```
p(3)
```

you are passing 3 to procedure p as a parameter. The variable x in the procedure is instantiated as 3 but only for the duration of this invocation of p. It would not be correct to think of the value 3 as being "stored" in a location called x; as soon as the procedure terminates, it is gone.

One uninstantiated variable can even be unified with another. When this happens, the two variables are said to SHARE, which means that they become alternative names for a single variable, and if one of them is subsequently given a value, the other one will have the same value at the same time. This situation is relatively uncommon, but there are programs in which it plays a crucial role. We will discuss unification and instantiation at greater length in Chapter 3.

Exercise 1.5.1

What would happen to GEO.PL if Clauses 5 and 6 were changed to the following?

```
located_in(Y,usa) :- located_in(Y,georgia).
located_in(Z,usa) :- located_in(Z,texas).   NOTHING
```

Exercise 1.5.2

Disregarding the wisdom of this section, a beginning Prolog student loads GEO.PL and has the following dialogue with the computer:

```
?- located_in(austin,X).
X = texas
?- write(X).
X is uninstantiated
```

Why didn't the computer print 'texas' the second time? Try this on your computer. What does your computer print when you try to write out an uninstantiated variable?

1.6. BACKTRACKING

If several rules can unify with a query, how does Prolog know which one to use? After all, if we unify

```
?- located_in(austin,usa).
```

with Clause 5, we generate

```
?- located_in(austin,georgia).
```

which fails. However, if we use Clause 6, we generate

```
?- located_in(austin,texas).
```

which succeeds. From the viewpoint of our query, Clause 5 is a blind alley that does not lead to a solution.

The answer is that Prolog does not know in advance which clause will succeed, but it does know how to back out of blind alleys. This process is called BACKTRACKING.

Prolog tries the rules in the order in which they are given in the knowledge base. If a rule does not lead to success, it backs up and tries another. Thus, the query '?- `located_in(austin,usa).`' will first try to unify with Clause 5 and then, when that fails, the computer will back up and try Clause 6.

A good way to conceive of backtracking is to arrange all possible paths of computation into a tree. Consider the query:

```
?- located_in(toronto,north_america).
```

Figure 1.2 shows, in tree form, all the paths that the computation might follow. We can prove that Toronto is in North America if we can prove that it is in either the U.S.A. or Canada. If we try the U.S.A., we have to try several states; fortunately, we only know about one Canadian province. Almost all of the paths are blind alleys, and only the rightmost one leads to a successful solution.

Figure 1.3 is the same diagram with arrows added to show the order in which the possibilities are tried. Whenever the computer finds that it has gone down a blind alley, it backs up to the most recent query for which there are still untried alternatives, and tries another path. Remember this principle:

Backtracking always goes back to the most recent untried alternative.

When a successful answer is found, the process stops, unless, of course, the user asks for alternatives, in which case the computer continues backtracking to look for another successful path.

This strategy of searching a tree is called DEPTH-FIRST SEARCH because it involves going as far along each path as possible before backing up and trying another path. Depth-first search is a powerful algorithm for solving almost any problem that involves trying alternative combinations. Programs based on depth-first search are easy to write in Prolog.

Note that, if we use only the features of Prolog discussed so far, any Prolog query gives the same answers regardless of the order in which the rules and facts are stated in the knowledge base. Rearranging the knowledge base affects the order in which alternative solutions are found, as well as the number of blind alleys that must be tried before finding a successful solution, but it does not affect the actual answers given. This is one of the most striking differences between Prolog and conventional programming languages.

Exercise 1.6.1

Make a diagram like Figure 1.3 showing how GEO.PL handles the query '?- `located_in(austin,north_america).`'

Exercise 1.6.2

With GEO.PL, which is faster to compute, '?- `located_in(atlanta,usa).`' or '?- `located_in(austin,usa).`'? Why?

Exercise 1.6.3

Without using the computer, predict the order in which the Prolog system will find the various solutions to the query '?- `located_in(I,usa).`' Then use the computer to verify your prediction.

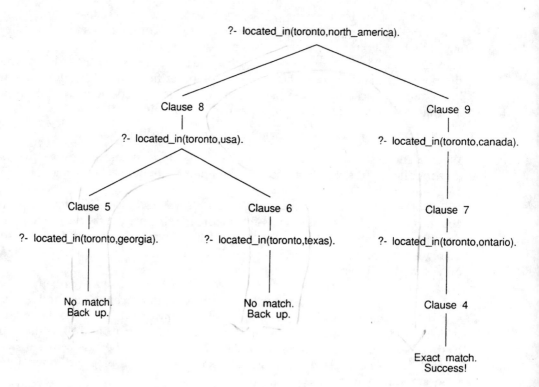

Figure 1.2   The solution to the query lies somewhere along one of these paths.

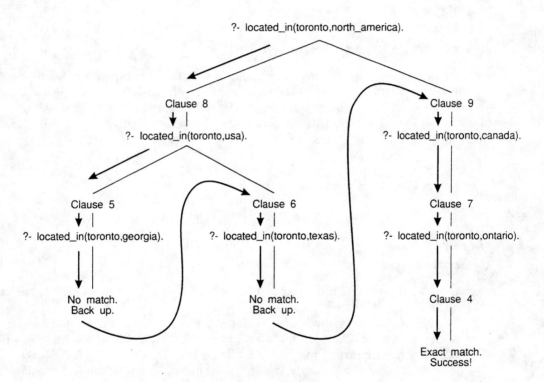

Figure 1.3   The computer searches the paths in this order.

1.7. PROLOG SYNTAX

The fundamental units of Prolog syntax are atoms, numbers, structures, and variables. We will discuss numbers and structures further in Chapter 3. Atoms, numbers, structures, and variables together are known as TERMS.

Atoms are used as names of individuals and predicates. An atom normally begins with a lowercase letter and can contain letters, digits, and the underscore mark (_). The following are examples of atoms:

```
x

georgia

ax123aBCD

abcd_x_and_y_a_long_example
```

If an atom is enclosed in single quotes, it can contain any characters whatsoever, but there are two points to note. First, a quote occurring within single quotes is normally written double. Second, in some implementations, a backslash within an atom has special significance; for details see Appendix A and your manual. Thus, the following are also atoms:

```
'Florida'

'a very long atom with blanks in it'

'12$12$'

'  a'

'don''t worry'

'back\\slashes'
```

In fact, '32' is an atom, not equal to the number 32. Even '' is an atom (the empty atom), although it is rarely used.

Atoms composed entirely of certain special characters do not have to be written between quotes; for example, '-->' (without quotes) is a legitimate atom. (We will explore this feature further in Chapter 6.) There is usually no limit on the length of an atom, with or without quotes, but check the manual for your implementation to be sure.

A structure normally consists of an atom, an opening parenthesis, one or more arguments separated by commas, and a closing parenthesis. However, an atom by itself is, strictly speaking, a structure with no arguments. All of the following are structures:

```
a(b,c,d)

located_in(atlanta,texas)

located_in(X,georgia)

mother_of(cathy,melody)

'a Weird!?! Atom'(xxx,yyy,zzz)

i_have_no_arguments
```

The atom at the beginning is called the FUNCTOR of the structure. (If some of the arguments are also structures, then the functor at the beginning of the whole thing is called the PRINCIPAL FUNCTOR.) So far we have used structures only in queries, facts, and rules. In all of these, the functor signified the name of a predicate. Functors have other uses that we will meet in Chapter 3.

Actually, even a complete rule is a structure; the rule

```
a(X)  :-  b(X).
```

could equally well be written

```
:-(a(X),b(X)).
```

or possibly, in some implementations,

```
':-'(a(X),b(X)).
```

The functor ':-' is called an INFIX OPERATOR because it is normally written between its arguments rather than in front of them. In Chapter 6 we will see how to create other functors with this special feature.

Variables begin with capital letters or the underscore mark, like these:

```
A               Result        Which_Ever
_howdy          _12345        Xx
```

A variable name can contain letters, digits, and underscores.

Prolog knowledge bases are written in free format. That is, you are free to insert spaces or begin a new line at any point, with two restrictions: You cannot break up an atom or a variable name, and you cannot put anything between a functor and the opening parenthesis that introduces its arguments. That is, in place of

```
located_in(atlanta,georgia).
```

you are welcome to write

```
located_in( atlanta,
            georgia ).
```

but not

```
located_in (at lanta,georgia).              % two syntax errors!
```

Most implementations of Prolog require all the clauses for a particular predicate to be grouped together in the file from which the clauses are loaded. That is, you can say

```
mother(melody,cathy).
mother(eleanor,melody).
father(michael,cathy).
father(jim,melody).
```

but not

```
mother(melody,cathy).                        % wrong!
father(michael,cathy).
mother(eleanor,melody).
father(jim,melody).
```

The results of violating this rule are up to the implementor. Many Prologs do not object at all. Quintus Prolog gives warning messages, but loads all the clauses properly. A few Prologs ignore some of the clauses with no warning. See Appendices A and B for more information about discontiguous sets of clauses.

Exercise 1.7.1

Identify each of these as an atom, number, structure, variable, or not a legal term:

asdfasdf   234   f(a,b)   _on

X(y,z)   in_out_   'X'(XX)   'X'

Exercise 1.7.2

What are the two syntax errors in the following?

```
located_in (at lanta,georgia).
```

Exercise 1.7.3

What does your Prolog system do if the clauses for a predicate are not grouped together? Does it give an error or warning message? Does it ignore any of the clauses? Experiment and see.

1.8. DEFINING RELATIONS

The file FAMILY.PL (Figure 1.4) contains some information about the family of one of the authors. It states facts in terms of the relations mother and father, each of which links two individuals. In each pair, we have decided to list the parent first and the son or daughter second.

FAMILY.PL can answer queries such as "Who is Cathy's mother?" —

```
?- mother(X,cathy).
X = melody
```

or "Who is Hazel the mother of?" —

```
?- mother(hazel,A).
A = michael
A = julie
```

More importantly, we can define other relations in terms of the ones already defined. For example, let's define "parent." A parent of X is the father or mother of X. Since there are two ways to be a parent, two rules are needed:

```
parent(X,Y) :- father(X,Y).
parent(X,Y) :- mother(X,Y).
```

```
% File FAMILY.PL
% Part of a family tree expressed in Prolog

% In father/2, mother/2, and parent/2,
% first arg. is parent and second arg. is child.

father(michael,cathy).
father(michael,sharon).
father(charles_gordon,michael).
father(charles_gordon,julie).
father(charles,charles_gordon).
father(jim,melody).
father(jim,crystal).
father(elmo,jim).
father(greg,stephanie).
father(greg,danielle).

mother(melody,cathy).
mother(melody,sharon).
mother(hazel,michael).
mother(hazel,julie).
mother(eleanor,melody).
mother(eleanor,crystal).
mother(crystal,stephanie).
mother(crystal,danielle).

parent(X,Y) :- father(X,Y).
parent(X,Y) :- mother(X,Y).
```

Figure 1.4   Part of a family tree in Prolog.

These two rules are alternatives. The computer will try one of them and then, if it doesn't work or if alternative solutions are requested, back up and try the other. If we ask

```
?- parent(X,michael).
```

we get X=charles_gordon, using the first definition of "parent," and then X=hazel, using the second definition.

Exercise 1.8.1

> Make a diagram like Figure 1.3 showing how Prolog answers the query
> `?- parent(X,danielle).`
> using FAMILY.PL as the knowledge base.

Exercise 1.8.2

> Make a modified copy of FAMILY.PL using information about your own family. Make sure that queries to **mother**, **father**, and **parent** are answered correctly.

1.9. CONJOINED GOALS ("AND")

We can even ask Prolog to satisfy two goals at once. Suppose we want to know the name of Michael's paternal grandfather. That is, we want to find out who Michael's father is, and then find out the name of that person's father. We can express this as:

```
?- father(F,michael), father(G,F).
F = charles_gordon   G = charles
```

In English: "Find F and G such that F is the father of Michael and G is the father of F." The computer's task is to find a single set of variable instantiations that satisfies both parts of this compound goal. It first solves **father(F,michael)**, instantiating F to **charles_gordon**, and then solves **father(G,charles_gordon)**, instantiating G to **charles**. This is consistent with what we said earlier about variable instantiations because F and G occur in the same invocation of the same clause.

We will get exactly the same answer if we state the subgoals in the opposite order:

```
?- father(G,F), father(F,michael).
F = charles_gordon   G = charles
```

In fact, this is intuitively easier to follow because G, F, and **michael** are mentioned in chronological order. However, it slows down the computation. In the first subgoal, G and F are both uninstantiated, so the computer can instantiate them by using any clause that says someone is someone's father. On the first try, it uses the very first clause in the knowledge base, which instantiates G to **michael** and F to **cathy**. Then it gets to the second subgoal and discovers that Cathy is not Michael's father, so it has to back up. Eventually, it gets to **father(charles_gordon,charles)** and can proceed.

The way we originally stated the query, there was much less backtracking because the computer had to find the father of Michael before proceeding to the second subgoal. It pays to think about the search order as well as the logical correctness of Prolog expressions. We will return to this point in Chapter 4.

We can use compound goals in rules, as in the following definition of "grandfather":

```
grandfather(G,C) :- father(F,C), father(G,F).
grandfather(G,C) :- mother(M,C), father(G,M).
```

The comma is pronounced "and" — in fact, there have been Prolog implementations that write it as an ampersand (`&`).

Exercise 1.9.1

> Add the predicates **grandfather**, **grandmother**, and **grandparent** to FAMILY.PL. (Hint: You will find **parent** useful.) Verify that your new predicates work correctly.

1.10. DISJOINT GOALS ("OR")

Prolog also provides a semicolon, meaning "or," but we do not recommend that you use it very much. The definition of **parent** in FAMILY.PL could be written as a single rule:

```
parent(X,Y) :- father(X,Y); mother(X,Y).
```

However, the normal way to express an "or" relation in Prolog is to state two rules, not one rule with a semicolon in it. The semicolon adds little or no expressive power to the language, and it looks so much like the comma that it often leads to typographical errors. In some Prologs you can use a vertical bar, '|', in place of a semicolon; this reduces the risk of misreading.

If you do use semicolons, we advocate that you use parentheses and/or distinctive indentation to make it crystal clear that they are not commas. If there are no parentheses to indicate otherwise, the semicolon has wider scope than the comma. For example,

```
f(X) :- a(X), b(X); c(X), d(X).
```

is equivalent to

```
f(X) :- (a(X), b(X)); (c(X), d(X)).
```

and means, "To satisfy `f(X)`, find an `X` that satisfies either `a(X)` and `b(X)`, or else `c(X)` and `d(X)`." The parentheses make it easier to understand. O'Keefe (1990:101) recommends that, instead, you should write:

```
f(X) :- (  a(X), b(X)
        ;  c(X), d(X)
        ).
```

to make the disjunction really prominent. In his style, the parentheses call attention to the disjunction itself, and the scope of the *and*s and *or*s is represented by rows and columns. But as a rule of thumb, we recommend that instead of mixing semicolons and commas together in a single predicate definition, you should usually break up the complex predicate into simpler ones.

Exercise 1.10.1

Go back to GEO.PL and add the predicate `eastern/1`, defined as follows: A place is eastern if it is in Georgia or in Ontario. Implement this predicate two different ways: first with a semicolon, and then without using the semicolon.

Exercise 1.10.2

Define a predicate equivalent to

`f(X) :- (a(X), b(X)); (c(X), d(X)).`

but without using semicolons. Use as many clauses as necessary.

1.11. NEGATIVE GOALS ("NOT")

The special predicate \+ is pronounced "not" or "cannot-prove" and takes any goal as its argument. (In earlier Prologs, \+ was written **not**; \+ is a typewritten representation of ⊬, which means "not provable" in formal logic.)

If *g* is any goal, then \+ *g* succeeds if *g* fails, and fails if *g* succeeds. For instance:

```
?- father(michael,cathy).
yes
?- \+ father(michael,cathy).
no
?- father(michael,melody).
no
?- \+ father(michael,melody).
yes
```

Notice that \+ does not require parentheses around its argument.

The behavior of \+ is called NEGATION AS FAILURE. In Prolog, you cannot state a negative fact ("Cathy is not Michael's father"); all you can do is conclude a negative statement if you cannot conclude the corresponding positive statement. More precisely, the computer cannot know that Cathy is not Michael's father; all it can know is that it has no proof that she *is* his father.

Rules can contain \+. For instance, "non-parent" can be defined as follows:

`non_parent(X,Y) :- \+ father(X,Y), \+ mother(X,Y).`

That is, X is a non-parent of Y if X is not the father of Y and X is also not the mother of Y.

In FAMILY.PL, the "non-parents" of Cathy are everyone except Michael and Melody. Sure enough, the following queries succeed:

```
?- non_parent(elmo,cathy).
yes
?- non_parent(sharon,cathy).
yes
?- non_parent(charles,cathy).
yes
```

and `non_parent` fails if its arguments are in fact a parent and his or her child:

```
?- non_parent(michael,cathy).
no
?- non_parent(melody,cathy).
no
```

So far, so good, but what happens if you ask about people who are not in the knowledge base at all?

```
?- non_parent(donald,achsa).
yes
```

Wrong! Actually, Donald (another of the authors of this book) *is* the father of Achsa, but FAMILY.PL doesn't know about it. Because the computer can't prove `father(donald,achsa)` nor `mother(donald,achsa)`, the `non_parent` query succeeds, giving a result that is false in the real world.

Here we see a divergence between Prolog and intuitively correct thinking. The Prolog system assumes that its knowledge base is complete (e.g., that there aren't any fathers or mothers in the world who aren't listed). This is called the CLOSED-WORLD ASSUMPTION. Under this assumption, \+ means about the same thing as "not," but without the closed-world assumption, \+ is merely a test of whether a query fails. That's why many Prolog users refuse to call \+ "not," pronouncing it "cannot-prove" or "fail-if" instead.

Note also that a query preceded by \+ never returns a value for its variables. You might think that the query

```
?- \+ father(X,Y).
```

would instantiate X and Y to two people, the first of which is not the father of the second. Not so. To solve \+ `father(X,Y)`, the computer attempts to solve `father(X,Y)` and then fails if the latter goal succeeds or succeeds if the latter goal fails. In turn, `father(X,Y)` succeeds by matching a clause in the knowledge base. Therefore, \+ `father(X,Y)` has to fail, and because it fails, it does not report variable instantiations.

As if this were not enough, the order of subgoals in a query containing \+ can affect the outcome. Let's add the fact

```
blue_eyed(cathy).
```

to the knowledge base. Now look at the results of the following queries:

```
?- blue_eyed(X),non_parent(X,Y).
X = cathy
yes
?- non_parent(X,Y),blue_eyed(X).
no
```

The first query succeeds because X gets instantiated to cathy before non_parent(X,Y) is evaluated, and non_parent(cathy,Y) succeeds because there are no clauses that list Cathy as a mother or father. But in the second query, X is uninstantiated when non_parent(X,Y) is evaluated, and non_parent(X,Y) fails as soon as it finds a clause that matches father(X,Y).

To make negation apply to a compound goal, put the compound goal in parentheses, and be sure to leave a space after the negation symbol. Here's a whimsical example:[2]

```
blue_eyed_non_grandparent(X) :-
   blue_eyed(X),
   \+ (parent(X,Y), parent(Y,Z)).
```

That is, you're a blue-eyed non-grandparent if you are blue-eyed, and you are not the parent of some person Y who is in turn the parent of some person Z.

Finally, note that \+ (with its usual Prolog meaning) can appear only in a query or on the right-hand side of a rule. It cannot appear in a fact or in the head of a rule. If you say

```
\+ father(cathy,michael).                              % wrong!
```

you are not denying that Cathy is Michael's father; you are merely redefining the built-in predicate \+, with no useful effect. Some Prolog implementations will allow this, with possibly unpleasant results, while others will display an error message saying that \+ is a built-in predicate and you cannot add clauses to it.

Exercise 1.11.1

Define non_grandparent(X,Y), which should succeed if X is not a grandparent of Y.

Exercise 1.11.2

Define young_parent(X), which should succeed if X has a child but does not have any grandchildren. Make sure it works correctly; consider the case of someone who has two children, one of whom, in turn, has a child of her own while the other one does not.

1.12. TESTING FOR EQUALITY

Now consider the problem of defining "sibling" (brother or sister). Two people are siblings if they have the same mother. (They also have the same father, but this is irrelevant because everyone has both a father and a mother — at least in *this* knowledge base.) So a first approximation is:

---

[2]Some Prologs will print a warning message that the value of Z in this clause is never put to any use. See "Anonymous Variables" (Sec. 1.13).

```
sibling(X,Y) :- mother(M,X), mother(M,Y).
```

If we put this rule into FAMILY.PL and then ask for all the pairs of siblings known to the computer, we get a surprise:

```
?- sibling(X,Y).
X = cathy     Y = cathy
X = cathy     Y = sharon
X = sharon    Y = cathy
X = sharon    Y = sharon      (etc.)
```

Cathy is not Cathy's sibling, yet Cathy definitely has the same mother as Cathy. We need to rephrase the rule: "X is a sibling of Y if M is the mother of X, and M is the mother of Y, and X is not the same as Y."

To express "not the same" we need an equality test: if X and Y are instantiated to the same value, then

```
X == Y
```

succeeds and, of course,

```
\+ X == Y
```

fails. The new rule is:

```
sibling(X,Y) :- mother(M,X), mother(M,Y), \+ X == Y.
```

With it, we get the desired result:

```
?- sibling(X,Y).
X = cathy     Y = sharon
X = sharon    Y = cathy      (etc.)
```

Wait a minute, you say. That's the same answer twice! We reply: No, it isn't. Remember that, as far as Prolog is concerned, the two conclusions `sibling(cathy,sharon)` and `sibling(sharon,cathy)` are separate pieces of knowledge. Both of them are true, so it's entirely correct to get them both.

Here's another example of equality testing. X is an *only child* if X's mother doesn't have another child different from X. In Prolog:

```
only_child(X) :- mother(M,X), \+ (mother(M,Y), \+ X == Y).
```

Note how the negations are nested. Given X, the first step is to find X's mother, namely M. Then we test whether M has another child Y different from X.

There are actually two "equal" predicates in Prolog. The predicate '==' tests whether its arguments *already* have the same value. The other equality predicate, '=', attempts to unify its arguments with each other, and succeeds if it can do so. Thus, you can use it not only to test equality, but also to give a variable a value: X = a will unify X with a. With both arguments instantiated, '=' and '==' behave exactly alike.

It's a waste of time to use an equality test if you can do the same job by simply putting a value in an argument position. Suppose, for instance, you want to define a predicate `parent_of_cathy(X)` that succeeds if X is a parent of Cathy. Here is one way to express it:

```
parent_of_cathy(X) :- parent(X,Y), Y = cathy.      % poor style
```

That is: first find a person Y such that X is a parent of Y, then check whether Y is Cathy. This involves an unnecessary step, since we can get the same answer in a single step with the rule:

```
parent_of_cathy(X) :- parent(X,cathy).             % better style
```

However, '=' and '==' are often necessary in programs that perform input from the keyboard or a file during the computation. We can have goals such as:

```
?- read(X), write(X), X = cathy.
```

This means: Instantiate X to a value read in from the keyboard, then write X on the screen, then test whether X equals cathy. It is necessary to use '=' or '==' here because we cannot predict what value X will have, and we don't want the computation to fail before printing X out. We will deal with input and output in Chapter 2.

Exercise 1.12.1

Does FAMILY.PL list anyone who satisfies only_child as defined in this section? Explain why or why not.

Exercise 1.12.2

Can a query such as '?- only_child(X).' retrieve a value for X? Explain why or why not. If necessary, add an instance of an only child to the knowledge base in order to test this.

Exercise 1.12.3

From the information in FAMILY.PL, can you tell for certain who is married to whom? Explain why or why not.

Exercise 1.12.4

Add to FAMILY.PL the definitions of *brother, sister, uncle,* and *aunt.* Verify that your predicate definitions work correctly. (Hint: Recall that you have two kinds of uncles: the brothers of your parents, and the husbands of your aunts. You will need to add facts to specify who is male, who is female, and who is married to whom.)

1.13. ANONYMOUS VARIABLES

Suppose we want to find out whether Hazel is a mother but we don't care whose mother she is. We can express the query this way:

```
?- mother(hazel,_).
```

Here the underscore mark stands for an ANONYMOUS VARIABLE, a special variable that matches anything, but never takes on a value. The values of anonymous variables are not printed out in response to a query. More importantly, successive anonymous variables in the same clause do not take on the same value; they behave as if they were different variables.

You should use an anonymous variable whenever a variable occurs only once in a clause and its value is never put to any use. For example, the rule

```
is_a_grandmother(X) :- mother(X,Y), parent(Y,Z).
```

is exactly equivalent to

```
is_a_grandmother(X) :- mother(X,Y), parent(Y,_).
```

but is less work for the computer because no value need be assigned to the anonymous variable. Here X and Y cannot be replaced with anonymous variables because each of them has to occur in two places with the same value.

Exercise 1.13.1

Modify `blue_eyed_non_grandparent` (p. 22) by putting an anonymous variable in the appropriate place.

Exercise 1.13.2

Why isn't the following a proper definition of *grandparent*?

```
grandparent(G,C) :- parent(G,_), parent(_,C).            % wrong!
```

1.14. AVOIDING ENDLESS COMPUTATIONS

Some Prolog rules, although logically correct, cause the computation to go on endlessly. Suppose, for example, we have the following knowledge base:

```
married(michael,melody).                                 [1]
married(greg,crystal).
married(jim,eleanor).
```

and we want to express the fact that if X is married to Y, then Y is married to X. We might try the rule:

```
married(X,Y) :- married(Y,X).                            [2]
```

Now suppose we type the query:

```
?- married(don,jane).
```

Don and Jane are not in the knowledge base. Accordingly, this query does not match any of the facts in [1], so rule [2] gets invoked and the new goal becomes:

```
?- married(jane,don).
```

Again, this does not match any of the facts in [1], so rule [2] is invoked and the new goal becomes:

```
?- married(don,jane).
```

Now we're back where we started. The loop continues until the computer runs out of stack space or the user interrupts the computation.

One way to prevent the loop is to have two "married" predicates, one for facts and one for rules. Given the facts in [1], we can define a predicate `couple/2` which, unlike `married`, will take its arguments in either order. The definition is as follows:

```
couple(X,Y) :- married(X,Y).
couple(Y,X) :- married(X,Y).
```

No loop can arise because no rule can call itself directly or indirectly; so now the query '`?- couple(don,jane).`' fails, as it should. (Only because they are not in the knowledge base; we hasten to assure readers who know us personally that they *are* married!)

Sometimes a rule has to be able to call itself in order to express repetition. To keep the loop from being endless, we must ensure that, when the rule calls itself, it does not simply duplicate the previous call.

For an example, let's go back to FAMILY.PL and develop a definition for "ancestor." One clause is easy, since parents are ancestors of their children:

```
ancestor(X,Y) :- parent(X,Y).                              [3]
```

But the relation of ancestor to descendant can span an unlimited number of generations. We might try to express this with the clause:

```
ancestor(X,Y) :- ancestor(X,Z), ancestor(Z,Y).    % wrong!  [4]
```

But this causes a loop. Consider the query:

```
?- ancestor(cathy,Who).
```

Cathy isn't an ancestor of anyone, and the query should fail. Instead, the computer goes into an infinite loop. To solve the query, the computer first tries clause [3], which fails because it can't satisfy `parent(cathy,Who)`. Then it tries clause [4], generating the new goal:

```
?- ancestor(cathy,Z), ancestor(Z,Who).
```

In order to solve `ancestor(cathy,Z)` the computer will do exactly the same things as for `ancestor(cathy,Who)`; in fact, since both `Z` and `Who` are uninstantiated, the new goal is in effect the same as the old one. The loop continues over and over until the computer runs out of stack space or the user interrupts the computation.

We can fix the problem by replacing [4] with the following:

```
ancestor(X,Y) :- parent(X,Z), ancestor(Z,Y).              [5]
```

This definition will still follow an ancestor-descendant chain down an unlimited number of generations, but now it insists on finding a parent-child relation in each step before calling itself again. As a result, it never gets into endless loops. Many, though not all, transitive relations can be expressed in this way in order to prevent looping.

Finally, and more obviously, Prolog can get into a loop whenever two rules call each other without imposing any additional conditions. For example:

```
human_being(X) :- person(X).
person(X) :- human_being(X).
```

The cure in this case is to recognize that the predicates **human_being** and **person** are equivalent, and use only one of them.

It is possible to have a computation that never halts but never repeats a query. For instance, with the rules:

```
positive_integer(1).
positive_integer(X) :- Y is X-1, positive_integer(Y).
```

the query '?- positive_integer(2.5).' generates the endless sequence:

```
?- positive_integer(1.5).
 ?- positive_integer(0.5).
  ?- positive_integer(-0.5).
    ?- positive_integer(-1.5).
```

and so on.

Exercise 1.14.1

Add to FAMILY.PL the predicate **related(X,Y)** such that **X** is related to **Y** if **X** and **Y** have any ancestor in common but are not the same person. (Note that when you ask for all the solutions, it will be normal to get many of them more than once, because if two people have one ancestor in common, they also have earlier ancestors in common, several of whom may be in the knowledge base.)

Verify that Michael and Julie are related, Cathy and Danielle are related, but Michael and Melody are not related.

Exercise 1.14.2

Describe how to fix **positive_integer** so that queries with noninteger arguments would fail rather than looping. (You haven't been given quite enough Prolog to actually implement your solution yet.)

1.15. USING THE DEBUGGER TO TRACE EXECUTION

Almost all Prolog systems have a DEBUGGER (perhaps it should be called a *tracer*) modeled on the one in Edinburgh Prolog. The debugger allows you to trace exactly what is happening as Prolog executes a query. Here's an example (using GEO.PL):

```
?- spy(located_in/2).    (specifies what predicate you are tracing)
yes
?- trace.   (turns on the debugger)
yes
?- located_in(toronto,canada).
** (0) CALL: located_in(toronto,canada) ?  > (press Return)
** (1) CALL: located_in(toronto,ontario) ?  > (press Return)
** (1) EXIT: located_in(toronto,ontario) ?  > (press Return)
** (0) EXIT: located_in(toronto,canada) ?  > (press Return)
yes
```

That is: to prove `located_in(toronto,canada)`, the computer first had to prove `located_in(toronto,ontario)`. Here's an example in which the backtracking is more complicated:

```
?- located_in(What,texas).
** (0) CALL: located_in(_0085,texas) ?  > (Return)
** (0) EXIT: located_in(houston,texas) ?  > (Return)
What = houston ->;
** (0) REDO: located_in(houston,texas) ?  > (Return)
** (0) EXIT: located_in(austin,texas) ?  > (Return)
What = austin ->;
** (0) REDO: located_in(austin,texas) ?  > (Return)
** (0) FAIL: located_in(_0085,texas) ?  > (Return)
no
```

Here _0085 denotes an uninstantiated variable. Notice that each step is marked one of four ways:

CALL marks the beginning of execution of a query;

REDO means an alternative solution is being sought for a query that has already succeeded once;

EXIT means that a query has succeeded;

FAIL means that a query has failed.

If you keep hitting Return you will see all the steps of the computation. If you hit s (for "skip"), the debugger will skip to the end of the current query (useful if the current query has a lot of subgoals which you don't want to see). If you hit a ("abort"), the computation will stop.

To turn off the debugger, type

```
?- notrace.
```

To learn more about what the debugger can do, consult your manual.

Exercise 1.15.1

Use the debugger to trace each of the following queries:
```
?- located_in(austin,What).   (using GEO.PL)
?- parent(michael,cathy).   (using FAMILY.PL)
?- uncle(Who,cathy).   (using your solution to Exercise 1.12.4)
?- ancestor(Who,cathy).   (using FAMILY.PL with [4] and [5] from section 1.14)
```
Describe what happens in each case.

1.16. STYLES OF ENCODING KNOWLEDGE

In FAMILY.PL, we took the relations "mother" and "father" as basic and defined all other relations in terms of them. We could equally well have taken "parent" as basic and used it (along with "male" and "female") to define "mother" and "father":

```
parent(michael,cathy).                        % This is not all of FAMILY.PL
parent(melody,cathy).
parent(charles_gordon,michael).
parent(hazel,michael).

male(michael).
male(charles_gordon).

female(cathy).
female(melody).
female(hazel).

father(X,Y) :- parent(X,Y), male(X).
mother(X,Y) :- parent(X,Y), female(X).
```

Is this an improvement? In one sense, definitely so, because now the information is broken down into simpler concepts. If you say "mother" you're asserting parenthood and femaleness at once; if you say "parent" and "female" separately, you're distinguishing these two concepts.

Not only that, but now you can tell without a doubt who is female and who is male. In FAMILY.PL, you could deduce that all the mothers are female and all the fathers are male, but you'd still have to state separately that Cathy is female (she's not a mother).

Which style is computationally more efficient depends on the kinds of queries to be answered. FAMILY.PL can answer "father" and "mother" queries more quickly, since they do not require any inference. But the representation that takes "parent" as basic can answer "parent" queries more quickly.

Unlike other knowledge representation languages, Prolog does not force the knowledge base builder to state information in a particular logical style. Information can be entered in whatever form is most convenient, and then appropriate rules can be added to retrieve the information in a different form. From the viewpoint of the user or higher- level rule issuing a query, information deduced through rules looks exactly like information entered as facts in the knowledge base.

Yet another style is sometimes appropriate. We could use a "data-record" format to encode the family tree like this:

```
person(cathy,female,michael,melody).
person(michael,male,charles_gordon,hazel).
person(melody,female,jim,eleanor).
```

Each record lists a person's name, gender, father, and mother. We then define predicates to pick out the individual pieces of information:

```
male(X) :- person(X,male,_,_).
female(X) :- person(X,female,_,_).
father(Father,Child) :- person(Child,_,Father,_).
mother(Mother,Child) :- person(Child,_,_,Mother).
```

The only advantage of this style is that the multiargument facts are often easy to generate from conventional databases, by simply printing out the data in a format that conforms to Prolog syntax. Human beings find the data-record format much less readable than the other formats, and it is, if anything, slower to process than a set of one- or two-argument facts.

Exercise 1.16.1

> Databases often contain names and addresses. Take the names and addresses of two or three people and represent them as a set of Prolog facts. Many different approaches are possible; be prepared to justify the approach you have taken.

1.17. BIBLIOGRAPHICAL NOTES

Two indispensable handbooks of Prolog practice are Sterling and Shapiro (1994) and O'Keefe (1990); the former concentrates on theory and algorithms, the latter on practical use of the language.

There is a large literature on detection and prevention of endless loops in Prolog; see, for example, Smith, Genesereth, and Ginsberg (1986) and Bol (1991). Most loops can be detected, but there may be no way to tell whether the looping computation should succeed or fail.

Chapter 2

Constructing Prolog Programs

2.1. DECLARATIVE AND PROCEDURAL SEMANTICS

In the previous chapter we viewed Prolog primarily as a way of representing knowledge. We saw that the crucial difference between a Prolog knowledge base and a conventional database is that, in Prolog, inferred or deduced knowledge has the same status as information stored explicitly in the knowledge base. That is, Prolog will tell you whether a query succeeds, and if so, with what variable instantiations. It does not normally tell you whether the answer was looked up directly or computed by inference.

Prolog interprets clauses as procedure definitions. As a result, the language has both a DECLARATIVE SEMANTICS and a PROCEDURAL SEMANTICS. Any Prolog knowledge base can be understood declaratively as representing knowledge, or procedurally as prescribing certain computational actions.

Even for knowledge representation, Prolog is not perfectly declarative; the programmer must keep some procedural matters in mind. For instance, as we saw, some declaratively correct knowledge bases produce endless loops. In other cases two declaratively equivalent knowledge bases may be vastly different in computational efficiency.

Moreover, a procedural approach is necessary if we want to go from writing knowledge bases, which can answer queries, to writing programs that interact with the user in other ways.

This chapter will concentrate on the procedural interpretation of Prolog. We will introduce built-in predicates for input and output, for modifying the knowledge base, and for controlling the backtracking process.

The programs in this chapter will contain both a knowledge base and a set of procedures. For brevity, we will usually use a trivially simple knowledge base. Bear in mind, however, that the powerful knowledge base construction techniques from the previous chapter are equally usable here.

The input-output predicates introduced in this chapter are those of Edinburgh Prolog. It is expected that commercial implementations will continue to support them even though the input-output system of ISO Prolog is not entirely the same. We'll look at the ISO Prolog input-output system in Chapter 5; it is described in detail in Appendix A.

2.2. OUTPUT: `write`, `nl`, `display`

The built-in predicate `write` takes any Prolog term as its argument and displays that term on the screen. The built-in predicate `nl`, with no arguments, advances to a new line. For example:

```
?- write('Hello'), write('Goodbye').
HelloGoodbye
yes
?- write('Hello'), nl, write('Goodbye').
Hello
Goodbye
yes
```

Recall that "yes" is printed after every successful query. We often use `write` to print out a value obtained by instantiating a variable:

```
?- mother(X,cathy), write('The mother of Cathy is '), write(X).
The mother of Cathy is melody
yes
```

Notice that `melody` is written in all lower case, just as in the knowledge base.

If its argument is an uninstantiated variable, `write` displays a symbol such as `_0001`, uniquely identifying the variable but not giving its name. Try a query such as

```
?- write(X).
```

to see what uninstantiated variables look like in your implementation.

Notice that `write` displays quoted atoms, such as `'Hello there'`, without the quotes. The omission of quotes means that terms written onto a file by `write` cannot easily be read back in using Prolog syntax. If you write `'hello there'` you get `hello there`, which will be read back in as two atoms, not one. To solve this problem, Prolog offers another predicate, called `writeq`, that includes quotes if they would be needed for reading the term back in:

```
?- writeq('hello there').
'hello there'
yes
```

Another predicate, called `display`, puts all functors in front of their arguments even if they were originally written in other positions. This makes `display` useful for investigating the internal representation of Prolog terms. For example:

```
?- display(2+2).
+(2,2)
yes
```

This shows that + is an infix operator. We will deal with arithmetic operators in Chapter 3. For now, be aware that 2+2 does not represent the number 4; it is a data structure consisting of a 2, a +, and another 2.

Still another predicate, `write_canonical`, combines the effects of `writeq` and `display`:

```
?- write_canonical(2+3).
+(2,3)
?- write_canonical('hello there').
'hello there'
```

Not all Prologs have `write_canonical`; Quintus Prolog and the ISO standard include it.

Exercise 2.2.1

Predict the output of each of the following queries, then try the queries on the computer to confirm your predictions:

```
?- write(aaa), write(bbb).
?- write(aaa), nl, write(bbb).
?- writeq(aaa).
?- display(aaa).
?- write('don''t panic').
?- writeq('don''t panic').
?- display('don''t panic').
?- write(Dontpanic).
?- writeq(Dontpanic).
?- display(Dontpanic).
?- write(3.14159*2).
?- display(3.14159*2).
?- write('an\\example').
?- display('an\\example').
```

Also try out `write_canonical` if your implementation supports it. If you're bursting with curiosity about how to do arithmetic in Prolog, try this query:

```
?- What is 3.14159*2.
```

2.3. COMPUTING VERSUS PRINTING

It's important to distinguish queries that perform input-output operations from queries that don't. For example, the query

```
?- mother(X,cathy), write(X).
```

tells the computer to figure out who is the mother of Cathy and print the result. By contrast, the query

```
?- mother(X,cathy).
```

tells the computer to identify the mother of Cathy, but does not say to print anything. If you type the latter query at the Prolog prompt, the value of X will get printed, because the Prolog system always prints the values of variables instantiated by queries that have not performed any output of their own. However, it's important to understand that mother/2 isn't doing the printing; the Prolog user interface is.

A common mistake is to construct a predicate that *prints* something when you were assigned to construct a predicate that *computes* it, or vice versa. Normally, in Prolog, any predicate that does a computation should deliver the result by instantiating an argument, not by writing on the screen directly. That way, the result can be passed to other subgoals in the same program.

Exercise 2.3.1

Add to FAMILY.PL the following two predicates:

- A predicate `cathys_father(X)` that instantiates X to the name of Cathy's father.
- A predicate `print_cathys_father` (with no arguments) that writes the name of Cathy's father on the screen.

2.4. FORCING BACKTRACKING WITH fail

The built-in predicate `fail` always fails; you can use it to force other predicates to backtrack through all solutions. For an example, consider the tiny knowledge base in Figure 2.1 (CAPITALS.PL). The query

```
?- capital_of(State,City),write(City),
        write(' is the capital of '),write(State),nl.
```

will display information about the first state it finds. A few Prolog systems will then invite you to type ';' to get alternative solutions, but most Prologs will not do this, because they assume that if you used `write`, you must have already written out whatever it was that you wanted to see.

That's where `fail` comes in. To print out all the alternatives, you can phrase the query like this:

```
% File CAPITALS.PL or KB.PL
% Knowledge base for several examples in Chapter 2

:- dynamic(capital_of/2).       % Omit this line if your Prolog
                                % does not accept it.

capital_of(georgia,atlanta).
capital_of(california,sacramento).
capital_of(florida,tallahassee).
capital_of(maine,augusta).
```

Figure 2.1   A small knowledge base about states and capitals.

```
?- capital_of(State,City),write(City),
         write(' is the capital of '),write(State),nl,fail.
atlanta is the capital of georgia
sacramento is the capital of california
tallahassee is the capital of florida
augusta is the capital of maine
no
```

In place of `fail` you could have used any predicate that fails, because any failure causes Prolog to back up to the most recent untried alternative. The steps in the computation are as follows:

1. Solve the first subgoal, `capital_of(State,City)`, by instantiating `State` as `georgia` and `City` as `atlanta`.

2. Solve the second, third, fourth, and fifth subgoals (the three `writes` and `nl`) by writing `atlanta is the capital of georgia` and starting a new line.

3. Try to solve the last subgoal, `fail`. This subgoal cannot be solved, so back up.

4. The most recent subgoal that has an alternative is the first one, so pick another state and city and try again.

Figure 2.2 shows part of this process in diagrammatic form. Notice that the `writes` are executed as the computer tries each path that passes through them, whether or not the whole query is going to succeed. In general, a query does not have to succeed in order to perform actions. We say that `write` has the SIDE EFFECT that whenever it executes, something gets written to the screen, regardless of whether the whole query is going to succeed.

Notice also that upon hitting `fail`, the computer has to back up all the way back to `capital_of(State,City)` to get an alternative. It is then free to move forward through the `writes` again, since it is now on a different path. Input-output predicates such as `write`, `writeq`, `nl`, and `display` do not yield alternative solutions upon backtracking. For instance, the query

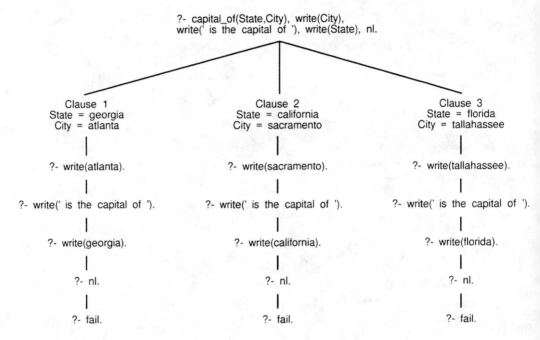

Figure 2.2 Queries to `write` and `nl` do not generate alternatives.

```
?- write('hello'),fail.
```

writes `hello` only once. That is, `write`, `writeq`, `nl`, and `display` are DETERMINISTIC (or, as some textbooks express it, they CANNOT BE RESATISFIED).

Exercise 2.4.1

Take the first example of `fail` given at the beginning of this section, and replace `fail` with some other query that will definitely fail. What happens?

Exercise 2.4.2

In your Prolog system, what happens if you try to query a predicate that doesn't exist? Does the query fail, or do you get an error message? Experiment and find out.

Exercise 2.4.3

Recall that CAPITALS.PL does not list Idaho. Assuming that CAPITALS.PL has been consulted, what is output by each of the following two queries? Explain the reason for the difference.

```
?- capital_of(idaho,C), write('The capital of Idaho is '), write(C).
?- write('The capital of Idaho is '), capital_of(idaho,C), write(C).
```

Exercise 2.4.4

Using FAMILY.PL and your knowledge from Chapter 1, construct a query that will print out the names of all the ancestors of Cathy like this:

> The ancestors of Cathy are: michael melody charles_gordon (etc.)
>
> Define the predicate `ancestor` and use it in the query.

2.5. PREDICATES AS SUBROUTINES

The query in the examples in the previous section was rather cumbersome. It can be encapsulated into a rule as follows:

```
print_capitals :- capital_of(State,City),
                  write(City),
                  write('is the capital of '),
                  write(State),
                  nl,
                  fail.
```

Then, the query

```
?- print_capitals.
```

will have the same effect as the much longer query that it stands for. In effect, the rule defines a subroutine; it makes it possible to execute all the subgoals of the original query by typing a single name.

In this case, there are advantages to defining two subroutines, not just one:

```
print_a_capital :- capital_of(State,City),
                   write(City),
                   write(' is the capital of '),
                   write(State),
                   nl.

print_capitals :- print_a_capital,
                  fail.
```

does the order of these comments in kB matter?

This makes the program structure clearer by splitting apart two conceptually separate operations — printing one state capital in the desired format, and backtracking through all alternatives.

Predicate definitions in Prolog correspond to subroutines in Fortran or procedures in Pascal. From here on, we will often refer to Prolog predicate definitions as PROCEDURES.

There's one more subtlety to consider. Any query to `print_capitals` will ultimately fail (although it will print out a lot of useful things along the way). By adding a second clause, we can make `print_capitals` end with success rather than failure:

```
print_capitals :- print_a_capital,       % Clause 1
                  fail.

print_capitals.                           % Clause 2
```

b/c this is a FACT.

Now any query to `print_capitals` will backtrack through all the solutions to `print_a_capital`, just as before. However, after the first clause has run out of solutions, execution will backtrack into the second clause, which succeeds without doing anything further.

Exercise 2.5.1

Get `print_capitals` working on your computer. Try the query
?- print_capitals, write('All done.').
with and without Clause 2. What difference does Clause 2 make?

Exercise 2.5.2

Go back to FAMILY.PL and your solution to Exercise 2.4.4. Define a predicate called `print_ancestors_of` that takes one argument (a person's name) and prints out the names of all the known ancestors of that person, in the same format as in Exercise 2.4.4.

2.6. INPUT OF TERMS: read

The built-in predicate `read` accepts any Prolog term from the keyboard. That term must be typed in the same syntax as if it were within a Prolog program, and it must be followed by a period. For example:

```
?- read(X).
hello.                    (typed by user)
X = hello
yes


?- read(X).
'hello there'.            (typed by user)
X = 'hello there'
yes


?- read(X).
hello there.              (typed by user)
--Syntax error--
```

Crucially, *if the period is left out, the computer will wait for it forever,* accepting line after line of input in the hope that the period will eventually be found.

If the argument of `read` is already instantiated, then `read` will try to unify that argument with whatever the user types, and will succeed if the unification succeeds, and fail if the unification fails:

```
?- read(hello).
hello.                    (typed by user)
yes


?- read(hello).
goodbye.                  (typed by user)
no
```

```
% File INTERAC.PL
% Simple interactive program

capital_of(georgia,atlanta).
capital_of(florida,tallahassee).

go :- write('What state do you want to know about?'),nl,
      write('Type its name, all lower case, followed by a period.'),nl,
      read(State),
      capital_of(State,City),
      write('Its capital is: '),write(City),nl.
```

Figure 2.3   An interactive program.

Note in particular that `read(yes)` will succeed if the user types 'yes.' and fail if the user types anything else. This can be a handy way to get answers to yes–no questions.

With `read`, the user can type any legal Prolog term, no matter how complex:

```
?- read(X).
mother(melody,cathy).
X = mother(melody,cathy)
yes
```

Exactly as in programs, unquoted terms that begin with upper case letters are taken to be variables:

```
?- read(X).
A.                              (typed by user)
X = _0091
yes
```

```
?- read(X).
f(Y) :- g(Y).                   (typed by user)
X = (f(_0089) :- g(_0089))
yes
```

Here _0091 and _0089 stand for uninstantiated variables.

Like `write`, `writeq`, `nl`, and `display`, `read` is deterministic, i.e., it does not yield alternative solutions upon backtracking.   *what if you use fail?*

Figure 2.3 shows a program, INTERAC.PL, that uses `read` to interact with the user. A dialogue with INTERAC.PL looks like this:

```
?- go.
What state do you want to know about?
Type its name, all lower case, followed by a period:
florida.
Its capital is: tallahassee
```

The need to follow Prolog syntax can be a real inconvenience for the user. The period is easy to forget, and bizarre errors can result from uppercase entries being taken as variables. In Chapter 5 we will show you how to get around this. In the meantime, note that read makes a good quick-and-dirty substitute for more elaborate input routines that will be added to your program later. Also, consult your manual for more versatile input routines that your implementation may supply.

Exercise 2.6.1

Try out INTERAC.PL. (Consult it and type '?- go.' to start it.) What happens if you begin the name of the state with a capital letter? Explain why you get the results that you do.

Exercise 2.6.2

If you wanted to mention South Carolina when running INTERAC.PL, how would you have to type it?

Exercise 2.6.3

Using FAMILY.PL, write an interactive procedure find_mother (with no arguments) that asks the user to type a person's name, then prints out the name of that person's mother.

Exercise 2.6.4

What does read(yes) do if the user responds to it by typing each of the following? Does it succeed, fail, or crash with an error message? Why?

```
yes.
no.
Yes.
No.
y.
n.
y e s.
```

Exercise 2.6.5

 Does read ignore comments in its input? Try it and see.

2.7. MANIPULATING THE KNOWLEDGE BASE

Much of the power of Prolog comes from the ability of programs to modify themselves. The built-in predicates asserta and assertz add clauses to the beginning and end, respectively, of the set of clauses for the predicate, and retract removes a clause. (Many Prologs accept assert as an alternative spelling for assertz; we will often refer to asserta and assertz generically as assert.)

The argument of asserta or assertz is a complete clause. For example,

```
?- asserta(capital_of(hawaii,honolulu)).
```

inserts `capital_of(hawaii,honolulu)` immediately before the other clauses for `capital_of`, and

```
?- assertz(capital_of(wyoming,cheyenne)).
```

adds a fact at the end of the clauses for `capital_of`.

The argument of `retract` is either a complete clause or a structure that matches the clause but contains some uninstantiated variables. The predicate must be instantiated and have the correct number of arguments. For example,

```
?- retract(mother(melody,cathy)).
```

removes `mother(melody,cathy)` from the knowledge base, and

```
?- retract(mother(X,Y)).
```

finds the first clause that matches `mother(X,Y)` and removes it, instantiating `X` and `Y` to the arguments that it found in that clause. If there is no clause matching `mother(X,Y)`, then `retract` fails.

Extra parentheses are required when the argument of `asserta`, `assertz`, or `retract` contains a comma or an "if" operator:

```
?- asserta((male(X) :- father(X))).
?- asserta((can_fly(X) :- bird(X), \+ penguin(X))).
?- retract((parent(X,Y) :- Z)).
```

The parentheses make it clear that the whole clause is just one argument.

The effects of `assert` and `retract` are not undone upon backtracking. These predicates thus give you a "permanent" way to store information. By contrast, variable instantiations store information only temporarily since variables lose their values upon backtracking. (Note that `assert` and `retract` modify only the knowledge base *in memory;* they don't affect the disk file from which that knowledge base was loaded.)

The predicate `abolish` removes *all* the clauses for a particular predicate with a particular arity, and succeeds whether or not any such clauses exist: [1]

```
?- abolish(mother/2).
```

Finally, to see the contents of the knowledge base in memory, type:

```
?- listing.
```

To see only a particular predicate, type, for example, '`?- listing(mother).`' or '`?- listing(mother/2).`' Note that `listing` is not in the ISO standard, and its exact behavior varies somewhat from one implementation to another.

Exercise 2.7.1

What would be in the knowledge base if you started with it empty and then performed the following queries in the order shown?

---

[1] In ALS Prolog and SWI Prolog, write `abolish(mother,2)` instead of `abolish(mother/2)`.

```
?- asserta(green(kermit)).
?- assertz(gray(gonzo)).
?- asserta(green(broccoli)).
?- assertz(green(asparagus)).
?- retract(green(X)).
```

Predict the result, then try the queries and use `listing` to see if your prediction was right.

Exercise 2.7.2

What does the following Prolog code do?

```
:- dynamic(f/0).        % Omit this line if your Prolog
                        % does not accept it

test :- f, write('Not the first time').

test :- \+ f, asserta(f), write('The first time').
```

[handwritten: can be changed in KB]

[handwritten: do you have to define all prod as Static or dynamic?]

Try the query '?- `test`.' several times and explain why it does not give the same result each time.

2.8. STATIC AND DYNAMIC PREDICATES

Back in DEC-10 days, all the clauses in the Prolog knowledge base were equal in status — any clause could be retracted, abolished, or examined at run time.

Nowadays, however, many Prolog implementations distinguish STATIC from DYNAMIC predicates. Dynamic predicates can be asserted and retracted. Static predicates cannot, because their clauses have been compiled into a form that runs faster but is no longer modifiable at run time.

In the ISO standard and many present-day implementations, all predicates are static unless you make them dynamic. In some Prologs, all predicates are dynamic. In others, predicates are dynamic if you load them `consult` or `reconsult`, or static if you load them with `compile`.

One way to make a predicate dynamic is to create it using `assert`. Another way is to create it in the usual way (by putting clauses in your program file), but precede those clauses with a declaration such as

```
:- dynamic(capital_of/2).
```

to tell the Prolog system that the predicate `capital_of/2` (or whatever) should be stored in a way that allows you to assert and retract its clauses.

That's the reason for the dynamic declaration in CAPITALS.PL (page 35). As you might guess, we're going to be asserting some additional clauses into `capital_of` at run time.

Dynamic declarations have another effect, too: They tell the Prolog system not to worry if you try to query a predicate that doesn't exist yet. In many Prologs, a query like

```
?- f(a,b).
```

will raise an error condition if there are no clauses for `f/2` in the knowledge base. The computer has, of course, no way of knowing that you are going to assert some clauses later and you just haven't gotten around to it. If you have declared '`:- dynamic(f/2).`' then the query will simply fail without raising an error condition.

Finally, note that `abolish` wipes out not only a predicate but also its dynamic declaration, if there is one. To retract all the clauses for a predicate without wiping out its dynamic declaration, you could do something like this:

```
clear_away_my_predicate :- retract(f(_,_)), fail.
clear_away_my_predicate :- retract(f(_,_) :- _), fail.
clear_away_my_predicate.
```

That is: Retract all the facts that match `f(_,_)`, then retract all the rules that begin with `f(_,_)`, and finally succeed with no further action.

Exercise 2.8.1

Does your Prolog allow you to use dynamic declarations? If so, do they affect whether or not you can assert and retract clauses? Try consulting CAPITALS.PL and then performing the queries:

```
?- retract(capital_of(X,Y)).
?- assertz(capital_of(kentucky,frankfort)).
```

Exercise 2.8.2

In your Prolog, does `listing` show all the predicates or only the dynamic ones? State how you found out.

Exercise 2.8.3

Does your Prolog let you use `compile` as an alternative to `consult` or `reconsult`? If so, does it affect whether predicates are static or dynamic?

2.9. MORE ABOUT `consult` AND `reconsult`

We can now say, with some precision, exactly what `consult` and `reconsult` do. Their job is to read a whole file of Prolog terms, using `read/1`, and assert each term into the Prolog knowledge base as a fact or rule.

There is one exception. Any terms that begin with `:-` are executed as queries the moment `consult` or `reconsult` sees them. We call such terms EMBEDDED QUERIES. If you consult this file,

```
:- write('Starting...'),nl.
green(kermit).
green(asparagus).
:- write('Finished'),nl.
```

the messages `Starting...` and `Finished` will appear at the beginning and the end of the consulting process, respectively. (A few Prologs use `?-` instead of `:-`, and some Prologs take either one.)

Can you use an embedded query to make your program start executing the moment it is loaded? Possibly. We often did this in the previous edition of this book, but we no longer recommend it because it is not compatible with all Prologs. The question of how to start execution really arises only when you are compiling your Prolog program into a stand-alone executable (an .EXE file or the like), and the manual for your compiler will tell you how to specify a starting query. For portable programs that are to be run from the query prompt, you could embed a query that gives instructions to the user, such as

```
:- write('Type ''go.'' to start.').
```

at the end of the program file. In this book, we will often use the names `go` or `start` for the main procedure of a program, but this is just our choice; those names have no special significance in Prolog.

The difference between `consult` and `reconsult`, as we noted in Chapter 1, is that upon encountering the first clause for each predicate in the file, `reconsult` throws away any preexisting definitions of that predicate that may already be in the knowledge base. Thus, you can `reconsult` the same file over and over again without getting multiple copies of it in memory. In fact, some Prologs no longer maintain this distinction; in Quintus Prolog, for example, `consult` is simply another name for `reconsult`. In SWI Prolog, `consult` acts like the old `reconsult`, and `reconsult` doesn't exist.

One very good use of embedded queries is to include one Prolog file into another. Suppose FILE1.PL contains a predicate that you want to use as part of FILE2.PL. You can simply insert the line

```
:- reconsult('file1.pl').
```

near the top of FILE2.PL. Then, whenever you consult or reconsult FILE2.PL, FILE1.PL will get reconsulted as well (provided, of course, it is in your current directory!). Better yet, if your Prolog permits it, use the embedded query

```
:- ensure_loaded('file1.pl').
```

which will reconsult FILE1.PL only if it is not already in memory at the time. Quintus Prolog and the ISO standard support `ensure_loaded`, but in order to accommodate other Prologs, we will generally use `reconsult` in this book.

Finally, what if the clauses for a single predicate are spread across more than one file? Recall that `reconsult` will discard one set of clauses as soon as it starts reading the other one. To keep it from doing so, you can use a declaration like this:

```
:- multifile(capital_of/2).
```

That is: "Allow clauses for `capital_of/2` to come from more than one file." This declaration must appear in every file that contains any of those clauses. At least, that's how it's done in Quintus Prolog and in the ISO standard; consult your manual to find out whether this applies to the Prolog that you are using.

Exercise 2.9.1

> Does your Prolog support embedded queries beginning with ':-'? With '?-'? Experiment and see.

Exercise 2.9.2

> By experiment, find out whether your Prolog supports `ensure_loaded` and whether it supports `multifile`.

2.10. FILE HANDLING: see, seen, tell, told

In this section we introduce the simple file operations that are supported by Edinburgh Prolog; most implementations support considerably more, and so does the ISO standard (see Chapter 5 and Appendix A).

The built-in predicate see takes a file name as an argument. It opens that file for input (if it is not already open) and causes Prolog to take input from that file rather than from the keyboard. The predicate seen closes all input files and switches input back to the keyboard. Thus, the following query reads the first three Prolog terms from file MYDATA:

```
?- see('mydata'),
   read(X),
   read(Y),
   read(Z),
   seen.
```

As long as a file is open, the computer keeps track of the position at which the next term will be read. By calling see repeatedly, you can switch around among several files that are open at once. To switch to the keyboard without closing the other input files, use see(user). Thus:

```
?- see('aaa'),
   read(X1),    % read first term from AAA
   see('bbb'),
   read(X2),    % read first term from BBB
   see(user),
   read(X3),    % read a term from the keyboard
   see('aaa'),
   read(X4),    % read second term from AAA
   seen.        % close all input files
```

On attempting to read past the end of a file, read returns the special atom end_of_file ('!EOF' in Cogent Prolog and Amzi Prolog).   If the attempt is repeated, some implementations return end_of_file over and over, and some raise an error condition.

The predicate tell opens a file for output and switches output to that file; told closes output files and switches output back to the console.   Here is how to create a file called YOURDATA and write Hello there on it:

```
?- tell('yourdata'),
   write('Hello there'),
   nl,
   told.
```

Like see, tell can have several files open at once:

```
?- tell('aaa'),
   write('First line of AAA'),nl,
   tell('bbb'),
   write('First line of BBB'),nl,
   tell(user),
   write('This goes on the screen'),nl,
   tell('aaa'),
   write('Second line of AAA'),nl,
   told.
```

The biggest disadvantage of tell is that if something goes wrong, the error messages appear on the file, not the screen. Likewise, if something goes wrong while see is in effect, you may not be able to make the computer accept any input from the keyboard. In general, see, seen, tell, and told are barely adequate as a file handling system; we will use them often in this book because of their great portability, but you should jump at every chance to use a better file input-output system (implementation-specific or ISO standard as the case may be).

Exercise 2.10.1

Use the following query to create a text file:

```
?- tell(myfile),
   write(green(kermit)), write('.'), nl,
   write(green(asparagus)), write('.'), nl,
   told.
```

What gets written on the file?

Exercise 2.10.2

Construct a query that will read both of the terms from the file you have just created.

2.11. A PROGRAM THAT "LEARNS"

Now we're ready to put together a program that "learns" — or more specifically, a program that adds new information to its knowledge base as it runs, then "remembers" that information at the next session.

Adding new information is easy — we'll use assert. To save the information until the next session, we'll use a trick: We'll redirect output to a file and do a listing of the modified predicate, thereby storing a set of clauses that can be reconsulted by the same program the next time it runs.

The program that learns is called LEARNER.PL (Figure 2.4). It attempts to name the capital of any state that the user asks about. If it cannot do so, it asks the user to name the capital and stores the information in its knowledge base. The knowledge base is stored on a separate file called KB.PL, which is initially a copy of CAPITALS.PL but gets rewritten every time the user terminates the program. A dialogue with LEARNER.PL looks like this:

```
?- start.
Type names all in lower case, followed by period.
Type "stop." to quit.

State? georgia.
The capital of georgia is atlanta

State? hawaii.
I do not know the capital of that state.
Please tell me.
Capital? honolulu.
Thank you.

State? maine.
The capital of maine is augusta

State? hawaii.
The capital of hawaii is honolulu

State? stop.
Saving the knowledge base...
Done.
```

Notice that the program has "learned" what the capital of Hawaii is. The "learning" is permanent — if you run the program again and ask for the capital of Hawaii, you will henceforth get the correct answer.

LEARNER.PL uses three predicates: start, process_a_query, and answer. Its structure is a recursive loop, since process_a_query calls answer and, under most conditions, answer then calls process_a_query. In Pascal or a similar language, this kind of loop would be very bad form, but in Prolog it is one of the normal ways of expressing repetition. Further, as we will see in Chapter 4, the program can be modified so that the recursive calls do not consume stack space.

The predicate start simply loads the knowledge base (using reconsult so that the program can be run again and again with impunity), prints the introductory message, and calls process_a_query for the first time. Then process_a_query asks the user to name a state, accepts a term as input, and passes it to answer.

The predicate answer does one of three things, depending on its argument. If the argument is stop, it saves a new copy of the knowledge base that contains any information added during the run, then prints Done and terminates successfully.

Otherwise, if the argument is a state that can be found in the knowledge base, answer looks up the capital and writes it on the screen. If the argument is a state that is not in the knowledge base, answer asks the user for the requisite information, constructs the appropriate fact, and adds it using `assertz`. In either of these latter cases `answer` then calls `process_a_query` to begin the cycle anew.

Exercise 2.11.1

Get LEARNER.PL working on your computer and confirm that it performs as described. In particular, confirm that LEARNER.PL remembers what it has learned even after you exit Prolog completely and start everything afresh. What does KB.PL look like after several states and capitals have been added?

Exercise 2.11.2

In LEARNER.PL, what is the effect of the following line?
```
write(':- dynamic(capital_of/2).'),nl,
```
Why is it needed?

2.12. CHARACTER INPUT AND OUTPUT: get, get0, put

The built-in predicate `put` outputs one character; its argument is an integer that gives the character's ASCII code. For example:

```
?- put(42).
*
yes
```

Here 42 is the ASCII code for the asterisk. You can use `put` to output not only printable characters, but also special effects such as code 7 (beep), code 8 (backspace), code 12 (start new page on printer), or code 13 (return without new line).

ASCII stands for American Standard Code for Information Interchange. Table 2.1 lists the 128 ASCII characters; some computers, including the IBM PC, use codes 128 to 255 for additional special characters. IBM mainframe computers use a different set of codes known as EBCDIC.

The opposite of `put` is `get`. That is, `get` accepts one character and instantiates its argument to that character's ASCII code, like this:

```
?- get(X).
*              (typed by user)
X = 42
```

Here you will encounter a distinction between *buffered* and *unbuffered* keyboard input. In the example just given, some Prologs will execute `get(X)` the moment you type the asterisk. Most Prologs won't see the asterisk until you have also hit Return.

We describe the keyboard as BUFFERED if the program does not receive any input until you hit Return, or UNBUFFERED (RAW) if all incoming keystrokes are available to the program immediately.

Note that `get` skips any blanks, returns, or other nonprinting characters that may precede the character it is going to read. If you want to read every keystroke that comes in or every byte in a file, use `get0` instead. For example, if you type

```
?- get0(X), get0(Y).
```

```
% File LEARNER.PL
% Program that modifies its own knowledge base

%  This program requires file KB.PL, which should be a copy of CAPITALS.PL.

start :-  reconsult('kb.pl'),
          nl,
          write('Type names entirely in lower case, followed by period.'), nl,
          write('Type "stop." to quit.'), nl,
          nl,
          process_a_query.

process_a_query :- write('State? '),
                   read(State),
                   answer(State).

   % If user typed "stop." then save the knowledge base and quit.

answer(stop) :-    write('Saving the knowledge base...'),nl,
                   tell('kb.pl'),
                   write(':- dynamic(capital_of/2).'),nl, % omit if not needed
                   listing(capital_of),
                   told,
                   write('Done.'),nl.

   % If the state is in the knowledge base, display it, then
   % loop back to process_a_query

answer(State) :-    capital_of(State,City),
                    write('The capital of '),
                    write(State),
                    write(' is '),
                    write(City),nl,
                    nl,
                    process_a_query.

   % If the state is not in the knowledge base, ask the
   % user for information, add it to the knowledge base, and
   % loop back to process_a_query

answer(State) :-    \+ capital_of(State,_),
                    write('I do not know the capital of that state.'),nl,
                    write('Please tell me.'),nl,
                    write('Capital? '),
                    read(City),
                    write('Thank you.'),nl,nl,
                    assertz(capital_of(State,City)),
                    process_a_query.
```

Figure 2.4   A program that "learns."

TABLE 2.1   ASCII CHARACTER SET, WITH DECIMAL NUMERIC CODES

0	Ctrl-@	32	Space	64	@	96	`
1	Ctrl-A	33	!	65	A	97	a
2	Ctrl-B	34	"	66	B	98	b
3	Ctrl-C	35	#	67	C	99	c
4	Ctrl-D	36	$	68	D	100	d
5	Ctrl-E	37	%	69	E	101	e
6	Ctrl-F	38	&	70	F	102	f
7	Ctrl-G	39	'	71	G	103	g
8	Backspace	40	(	72	H	104	h
9	Tab	41	)	73	I	105	i
10	Ctrl-J	42	*	74	J	106	j
11	Ctrl-K	43	+	75	K	107	k
12	Ctrl-L	44	,	76	L	108	l
13	Return	45	-	77	M	109	m
14	Ctrl-N	46	.	78	N	110	n
15	Ctrl-O	47	/	79	O	111	o
16	Ctrl-P	48	0	80	P	112	p
17	Ctrl-Q	49	1	81	Q	113	q
18	Ctrl-R	50	2	82	R	114	r
19	Ctrl-S	51	3	83	S	115	s
20	Ctrl-T	52	4	84	T	116	t
21	Ctrl-U	53	5	85	U	117	u
22	Ctrl-V	54	6	86	V	118	v
23	Ctrl-W	55	7	87	W	119	w
24	Ctrl-X	56	8	88	X	120	x
25	Ctrl-Y	57	9	89	Y	121	y
26	Ctrl-Z	58	:	90	Z	122	z
27	Escape	59	;	91	[	123	{
28	Ctrl-\	60	<	92	\	124		
29	Ctrl-]	61	=	93	]	125	}
30	Ctrl-^	62	>	94	^	126	~
31	Ctrl-_	63	?	95	_	127	Delete

and type * and Return, you'll see the code for * (42) followed by the code for Return (13 or 10 depending on your implementation).

In the ISO standard, put and get0 are called put_code and get_code respectively; get is not provided, but you can define it as:

```
get(Code) :- repeat, get_code(Code), Code>32, !.
```

The use of repeat and ! (pronounced "cut") will be discussed in Chapter 4.

As you may surmise, get0 and put are used mainly to read arbitrary bytes from files, send arbitrary control codes to printers, and the like. We'll explore byte-by-byte file handling in Chapter 5. On trying to read past end of file, both get and get0 return −1, except in Arity Prolog, in which they simply fail, and Cogent and Amzi Prolog, in which they return the atom '!EOF'.

Exercise 2.12.1

What does the following query do? Explain, step by step, what happens.

```
?- write(hello), put(13), write(bye).
```

Exercise 2.12.2

Is Prolog keyboard input on your computer buffered or unbuffered? Explain how you found out.

Exercise 2.12.3

When you hit Return, does get0 see code 10, code 13, or both? Explain how you found out.

2.13. CONSTRUCTING MENUS

Figure 2.5 (MENUDEMO.PL) shows how to use get to accept single-keystroke responses to a menu. A dialogue with this program looks like this:

```
Which state do you want to know about?
   1   Georgia
   2   California
   3   Florida
   4   Maine
Type a number, 1 to 4 --- 4
The capital of maine is augusta
```

Similar menus can be used in other types of programs.

Note that MENUDEMO.PL reads each response by executing both get and get0, like this:

```
get_from_menu(State) :-  get(Code),   % read a character
                         get0(_),     % consume the Return keystroke
                         interpret(Code,State).
```

```
% File  MENUDEMO.PL
% Illustrates accepting input from a menu

% Knowledge base

capital_of(georgia,atlanta).
capital_of(california,sacramento).
capital_of(florida,tallahassee).
capital_of(maine,augusta).

% Procedures to interact with user

start :-  display_menu,
          get_from_menu(State),
          capital_of(State,City),
          nl,
          write('The capital of '),
          write(State),
          write(' is '),
          write(City),
          nl.

display_menu :- write('Which state do you want to know about?'),nl,
                write(' 1  Georgia'),nl,
                write(' 2  California'),nl,
                write(' 3  Florida'),nl,
                write(' 4  Maine'),nl,
                write('Type a number, 1 to 4 -- ').

get_from_menu(State) :-  get(Code),  % read a character
                         get0(_),    % consume the Return keystroke
                         interpret(Code,State).

interpret(49,georgia).      /* ASCII 49 = '1' */
interpret(50,california).   /* ASCII 50 = '2' */
interpret(51,florida).      /* ASCII 51 = '3' */
interpret(52,maine).        /* ASCII 52 = '4' */
```

Figure 2.5 Example of a program that uses a menu.

```
% File GETYESNO.PL
% Menu that obtains 'yes' or 'no' answer

get_yes_or_no(Result) :- get(Char),              % read a character
                         get0(_),                % consume the Return after it
                         interpret(Char,Result),
                         !.                       % cut -- see text

get_yes_or_no(Result) :- nl,
                         put(7),  % beep
                         write('Type Y or N:'),
                         get_yes_or_no(Result).

interpret(89,yes).   % ASCII 89  = 'Y'
interpret(121,yes).  % ASCII 121 = 'y'
interpret(78,no).    % ASCII 78  = 'N'
interpret(110,no).   % ASCII 110 = 'n'
```

Figure 2.6   A menu routine that gets the user to answer "yes" or "no."

Here get(Code) skips any preceding nonprinting codes, then reads the digit 1, 2, 3, or 4 typed by the user. Then get0(_) reads the Return keystroke that follows the letter. If your Prolog accesses the keyboard without buffering, you can remove get0(_) and the user will get an instant response upon typing the digit.

The kind of menu that we'll use most often is one that gets a "yes" or "no" answer to a question, and won't accept any other answers (Fig. 2.6, file GETYESNO.PL). The idea is that from within a program, you can execute a query such as

```
?- get_yes_or_no(Response).
```

and Response will come back instantiated to yes if the user typed y or Y, or no if the user typed n or N. If the user types anything else, he or she gets prompted to type Y or N.

The first clause of get_yes_or_no reads a character, then calls interpret to translate it to yes or no. If the user typed y, Y, n, or N, the call to interpret succeeds, and get_yes_or_no then executes a "cut" (written '!'). We'll introduce cuts in Chapter 4; for now, all you need to know is that cut prevents execution from backtracking into the other clause.

If the user doesn't type y, Y, n, or N, then interpret won't succeed and the cut won't get executed. In that case, get_yes_or_no will backtrack into the other clause, beep, print Type Y or N, and call itself recursively to begin the whole process again.

Exercise 2.13.1

Adapt MENUDEMO.PL to use the first letter of the name of each state, rather than the digits 1–4, to indicate choices.

Exercise 2.13.2

Using `get_yes_or_no`, define another predicate `succeed_if_yes` that asks the user to type Y or N (upper or lower case), then succeeds if the answer was Y and fails if the answer was N.

Exercise 2.13.3

What would go wrong with `get_yes_or_no` if the cut were omitted?

2.14. A SIMPLE EXPERT SYSTEM

We are now ready to write an expert system, albeit a simple one. CAR.PL (Figure 2.7, p. 57) is a program that tells the user why a car won't start. Here is one example of a dialogue with it:

```
?- start.
This program diagnoses why a car won't start.
Answer all questions with Y for yes or N for no.

When you first started trying to start the car,
did the starter crank the engine normally?
y

Does the starter crank the engine normally now?
n

Your attempts to start the car have run down the battery.
Recharging or jump-starting will be necessary.
But there is probably nothing wrong with the battery itself.

Look in the carburetor.  Can you see or smell gasoline?
n

Check whether there is fuel in the tank.
If so, check for a clogged fuel line or filter
or a defective fuel pump.
```

CAR.PL has two features that would be difficult to implement in a conventional programming language: it lists all possible diagnoses, not just one, and it does not ask questions unless the information is actually needed. Both of these features are exemplified in the following dialogue.

```
?- start.
This program diagnoses why a car won't start.
Answer all questions with Y for yes or N for no.

When you first started trying to start the car,
```

```
did the starter crank the engine normally?
n
```

```
Check that the gearshift is set to Park or Neutral.
Try jiggling the gearshift lever.
```

```
Check for a defective battery, voltage
regulator, or alternator; if any of these is
the problem, charging the battery or jump-
starting may get the car going temporarily.
Or the starter itself may be defective.
```

If the starter is obviously inoperative, the other diagnoses do not come into consideration and there is no point collecting the information needed to try them.

CAR.PL has two knowledge bases. The diagnostic knowledge base specifies what diagnoses can be made under what conditions, and the case knowledge base describes the particular car under consideration. The diagnostic knowledge base resides in `defect_may_be/1`. The case knowledge base resides in `stored_answer/2`, whose clauses get asserted as the program runs. For convenience, we have assigned names both to the diagnoses (e.g., `drained_battery`) and the conditions that the user observes and reports (e.g., `fuel_is_ok`). Separate predicates (`explain/1` and `ask_question/1`) display the text associated with each diagnosis or observation.

The diagnoses themselves are straightforward. The battery may be drained if the starter worked originally and does not work now; the gearshift may be set incorrectly if the starter never worked; and so on. Notice that the diagnoses are not mutually exclusive — in particular, `wrong_gear` and `starting_system` have the same conditions — and are not arranged into any kind of "logic tree" or flowchart. One of the strengths of Prolog is that the contents of a knowledge base need not be organized into a rigorous form in order to be usable.

The case knowledge base is more interesting since the information has to be obtained from the user, but we do not want to ask for information that is not needed nor repeat requests for information that was already obtained when trying another diagnosis.

To take care of this, the program does not call `stored_answer` directly but rather calls `user_says`, which either retrieves a stored answer or asks a question, as appropriate. Consider what happens upon a call to `user_says(fuel_is_ok,no)`. The first clause of `user_says` immediately looks for `stored_answer(fuel_is_ok,no)`; if that stored answer is found, the query succeeds. Otherwise, there are two other possibilities. Maybe there is no `stored_answer(fuel_is_ok,...)` at all; in that case, `user_says` will ask the question, store the answer, and finally compare the answer that was received to the answer that was expected (`no`). If there is already a `stored_answer(fuel_is_ok,...)` whose second argument is not `no`, the query fails and the question is not asked.

The top-level procedure `try_all_possibilities` manages the whole process:

```
try_all_possibilities :- defect_may_be(D),
                         explain(D),
                         fail.


try_all_possibilities.
```

The first clause finds a possible diagnosis — that is, a clause for `defect_may_be` that succeeds, instantiating `D` to some value. Then it prints the explanation for `D`. Next it hits `fail` and backs up. Since `explain` has only one clause for each value of `D`, the computation has to backtrack to `defect_may_be`, try another clause, and instantiate `D` to a new value. In this manner, all possible diagnoses are found.

The second clause succeeds with no further action after the first clause has failed. This enables the program to terminate with success rather than with failure.

Although small and simple, CAR.PL can be expanded to perform many kinds of diagnosis. It is much more versatile than the flowcharts or logic trees that would be required to implement a diagnostic program easily in a conventional programming language.

Exercise 2.14.1

Get CAR.PL working on your computer and demonstrate that it works as described.

Exercise 2.14.2

Modify CAR.PL to diagnose defects in some other kind of machine that you are familiar with.

```
% File CAR.PL
% Simple automotive expert system

:- reconsult('getyesno.pl').  % Use ensure_loaded if available.

%
% Main control procedures
%

start :-
    write('This program diagnoses why a car won''t start.'),nl,
    write('Answer all questions with Y for yes or N for no.'),nl,
    clear_stored_answers,
    try_all_possibilities.

try_all_possibilities :-      % Backtrack through all possibilities...
    defect_may_be(D),
    explain(D),
    fail.

try_all_possibilities.        % ...then succeed with no further action.

%
% Diagnostic knowledge base
%    (conditions under which to give each diagnosis)
%

defect_may_be(drained_battery) :-
    user_says(starter_was_ok,yes),
    user_says(starter_is_ok,no).

defect_may_be(wrong_gear) :-
    user_says(starter_was_ok,no).

defect_may_be(starting_system) :-
    user_says(starter_was_ok,no).

defect_may_be(fuel_system) :-
    user_says(starter_was_ok,yes),
    user_says(fuel_is_ok,no).

defect_may_be(ignition_system) :-
    user_says(starter_was_ok,yes),
    user_says(fuel_is_ok,yes).
```

Figure 2.7   A simple expert system in Prolog (continued on following pages).

```
%
% Case knowledge base
%   (information supplied by the user during the consultation)
%

:- dynamic(stored_answer/2).

    % (Clauses get added as user answers questions.)

%
% Procedure to get rid of the stored answers
% without abolishing the dynamic declaration
%

clear_stored_answers :- retract(stored_answer(_,_)),fail.
clear_stored_answers.

%
% Procedure to retrieve the user's answer to each question when needed,
% or ask the question if it has not already been asked
%

user_says(Q,A) :- stored_answer(Q,A).

user_says(Q,A) :- \+ stored_answer(Q,_),
                  nl,nl,
                  ask_question(Q),
                  get_yes_or_no(Response),
                  asserta(stored_answer(Q,Response)),
                  Response = A.

%
% Texts of the questions
%

ask_question(starter_was_ok) :-
   write('When you first started trying to start the car,'),nl,
   write('did the starter crank the engine normally? '),nl.

ask_question(starter_is_ok) :-
   write('Does the starter crank the engine normally now? '),nl.

ask_question(fuel_is_ok) :-
   write('Look in the carburetor.  Can you see or smell gasoline?'),nl.
```

Figure 2.7 (Continued).

```
%
%  Explanations for the various diagnoses
%

explain(wrong_gear) :-
   nl,
   write('Check that the gearshift is set to Park or Neutral.'),nl,
   write('Try jiggling the gearshift lever.'),nl.

explain(starting_system) :-
   nl,
   write('Check for a defective battery, voltage'),nl,
   write('regulator, or alternator; if any of these is'),nl,
   write('the problem, charging the battery or jump-'),nl,
   write('starting may get the car going temporarily.'),nl,
   write('Or the starter itself may be defective.'),nl.

explain(drained_battery) :-
   nl,
   write('Your attempts to start the car have run down the battery.'),nl,
   write('Recharging or jump-starting will be necessary.'),nl,
   write('But there is probably nothing wrong with the battery itself.'),nl.

explain(fuel_system) :-
   nl,
   write('Check whether there is fuel in the tank.'),nl,
   write('If so, check for a clogged fuel line or filter'),nl,
   write('or a defective fuel pump.'),nl.

explain(ignition_system) :-
   nl,
   write('Check the spark plugs, cables, distributor,'),nl,
   write('coil, and other parts of the ignition system.'),nl,
   write('If any of these are visibly defective or long'),nl,
   write('overdue for replacement, replace them; if this'),nl,
   write('does not solve the problem, consult a mechanic.'),nl.


% End of CAR.PL
```

Figure 2.7 (Continued).

Chapter 3

Data Structures and Computation

3.1. ARITHMETIC

Here are some examples of how to do arithmetic in Prolog:

```
?- Y is 2+2.
Y = 4
yes


?- 5 is 3+3.
no


?- Z is 4.5 + (3.9 / 2.1).
Z = 6.3571428
yes
```

The built-in predicate is takes an arithmetic expression on its right, evaluates it, and unifies the result with its argument on the left. Expressions in Prolog look very much like those in any other programming language; consult your manual and Table 3.1 (p. 62) for details.[1] The simplest expression consists of just a number; you can say

```
?- What is 2.
```

---

[1]Older versions of Arity Prolog, and possibly some other Prologs, do not let you write an infix operator immediately before a left parenthesis. You have to write 4.5 + (3.9/2.1) (with spaces), not 4.5+(3.9/2.1).

61

TABLE 3.1 FUNCTORS THAT CAN BE USED IN EVALUABLE EXPRESSIONS.

(Many implementations include others. Pre-ISO versions of Quintus Prolog lack `sqrt()`, `log()`, `exp()`, and `floor()`; see note on p. 66.)

Infix operators	+	Addition
	−	Subtraction
	*	Multiplication
	/	Floating-point division
	//	Integer division
	mod	Modulo
Functions	abs( )	Absolute value
	sqrt( )	Square root
	log( )	Logarithm, base e
	exp( )	Antilogarithm, base e
	floor( )	Largest integer $\leq$ argument

if you want to, but it's a needlessly roundabout way to do a simple thing.

The precedence of operators is about the same as in other programming languages: ^ is performed first, then * and /, and finally + and -. Where precedences are equal, operations are performed from left to right. Thus, 4+3*2+5 is equivalent to (4+(3*2))+5.

Prolog supports both integers and floating-point numbers, and interconverts them as needed. Floating-point numbers can be written in E format (e.g., 3.45E-6 for 3.45×10^{-6}).

Notice that *Prolog is not an equation solver.* That is, Prolog does not solve for unknowns on the right side of `is`:

```
?- 5 is 2 + What.          % wrong!
instantiation error
```

Beginners are sometimes surprised to find that Prolog can solve for the unknown in `father(michael,Who)` but not in `5 is 2 + What`. Think a moment about the difference between the two cases. The query `father(michael,Who)` can be solved by trying all the clauses that match it. The query `5 is 2 + What` can't be solved this way because there are no clauses for `is`, and anyhow, if you wanted to do arithmetic by trying all the possible numbers, the search space would be infinite in several dimensions.

The only way to solve `5 is 2 + What` is to manipulate the equation in some way, either algebraically (5 − 2 =*What*) or numerically (by doing a guided search for the right value of *What*). This is particularly easy to do in Prolog because `is` can accept an expression created at run time. We will explore numerical equation solving in Chapter 7. The point to remember, for now, is that the ordinary Prolog search strategy doesn't work for arithmetic because there would be an infinite number of numbers to try.

Exercise 3.1.1

Try out expressions containing each of the functors in Table 3.1. Do they all work in your Prolog?

Exercise 3.1.2

Use Prolog to evaluate each of the following expressions. Indicate how you did so.
$234 + (567.8 \times 3) - 0.0001$
$|5 - 6|$
$9^3 \bmod 12$

Exercise 3.1.3

In your Prolog, what happens if you try to do arithmetic on an expression that contains an uninstantiated variable? Does the query simply fail, or is there an error message? Try it and see.

3.2. CONSTRUCTING EXPRESSIONS

A big difference between Prolog and other programming languages is that other languages evaluate arithmetic expressions wherever they occur, but Prolog evaluates them only in specific places. For example, 2+2 evaluates to 4 only when it is an argument of the predicates in Table 3.2; the rest of the time, it is just a data structure consisting of 2, +, and 2. Actually, that's a feature, not a limitation; it allows us to manipulate the expression as data before evaluating it, as we'll see in Chapter 7. Make sure you distinguish clearly between:

- is, which takes an expression (on the right), evaluates it, and unifies the result with its argument on the left;

- =:=, which evaluates two expressions and compares the results;

- =, which unifies two terms (which need not be expressions and, if expressions, will not be evaluated).

Thus:

```
?- What is 2+3.      % Evaluate 2+3, unify result with What
What = 5

?- 4+1 =:= 2+3.      % Evaluate 4+1 and 2+3, compare results
yes

?- What = 2+3        % Unify What with the expression 2+3
What = 2+3
```

The other comparisons, <, >, =<, and >=, work just like =:= except that they perform different tests. Notice that we write =< and >=, not => and <=. This is because the latter two symbols look like arrows, and the designers of standard Prolog chose to keep them undefined so that you could redefine them for other purposes.

TABLE 3.2 BUILT-IN PREDICATES THAT EVALUATE EXPRESSIONS

R is Expr	Evaluates **Expr** and unifies result with **R**
Expr1 =:= Expr2	Succeeds if results of both expressions are equal
Expr1 =\= Expr2	Succeeds if results of the expressions are not equal
Expr1 > Expr2	Succeeds if $Expr1 > Expr2$
Expr1 < Expr2	Succeeds if $Expr1 < Expr2$
Expr1 >= Expr2	Succeeds if $Expr1 \geq Expr2$
Expr1 =< Expr2	Succeeds if $Expr1 \leq Expr2$

Note syntax: =< and >=, not <= and =>.

Notice also that the arithmetic comparison predicates require their arguments to be fully instantiated. You cannot say "Give me a number less than 20" because such a request would have an infinite number of possible answers.

Speaking of comparisions, another trap for the unwary, present in all programming languages but easier to fall into in Prolog than in most, is the following:

> *A floating-point number obtained by computation is almost never truly equal to any other floating-point number, even if the two look the same when printed out.*

This is because computers do arithmetic in binary, but we write numbers in decimal notation. Many decimal numbers, such as 0.1, have no binary equivalent with a finite number of digits. (Expressing 1/10 in binary is like expressing 1/3 or 1/7 in decimal — the digits to the right of the point repeat endlessly.) As a result, floating-point calculations are subject to rounding error, and $0.1 + 0.1$ does not evaluate to precisely 0.2. Some Prologs work around this problem by treating numbers as equal if they are sufficiently close, even though their internal representations are different.

Exercise 3.2.1

Explain which of the following queries succeed, fail, or raise error conditions, and why:
```
?- 5 is 2+3.
?- 5 =:= 2+3.
?- 5 = 2+3.
?- 4+1 is 2+3.
?- 4+1 =:= 5.
?- What is 2+3.
?- What =:= 2+3.
?- What is 5.
?- What = 5.
```

Exercise 3.2.2

Try each of the following queries and explain the results you get:
```
?- 4 is sqrt(16).
?- 2.0E-1 is sqrt(4.0E-2).
?- 11.0 is sqrt(121.0).
?- 0.5 is 0.1 + 0.1 + 0.1 + 0.1 + 0.1.
?- 0.2 * 100 =:= 2 * 10.
```

If you have the time and the inclination, try similar tests in other programming languages.

3.3. PRACTICAL CALCULATIONS

The alert reader will have surmised that when we use expressions in Prolog, we are mixing styles of encoding knowledge. From a logical point of view, "sum" and "product" are relations between numbers, just as "father" and "mother" are relations between people. From a logical point of view, instead of

```
?- What is 2 + 3*4 + 5.
```

we should write

```
?- product(3,4,P), sum(2,P,S), sum(S,5,What).    % Not standard Prolog!
```

and in fact that's how some early Prologs did it. However, the older approach has two problems: It's unwieldy, and it gives the impression that Prolog has a search strategy for numbers, which it doesn't. Thus, we use expressions instead.

If you want to implement numerical algorithms, you *do* have to define Prolog predicates because there's usually no way to define additional functions that can appear within expressions. Thus, you have to revert to a purely logical style when dealing with things you've defined for yourself.[2]

For example, let's define a predicate `close_enough/2` that succeeds if two numbers are equal to within 0.0001. That will let us compare the results of floating-point computations without being thrown off by rounding errors. Here's how it's done:

```
close_enough(X,X)  :-  !.

close_enough(X,Y)  :-  X < Y,
                       Y-X < 0.0001.

close_enough(X,Y)  :-  X > Y,
                       close_enough(Y,X).
```

The first clause takes care of the case where the two arguments, by some miracle, really are equal. It also handles the case where one argument is uninstantiated, by unifying it with the other argument. This enables us to use `close_enough` as a complete substitute for = when working with floating-point numbers. The cut ('!') ensures that if clause 1 succeeds in a particular case, the other two clauses will never be tried.

The second clause is the heart of the computation: compare X and Y, subtract the smaller from the larger, and check whether the difference is less than 0.0001.

---

[2]Unless, of course, you want to write your own replacement for `is`, which can be well worth doing; see Chapter 7.

The third clause deals with arguments in the opposite order; it simply swaps them and calls `close_enough` again, causing the second clause to take effect the second time. Notice that no loop is possible here.

Now let's do some computation. The following predicate instantiates Y to the real square root of X if it exists, or to the atom `nonexistent` if not:[3]

```
real_square_root(X,nonexistent) :- X < 0.0.

real_square_root(X,Y) :- X >= 0.0,
                         Y is sqrt(X).
```

Some examples of its use:

```
?- real_square_root(9.0,Root).
Root = 3.0
yes

?- real_square_root(-1.0,Root).
Root = nonexistent
yes
```

Notice, however, that the query `real_square_root(121.0,11.0)` will probably fail because 11.0 does not exactly match the floating-point result computed by `sqrt`, even though $\sqrt{121} = 11$ exactly. We can remedy this by doing the comparison with `close_enough` rather than letting the unifier do it directly. This requires redefining `real_square_root` as follows:

```
real_square_root(X,nonexistent) :- X < 0.0.          % Clause 1

real_square_root(X,Y) :- X >= 0.0,                   % Clause 2
                         R is sqrt(X),
                         close_enough(R,Y).
```

Now we get the result we wanted:

```
?- real_square_root(121.0,11.0).
yes
```

Finally, let's exploit Prolog's ability to return alternative answers to the same question. Every positive real number has *two* square roots, one positive and the other negative. For example, the square roots of 1.21 are 1.1 and −1.1. We'd like `real_square_root` to get both of them.

---

[3]Versions of Quintus Prolog and Cogent (Amzi) Prolog that predate the ISO standard do not let you write `sqrt(...)` in expressions. In Cogent (Amzi) Prolog, for `sqrt(X)` simply write `exp(ln(X)/2)`. In Quintus, `sqrt/2` is a Prolog predicate found in the math library, and to make `real_square_root` work, you'll have to change it as follows:

(1) Add ':- `ensure_loaded(library(math))`.' at the beginning of your program.

(2) Replace `R is sqrt(X)` with the goal `sqrt(X,R)`.

(3) In clause 3, replace `R is -sqrt(X)` with the two goals `sqrt(X,S)`, `R is -S`.

That's easy to do, but we need separate clauses for the alternatives because the arithmetic itself, in Prolog, is completely deterministic. All we have to add is the following clause:

```
real_square_root(X,Y) :- X > 0.0,                    % Clause 3
                         R is -sqrt(X),
                         close_enough(R,Y).
```

This gives an alternative way of finding a real square root. Now every call to `real_square_root` with a positive first argument will return two answers on successive tries:

```
?- real_square_root(9.0,Root).
Root = 3.0
Root = -3.0
yes
```

Nondeterminism is a useful mathematical tool because many mathematical problems have multiple solutions that can be generated algorithmically. Even if the mathematical computation is deterministic, Prolog lets you package the results so that they come out as alternative solutions to the same query.

Exercise 3.3.1

Get `close_enough` and `real_square_root` working and verify that they work as described.

Exercise 3.3.2

What guarantees that the recursion in `close_enough` will not continue endlessly?

Exercise 3.3.3

Modify `close_enough` so that it tests whether two numbers are equal to within 0.1% (i.e., tests whether the difference between them is less than 0.1% of the larger number).

Exercise 3.3.4

What does `real_square_root` do if you ask for the square root of a negative number? Why? Explain which clauses are tried and what happens in each.

3.4. TESTING FOR INSTANTIATION

So far, `real_square_root` still requires its first argument to be instantiated, but with some minor changes we can even endow `real_square_root` with interchangeability of unknowns. Using the two arguments X and Y, the strategy we want to follow is this:

- If X is known, unify Y with $\sqrt{X}$ or $-\sqrt{X}$ (these are two alternative solutions).

- If Y is known, unify X with Y^2.

To do this, we need a way to test whether X and Y are instantiated. Prolog provides two predicates to do this: var, which succeeds if its argument is an uninstantiated variable, and nonvar, which succeeds if its argument has a value. We can thus rewrite real_square_root as follows:[4]

```
real_square_root(X,nonexistent) :-                    % Clause 1
                    nonvar(X),
                    X < 0.0.


real_square_root(X,Y) :- nonvar(X),                   % Clause 2
                    X >= 0.0,
                    R is sqrt(X),
                    close_enough(R,Y).


real_square_root(X,Y) :- nonvar(X),                   % Clause 3
                    X > 0.0,
                    R is -sqrt(X),
                    close_enough(R,Y).


real_square_root(X,Y) :- nonvar(Y),                   % Clause 4
                    Ysquared is Y*Y,
                    close_enough(Ysquared,X).
```

Here clause 4 provides a way to compute X from Y, and the use of nonvar throughout ensures that the correct clause will be chosen and that we will not try to do computations or comparisons on uninstantiated variables.

Now, however, there is some spurious nondeterminism. If both X and Y are instantiated, then either clause 2 or clause 3 will succeed, and so will clause 4. This may produce unwanted multiple results when a call to real_square_root is embedded in a larger program. The spurious nondeterminism can be removed by adding still more tests to ensure that only one clause succeeds in such a case.

Exercise 3.4.1

Demonstrate that the latest version of real_square_root works as described (i.e., that it can solve for either argument given the other).

Exercise 3.4.2

Remove the spurious nondeterminism in real_square_root. That is, ensure that a query such as real_square_root(1.21,1.1) succeeds only once and does not have an alternative way of succeeding.

Exercise 3.4.3

Define the predicate sum(X,Y,Z) such that $X + Y = Z$. Give it the ability to solve for any of its three arguments given the other two. You can assume that at least two arguments will be instantiated.

---

[4]Quintus and Cogent (Amzi) Prolog users, see footnote 3 (page 66).

Exercise 3.4.4

> Implement a solver for Ohm's Law in Prolog with full interchangeability of unknowns. That is, define ohm(E,I,R) such that E = I × R and such that any of the three arguments will be found if the other two are given. You can assume that all arguments will be nonzero.

3.5. LISTS

One of the most important Prolog data structures is the LIST. A list is an ordered sequence of zero or more terms written between square brackets and separated by commas, thus:

```
[alpha,beta,gamma,delta]
[1,2,3,go]
[(2+2),in(austin,texas),-4.356,X]
[[a,list,within],a,list]
```

The elements of a list can be Prolog terms of any kind, including other lists. The empty list is written []. Note especially that the one-element list [a] is not equivalent to the atom a.

Lists can be constructed or decomposed through unification. An entire list can, of course, match a single variable:

Unify	With	Result
[a,b,c]	X	X=[a,b,c]

Also, not surprisingly, corresponding elements of two lists can be unified one by one:

Unify	With	Result
[X,Y,Z]	[a,b,c]	X=a, Y=b, Z=c
[X,b,Z]	[a,Y,c]	X=a, Y=b, Z=c

This applies even to lists or structures embedded within lists:

Unify	With	Result
[[a,b],c]	[X,Y]	X=[a,b], Y=c
[a(b),c(X)]	[Z,c(a)]	X=a, Z=a(b)

More importantly, any list can be divided into head and tail by the symbol '|'. (On your keyboard, the character | may have a gap in the middle.) The head of a list is the first element; the tail is a list of the remaining elements (and can be empty).

The tail of a list is always a list; the head of a list is an element.

Every nonempty list has a head and a tail. Thus,

```
[a|[b,c,d]]  =  [a,b,c,d]
[a|[]]  =  [a]
```

(The empty list, [], cannot be divided into head and tail.)

The term [X|Y] unifies with any nonempty list, instantiating X to the head and Y to the tail, thus:

Unify	With	Result
[X|Y]	[a,b,c,d]	X=a, Y=[b,c,d]
[X|Y]	[a]	X=a, Y=[]

So far, | is like the CAR–CDR distinction in Lisp, but unlike CAR and CDR, | can pick off more than one initial element in a single step. Thus:

[a,b,c|[d,e,f]]   =   [a,b,c,d,e,f]

and this feature really proves its worth in unification, as follows:

Unify	With	Result
[X,Y|Z]	[a,b,c]	X=a, Y=b, Z=[c]
[X,Y|Z]	[a,b,c,d]	X=a, Y=b, Z=[c,d]
[X,Y,Z|A]	[a,b,c]	X=a, Y=b, Z=c, A=[]
[X,Y,Z|A]	[a,b]	fails
[X,Y,a]	[Z,b,Z]	X=Z=a, Y=b
[X,Y|Z]	[a|W]	X=a, W=[Y|Z]

The work of constructing and decomposing lists is done mostly by unification, not by procedures. This means that the heart of a list processing procedure is often in the notation that describes the structure of the arguments.

To accustom ourselves to this notation, let's define a simple list processing predicate:

```
third_element([A,B,C|Rest],C).
```

This one succeeds if the first argument is a list and the second argument is the third element of that list. It has complete interchangeability of unknowns, thus:

```
?- third_element([a,b,c,d,e,f],X).
X = c
yes


?- third_element([a,b,Y,d,e,f],c).
Y = c
yes


?- third_element(X,a).
X = [_0001,_0002,a|_0003]
yes
```

In the last of these, the computer knows nothing about X except that it is a list whose third element is a. Therefore, it constructs a list with uninstantiated first and second elements, followed by a and then an uninstantiated tail.

Exercise 3.5.1

Define a predicate `first_two_same` that succeeds if its argument is a list whose first two elements match (are unifiable), like this:

```
?- first_two_same([a,a,b,c]).
yes
?- first_two_same([a,X,b,c]).        % here a can unify with X
X=a
yes
?- first_two_same([a,b,c,d]).
no
```

Exercise 3.5.2

Define a predicate `swap_first_two` which, given a list of any length ≥ 2, constructs another list like the first one but with the first two elements swapped:

```
?- swap_first_two([a,b,c,d],What).
What = [b,a,c,d]
```

Hint: The definition of `swap_first_two` can consist of a single Prolog fact.

3.6. STORING DATA IN LISTS

Lists can contain data in much the same way as records in COBOL or Pascal. For example,

```
['Michael Covington',
 '285 Saint George Drive',
 'Athens',
 'Georgia',
 '30606']
```

is a reasonable way to represent an address, with fields for name, street, city, state, and zip code. Procedures like `third_element` in the previous section can extract or insert data into such a list.

One important difference between a list and a data record is that the number of elements in a list need not be declared in advance. At any point in a program, a list can be created with as many elements as available memory can accommodate. (If the number of elements that you want to accommodate is fixed, you should consider using not a list but a STRUCTURE, discussed in section 3.14.)

Another difference is that the elements of a list need not be of any particular type. Atoms, structures, and numbers can be used freely in any combination. Moreover, a list can contain another list as one of its elements:

```
['Michael Covington',
 [['B.A',1977],
 ['M.Phil.',1978],
 ['Ph.D.',1982]],
 'Associate Research Scientist',
 'University of Georgia']
```

Here the main list has four elements: name, list of college degrees, current job title, and current employer. The list of college degrees has three elements, each of which is a two-element list of degree and date. Note that the number of college degrees per person is not fixed; the same structure can accommodate a person with no degrees or a person with a dozen.

This, of course, raises a wide range of issues in data representation. Recall the contrast between "data-record style" and other uses of predicates that we pointed out at the end of Chapter 1. The best representation of a database cannot be determined without knowing what kind of queries it will most often be used to answer.

Lists in Prolog can do the work of arrays in other languages. For instance, a matrix of numbers can be represented as a list of lists:

```
[[1,2,3],
 [4,5,6],
 [7,8,9]]
```

There is, however, an important difference. In an array, any element can be accessed as quickly as any other. In a list, the computer must always start at the beginning and work its way along the list element by element. This is necessary because of the way lists are stored in memory. Whereas an array occupies a sequence of contiguous locations, a list can be discontinuous. Each element of a list is accompanied by a pointer to the location of the next element, and the entire list can be located only by following the whole chain of pointers. We will return to this point in Chapter 7.

Exercise 3.6.1

Define a predicate `display_degrees` that will take a list such as

```
['Michael Covington',
 [['B.A',1977],
  ['M.Phil.',1978],
  ['Ph.D.',1982]],
 'Associate Research Scientist',
 'University of Georgia']
```

and will write out only the list of degrees (i.e., the second element of the main list).

3.7. RECURSION

To fully exploit the power of lists, we need a way to work with list elements without specifying their positions in advance. To do this, we need repetitive procedures that will work their way along a list, searching for a particular element or performing some operation on every element encountered.

Repetition is expressed in Prolog by using RECURSION, a program structure in which a procedure calls itself. The idea is that, in order to solve a problem, we will perform some action and then solve a smaller problem of the same type using the same procedure. The process terminates when the problem becomes so small that the procedure can solve it in one step without calling itself again.

Let's define a predicate `member(X,Y)` that succeeds if X is an element of the list Y. We do not know in advance how long Y is, so we can't try a finite set of predetermined positions. We need to keep going until we either find X or run out of elements to examine.

Before thinking about how to perform the repetition, let's identify two special cases that aren't repetitive.

- If Y is empty, fail with no further action (because nothing is a member of the empty list).

- If X is the first element of Y, succeed with no further action (because we've found it).

We will deal with the first special case by making sure that, in all of our clauses, the second argument is something that will not unify with an empty list. An empty list has no tail, so we can rule out empty lists by letting the second argument be a list that has both a head and a tail.

We can express the second special case as a simple clause:[5]

```
member(X,[X|_]).                                  % Clause 1
```

Now for the recursive part. Think about this carefully to see why it works:

X *is a member of* Y *if* X *is a member of the tail of* Y.

This is expressed in Prolog as follows:

```
member(X,[_|Ytail]) :- member(X,Ytail).          % Clause 2
```

Let's try an example.

```
?- member(c,[a,b,c]).
```

This does not match clause 1, so proceed to clause 2. This clause generates the new query

```
?- member(c,[b,c]).
```

We're making progress — we have transformed our original problem into a smaller problem of the same kind. Again, clause 1 does not match, but clause 2 does, and we get a new query:

```
?- member(c,[c]).
```

Now we're very close indeed. Remember that [c] is equivalent to [c|[]]. This time, clause 1 works and the query succeeds.

If we had asked for an element that wasn't there, clause 2 would have applied one more time, generating a query with an empty list as the second argument. Since an empty list has no tail, that query would match neither clause 1 nor clause 2, so it would fail — exactly the desired result.

This process of trimming away list elements from the beginning is often called "CDRing down" the list. (CDR, pronounced "could-er," is the name of the Lisp function that retrieves the tail of a list; it originally stood for "contents of the decrement register.")

---

[5]If **member** is a built-in predicate in the implementation of Prolog that you are using, give your version of it a different name, such as **mem**.

Exercise 3.7.1

Describe exactly what happens, step by step, when the computer solves each of these queries:

```
?- member(c,[a,b,c,d,e]).
?- member(q,[a,b,c,d,e]).
```

Exercise 3.7.2

What does each of the following queries do?

```
?- member(What,[a,b,c,d,e]).
?- member(a,What).
```

How many solutions does each of them have?

Exercise 3.7.3

What does each of the following predicates do? Try them on the computer (with various lists as arguments) before jumping to conclusions. Explain the results.

```
test1(List) :- member(X,List), write(X), nl, fail.
test1(_).

test2([First|Rest]) :- write(First), nl, test2(Rest).
test2([]).
```

3.8. COUNTING LIST ELEMENTS

Here is a recursive algorithm to count the elements of a list:

- If the list is empty, it has 0 elements.

- Otherwise, skip over the first element, count the number of elements remaining, and add 1.

The second of these clauses is recursive because, in order to count the elements of a list, you have to count the elements of another, smaller list. The algorithm expressed in Prolog is the following:[6]

```
list_length([],0).

list_length([_|Tail],K) :- list_length(Tail,J),
                            K is J+1.
```

The recursion terminates because the list eventually becomes empty as elements are removed one by one. The order in which the computations are done is shown as follows. (Variable names are marked with subscripts to show that variables in different invocations of the clause are not identical.)

---

[6]We call it list_length because there is already a built-in predicate called length that does the same thing.

```
?- list_length([a,b,c],K₀).
 ?- list_length([b,c],K₁).
  ?- list_length([c],K₂).
   ?- list_length([],0).
  ?- K₂ is 0+1.
 ?- K₁ is 1+1.
?- K₀ is 2+1.
```

This recursive procedure calls itself in the middle: shorten the list, find the length of the shorter list, and then add 1. Work similar examples by hand until you are at ease with this kind of program execution.

Exercise 3.8.1

Define a predicate count_occurrences(X,L,N) that instantiates N to the number of times that element X occurs in list L:

```
?- count_occurrences(a,[a,b,r,a,c,a,d,a,b,r,a],What).
What = 5
?- count_occurrences(a,[n,o,t,h,e,r,e],What).
What = 0
```

Start by describing the recursive algorithm in English. Consider three cases: the list is empty, the first element matches what you are looking for, or the first element does not match what you are looking for.

Exercise 3.8.2

Define a predicate last_element(L,E) that instantiates E to the last element of list L, like this:

```
?- last_element([a,b,c,d],What).
What = d
```

3.9. CONCATENATING (APPENDING) LISTS

What if we want to concatenate (APPEND) one list to another? We'd like to combine [a,b,c] with [d,e,f] to get [a,b,c,d,e,f].

Notice that | will not do the job for us; [[a,b,c]|[d,e,f]] is equivalent to [[a,b,c],d,e,f], which is not what we want. We'll have to work through the first list element by element, adding the elements one by one to the second list.

First, let's deal with the limiting case. Since we'll be shortening the first list, it will eventually become empty, and to append an empty list to the beginning of another list, you don't have to do anything. So:

```
append([],X,X).                                    % Clause 1
```

The recursive clause is less intuitive, but very concise:

```
append([X1|X2],Y,[X1|Z]) :- append(X2,Y,Z).       % Clause 2
```

Describing clause 2 declaratively: The first element of the result is the same as the first element of the first list. The tail of the result is obtained by concatenating the tail of the first list with the whole second list.[7]

Let's express this more procedurally. To concatenate two lists:

1. Pick off the head of the first list (call it X1).

2. Recursively concatenate the tail of the first list with the whole second list. Call the result Z.

3. Add X1 to the beginning of Z.

Note that the value of X1 from step 1 is held somewhere while the recursive computation (step 2) is going on, and then retrieved in step 3. The place where it is held is called the RECURSION STACK.

Note also that the Prolog syntax matches the declarative rather than the procedural English description just given. From the procedural point of view, the term [X1|X2] in the argument list represents the first step of the computation — decomposing an already instantiated list — while the term [X1|Z] in the same argument list represents the last step in the whole procedure, putting a list together after Z has been instantiated.

Because of its essentially declarative nature, append enjoys complete interchangeability of unknowns:

```
?- append([a,b,c],[d,e,f],X).
X = [a,b,c,d,e,f]
yes

?- append([a,b,c],X,[a,b,c,d,e,f]).
X = [d,e,f]
yes

?- append(X,[d,e,f],[a,b,c,d,e,f]).
X = [a,b,c]
yes
```

Each of these is deterministic; there is only one possible solution. However, if we leave the first two arguments uninstantiated, we get, as alternative solutions, all of the ways of splitting the last argument into two sublists:

```
?- append(X,Y,[a,b,c,d]).
X=[] Y=[a,b,c,d]
X=[a]   Y=[b,c,d]
X=[a,b]   Y=[c,d]
X=[a,b,c]   Y=[d]
X=[a,b,c,d] Y=[]
```

---

[7]Like member, append is a built-in predicate in some implementations. If you are using such an implementation, use a different name for your predicate, such as app.

This can be useful for solving problems that involve dividing groups of objects into two sets.

Exercise 3.9.1

> What is the result of this query?
> ```
> ?- append([J,b,K],[d,L,f],[a,M,c,N,e,P]).
> ```

Exercise 3.9.2

> Define a predicate `append3` that concatenates *three* lists and has complete interchangeability of unknowns. You can refer to `append` in its definition.

Exercise 3.9.3

> Write a procedure called `flatten` that takes a list whose elements may be either atoms or lists (with any degree of embedding) and returns a list of all the atoms contained in the original list, thus:
> ```
> ?- flatten([[a,b,c],[d,[e,f],g],h],X).
> X = [a,b,c,d,e,f,g,h]
> ```
> Make sure your procedure does not generate spurious alternatives upon backtracking. (What you do with empty lists in the input is up to you; you can assume that there will be none.)

3.10. REVERSING A LIST RECURSIVELY

Here is a classic recursive algorithm for reversing the order of elements in a list:

1. Split the original list into head and tail.

2. Recursively reverse the tail of the original list.

3. Make a list whose only element is the head of the original list.

4. Concatenate the reversed tail of the original list with the list created in step 3.

Since the list gets shorter every time, the limiting case is an empty list, which we want to simply return unchanged. In Prolog:[8]

```
reverse([],[]).                                    % Clause 1

reverse([Head|Tail],Result) :-                     % Clause 2
            reverse(Tail,ReversedTail),
            append(ReversedTail,[Head],Result).
```

This is a translation of the classic Lisp list-reversal algorithm, known as "naive reversal" or NREV and frequently used to test the speed of Lisp and Prolog implementations. Its naiveté consists in its great inefficiency. You might think that an

---

[8] Again, `reverse` may be a built-in predicate in your implementation. If so, name your predicate `rev`.

eight-element list could be reversed in eight or nine steps. With this algorithm, however, reversal of an eight-element list takes 45 steps — 9 calls to `reverse` followed by 36 calls to `append`.

One thing to be said in favor of this algorithm is that it enjoys interchangeability of unknowns — at least on the first solution to each query. If the first argument is uninstantiated, the second argument is a list, and we ask for more than one solution, a strange thing happens. Recall that in order to solve

```
?- reverse(X,[a,b,c]).
```

the computer must solve the subgoal

```
?- reverse(Tail,ReversedTail).
```

where `[Head|Tail]=X` but neither `Tail` nor `ReversedTail` is instantiated. The computer first tries the first clause, instantiating both `Tail` and `ReversedTail` to `[]`. This can't be used in further computation, so the computer backtracks, tries the next clause, and eventually generates a list of uninstantiated variables of the proper length. So far so good; computation can then continue, and the correct answer is produced. When the user asks for an alternative solution, Prolog tries a yet longer list of uninstantiated variables, and then a longer one, ad infinitum. The computation backtracks endlessly until it generates a list so long that it uses up all available memory.

Exercise 3.10.1

By inserting some `writes` and `nls`, get `reverse` to display the arguments of each call to itself and each call to `append`. Then try the query `reverse(What,[a,b,c])`, ask for alternative solutions, and watch what happens. Show your modified version of `reverse` and its output.

Exercise 3.10.2   (for students with mathematical background)

Devise a formula that predicts how many procedure calls are made by `reverse` as a function of the length of the list.

Exercise 3.10.3

Why is NREV not a good algorithm for testing Prolog implementations?
Hint: Consider what Prolog is designed for.

3.11. A FASTER WAY TO REVERSE LISTS

Here is an algorithm that reverses a list much more quickly but lacks interchangeability of unknowns.

```
fast_reverse(Original,Result) :-
   nonvar(Original),
   fast_reverse_aux(Original,[],Result).
```

```
fast_reverse_aux([Head|Tail],Stack,Result) :-
    fast_reverse_aux(Tail,[Head|Stack],Result).

fast_reverse_aux([],Result,Result).
```

The first clause checks that the original list is indeed instantiated, then calls a three-argument procedure named `fast_reverse_aux`. The idea is to move elements one by one, picking them off the beginning of the original list and adding them to a new list that serves as a stack. The new list, of course, becomes a backward copy of the original list. Through all of the recursive calls, `Result` is uninstantiated; at the end, we instantiate it and pass it back to the calling procedure. Thus:

```
?- fast_reverse_aux([a,b,c],[],Result).
 ?- fast_reverse_aux([b,c],[a],Result).
  ?- fast_reverse_aux([c],[b,a],Result).
   ?- fast_reverse_aux([],[c,b,a],[c,b,a]).
```

This algorithm reverses an n-element list in $n + 1$ steps.

We included `nonvar` in the first clause to make `fast_reverse` fail if its first argument is uninstantiated. Without this, an uninstantiated first argument would send the computer into an endless computation, constructing longer and longer lists of uninstantiated variables, none of which leads to a solution.

Exercise 3.11.1

Demonstrate that `fast_reverse` works as described. Modify it to print out the arguments of each recursive call so that you can see what it is doing.

Exercise 3.11.2

Compare the speed of `reverse` and `fast_reverse` in reversing a long list.
Hint: On a microcomputer, you will have to do this with stopwatch in hand. On UNIX systems, the Prolog built-in predicate `statistics` will tell you how much CPU time and memory the Prolog system has used.

3.12. CHARACTER STRINGS

There are three ways to represent a string of characters in Prolog:

- As an atom. Atoms are compact but hard to take apart or manipulate.

- As a list of ASCII codes. You can then use standard list processing techniques on them.

- As a list of one-character atoms. Again, you can use standard list processing techniques.

In Prolog, if you write a string with double quotes (`"like this"`), the computer interprets it as a list of ASCII codes. Thus, `"abc"` and `[97,98,99]` are exactly the same Prolog term. Such lists of ASCII codes are traditionally called STRINGS.[9]

---

[9]In ISO Prolog, to ensure that strings are interpreted in the way described here, add the declaration "`:- set_prolog_flag(double_quotes,codes).`" at the beginning of your program.

An immediate problem is that there is no standard way to output a character string, since `write` and `display` both print the list of numbers:

```
?- write("abc").
[97,98,99]
yes
```

We will define a string input routine presently and refine it in Chapter 5, but here is a simple string output procedure:

```
write_str([Head|Tail]) :- put(Head), write_str(Tail).
write_str([]).
```

The recursion is easy to follow. If the string is nonempty (and thus will match [Head|Tail]), print the first item and repeat the procedure for the remaining items. When the string becomes empty, succeed with no further action.

Strings are lists, in every sense of the word, and all list processing techniques can be used on them. Thus `reverse` will reverse a string, `append` will concatenate or split strings, and so forth.

Exercise 3.12.1

Define a Prolog predicate `print_splits` which, when given a string, will print out all possible ways of dividing the string in two, like this:

```
?- print_splits("university").
 university
u niversity
un iversity
uni versity
univ ersity
unive rsity
univer sity
univers ity
universi ty
universit y
university
yes
```

Feel free to define and call other predicates as needed.

Exercise 3.12.2

Define a predicate `ends_in_s` that succeeds if its argument is a string whose last element is the character s (or, more generally, a list whose last element is the ASCII code for s), like this:

```
?- ends_in_s("Xerxes").
yes
?- ends_in_s("Xenophon").
no
?- ends_in_s([an,odd,example,115]).        % 115 is code for s
yes
```

Hint: This can be done in two ways: using `append` or using the algorithm of Exercise 3.8.2.

3.13. INPUTTING A LINE AS A STRING OR ATOM

It's easy to make Prolog read a whole line of input into a single string without caring whether the input follows Prolog syntax. The idea is to avoid using `read`, and instead use `get0` to input characters until the end of the line is reached.[10] It turns out that the algorithm requires one character of LOOKAHEAD — it can't decide what to do with each character until it knows whether the *next* character marks the end of the line. Here's how it's done:

```
% read_str(String)
%    Accepts a whole line of input as a string (list of ASCII codes).
%    Assumes that the keyboard is buffered.

read_str(String) :- get0(Char),
                     read_str_aux(Char,String).

read_str_aux(-1,[]) :- !.    % end of file
read_str_aux(10,[]) :- !.    % end of line (UNIX)
read_str_aux(13,[]) :- !.    % end of line (DOS)

read_str_aux(Char,[Char|Rest]) :- read_str(Rest).
```

Notice that this predicate begins with a brief comment describing it. From now on such comments will be our standard practice.

The lookahead is achieved by reading one character and then passing that character to `read_str_aux`, which makes a decision and then finishes inputting the line. Specifically:

- If `Char` is 10 or 13 (end of line) or −1 (end of file), don't input anything else; the rest of the string is empty.

- Otherwise, put `Char` at the beginning of the string, and recursively input the rest of it the same way.

The cuts in `read_str_aux` ensure that if any of the first three clauses succeeds, the last clause will never be tried. We'll explain cuts more fully in Chapter 4. Their purpose here is to keep the last clause from matching unsuitable values of `Char`.

Note that `read_str` assumes that keyboard input is buffered. If the keyboard is unbuffered, `read_str` will still work, but if the user hits Backspace while typing, the Backspace key will not "untype" the previous key — instead, the Backspace character will appear in the string.[11]

We often want to read a whole line of input, not as a string, but as an atom. That's easy, too, because the built-in predicate `name/2` interconverts strings and atoms:

----

[10]Recall that in ISO Prolog, `get0` is called `get_code`.

[11]In Arity Prolog, which uses unbuffered input, you can define `read_str` this way:
```
read_str(String) :- read_line(0,Text), list_text(String,Text).
```
This relies on two built-in Arity Prolog predicates. There is also a built-in predicate `read_string`, which reads a fixed number of characters.

```
?- name(abc,What).
What = [97,98,99]    % equivalent to "abc"

?- name(What,"abc").
What = abc

?- name(What,"Hello there").
What = 'Hello there'
yes

?- name(What,[97,98]).
What = ab
```

(Remember that a string *is* a list of numbers, nothing more, nothing less. The Prolog system neither knows nor cares whether you have typed "abc" or [97,98,99].) An easy way to read lines as atoms is this:

```
% read_atom(Atom)
%    Accepts a whole line of input as a single atom.

read_atom(Atom) :- read_str(String), name(Atom,String).
```

Implementations differ as to what name does when the string can be interpreted as a number (such as "3.1416"). In some implementations, name would give you the number 3.1416, and in others, the atom '3.1416'. That's one reason name isn't in the ISO standard.   In its place are two predicates, atom_codes and number_codes, which produce atoms and numbers respectively.   Alongside them are two more predicates, atom_chars and number_chars, which use lists of one-character atoms instead of strings.[12] We will deal with input of numbers in Chapter 5.

Exercise 3.13.1

Get read_str and read_atom working on your computer and verify that they function as described.

Exercise 3.13.2

In your Prolog, does '?- name(What,"3.1416").' produce a number or an atom? State how you found out.

Exercise 3.13.3

Based on read_str, define a predicate read_charlist that produces a list of one-character atoms [l,i,k,e,' ',t,h,i,s] instead of a string.

Exercise 3.13.4

Modify read_str to skip blanks in its input. Call the new version read_str_no_blanks. It should work like this:

---

[12]Pre-ISO versions of Quintus Prolog have **atom_chars** and **number_chars**, but they produce strings, not character lists; that is, they have the behavior prescribed for atom_codes and number_codes respectively.

```
?- read_str_no_blanks(X).
a     b c     d      (typed by user)
X = [97,98,99,100]  % equivalent to "abcd"
```

Do not use **get**; instead, read each character with **get0** and skip it if it is a blank.

3.14. STRUCTURES

Many Prolog terms consist of a functor followed by zero or more terms as arguments:

```
a(b,c)
```

```
alpha([beta,gamma],X)
```

```
'this and'(that)
```

```
f(g,h,i,j,k,l,m,n,o,p,q,r,s,t,u,v)
```

```
i_have_no_arguments
```

Terms of this form are called STRUCTURES. The functor is always an atom, but the arguments can be terms of any type whatever. A structure with no arguments is simply an atom.

So far we have used structures in facts, rules, queries, and arithmetic expressions. Structures are also data items in their own right; alongside lists, they are useful for representing complex data. For example:

```
person(name('Michael Covington'),
       gender(male),
       birthplace(city('Valdosta'),
                  state('Georgia'))))
```

```
sentence(noun_phrase(determiner(the),
                     noun(cat)),
         verb_phrase(verb(chased),
                     noun_phrase(determiner(the),
                                 noun(dog))))
```

Structures work much like lists, although they are stored differently (and more compactly) in memory. The structure `a(b,c)` contains the same information as the list `[a,b,c]`. In fact, the two are interconvertible by the predicate '`=..`' (pronounced "univ" after its name in Marseilles Prolog):

```
?- a(b,c,d) =.. X.
X = [a,b,c,d]
yes
```

```
?- X =.. [w,x,y,z].
X = w(x,y,z)
yes
```

```
?- alpha =.. X.
X = [alpha]
yes
```

Notice that the left-hand argument is always a structure, while the right-hand argument is always a list whose first element is an atom.

One important difference is that a list is decomposable into head and tail, while a structure is not. A structure will unify with another structure that has the same functor and the same number of arguments. Of course, the whole structure will also unify with a single variable:

Unify	With	Result
a(b,c)	X	X=a(b,c)
a(b,c)	a(X,Y)	X=b, Y=c
a(b,c)	a(X)	fails
a(b,c)	a(X,Y,Z)	fails

In addition to =.. Prolog provides two other built-in predicates for decomposing structures:

- `functor(S,F,A)` unifies F and A with the functor and arity, respectively, of structure S. Recall that the arity of a structure is its number of arguments.

- `arg(N,S,X)` unifies X with the Nth argument of structure S.

For example:

```
?- functor(a(b,c),X,Y).
X = a
Y = 2

?- arg(2,a(b,c,d,e),What).
What = c
```

These are considerably faster than =.. because they don't have to construct a list.

Do not confuse Prolog *functors* with *functions* in other programming languages. A Pascal or FORTRAN function always stands for an operation to be performed on its arguments. A Prolog functor is not an operation but merely the head of a data structure.

Exercise 3.14.1

Using what you know about list processing, construct a predicate `reverse_args` that takes any structure and reverses the order of its arguments:
```
?- reverse_args(a(b,c,d,e),What).
What = a(e,d,c,b)
```

Exercise 3.14.2

Which arguments of `functor` have to be instantiated in order for it to work? Try various combinations and see.

Exercise 3.14.3

Construct a predicate `last_arg(S,A)` that unifies `A` with the last argument of structure `S`, like this:

```
?- last_arg(a(b,c,d,e,f),What).
What = f
```

Use `functor` and `arg`.

3.15. THE "OCCURS CHECK"

You can create bizarre, loopy structures by unifying a variable with a structure or list that contains that variable. Such structures contain pointers to themselves, and they lead to endless loops when the print routine, or anything else, tries to traverse them. For example:

```
?- X = f(X).
X = f(f(f(f(f(f(f(f(f(f(f(f(f(f(f(f(f(f(f(f(f(f(f(f(f(f(f(f(f(f(f(f(f...
```

```
?- X = [a,b,X]
X = [a,b,[a,b,[a,b,[a,b,[a,b,[a,b,[a,b,[a,b[a,b,[a,b[a,b,[a,b...
```

```
?- f(X) = f(f(X))
X = f(f(f(f(f(f(f(f(f(f(f(f(f(f(f(f(f(f(f(f(f(f(f(f(f(f(f(f(f(...
```

The ISO standard includes a predicate, `unify_with_occurs_check`, that checks whether one term contains the other before attempting unification, and fails if so:

```
?- unify_with_occurs_check(X,f(X)).
no.
```

```
?- unify_with_occurs_check(X,f(a)).
X = f(a)
```

Our experience has been that the occurs check is rarely needed in practical Prolog programs, but it is something you should be aware of.

Exercise 3.15.1

Which of the following queries creates a loopy structure?

```
?- X=Y, Y=X.
?- X=f(Y), Y=X.
?- X=f(Y), Y=f(X).
?- X=f(Y), Y=f(Z), Z=a.
```

3.16. CONSTRUCTING GOALS AT RUNTIME

Because Prolog queries are structures, you can treat them as data and construct them as the program runs. The built-in predicate `call` executes its argument as a query.

Thus, `call(write('hello there'))` is exactly equivalent to `write('hello there')`.

The power of `call` comes from the fact that a goal can be created by computation and then executed. For example:

```
answer_question :-
        write('Mother or father? '),
        read_atom(X),
        write('Of whom? '),
        read_atom(Y),
        Q =.. [X,Who,Y],
        call(Q),
        write(Who),
        nl.
```

If the user types `mother` and `cathy`, then `Q` becomes `mother(Who,cathy)`. This is then executed as a query and the value of `Who` is printed out. Thus (assuming the knowledge base from FAMILY.PL):

```
?- answer_question.
Mother or father?  father
Of whom?  michael
charles_gordon
yes


?- answer_question.
Mother or father?  mother
Of whom?  melody
eleanor
yes
```

We can make this slightly more convenient by defining a predicate `apply` (similar to APPLY in Lisp) that takes an atom and a list, constructs a query using the atom as the functor and the list as the arguments, and then executes the query.

```
% apply(Functor,Arglist)
%    Constructs and executes a query.

apply(Functor,Arglist) :-
        Query =.. [Functor|Arglist],
        call(Query).
```

The goal `apply(mother, [Who,melody])` has the same effect as `mother(Who,melody)`. The arguments are given in a list because the number of them is unpredictable; the list, containing an unspecified number of elements, is then a single argument of `apply`. Prolog provides no way to define a predicate with an arbitrarily variable number of arguments.

Many Prologs, including the ISO standard, let you omit the word `call` and simply write a variable in place of a subgoal:

```
apply(Functor,Arglist) :-
        Query =.. [Functor|Arglist],
        Query.
```

Exercise 3.16.1

Does your Prolog let you write a variable as a goal instead of using `call`?

Exercise 3.16.2

Get `answer_question` working (in combination with FAMILY.PL) and then modify `answer_question` to use `apply`.

Exercise 3.16.3   (small project)

Define `map(Functor,List,Result)` (similar to MAPCAR in Lisp) as follows: `Functor` is a 2-argument predicate, `List` is a list of values to be used as the first argument of that predicate, and `Result` is the list of corresponding values of the second argument. For example, using the knowledge base of CAPITALS.PL, the following query should succeed:

```
?- map(capital_of,[georgia,california,florida],What).
What = [atlanta,sacramento,tallahassee]
```

3.17. DATA STORAGE STRATEGIES

There are three places you can store data in a Prolog program:

- *In the instantiation of a variable.* This is the least permanent way of storing information, because a variable exists only within the clause that defines it. Further, variables lose their values upon backtracking. That is, if a particular subgoal instantiates a variable and execution then backs up past that subgoal, the variable will revert to being uninstantiated.

- *In arguments of predicates.* The argument list is the only way a Prolog procedure normally communicates with the outside world. (Input/output predicates and predicates that modify the knowledge base are exceptions, of course.) By passing arguments to itself when calling itself recursively, a procedure can perform a repetitive process and save information from one repetition to the next.

- *In the knowledge base.* This is the most permanent way of storing information. Information placed in the knowledge base by **asserta** or **assertz** remains there until explicitly retracted and is unaffected by backtracking.

A simple example of storing knowledge in the knowledge base is the predicate `count` (Figure 3.1), which tells you how many times it has been called. (A call to such a procedure might be inserted into another procedure in order to measure the number of times a particular step is executed.) For example:

```
% count(X)
%    Unifies X with the number of times count/1 has been called.

count(X) :- retract(count_aux(N)),
            X is N+1,
            asserta(count_aux(X)).

:- dynamic(count_aux/1).

count_aux(0).
```

Figure 3.1   A predicate that tells you how many times it has been called.

```
?- count(X).
X = 1
yes

?- count(X).
X = 2
yes

?- count(X).
X = 3
yes
```

Because count has to remember information from one call to the next, regardless of backtracking or failure, it must store this information in the knowledge base using assert and retract. There is no way the information could be passed from one procedure to another through arguments, because there is no way to predict what the path of execution will be.

In almost all Prologs, including the ISO standard, count is deterministic, but in LPA Prolog, it is nondeterministic because LPA Prolog considers that performing the assert creates a new alternative solution.

There are several reasons to use assert only as a last resort. One is that assert usually takes more computer time than the ordinary passing of an argument. The other is that programs that use assert are much harder to debug and prove correct than programs that do not do so. The problem is that the flow of control in a procedure can be altered when the program modifies itself. Thus, it is no longer possible to determine how a predicate behaves by looking just at the definition of that predicate; some other part of the program may contain an assert that modifies it.

There are, however, legitimate uses for assert. One of them is to record the results of computations that would take a lot of time and space to recompute. For instance, a graph-searching algorithm might take a large number of steps to find each path through the graph. As it does so, it can use assert to add the paths to the knowledge base so that if they are needed again, the computation need not be repeated. Thus:

```
find_path(...) :- ...computation...,
                  asserta(find_path(...)).
```

Each time `find_path` computes a solution, it inserts into the knowledge base, ahead of itself, a fact giving the solution that it found. Subsequent attempts to find the same path will use the stored fact rather than performing the computation. Procedures that "remember their own earlier results" in this way are sometimes called MEMO PROCEDURES, and are much easier to create in Prolog than in other languages (compare Abelson and Sussman 1985:218-219).

Another legitimate use of **assert** is to set up the controlling parameters of a large and complex program, such as an expert system, which the user can use in several modes. By performing appropriate **assert**s, the program can set itself up to perform the function that the user wants in a particular session. For example, asserting **test_mode(yes)** might cause a wide range of testing actions to be performed as the program runs.

Exercise 3.17.1

Define a procedure **gensym(X)** (like GENSYM in Lisp) which generates a new atom every time it is called. One possibility would be to have it work like this:

```
?- gensym(What).
What = a
?- gensym(What).
What = b
...
?- gensym(What).
What = z
?- gensym(What).
What = za
```

However, you are free to generate any series of Prolog atoms whatsoever, so long as each atom is generated only once.

Exercise 3.17.2   (small project)

Use a memo procedure to test whether integers are prime numbers. Show that this procedure gets more efficient the more it is used.

3.18. BIBLIOGRAPHICAL NOTES

Sterling and Shapiro (1994) give many useful algorithms for processing lists and structures. There is little literature on arithmetic in Prolog, partly because Prolog has little to contribute that is new and partly because the lack of language standardization has severely hampered sharing of arithmetic routines. This situation should change once the ISO standard is widely accepted.

Chapter 4

Expressing Procedural Algorithms

4.1. PROCEDURAL PROLOG

We have noted already that Prolog combines procedural and nonprocedural programming techniques. This chapter will discuss Prolog from the procedural standpoint. We will tell you how to express in Prolog algorithms that were originally developed in other languages, as well as how to make your Prolog programs more efficient.

Some purists may object that you should not program procedurally in Prolog — that the only proper Prolog is "pure" Prolog that ignores procedural considerations. We disagree. Prolog was never meant to be a wholly nonprocedural language, but rather a practical *compromise* between procedural and nonprocedural programming. Colmerauer's original idea was to implement not a general-purpose theorem prover, but a streamlined, trimmed-down system that sacrificed some of the power of classical logic in the interest of efficiency.

Any automated reasoning system consists of a system of logic plus a control strategy that tells it what inferences to make when. Prolog's control strategy is a simple depth-first search of a tree that represents paths to solutions. This search is partly under the programmer's control: The clauses are tried in the specified order, and the programmer can even specify that some potential solutions should not be tried at all. This makes it possible to perform efficiently some types of computations that would be severely inefficient, or even impossible, in a purely nonprocedural language.

Exercise 4.1.1

How does Prolog arithmetic (Chapter 3) differ from what you would expect in a programming language based purely on logic? Explain the practical reason(s) for the difference(s).

4.2. CONDITIONAL EXECUTION

An important difference between Prolog and other programming languages is that Prolog procedures can have multiple definitions (clauses), each applying under different conditions. In Prolog, conditional execution is normally expressed not with `if` or `case` statements but with alternative definitions of procedures.

Consider, for example, how we might translate into Prolog the following Pascal procedure:

```
procedure writename(X:integer);              { Pascal, not Prolog }
begin
   case X of
      1: write('One');
      2: write('Two');
      3: write('Three')
   end
end;
```

The Prolog translation has to give `writename` three definitions:

```
writename(1) :- write('One').
writename(2) :- write('Two').
writename(3) :- write('Three').
```

Each definition matches in exactly one of the three cases. A common mistake is to write the clauses as follows:

```
writename(X) :- X=1, write('One').     % Inefficient!
writename(X) :- X=2, write('Two').
writename(X) :- X=3, write('Three').
```

This gives correct results but wastes time. It is wasteful to start executing each clause, perform a test that fails, and backtrack out, if the inapplicable clauses could have been prevented from matching the goal in the first place.

A key to effective programming in Prolog is making each logical unit of the program into a separate procedure. Each `if` or `case` statement should, in general, become a procedure call so that decisions are made by the procedure-calling process. For example, the Pascal procedure

```
procedure a(X:integer);                          { Pascal, not Prolog }
begin
  b;
  if X=0 then c else d;
  e
end;
```

should go into Prolog like this:

```
a(X) :- b,
        cd(X),
        e.


cd(0) :- c.
cd(X) :- X<>0, d.
```

Crucially,

> *Every time there is a decision to be made, Prolog calls a procedure and makes the decision by choosing the right clause.*

In this respect, Prolog goes further than ordinary structured programming. A major goal of structured programming is to make it easy for the programmer to visualize the conditions under which any given statement will be executed. Thus, structured languages such as Pascal restrict the use of goto statements and encourage the programmer to use block structures such as if–then–else, while, and repeat, in which the conditions of execution are stated explicitly. Still, these structures are merely branches or exceptions embedded in a linear stream of instructions. In Prolog, by contrast, the conditions of execution are the most visible part of the program.

Exercise 4.2.1

Define a predicate absval which, given a number, computes its absolute value:

```
?- absval(0,What).
What = 0
?- absval(2.34,What).
What = 2.34
?- absval(-34.5,What).
What = 34.5
```

Do not use the built-in abs() function. Instead, test whether the number is negative, and if so, multiply it by −1; otherwise return it unchanged.

Make sure absval is deterministic, i.e., does not have unwanted alternative solutions. Do not use cuts.

Exercise 4.2.2

Define a predicate classify that takes one argument and prints odd, even, not an integer, or not a number at all, like this:

```
?- classify(3).
odd
```

```
?- classify(4).
even

?- classify(2.5).
not an integer

?- classify(this(and,that)).
not a number at all
```

Hint: You can find out whether a number is even by taking it modulo 2. For example, 13 mod 2 = 1 but 12 mod 2 = 0 and −15 mod 2 = −1.

Make sure that `classify` is deterministic. Do not use cuts.

4.3. THE "CUT" OPERATOR (!)

Consider another version of `writename` that includes a catchall clause to deal with numbers whose names are not given. In Pascal, this can be expressed as:

```
procedure writename(X:integer);                    { Pascal, not Prolog }
begin
  case X of
    1: write('One');
    2: write('Two');
    3: write('Three')
  else
    write('Out of range')
  end
end;
```

Here is approximately the same algorithm in Prolog:

```
writename(1) :- write('One').
writename(2) :- write('Two').
writename(3) :- write('Three').
writename(X) :- X<1, write('Out of range').
writename(X) :- X>3, write('Out of range').
```

This gives correct results but lacks conciseness. In order to make sure that only one clause can be executed with each number, we have had to test the value of X in both of the last two clauses. We would like to tell the program to print "Out of range" for any number that did not match any of the first three clauses, without performing further tests. We could try to express this as follows, with some lack of success:

```
writename(1) :- write('One').              % Wrong!
writename(2) :- write('Two').
writename(3) :- write('Three').
writename(_) :- write('Out of range').
```

The problem here is that, for example, the goal

```
?- writename(1).
```

matches both the first clause and the last clause. Thus it has two alternative solutions, one that prints "One" and one that prints "Out of range."

> *Unwanted alternatives are a common error in Prolog programs. Make sure your procedures do the right thing, not only on the first try but also upon backtracking for an alternative.*

We want `writename` to be DETERMINISTIC, i.e., to give exactly one solution for any given set of arguments, and not give alternative solutions upon backtracking.   We therefore need to specify that if any of the first three clauses succeeds, the computer should not try the last clause. This can be done with the "cut" operator (written '!').

The cut operator makes the computer discard some alternatives (backtrack points) that it would otherwise remember. Consider, for example, this knowledge base:

```
b :- c, d, !, e, f.
b :- g, h.
```

and suppose that the current goal is b. We will start by taking the first clause. Suppose further that c and d succeed and the cut is executed. When this happens, it becomes impossible to look for alternative solutions to c and d (the goals that precede the cut in the same clause) or to try the other clause for b (the goal that invoked the clause containing the cut). We are committed to sticking with the path that led to the cut. It remains possible to try alternatives for e and f in the normal manner.

More precisely, *at the moment the cut is executed, the computer forgets about any alternatives that were discovered upon, or after, entering the current clause.* Thus, the cut "burns your bridges behind you" and commits you to the choice of a particular solution.

The effect of a cut lasts only as long as the clause containing it is being executed. To see how this works, add to the knowledge base the following clauses:

```
a :- p, b, q.
a :- r, b.
```

Leave b defined as shown above, and let the current goal be a. There are two clauses for a. Take the first one, and assume that p succeeds, and then b succeeds using the first of its clauses (with the cut), and then q fails. What can the computer do?

It can't try an alternative for b because the cut has ensured that there are none. It can, however, backtrack all the way past b, outside the scope of the cut, and look for alternatives for p and for a, which the cut didn't affect. When this is done, the effect of the cut is forgotten (because that particular call to b is over), and if execution reenters b, the search for solutions for b will start afresh.

We can make `writename` deterministic by putting a cut in each of the first three clauses. This changes their meaning slightly, so that the first clause, for example, says, "If the argument is 1, then write 'One' and do not try any other clauses."

```
writename(1) :- !, write('One').
writename(2) :- !, write('Two').
writename(3) :- !, write('Three').
writename(_) :- write('Out of range').
```

Since `write` is deterministic, it does not matter whether the cut is written before or after the call to `write`. The alternatives that get cut off are exactly the same. However, programs are usually more readable if cuts are made as early as possible. That is: Make the cut as soon as you have determined that the alternatives won't be needed.

Exercise 4.3.1

Make `absval` (from the previous section) more efficient by using one or more cuts. State exactly what unwanted computation the cut(s) prevent(s).

Exercise 4.3.2

Make `classify` (from the previous section) more efficient by using one or more cuts.

Exercise 4.3.3

Consider a predicate `my_cut` defined as follows:
```
my_cut :- !.
```
Given the following knowledge base:
```
fact(1).
fact(2).
cuttest0(X) :- fact(X), !.
cuttest1(X) :- fact(X), my_cut.
```
What is printed by each of the following queries?
```
?- cuttest0(X), write(X), fail.
?- cuttest1(X), write(X), fail.
```
Explain why this happens. Why isn't `my_cut` equivalent to cut?

4.4. RED CUTS AND GREEN CUTS

A green cut makes a program more efficient without affecting the set of solutions that the program generates; a red cut prevents the program from generating solutions it would otherwise give. For example, let's return to `writename`. In "pure" Prolog, the definition is as follows:

```
writename(1) :- write('One').
writename(2) :- write('Two').
writename(3) :- write('Three').
writename(X) :- X<1, write('Out of range').
writename(X) :- X>3, write('Out of range').
```

To this we can add some green cuts to eliminate backtracking:

```
writename(1) :- !, write('One').
writename(2) :- !, write('Two').
writename(3) :- !, write('Three').
writename(X) :- X<1, !, write('Out of range').
writename(X) :- X>3, write('Out of range').
```

These cuts have no effect if only one solution is being sought. However, they ensure that, if a later goal fails, no time will be wasted backtracking into this predicate to look for another solution. The programmer knows that only one of these clauses will succeed with any given value of X; the cuts enable him or her to communicate this knowledge to the computer. (No cut is needed in the last clause because there are no more alternatives after it.)

Red cuts can save time even when looking for the first solution:

```
writename(1)  :-  !, write('One').
writename(2)  :-  !, write('Two').
writename(3)  :-  !, write('Three').
writename(_)  :-  write('Out of range').
```

Here, we need never test explicitly whether X is out of range. If X = 1, 2, or 3, one of the first three clauses will execute a cut and execution will never get to the last clause. Thus, we can assume that if the last clause executes, X must have been out of range. These cuts are considered red because the same clauses without the cuts would not be logically correct.

Use cuts cautiously. Bear in mind that the usual use of cuts is to make a specific predicate deterministic. Resist the temptation to write an imprecise predicate and then throw in cuts until it no longer gives solutions that you don't want. Instead, get the logic right, *then* add cuts if you must. "Make it correct before you make it efficient" is a maxim that applies to Prolog at least as much as to any other computer language.

Exercise 4.4.1

Classify as red or green the cuts that you added to `absval` and `classify` in the previous section.

4.5. WHERE NOT TO PUT CUTS

In general, you should not put cuts within the scope of negation   (\+), nor in a variable goal, nor in a goal that is the argument of another predicate (such as `call`, `once`, or `setof` — don't panic, you're not supposed to have seen all of these yet).

If you do, the results will vary depending on which implementation of Prolog you're using. Appendices A and B tell the whole messy story. Suffice it to say that the usual purpose of a cut is to prevent backtracking within and among the clauses of a predicate. It's not surprising that if you put a cut in a goal that does not belong to a specific clause, there's little consensus as to what the cut should do.

Exercise 4.5.1

Does your Prolog allow cuts within the scope of negation? If so, does the cut work like an ordinary cut or does it only prevent backtracking within the negated goals? Experiment and see. You might want to base your experiment on a clause such as

```
f(X)  :-  g(X), \+ (h(X), !).
```

where both `g(X)` and `h(X)` have multiple solutions.

4.6. MAKING A GOAL DETERMINISTIC WITHOUT CUTS

The trouble with extensive use of cuts is that it can be difficult to figure out whether all of the cuts are in the right places. Fortunately, there is another way to make goals deterministic. Instead of creating deterministic predicates, you can define nondeterministic predicates in the ordinary manner and then block backtracking when you call them.

This is done with the special built-in predicate `once/1`, which is built into most Prologs (including the ISO standard). If it's not built into yours, you can define it as follows:

```
once(Goal) :- call(Goal), !.
```

Then the query '`?- once(Goal).`' means "Find the first solution to `Goal`, but not any alternatives." For example (using FAMILY.PL from Chapter 2):

```
?- parent(Who,cathy).
Who = michael ;
Who = melody


?- once(parent(Who,cathy)).
Who = michael
```

No matter how many possible solutions there are to a goal such as `f(X)`, the goal `once(f(X))` will return only the first solution. If `f(X)` has no solutions, `once(f(X))` fails.

The argument of `once` can be a series of goals joined by commas. In such a case, extra parentheses are necessary:

```
?- once( (parent(X,cathy), parent(G,X)) ).
```

Of course, you can use `once` in predicate definitions. Here's a highly hypothetical example:

```
f(X) :- g(X), once( (h(X), i(X)) ), j(X).
```

Here `once` serves as a limited-scope cut (like Arity Prolog's "snips"); it ensures that, each time through, only the first solution of `(h(X), i(X))` will be taken, although backtracking is still permitted on everything else.

Use `once` sparingly. It is usually better to make your predicates deterministic, where possible, than to make a deterministic call to a nondeterministic predicate.

Exercise 4.6.1

Rewrite `absval` and `classify` (from several previous sections) to use `once` instead of cuts. Is this an improvement? (Not necessarily. Compare the old and new versions carefully and say which you prefer. Substantial reorganization of the Prolog code may be necessary.)

4.7. THE "IF-THEN-ELSE" STRUCTURE (->)

Another way to express deterministic choices in Prolog is to use the "if-then-else" structure,

```
Goal1 -> Goal2 ; Goal3
```

This means "if `Goal1` then `Goal2` else `Goal3`," or more precisely, "Test whether `Goal1` succeeds, and if so, execute `Goal2`; otherwise execute `Goal3`." For example:

```
writename(X) :-   X = 1 -> write(one) ;   write('not one').
```

You can nest if-then-else structures, like this:

```
writename(X) :-     (  X = 1   ->   write(one)
                    ;  X = 2   ->   write(two)
                    ;  X = 3   ->   write(three)
                    ;               write('out of range') ).
```

That is: "Try X = 1, then X = 2, then X = 3, until one of them succeeds; then execute the goal after the arrow, and stop." You can leave out the semicolon and the "else" goal.

The if-then-else structure gives Prolog a way to make decisions without calling procedures; this gives an obvious gain in efficiency. (Some compilers generate more efficient code for if-then-else structures than for the same decisions expressed any other way.) However, we have mixed feelings about if-then-else. To us, it looks like an intrusion of ordinary structured programming into Prolog. It's handy and convenient, but it collides head-on with the idea that Prolog clauses are supposed to be logical formulas.

We also have more substantial reasons for not using if-then-else in this book. First, if-then-else is unnecessary; anything that can be expressed with it can be expressed without it. Second, one of the major Prologs (Arity) still lacks the usual if-then-else structure (although it has a different if-then-else of its own). Third, and most seriously, Prolog implementors do not agree on what "if-then-else" structures should do in all situations; see Appendix B for the details.

Exercise 4.7.1

Rewrite `absval` and `classify` (again!), this time using if-then-else structures.

4.8. MAKING A GOAL ALWAYS SUCCEED OR ALWAYS FAIL

In order to control the flow of program execution, it is sometimes necessary to guarantee that a goal will succeed regardless of the results of the computation that it performs. Occasionally, it may be necessary to guarantee that a goal will always fail.

An easy way to make any procedure succeed is to add an additional clause to it that succeeds with any arguments and is tried last, thus:

```
f(X,Y) :- X<Y, write('X is less than Y'), !.
f(_,_).
```

A call to f succeeds with any arguments; it may or may not print its message, but it will certainly not fail and hence will not cause backtracking in the procedure that invoked it. Moreover, because of the cut, f is deterministic. The cut prevents the second clause from being used to generate a second solution with arguments that have already succeeded with the first clause.

Another way to make a query succeed is to put it in disjunction with true, which always succeeds:

```
?- (f(A,B) ; true).
```

(Recall that the semicolon means "or.") If the original query doesn't succeed, the call to true certainly will. Better yet, wrap the whole thing in once so that it doesn't give two solutions when you're expecting only one:

```
?- once( (f(A,B) ; true) ).
```

You can guarantee that any procedure will fail by adding !, fail at the end of each of its definitions, thus:

```
g(X,Y) :- X<Y, write('X less than Y'), !, fail.
g(X,Y) :- Y<X, write('Y less than X'), !, fail.
```

Any call to g ultimately returns failure for either of two reasons: either it doesn't match any of the clauses, or it matches one of the clauses that ends with cut and fail. The cut is written next to last so that it won't be executed unless all the other steps of the clause have succeeded; as a result, it is still possible to backtrack from one clause of g to the other as long as the cut has not yet been reached.

You can define predicates make_succeed and make_fail that make any goal succeed or fail, thus:

```
make_succeed(Goal) :- Goal, !.
make_succeed(_).
```

```
make_fail(Goal) :- call(Goal), !, fail.
```

Related to make_fail is the technique of making a rule fail conclusively. Think back to GEO.PL, the geographical knowledge base in Chapter 1. Suppose we found that, in practice, we were constantly getting queries from people wanting to know whether Toronto is in the United States. Rather than letting the computer calculate the answer each time, we might introduce, at the beginning of the knowledge base, the rule:

```
located_in(toronto,usa) :- !, fail.
```

Now the query '?- located_in(toronto,usa).' will hit this rule and fail immediately with no alternatives, thus saving computer time.

Finally, note that cut can be used to define not, thus:

```
not(Goal) :- call(Goal), !, fail.
not(_).
```

That is: If a call to `Goal` succeeds, then reject alternatives and fail. Otherwise, succeed regardless of what `Goal` is.

Exercise 4.8.1

Rewrite `writename` so that instead of printing "out of range" it succeeds without printing anything if its argument is not 1, 2, or 3. Make sure it is still deterministic.

Exercise 4.8.2

Using only two clauses, and not using \+, define a deterministic predicate `non_integer` that fails if its argument is an integer but succeeds if its argument is anything else whatsoever. (*Hint:* Use '`!, fail.`')

4.9. REPETITION THROUGH BACKTRACKING

Prolog offers two ways to perform computations repetitively: backtracking and recursion. Of the two, recursion is by far the more versatile. However, there are some interesting uses for backtracking, among them the construction of `repeat` loops. In Prolog implementations that lack tail recursion optimization (see below), `repeat-fail` looping is the only kind of iteration that can be performed ad infinitum without causing a stack overflow.

The built-in predicate `repeat` always succeeds and has an infinite number of solutions. If execution backtracks to a `repeat`, it can always go forward again. For example, here's how to print an infinite number of asterisks:

```
?- repeat, write('*'), fail.
```

Here's a procedure that turns the computer into a typewriter, accepting characters from the keyboard ad infinitum until the user hits the break key to abort the program:[1]

```
typewriter :- repeat,              % unreliable!
              get0(C),
              fail.
```

The loop can be made to terminate by allowing it to succeed eventually, so that backtracking stops. The following version of `typewriter` stops when the user presses Return (ASCII code 13):

```
typewriter :- repeat,              % unreliable!
              get0(C),
              C = 13.
```

---

[1]We assume that the computer displays each character as it is typed. If your Prolog doesn't do this, add `put(C)` after `get0(C)`. Remember that in ISO Prolog, `get0` and `put` are called `get_code` and `put_code` respectively.

If C is equal to 13, execution terminates; otherwise, execution backtracks to repeat and proceeds forward again through get0(C). (Note that in some Prologs you should test for code 10, not 13.)

Even with this change, the looping in typewriter can be restarted by the failure of a subsequent goal, as in the compound query

```
?- typewriter, write('Got it'), fail.
```

Try it. To prevent the loop from restarting unexpectedly, we need to add a cut as follows:

```
typewriter :- repeat,
              get0(C),
              C = 13,            %  10 under UNIX
              !.
```

In effect, this forbids looking for alternative solutions to anything in typewriter once one solution has succeeded. To sum up:

> *Every* repeat *loop begins with a* repeat *goal and ends with a test that fails, followed by a cut.*

Note that repeat loops in Prolog are quite different from repeat loops in Pascal. The biggest difference is that in Pascal, the loop always starts over and over from the beginning, whereas in Prolog, backtracking can take you to any subgoal that has an untried alternative — which need not be repeat. Moreover, if any goal in a Prolog loop fails, backtracking takes place immediately; subsequent goals are not attempted.

A serious limitation of repeat loops is that there is no convenient way to pass information from one iteration to the next. Prolog variables lose their values upon backtracking. Thus, there is no easy way to make a repeat loop accumulate a count or total. (Information can be preserved by storing it in the knowledge base, using assert and retract, but this process is usually inefficient and always logically inelegant.) With recursion, information can be transmitted from one pass to the next through the argument list. This is the main reason for preferring recursion as a looping mechanism.

Exercise 4.9.1

Modify typewriter so that it will stop whenever it gets code 10 or code 13.

Exercise 4.9.2

Using repeat, define a predicate skip_until_blank that reads characters from standard input, one by one, until it gets either a blank or an end-of-line mark. Demonstrate that it works correctly. If you are using the keyboard for input, note the effect of buffering.

Exercise 4.9.3

Using repeat, see, read, and assertz, write your own version of consult. That is, define a predicate which, when given a file name, will read terms from that file and assert them into the knowledge base. (This can be extremely handy if you want to preprocess the terms in some way before asserting them.)

4.10. RECURSION

Most programmers are familiar with recursion as a way to implement task-within-a-task algorithms such as tree searching and Quicksort. Indeed, Prolog lends itself well to expressing recursive algorithms developed in Lisp. What is not widely appreciated is that any iterative algorithm can be expressed recursively.

Suppose for example we want to print a table of the integers 1 to 5 and their squares, like this:

```
1   1
2   4
3   9
4   16
5   25
```

This is obviously a job for a loop. We could describe the computation in Pascal as:

```
for i:=1 to 5 do                          { Pascal, not Prolog }
  writeln(i,'   ',i*i)
```

or, breaking the `for` loop down into simpler components,

```
i:=1;
while not(i>5) do
  begin
    writeln(i,'   ',i*i);
    i:=i+1
  end;
```

but the same computation can also be described recursively. Let's first describe the recursive algorithm in English:

To print squares beginning with I:

- If $I > 5$, do nothing.

- Otherwise, print I and I^2, then print squares beginning with $I + 1$.

In Pascal this works out to the following:

```
procedure PrintSquares(i:integer);        { Pascal, not Prolog }
begin
  if not(i>5) then
    begin
      writeln(i,'   ',i*i);
      PrintSquares(i+1)
    end
end;
```

The procedure prints one line of the table, then invokes itself to print the next. Here is how it looks in Prolog:

```
print_squares(I) :- I > 5, !.

print_squares(I) :-
  S is I*I,
  write(I), write(' '), write(S), nl,
  NewI is I+1,
  print_squares(NewI).
```

We then start the computation with the query:

```
?- print_squares(1).
```

Notice that there is no loop variable. In fact, in Prolog, it is impossible to change the value of a variable once it is instantiated, so there is no way to make a single variable I take on the values 1, 2, 3, 4, and 5 in succession. Instead, the information is passed from one recursive invocation of the procedure to the next in the argument list.

Exercise 4.10.1

Define a predicate `print_stars` which, given an integer as an argument, prints that number of asterisks:

```
?- print_stars(40).
****************************************
yes
```

Hint: Consider carefully whether you should count up or count down.

4.11. MORE ABOUT RECURSIVE LOOPS

Let's take another example. Here is the classic recursive definition of the factorial function:

- The factorial of 0 is 1.

- The factorial of any larger integer N is N times the factorial of $N - 1$.

or, in Pascal:

```
function factorial(N:integer):integer;          { Pascal, not Prolog }
begin
  if N=0 then
    factorial:=1
  else
    factorial:=N*factorial(N-1);
end;
```

Finally, here's how it looks in Prolog:

```
factorial(0,1) :- !.

factorial(N,FactN) :-
  N > 0,
  M is N-1,
  factorial(M,FactM),
  FactN is N*FactM.
```

This is straightforward; the procedure `factorial` calls itself to compute the factorial of the next smaller integer, then uses the result to compute the factorial of the integer that you originally asked for. The recursion stops when the number whose factorial is to be computed is 0.

This definition is logically elegant. Mathematicians like it because it captures a potentially infinite number of multiplications by distinguishing just two cases, $N = 0$ and $N > 0$. In this respect, the recursive definition matches the logic of an inductive proof: the first step establishes the starting point, and the second step applies repeatedly to get from one instance to the next.

However, that is not the usual way to calculate factorials. Most programmers would quite rightly use iteration rather than recursion: "Start with 1 and multiply it by each integer in succession up to N." Here, then, is an iterative algorithm to compute factorials (in Pascal):

```
function factorial(N:integer):integer;        { Pascal, not Prolog }
var I,J:integer;
begin
  I:=0;                    { Initialize }
  J:=1;
  while I<N do
    begin                  { Loop }
      I:=I+1;
      J:=J*I
    end;
  factorial:=J           { Return result }
end;
```

In Pascal, this procedure does not call itself. Its Prolog counterpart is a procedure that calls itself as its very last step — a procedure that is said to be TAIL RECURSIVE:

```
factorial(N,FactN) :- fact_iter(N,FactN,0,1).

fact_iter(N,FactN,N,FactN) :- !.

fact_iter(N,FactN,I,J) :-
  I<N,
  NewI is I+1,
  NewJ is J*NewI,
  fact_iter(N,FactN,NewI,NewJ).
```

Here the third and fourth arguments of `fact_iter` are *state variables* or *accumulators* that pass values from one iteration to the next. State variables in Prolog correspond to variables that change their values repeatedly in Pascal.

Let's start by examining the recursive clause of `fact_iter`. This clause checks that I is still less than N, computes new values for I and J, and finally calls itself with the new arguments.

Because Prolog variables cannot change their values, the additional variables NewI and NewJ have to be introduced. In Prolog (as in arithmetic, but not in most programming languages), the statement

```
X is X+1                                            % wrong!
```

is never true. So NewI and NewJ contain the values that will replace I and J in the next iteration.

The first clause of `fact_iter` serves to end the iteration when the state variables reach their final values. A more Pascal-like but less efficient way of writing this clause is:

```
fact_iter(N,FactN,I,J) :- I = N, FactN = J.
```

That is, if I is equal to N, then FactN (uninstantiated until now) should be given the value of J. By writing this same clause more concisely, as we did above, we make Prolog's unification mechanism perform work that would require explicit computational steps in other languages.

Most iterative algorithms can be expressed in Prolog by following this general pattern. First transform other types of loops (e.g., `for` and `repeat–until`) into Pascal-like `while` loops. Then break the computation into three stages: the initialization, the loop itself, and any final computations needed to return a result.

Then express the loop as a tail recursive clause (like the second clause of `fact_iter`) with the `while`-condition at the beginning. Place the final computations in another nonrecursive clause of the same procedure that is set up so that it executes only after the loop is finished.

Finally, hide the whole thing behind a front-end procedure (`factorial` in this example) which is what the rest of the program actually calls. The front-end procedure passes its arguments into the tail recursive procedure along with initial values of the state variables.

Exercise 4.11.1

Define a recursive predicate `sum(J,K,N)` that instantiates N to the sum of the integers from J to K inclusive:

```
?- sum(-1,1,What).
What = 0
?- sum(1,3,What).
What = 6
?- sum(6,7,What).
What = 13
```

Exercise 4.11.2

Is your version of `sum` tail recursive? If not, modify it to make it so.

Exercise 4.11.3

   The Fibonacci series is the series of numbers obtained by starting with $\langle 1, 1 \rangle$ and forming each subsequent member by adding the previous two: $\langle 1, 1, 2, 3, 5, 8, 13, 21 \ldots \rangle$. The following procedure computes the Nth Fibonacci number in an elegant but inefficient way:

```
fib(1,1) :- !.
fib(2,1) :- !.
fib(N,F) :- N>2,
            N1 is N-1, fib(N1,F1),
            N2 is N-2, fib(N2,F2),
            F is F1+F2.
```

Explain what is inefficient about this. Then write a more efficient procedure (named fib2) that uses state variables to remember the previous two Fibonacci numbers when computing each one.

Exercise 4.11.4

   Are the cuts in fib (previous exercise) red or green?

4.12. ORGANIZING RECURSIVE CODE

Many programmers report that recursive Prolog procedures are harder to write than loops in conventional languages but, once written, are less likely to contain errors. This may be because Prolog forces the programmer to think more clearly about how the repetition is carried out.

   The first step in defining a recursive predicate is to decide how many situations have to be distinguished: always at least two (continue looping or stop looping), and sometimes more. There will be a clause for each situation.

   The second step is to focus on the loop itself. To know that a loop works correctly is to know three things:

- that it starts in the correct state;

- that it finishes in the correct state;

- that it proceeds correctly from each state to the next.

For instance, a loop to print the integers from 1 to 100 must start at 1 (not 0 or 2); must stop at 100 (not 99 or 101); and must, on each iteration, print the next integer greater than the one previously printed.

   If the loop is expressed as a recursive Prolog procedure, the state in which it starts is determined by the arguments passed to it. Starting in the wrong state is therefore unlikely.

   A more important question is whether the loop terminates, and if so, when. It can terminate in two ways: by successfully executing a nonrecursive clause, or by failing in the recursive clause prior to the recursive call. The following procedure can terminate either way:

```
f(81) :- !.
f(X)  :- X =< 100, NewX is X*X, f(NewX).
```

The idea is to start with a number and keep squaring it until either 81 or a number greater than 100 is reached. If 81 is encountered, the query succeeds; if not, the query fails, but in either case, the loop terminates, and the conditions under which it terminates are obvious from the way the program is written.

Finally, make sure that each of the clauses that you've written will actually execute in some situation. A common error is to have, say, three or four clauses, the last of which is never executed.

Exercise 4.12.1

Define a predicate `even_length` that takes one argument, a list, and succeeds if that list has an even number of elements. Do not use arithmetic; do the computation entirely by picking off elements of the list two at a time.

Exercise 4.12.2

Define a predicate `remove_duplicates(X,Y)` that removes duplicated members from list X giving list Y thus:

```
?- remove_duplicates([a,b,r,a,c,a,d,a,b,r,a],X).
X = [c,d,b,r,a]
```

That is, only one occurrence of each element is to be preserved. (Whether to preserve the first or the last occurrence is up to you.)

You can assume that the first argument is instantiated. Check that your procedure does not generate spurious alternatives.

Exercise 4.12.3

Write a predicate that produces a list of the members that two other lists have in common, thus:

```
?- members_in_common([a,b,c],[c,d,b],X).
X= [b,c]
```

Assume that the first two arguments are instantiated. The order of elements in the computed list is not important.

Exercise 4.12.4

Define a predicate `my_square_root(X,Y)` that unifies Y with the square root of X. Find the square root by successive approximations based on the principle that if G is a reasonably good guess for the square root of X, then $(X/G + G)/2$ is a better guess. Start with $G = 1$, and stop when G no longer changes very much from one iteration to the next.

4.13. WHY TAIL RECURSION IS SPECIAL

Whenever one Prolog procedure calls another, the computer has to save, on a push-down stack, information about what to do when the called procedure terminates. Since the called procedure may either succeed or fail, the computer must keep track of two things: the CONTINUATION, which tells how to continue with the current clause after the called procedure succeeds, and the BACKTRACK POINTS, which indicate where to look for alternatives if the current clause fails. Here's an example:

```
a :- b, c.
a :- d.


?- a.
```

When b is called, the computer must save information telling it to continue with c if b succeeds and to try the second clause of a if b fails. In this case there is only one backtrack point, but if b had been preceded by a subgoal that had more than one solution, there would have been a backtrack point for that subgoal as well. The stack space is released when the procedure terminates.

Since a recursive call places more information onto the stack without releasing what was already there, it would seem that repeated recursion would lead inevitably to stack overflow. However, almost all Prolog implementations recognize a special case. If the continuation is empty and there are no backtrack points, nothing need be placed on the stack; execution can simply jump to the called procedure without storing any record of how to come back. This is called LAST-CALL OPTIMIZATION.

If the procedure is recursive, then instead of calling the same procedure again, the computer simply places new values into its arguments and jumps back to the beginning. In effect, this transforms recursion into iteration. We have now come full circle: To make the logic clearer, we transformed iteration into recursion, and to make the execution more efficient, the interpreter or compiler transforms it back into iteration.

A procedure that calls itself with an empty continuation and no backtrack points is described as TAIL RECURSIVE, and last-call optimization is sometimes called TAIL-RECURSION OPTIMIZATION. For example, this procedure is tail recursive:

```
test1(N) :- write(N), nl, NewN is N+1, test1(NewN).
```

Its continuation is empty because the recursive call is the last subgoal in the clause. There is no backtrack point because there are no other clauses for test1 and no alternative solutions to write(N), nl, or NewN is N+1. By contrast, the following procedure is not tail recursive:

```
test2(N) :- write(N), nl, NewN is N+1, test2(NewN), nl.
```

Here the continuation is not empty; the second nl remains to be executed after the recursive call succeeds.

Here is a clause that has an empty continuation but still has a backtrack point:

```
test3(N) :- write(N), nl, NewN is N+1, test3(NewN).
test3(N) :- N<0.
```

Every time the first clause calls itself, the computer has to remember that (on that call) the second clause has not been tried yet. Accordingly, test3 is not tail recursive.

The fact that test3 has two clauses is not the point here. A procedure with many clauses can be tail recursive as long as there are no clauses remaining to be tried *after the recursive call*. If we rearrange the clauses of test3, we get a perfectly good tail recursive procedure:

```
test3a(N) :- N<0.
test3a(N) :- write(N), nl, NewN is N+1, test3a(NewN).
```

Nor does a one-clause procedure always lack backtrack points. The following procedure is not tail recursive because of untried alternatives within the clause:

```
test4(N) :- write(N), nl, m(N,NewN), test4(NewN).
```

```
m(N,NewN) :- N>=0, NewN is N+1.
m(N,NewN) :- N<0, NewN is (-1)*N.
```

There is only one clause for `test4`, but `m` has two clauses, and only the first of them has been tried when `test4` first calls itself recursively. The computer must therefore record, on the stack, the fact that another path of computation is possible. Never mind that both clauses cannot succeed with any given number; when the recursive call takes place, the second one has not even been tried.

A quick way to confirm that your Prolog system has tail recursion optimization is to type in the clauses above and try the queries:

```
?- test1(0).
?- test2(0).
?- test3(0).
?- test4(0).
```

If tail recursion optimization is taking place, `test1` will run indefinitely, printing ever-increasing integers until stopped by some external cause such as a numeric overflow or a finger on the Break key. However, `test2`, `test3`, and `test4` will run out of stack space after a few thousand iterations. Use them to gauge your machine's limits.

In almost all implementations of Prolog, a procedure can become tail recursive by executing a cut. Recall that a tail recursive procedure must have an empty continuation and no backtrack points. The purpose of the cut is to discard backtrack points. Accordingly, the following procedures `test5` and `test6` should be tail recursive:

```
test5(N) :- write(N), nl, NewN is N+1, !, test5(NewN).
test5(N) :- N<0.
```

```
test6(N) :- write(N), nl, m(N,NewN), !, test6(NewN).
```

Except for the cuts, these predicates are identical to `test3` and `test4`. (Recall that `m` was defined earlier.)

Finally, notice that tail recursion can be indirect. Unneeded stack space is freed whenever one procedure calls another with an empty continuation and no backtrack points, whether or not the call is recursive. That's why tail-recursion optimization is also called last-call optimization, although naturally it is of little practical importance except in tail recursive procedures. Thus, the following procedure is tail recursive:

```
test7(N) :- write(N), nl, test7a(N).
test7a(N) :- NewN is N+1, test7(NewN).
```

Each procedure calls the other without placing anything on the stack. The result is a recursive loop spread across more than one procedure.

Exercise 4.13.1

(Not recommended for multiuser computers.) Test tail recursion on your machine. How many iterations of `test2` can you execute without running out of stack space? How about `test3`?

Exercise 4.13.2

Rework `fib2` (from Exercise 4.11.3, p. 107) to make it tail recursive. (If your version of `fib2` is already tail recursive, say so.)

4.14. INDEXING

When a Prolog system executes a query, it doesn't have to search the entire knowledge base for a matching clause. All Prologs use INDEXING (a hashing function or lookup table) to go directly to the right predicate. For example, with FAMILY.PL, a query to `mother/2` does not search the clauses for `father/2`.

Most modern Prologs use indexing to go further than that. They index, not only on the predicate and arity, but also on the principal functor of the first argument. For example, if you have the knowledge base

```
a(b).
a(c).

d(e).
d(f).
```

then the query '`?- d(f).`' not only won't search the clauses for `a/1`, it also won't look at `d(e)`. It goes straight to `d(f)`, which is the only clause whose predicate, arity, and first argument match those in the query.

Indexing can speed up queries tremendously. It can also make predicates tail recursive when they otherwise wouldn't be. Here's an example:

```
test8(0) :- write('Still going'), nl, test8(0).
test8(-1).
```

The query '`?- test8(0).`' executes tail recursively because indexing always takes it right to the first clause, and the second clause is never even considered (and hence does not generate a backtrack point). Notice that:

- Indexing looks at the *principal functor of the first argument* (or the whole first argument if the first argument is a constant).

- First-argument indexing can distinguish [] from a nonempty list, but cannot distinguish one nonempty list from another.

- First-argument indexing works only when the first arguments of all the clauses, and also of the query, are instantiated (or at least have instantiated principal functors).

Indexing does not predict whether clauses will succeed. Nor does it necessarily predict whether the entire unification process, including the inner parts of lists and structures, can be carried out. Its only purpose is to rule out some obvious mismatches without wasting too much time.

> *To take advantage of indexing, you should design your predicates so that the first argument is the one that is most often used to select the right clause.*

That means that, commonly, you will organize Prolog predicates so that the first argument contains the known information, and the subsequent arguments contain information to be looked up or computed. Of course, this is not a hard and fast rule; if it were, Prolog wouldn't be nearly as versatile as it is.

Consider now the familiar list concatenation procedure:

```
append([Head|Tail],X,[Head|Y]) :- append(Tail,X,Y).
append([],X,X).
```

This procedure is tail recursive in Prolog even though its Lisp counterpart is not. It is easy to make the mistake of thinking that the Prolog procedure works in the following non-tail-recursive way:

(Misinterpreted algorithm:)

1. Split the first list into **Head** and **Tail**.

2. Recursively append **Tail** to **X** giving **Y**.

3. Join **Head** to **Y** giving the answer.

This is, after all, how the corresponding procedure would work in Lisp:

```
(DEFUN APPEND (LIST1 LIST2)
   (IF (NULL LIST1)
       LIST2
       (CONS (CAR LIST1) (APPEND (CDR LIST1) LIST2)))))
```

That is: if **LIST1** is empty, then return **LIST2**; otherwise join the first element of **LIST1** with the result of appending the tail of **LIST1** to **LIST2**. The joining operation (the **CONS**) is performed after returning from the recursive call; hence the recursive call is not the last step, and the procedure is not tail recursive in Lisp.

The catch is that in Prolog, the joining of **Head** to **Y** does not have to wait until the list **Y** has been constructed. Rather, the procedure operates as follows:

- Split the first list into **Head** and **Tail**; unify the second list with **X**; and create a third list whose head is **Head** and whose tail is **Y**, an uninstantiated variable.

- Recursively append **Tail** to **X**, instantiating **Y** to the result.

Internally, the third list is created with its tail pointing to a memory location where the rest of the list will be constructed; the recursive call then builds the rest of the list there. The ability to use uninstantiated variables in this way distinguishes Prolog from other list processing languages.

Exercise 4.14.1

In FAMILY.PL, which of the following queries executes faster?

```
?- father(Who,michael).
```

```
?- father(charles_gordon,Who).
```

You will probably not be able to measure the difference; give your answer based on what you know about indexing.

Exercise 4.14.2

Would `append` (as shown in this section) be tail recursive in a Prolog system that did not have first-argument indexing? Explain.

Exercise 4.14.3

Based on what you now know, take `flatten` (from exercise 3.9.3, p. 77) and make it tail recursive. (This is not easy; if you're stuck, make it as close to tail recursive as possible.)

4.15. MODULARITY, NAME CONFLICTS, AND STUBS

As far as possible, programs in any language should be MODULAR. This means that the program is broken up into sections that interact in clearly specified ways. In order to find out what a section of the program does, you need only look at that section and, perhaps, some other sections to which it refers explicitly. Many programmers discovered modularity when they moved from BASIC to Pascal and learned to write small, isolable procedures instead of creating a vast expanse of sequential statements.

Prolog facilitates modular programming because it has no global variables. A variable has a value only as long as a particular clause is being executed; clauses communicate with each other through arguments. If there are no `asserts` or `retracts`, the behavior of any predicate is predictable from its definition and the definitions of the predicates it calls. This makes it possible to break Prolog programs up into sections for execution on separate CPUs — a major motive behind the choice of Prolog for the Fifth Generation Project.

Predicate names, however, are global. You cannot have two separate predicates named `f`, with the same arity, in different parts of the same program. This presents a problem when parts of a large program are written by different programmers. If you want to call a predicate `f`, how can you be sure that no one else is using the name `f` for one of his predicates somewhere else?

Some Prologs, including the ISO standard, let you divide a program into "modules." Predicates defined in one module cannot be called from other modules unless you "export" them. Thus, you can have two predicates called `f` that do not conflict because there is no place from which they can both be called.

Our solution in this book is much simpler. If we are defining a procedure named f that will be embedded in larger programs, we will use names such as f_aux, f_start, and the like for any other predicates that are needed to make f complete. In this way, the programmer using f need not look at the names of all the predicates defined in the f package; he or she need only refrain from using predicate names that begin with "f_".

Prolog also facilitates top-down design. A program can be designed by writing the main procedure first, then filling in the other procedures that it will call. The interchangeability of facts and rules makes it easy to write STUBS, or substitutes, for procedures that are to be written later.

Suppose for example that the main body of the program requires a predicate permute(List1,List2) that succeeds if List2 is a permutation of List1. The following quick-and-dirty stub works with lists of three or fewer elements:

```
permute(X,X).
permute([A,B],[B,A]).
permute([A,B,C],[A,C,B]).
permute([A,B,C],[B,A,C]).
permute([A,B,C],[B,C,A]).
permute([A,B,C],[C,A,B]).
permute([A,B,C],[C,B,A]).
permute([A,B,C,D|Rest],[A,B,C,D|Rest]) :- write('List too long!').
```

A more general definition of permute can be substituted later without any other change to the program. In a similar way, Prolog facts with canned data can substitute for procedures that will be written later to obtain or compute the real data.

Exercise 4.15.1

Suppose you needed append but didn't have it. Write a stub for append that works for lists of up to 3 elements (giving a concatenated list up to 6 elements long).

Does writing the stub help you recognize the recursive pattern that would have to be incorporated into the real append predicate?

Exercise 4.15.2

Does your Prolog have a module system? Check the manuals and Appendix A. If so, describe it briefly.

4.16. HOW TO DOCUMENT PROLOG PREDICATES

In the remainder of this book, we will document all Prolog predicates by putting a comment at the beginning of each, in the format illustrated in Figure 4.1. Notice that:

- The first line gives descriptive names to the arguments and says whether or not they are instantiated, as follows:

    + denotes an argument that should already be instantiated when this predicate is called;

```
% writename(+Number)
%   Writes "One", "Two", or "Three" to describe Number.
%   Fails if Number is not 1, 2, or 3.

writename(1) :- write('One').
writename(2) :- write('Two').
writename(3) :- write('Three').


% writeq_string(+String)
%   Given a list of ASCII codes, writes the
%   corresponding characters in quotes.

writeq_string(String) :-
   write('"'), write_string_aux(String), write('"').

writeq_string_aux([First|Rest]) :-
   put(First), write_string_aux(Rest).

writeq_string_aux([]).


% square(+X,-S)
%   Given X, computes X squared.

square(X,S) :-
   S is X*X.


% append(?List1,?List2,?List3)
%   Succeeds if List1 and List2, concatenated, make List3.

append([Head|Tail],X,[Head|Y]) :- append(Tail,X,Y).

append([],X,X).
```

Figure 4.1 Examples of comments in the prescribed format.

– denotes an argument that is normally not instantiated until this predicate instantiates it;

? denotes an argument that may or may not be instantiated.

Some programmers use @ to denote arguments that contain variables which must not become instantiated.

- The next two lines describe, in English, what the predicate does. This description is as concise as possible.

- Then comes the predicate definition itself, followed by any auxiliary predicates that it uses internally.

Note that +, -, and ? (and @, if you use it) describe how the predicate is normally meant to be called; we don't guarantee that it will go wrong if called with the wrong set of instantiations (but we don't guarantee that it will go right, either).

Exercise 4.16.1

Add comments, in the prescribed format, to `mother` and `father` in FAMILY.PL.

Exercise 4.16.2

Add comments, in the prescribed format, to your latest versions of `absval` and `flatten` (from previous exercises).

Exercise 4.16.3

Add a comment, in the prescribed format, to the following predicate (which should be familiar from Chapter 3):

```
fast_reverse(Original,Result) :-
    nonvar(Original),
    fast_reverse_aux(Original,[],Result).
fast_reverse_aux([Head|Tail],Stack,Result) :-
    fast_reverse_aux(Tail,[Head|Stack],Result).
fast_reverse_aux([],Result,Result).
```

Is `fast_reverse_aux` tail recursive?

4.17. SUPPLEMENT: SOME HAND COMPUTATIONS

Skip this section if you are having no trouble visualizing how Prolog solves a query. However, if recursively defined predicates occasionally leave you mystified, you will probably find it helpful to work through the detailed examples presented here. Note also that the debugger (described briefly in Chapter 1) can show you the exact steps of any computation.

This material will also be useful if you are building a Prolog interpreter, since it suggests a way to implement backtracking and cuts. Moreover, tracing Prolog computations by hand is an excellent way to debug tricky code.

4.17.1. Recursion

First let's compute by hand the Prolog query

```
?- member(c,[a,b,c,X]).
```

Our definition of member has two clauses:

```
[1]   member(X,[X|_]).
[2]   member(X,[_|Y]) :- member(X,Y).
```

Our first goal is

```
(1) ?- member(c,[a,b,c,X]).
```

This does not match clause [1], but it matches the head of clause [2]. We must remember that the variable X in clause [2] and the variable X in our goal (1) are really different variables. So we will begin by rewriting clause [2] so the variables not only are different but also look different. Since we are matching goal (1) with clause [2], we will attach the digit 1 to each of the variables in clause [2] to distinguish them. This will also make it easier for us to remember at which step in our computation this invocation of clause [2] occurred. Rewritten, clause [2] looks like this:

```
[2.1] member(X1,[_|Y1]) :- member(X1,Y1).
```

(By '[2.1]' we mean 'the instance of clause [2] used in satisfying goal (1).') Now the goal matches the head of [2.1] with the following unifications:

```
X1 = c              _ = a              Y1 = [b,c,X]
```

In what follows we will usually omit anonymous variables because their values are not saved.

4.17.2. Saving Backtrack Points

Later we may be forced to backtrack and look for an alternative way to satisfy goal (1). If we do, we will need to know which clause to try next. We record this information by setting a pointer in the knowledge base to show the last rule with which (1) has been matched:[2]

```
[1]   member(X,[X|_]).
[2]   member(X,[_|Y]) :- member(X,Y). <-(1)
```

Recall that the unifications we just made apply to the body of [2.1] as well as to its head. The body of [2.1], with these unifications in effect, becomes our new goal, designated (2):

---

[2]Our pointers are one step behind those that would actually be used in an implementation of Prolog. Practical Prolog systems store pointers to the *next* clause that should be tried, rather than the clause that has just been used. If the last clause that has just been used is the last clause of the predicate (as in this case), no pointer is stored at all. That's the key to tail-recursion optimization.

```
(1) ?- member(c,[a,b,c,X]).
   (2) ?- member(c,[b,c,X]).
```

Goal (2) will not match clause [1]. It does match the head of clause [2], which we rewrite as

```
[2.2] member(X2,[_|Y2]) :- member(X2,Y2).
```

(This is another invocation of [2], distinct from [2.1].) To get the match, we must unify some variables. We add these new instantiations to our previous set:

```
X1 = c            Y1 = [b,c,X]
X2 = c            Y2 = [c,X]
```

Next, we set the pointer for goal (2) at clause [2] so we can remember which clause we used to satisfy (2).

```
[1]  member(X,[X|_]).
[2]  member(X,[_|Y]) :- member(X,Y). <-(1) <-(2)
```

We replace our current goal with the instantiated body of [2.2].

```
(1) ?- member(c,[a,b,c,X]).
   (2) ?- member(c,[b,c,X]).
      (3) ?- member(c,[c,X]).
```

Goal (3) matches clause [1], rewritten

```
[1.3] member(X3,[X3|_]).
```

when we unify X3 with c and X with the anonymous variable:

```
X1 = c            Y1 = [b,c,X]
X2 = c            Y2 = [b,c,X]
X3 = c
```

We set the pointer for (3):

```
[1]  member(X,[X|_]). <-(3)
[2]  member(X,[_|Y]) :- member(X,Y). <-(1) <-(2)
```

and we replace goal (3) with the instantiated body of [1.3]. However, [1.3] has no body, so we have no goals left to satisfy. *Success!* The original query, goal (1), has been satisfied. Since the variable X in the original query was never instantiated, Prolog prints something like X = _0021 as the solution to the query.

4.17.3. Backtracking

Suppose we ask Prolog to look for another solution. Then it will try to resatisfy (3). Before trying to resatisfy goal (3), it must undo all the variable instantiations that were established when it last satisfied (3). In particular, X3 loses its value and the list of instantiations reverts to:

```
X1 = c             Y1 = [b,c,X]
X2 = c             Y2 = [c,X]
```

We see that the pointer for (3) is pointing to clause [1], so we must now try a clause subsequent to [1]. Goal (3) will match clause [2], rewritten

```
[2.3] member(X3,[_|Y3]) :- member(X3,Y3).
```

New instantiations, moving the pointer for (3), and replacing the current goal with the instantiated body of the rule just invoked gives us this situation:

```
X1 = c             Y1 = [b,c,X]
X2 = c             Y2 = [c,X]
X3 = c             Y3 = [X]
```

```
[1]  member(X,[X|_]).
[2]  member(X,[_|Y]) :- member(X,Y). <-(1) <-(2) <-(3)

(1) ?- member(c,[a,b,c,X]).
    (2) ?- member(c,[b,c,X]).
        (3) ?- member(c,[c,X]).
            (4) ?- member(c,[X]).
```

Now that we have the general idea, let's move a little faster. Matching (4) with [1] rewritten

```
[1.4] member(X4,[X4|_]).
```

produces

```
X1 = c             Y1 = [b,c,c]
X2 = c             Y2 = [c,X]
X3 = c             Y3 = [c]
X4 = X = c
```

```
[1]  member(X,[X|_]). <-(4)
[2]  member(X,[_|Y]) :- member(X,Y). <-(1) <-(2) <-(3)
```

We have no new goal since [1] is a fact. Prolog prints the solution X = c.

Again we ask for additional solutions. Prolog tries to resatisfy (4), first deinstantiating X4 and X. Now (4) will match [2], rewritten as

```
[2.4] member(X4,[_|Y4]) :- member(X4,Y4).
```

producing this situation:

```
X1 = c             Y1 = [b,c,X]
X2 = c             Y2 = [c,X]
X3 = c             Y3 = [X]
X4 = c             Y4 = []
X = _
```

```
[1]  member(X,[X|_]).
[2]  member(X,[_|Y]) :- member(X,Y). <-(1) <-(2) <-(3) <-(4)
```

```
(1) ?- member(c,[a,b,c,X]).
    (2) ?- member(c,[b,c,X]).
        (3) ?- member(c,[c,X]).
            (4) ?- member(c,[X]).
                (5) ?- member(c,[]).
```

Goal (5) fails since it will match neither [1] nor the head of [2]. There are no more rules for (4) to match, so Prolog backs up and tries to resatisfy (3). After undoing the appropriate instantiations, the situation is this:

```
X1 = c              Y1 = [b,c,X]
X2 = c              Y2 = [c,X]

[1]  member(X,[X|_]).
[2]  member(X,[_|Y]) :- member(X,Y). <-(1) <-(2) <-(3)
```

There are no more rules for **member**, and there is nothing else that (3) can match, so it's time to redo goal (2). Prolog deinstantiates X2 and Y2, producing:

```
X1 = c              Y1 = [b,c,X]

[1]  member(X,[X|_]).
[2]  member(X,[_|Y]) :- member(X,Y). <-(1) <-(2)
```

and tries to resatisfy (2). There are no more rules for (2) to try, so Prolog backs up and tries to resatisfy (1) with the following situation:

```
No instantiations (all undone due to backtracking).

[1]  member(X,[X|_]).
[2]  member(X,[_|Y]) :- member(X,Y). <-(1)
```

Now there are no more clauses for (1) to try, so there are no more alternatives. Prolog has failed to find another solution for our query, so it prints **no**.

4.17.4. Cuts

Let's compute the same query '?- **member(c,[a,b,c,X])**.' again, but with a slightly different definition of **member**:

```
[1] member(X,[X|_]) :- !.
[2] member(X,[_|Y]) :- member(X,Y).
```

This example will show us how to do a hand computation where a cut is involved.

This computation will look exactly like our previous computation until the following situation is reached:

```
X1 = c              Y1 = [b,c,X]
X2 = c              Y2 = [c,X]
```

```
[1]   member(X,[X|_]) :- !.
[2]   member(X,[_|Y]) :- member(X,Y). <-(1) <-(2)
```

```
(1) ?- member(c,[a,b,c,X]).
    (2) ?- member(c,[b,c,X]).
        (3) ?- member(c,[c,X]).
```

Then (3) will match [1] to produce this situation:

```
X1 = c              Y1 = [b,c,X]
X2 = c              Y2 = [c,X]
X3 = c
```

```
[1]   member(X,[X|_]) :- !. <-(3)
[2]   member(X,[_|Y]) :- member(X,Y). <-(1) <-(2)
```

```
(1) ?- member(c,[a,b,c,X]).
    (2) ?- member(c,[b,c,X]).
        (3) ?- member(c,[c,X]).
            (4) ?- !.
```

Now the current goal is a cut. Recall that the cut is supposed to prevent backtracking. When we execute it, we promise that we will not try to resatisfy any previous goals until we backtrack above the goal that introduced the cut into the computation. This means that we must now mark some of the lines in our goal stack to indicate that we cannot try to resatisfy them. The lines that we must mark comprise the current line and all lines above it until we get to the line that introduced the cut into the computation — in this case, line (3). We will use exclamation marks for markers.[3]

```
(1) ?- member(c,[a,b,c,X]).
    (2) ?- member(c,[b,c,X]).
    ! (3) ?- member(c,[c,X]).
        ! (4) ?- !.
```

We have no more goals to satisfy, so our query has succeeded. The X in the topmost goal was never instantiated, so Prolog prints out something like X = _0021 as a solution to the query.

Suppose we ask for an alternative solution. Then we must backtrack. Lines (3) and (4) are marked as not resatisfiable, so we try to resatisfy (2). The situation is then:

```
X1 = c              Y1 = [b,c,X]
X2 = c              Y2 = [c,X]
```

```
[1]   member(X,[X|_]) :- !.
[2]   member(X,[_|Y]) :- member(X,Y). <-(1) <-(2)
```

---

[3]Note that we could get the same effect by moving <-(3) to the end of the last clause, which would mean, in effect, that <-(3) would no longer be a backtrack point. That's how a real Prolog interpreter does it: All backtrack points introduced after entering goal 3 get discarded by the cut.

```
(1) ?- member(c,[a,b,c,X]).
   (2) ?- member(c,[b,c,X]).
```

There are no more clauses for (2) to match, so it fails and we backtrack to (1). The pointer for (1) also drops off the bottom of the database, and our original query fails.

The difference between this computation and the earlier one is that the cut in clause [1] prevents us from finding the second solution. Instead of the two solutions X = _0021 and X = c that the first computation produced, this second computation produces only the second of these results.

4.17.5. An Unexpected Loop

Let's look at another example. The query

```
?- reverse(X,[a,b]).
```

will produce the result X = [b,a]. If we ask for alternative solutions, a curious thing happens: Computation continues until we interrupt it or until a message tells us that Prolog has run out of memory.

What has gone wrong? We can determine the answer by doing a hand computation of our query. The relevant clauses in our knowledge base are

```
[1]  reverse([],[]).
[2]  reverse([H|T],L) :- reverse(T,X), append(X,[H],L).
[3]  append([],X,X).
[4]  append([H|T],L,[H|TT]) :- append(T,L,TT).
```

and our initial goal is

```
(1) ?- reverse(X,[a,b]).
```

This will match [2], producing the situation:

```
X = [H1|T1]
L1 = [a,b]
```

```
[1]
[2] <-(1)
[3]
[4]
```

```
(2) ?- reverse(T1,X1), append(X1,[H1],L1).
```

(For brevity, we are no longer listing the whole goal stack or the bodies of the clauses, although if you are following along with pencil and paper, you may want to write them in.)

Goal (2) consists of two goals joined by a comma. Our first task is therefore to satisfy the first part of (2). This matches [2] producing:

```
X = [H1|[H2|T2]]
L1 = [a,b]            T1 = [H2|T2]          X1 = L2
```

```
[1]
[2] <-(1) <-(2)
[3]
[4]
```

(3) ?- (reverse(T2,X2), append(X2,[H2],L2)), append(L2,[H1],[a,b]).

Notice that (3) is the result of replacing the first goal in (2) with the instantiated body of [2]. The remainder of (2) is just recopied, becoming the final goal in (3). Our current goal is now the first goal in (3), which matches [1] producing:

```
X = [H1|[H2|T2]] = [H1,H2]
L1 = [a,b]           T1 = [H2|[]] = [H2]         X1 = L2
T2 = X2 = [].
```

```
[1] <-(3)
[2] <-(1) <-(2)
[3]
[4]
```

(4) ?- append([],[H2],L2), append(L2,[H1],[a,b]).

We have simplified the value of X in our list of instantiations. We will do this without further comment in subsequent steps. Since [1] is a fact, the first goal in (3) disappears, and (4) consists of the two remaining goals.

Now for the first goal in (4). This matches [3] producing the situation:

```
X = [H1,H2]
L1 = [a,b]            T1 = [H2]            X1 = [H2]
L2 = [H3] = [H2]      T2 = []             H2 = H3
```

```
[1] <-(3)
[2] <-(1) <-(2)
[3] <-(4)
[4]
```

(5) ?- append([H2],[H1],[a,b]).

We lost a goal going from (4) to (5) because we matched the first goal in (4) with a fact. The new current goal will not match [3] since [H2] will only match a list with at least one member. So our current goal matches [4] to produce:

```
X = [H1,H2] = [H1,a]
L1 = [a,b]            T1 = [H2] = [a]      X1 = [H2] = [a]
L2 = [H2] = [a]       T2 = []             H2 = H3 = H5 = a
L5 = [H1]             T5 = []             TT5 = [b]
```

```
[1] <-(3)
[2] <-(1) <-(2)
[3] <-(4)
[4] <-(5)
```

(6) ?- append([],[H1],[b]).

Goal (6) matches [3] with H1 = H6 = b. Since [3] is a fact, we have no goals left and our query succeeds. The final situation is:

```
X = [H1,a] = [b,a]
L1 = [a,b]                T1 = [a]              X1 = [a]
L2 = [a]                  T2 = []               H2 = H3 = H5 = a
L5 = [H1] = [b]           T5 = []               TT5 = [b]
H6 = H1 = b
```

```
[1] <-(3)
[2] <-(1) <-(2)
[3] <-(4) <-(6)
[4] <-(5)
```

Notice that every variable has been instantiated to some constant or list of constants. Prolog prints the solution, which comprises the instantiations for all variables occurring in the original query '?- reverse(X,[a,b]).' — namely X = [b,a].

What happens if we ask for another solution? We retry (6), first deinstantiating H6. Goal (6) will not match [4] since [] has no first member. So the pointer for (6) disappears and we retry (5) after deinstantiating H5, T5, L5, and TT5. The pointer is at the bottom of the database, so there are no more clauses to try. Backtrack to (4), moving the pointer for (4) down to [4]. The situation is then:

```
X = [H1|[H2]] = [H1,H2]
L1 = [a,b]            T1 = [H2|[]] = [H2]              X1 = L2
T2 = X2
```

```
[1] <-(3)
[2] <-(1) <-(2)
[3]
[4] <-(4)
```

Goal (4) doesn't match [4], so (4) fails and we backtrack to (3). Goal (3) matches [2] producing:

```
X = [H1|[H2|T2]] = [H1,H2|T2] = [H1,H2|[H3|T3]] = [H1,H2,H3|T3]
L1 = [a,b]
T1 = [H2|T2] = [H2|[H3|T3]] = [H2,H3|T3]
X1 = L2
T2 = [H3|T3]
X2 = L3
```

```
[1]
[2] <-(1) <-(2) <-(3)
[3]
[4]
```

(4) ?- reverse(T3,X3), append(X3,[H3],L3), append(X2,[H2],L2),
        append(L2,[H1],[a,b]).

The current goal matches [1] giving us:

```
X = [H1,H2,H3|T3] = [H1,H2,H3|[]] = [H1,H2,H3]
L1 = [a,b]
T1 = [H2,H3|T3] = [H2,H3|[]] = [H2,H3]
X1 = L2
T2 = [H3|T3] = [H3|[]] = [H3]
X2 = L3
T3 = []
X3 = []
```

```
[1] <-(4)
[2] <-(1) <-(2) <-(3)
[3]
[4]
```

(5) ?- append([],[H3],L3), append(L3,[H2],L2), append(L2,[H1],[a,b]).

The current goal matches [3] giving us:

```
X = [H1,H2,H3]
L1 = [a,b]          T1 = [H2,H3]
L2 = X1             T2 = [H3]
L3 = X2 = [H3]      T3 = []           X3 = []
```

```
[1] <-(4)
[2] <-(1) <-(2) <-(3)
[3] <-(5)
[4]
```

(6) ?- append([H3],[H2],L2), append(L2,[H1],[a,b]).

The current goal matches [4] to give us:

```
X = [H1,H2,H6]
L1 = [a,b]              T1 = [H2,H6]
L2 = X1 = [H6|TT6]      T2 = [H6]         X2 = [H6]
H3 = H6                 T3 = []           X3 = []
L6 = [H2]               T6 = []
```

```
[1] <-(4)
[2] <-(1) <-(2) <-(3)
[3] <-(5)
[4] <-(6)
```

(7) ?- append([],[H2],TT6), append(L2,[H1],[a,b]).

The current goal matches [3] producing:

```
X = [H1,H2,H6]
L1 = [a,b]
T1 = [H2,H6]
L2 = X1 = [H6|TT6] = [H6|[H2]] = [H6,H2]
T2 = [H6]
L3 = X2 = [H6]        T3 = []          X3 = []            H3 = H6
L6 = [H2]             T6 = []          TT6 = [H2]
```

```
[1] <-(4)
[2] <-(1) <-(2) <-(3)
[3] <-(5) <-(7)
[4] <-(6)
```

(8) ?- append([H6,H2],[H1],[a,b]).

Without tracing further, we can see that (8) must fail. We cannot append a list with two members and a list with one member to produce a list with only two members. Also, we cannot resatisfy (7) since one of the arguments is [] and therefore will not unify with [4]. The marker for (6) drops off the database. We cannot resatisfy (5) because of []. So we backtrack all the way to (4), deinstantiate all the variables with subscripts higher than 3, move the pointer for (4) down to [2], and the situation is:

```
X = [H1,H2,H3|T3]
L1 = [a,b]          T1 = [H2,H3|T3]          X1 = L2
X2 = L3             T2 = [H3|T3]
```

```
[1]
[2] <-(1) <-(2) <-(3) <-(4)
[3]
[4]
```

(4) ?- reverse(T3,X3), append(X3,[H3],L3), append(X2,[H2],L2),
         append(L2,[H1],[a,b]).

Notice that the current goal is now the same as when we were at (3). If we continue, we will reach a situation where X = [H1,H2,H3,H4|T4] and the current goal will be reverse(T4,X4). Of course, the reverse of [a,b] can't have four members any more than it could have three. A new variable will be added to the list X and the process will repeat until we fill the stack and the machine stops.

This last example shows how we can use hand computations to discover why Prolog behaves the way it does when it does something unexpected. Sometimes using the trace facility built into a Prolog interpreter is confusing since we only see the current goal and cannot at the same time view either the preceding goals or the knowledge base with the pointers to the clauses used to satisfy the preceding goals. A good method to better understand what the trace is telling you is to carry on a hand computation on paper as you run the trace.

Exercise 4.17.1

Try some of the hand computations in this section and trace the same computations using the Prolog debugger. Compare the results. Does your debugger display numbers that indicate which clauses are involved in each query?

4.18. BIBLIOGRAPHICAL NOTES

On the art of expressing iteration through tail recursion, see Abelson and Sussman (1985), who use Scheme, a Lisp dialect. Tail recursion optimization appears to have originated with Scheme (Steele 1978); it has spread to Common Lisp as well as Prolog. The implementation of tail recursion optimization is discussed by Warren (1986), who points out that **append** is tail recursive.

For detailed information on how a Prolog interpreter works, read Hogger (1984:181-221), then Maier and Warren (1988), and finally Campbell (1984, a collection of articles) and Aït-Kaci (1991).

Chapter 5

Reading Data in Foreign Formats

5.1. THE PROBLEM OF FREE-FORM INPUT

We noted in Chapter 2 that the usual Prolog input routine, `read/1`, expects all data to be written with Prolog syntax. Obviously, in the real world of commercial software, this is an unrealistic demand. In this chapter we show you how to make Prolog read data in any format you choose; as a grand finale we present a Prolog program that reads Lotus .WKS spreadsheets.

The amount of attention you devote to this chapter will depend on your needs. There's no logic programming theory here — only practical algorithms. If you're an AI experimenter, you may want to take it somewhat lightly, looking back at it later if the need arises. If you're a commercial software developer, this may well be the chapter that makes Prolog usable in your application.

> *The procedures defined in this chapter are not meant to be used blindly. They are instructive examples, and we assume that before incorporating them into your programs, you will study how they work and adapt them to meet your needs more exactly.*

5.2. CONVERTING STRINGS TO ATOMS AND NUMBERS

Let's start with keyboard input. We'd like for the user to be able to type anything at the keyboard and have it go into Prolog as an atom or number, like this:

```
?- read_atom(What).
this is an atom   (typed by user)
What = 'this is an atom'
?- read_num(What).
3.1416   (typed by user)
What = 3.1416
```

To make this work, we'll rely on `read_str`, defined in Chapter 3 and shown, along with some other predicates, in Figure 5.1. Many programs later in this book will assume that the predicates in this file (READSTR.PL) are available and have been debugged to run properly on your computer.

Usually, what you want from the input is not a list of character codes, but an atom or number. As we will see in Chapter 7, strings (lists) are bulky, and character-string data should be stored as atoms where feasible. Conversion of strings to numbers is obviously essential if you want to read numeric data from the keyboard or from text files.

There are three ways to approach the conversion process. First, the ISO Prolog standard defines two built-in predicates, `atom_codes` and `number_codes`, which interconvert, respectively, atoms with strings and numbers with strings, like this:

```
?- atom_codes(abc,What).
What = [97,98,99]
?- atom_codes(What,"abc").
What = abc
?- number_codes(3.14,What).
What = [51,46,49,52]
?- number_codes(What,"3.14").
What = 3.14
```

If `number_codes` is given a string that doesn't make a valid number, or if either of its arguments is of the wrong type, it raises a runtime error condition. We will explore how to deal with these errors in the next section.[1]

Many older Prologs use `name/2` to perform both kinds of conversions:

```
?- name(abc,What).
What = [97,98,99]
?- name(What,"abc").
What = abc
?- name(3.14,What).
What = [51,46,49,52]
?- name(What,"3.14").
What = 3.14
```

There are a few Prologs in which `name` has the behavior prescribed for `atom_codes` and the conversion of numbers is done some completely different way. Moreover,

---

[1]Pre-ISO versions of Quintus Prolog have these same predicates, but they are called `atom_chars` and `number_chars`. The ISO standard has predicates called `atom_chars` and `number_chars`, but they produce lists of characters [l,i,k,e,' ',t,h,i,s] rather than strings.

```
% File READSTR.PL
% Reading and writing lines of text

% Uses get0, and works in almost all Prologs (not Arity).


% read_str(-String)
%    Accepts a whole line of input as a string (list of ASCII codes).
%    Assumes that the keyboard is buffered.

read_str(String) :- get0(Char),
                    read_str_aux(Char,String).

read_str_aux(-1,[]) :- !.     % end of file
read_str_aux(10,[]) :- !.     % end of line (UNIX)
read_str_aux(13,[]) :- !.     % end of line (DOS)

read_str_aux(Char,[Char|Rest]) :- read_str(Rest).


% read_atom(-Atom)
% Reads a line of input and converts it to an atom.
% See text concerning name/2 vs. atom_codes/2.

read_atom(Atom) :-
   read_str(String),
   name(Atom,String).     % or preferably atom_codes(Atom,String).


% read_num(-Number)
% Reads a line of input and converts it to a number.
% See text concerning name/2 vs. number_codes/2.

read_num(Atom) :-
   read_str(String),
   name(Atom,String).     % or preferably number_codes(Atom,String).


% write_str(+String)
% Outputs the characters corresponding to a list of ASCII codes.

write_str([Code|Rest]) :- put(Code), write_str(Rest).
write_str([]).
```

Figure 5.1 Routines to read free-form input.

name generally deals with errors by simply failing, but check your implementation to be sure.

In what follows, we'll assume that you've successfully implemented `read_atom` and `read_num`, defined roughly as follows:

```
read_atom(Atom) :- read_str(String), atom_codes(Atom,String).

read_num(Num) :- read_str(String), number_codes(Number,String).
```

and that these are in the file READSTR.PL (Figure 5.1). Be sure to check that they work correctly in your Prolog.[2]

There is a third way to convert strings into numbers: Pick off the digits one by one, convert them to their numeric values, and do the arithmetic. Specifically, what you do is maintain a running total, which starts as 0. Each time you get another digit, multiply the total by 10, then add to it the value of that digit. For example, converting the string "249", you'd do the following computations:

Digit '2' $(0 \times 10) + 2 = 2$
Digit '4' $(2 \times 10) + 4 = 24$
Digit '9' $(24 \times 10) + 9 = 249$

You may never have to do this, but the algorithm is worth remembering in case you have to deal with digits in an unusual base or format (e.g., hexadecimal or separated by commas).

Exercise 5.2.1

On your computer, when you hit Return on the keyboard, does `get0` (ISO `get_code`) read it as code 10, code 13, or both? What if you read from a text file using `see`? Explain how you found out. Does `read_str` need any modification in order to work reliably when reading from files on your computer? If so, indicate what changes should be made.

Exercise 5.2.2

Are `read_str` and `write_str` tail recursive? Explain.

Exercise 5.2.3

Get `read_atom` and `read_num` working on your computer. Store the working versions in file READSTR.PL. What does `read_num` do when its input is not a validly written number?

Exercise 5.2.4

Put `read_atom` to practical use by modifying LEARNER.PL (Chapter 2) to accept input without requiring the user to use Prolog syntax.

---

[2]In ALS Prolog, use `name` to convert atoms, and deal with numbers thus:

```
read_num(Num) :- read_str(String), buf_read(String,[Num]).
```

In Arity Prolog, do this:

```
read_str(String) :- read_line(0,Text), list_text(String,Text).
read_atom(Atom) :- read_line(0,Text), atom_string(Atom,Text).
read_num(Num) :- read_line(0,Text),
                 ((int_text(Num,Text), !) ; float_text(Num,Text,general)).
```

Exercise 5.2.5

Modify `read_atom` to convert all letters to lowercase as they are read in.   Call the modified procedure `read_lc_atom`.

Exercise 5.2.6

Define a procedure, `read_hex_num`, that is like `read_num` except that it reads hexadecimal numbers:

```
?- read_hex_num(What).
20
What = 32
?- read_hex_num(What).
10fe
What = 4350
```

Use a digit-by-digit conversion algorithm similar to the one described in this section, but adapted for hexadecimal.

5.3. COMBINING OUR CODE WITH YOURS

Suppose you're writing a program in which you want to use the predicates that are defined in READSTR.PL. You have two choices:

- You can copy READSTR.PL, entire, into your program.

- You can insert a directive in your program that causes READSTR.PL to be consulted.

The second of these is what we'll explore here. In ISO Prolog, and in many existing implementations (including Quintus, SWI, and LPA), the directive

```
:- ensure_loaded('readstr.pl').
```

means, "If READSTR.PL has not already been consulted, consult it now."   That's exactly what you need. (Of course it works only if READSTR.PL is in the current directory.)

Other Prologs don't have `ensure_loaded`.   A reasonable substitute is to use `reconsult`, like this:

```
:- reconsult('readstr.pl').
```

On encountering this line in your program, the Prolog system will reconsult READSTR.PL, whether or not READSTR.PL has been consulted before. This wastes a bit of time, but nothing serious goes wrong.

Early versions of Arity Prolog (before 5.0) have trouble with nested `reconsult`s. If you find that you cannot include a `reconsult` directive in a file that is being `reconsult`ed, your best option is to copy one program, whole, into the other, thus bypassing the problem of how to reconsult it.

Exercise 5.3.1

Does your Prolog support `ensure_loaded`? If not, do embedded `reconsult` directives work correctly? Experiment and see.

5.4. VALIDATING USER INPUT

Any time a program accepts input from the user at the keyboard, two problems can arise:

- The user may type something that is not an acceptable answer (e.g., 4 when the menu choices are 1, 2, and 3).

- The user may type something that is not even interpretable (e.g., xyz when a number is expected).

In either case the program should do something sensible. It's convenient to use a repeat loop to validate user input, like this:

```
get_number(N)  :- repeat,
                  write('Type a number between 1 and 3: '),
                  read_num(N),
                  N =< 3,
                  N >= 1,
                  !.
```

If the user types a number that is out of range, execution backtracks to the repeat goal, the computer prints the prompt again, and the user gets another chance. If there are several discrete choices, it's convenient to use member with a list of alternatives:

```
get_choice(C)  :- repeat,
                  write('Type a, b, or c: '),
                  read_atom(C),
                  member(C,[a,b,c]),
                  !.
```

Still faster, but bulkier, is the following approach:

```
get_ok(C)  :- repeat,
              write('Type a, b, or c: '),
              read_atom(C),
              ok(C),
              !.
```

```
ok(a).
ok(b).
ok(c).
```

The last example shows that you can use all the power of Prolog inference to decide what answers are acceptable.

A greater challenge arises when the user types uninterpretable input, such as letters where a number is expected. In some Prologs, read_num will simply fail in such a case:

```
?- read_num(N).
asdf     (typed by user)
no.
```

That's simple enough: You can use **repeat** loops, and execution will backtrack from uninterpretable answers the same way as from answers that have been examined and found unacceptable.

In other Prologs, uninterpretable numbers cause runtime errors, stopping the program. Fortunately, the ISO standard includes a built-in predicate, **catch**, which can catch these errors and keep them from interrupting the program. If you have ISO Prolog available, try this:

```
read_num_or_fail(N) :-  catch(read_num(N),_,fail).
```

That is: "Execute **read_num(N)**, or if any error arises, simply fail."

Exercise 5.4.1

Try out **get_number**, **get_choice**, and **get_ok** (the examples just given) on your computer and verify that they work as intended.

Exercise 5.4.2

Rework GETYESNO.PL from Chapter 2 so that it uses **repeat** rather than recursion.

Exercise 5.4.3

On your computer, what does **read_num** do if the user types something that is not a valid number? If needed, check your manual and see if you can implement **read_num_or_fail**.

5.5. CONSTRUCTING MENUS

Because Prolog is good at handling complex data structures, it is a simple matter to write a procedure that will create and display a menu when you tell it what the menu choices should be. Figure 5.2 shows one example. The menu generator defined there is called by queries such as this:

```
?- menu([item('Georgia',ga),item('Florida',fl),item('Hawaii',hi)], What).

   1 Georgia
   2 Florida
   3 Hawaii
Your choice (1 to 3):  2

What = fl
```

Naturally, **menu/2** would normally be called from another procedure that needs to display a menu. Its first argument consists of a list of the form

```
[item(Message1,Value1),item(Message2,Value2),item(Message3,Value3)]
```

with up to 9 items, each consisting of a message to be displayed and a result to be returned (in the second argument position) if the user chooses that item. The message is normally an atom; the "value" can be a term of any kind.

The menus that you get this way are very unsophisticated. In fact, they ask the user to choose an arbitrary number, which is a relatively error-prone kind of choice. Menus that use initial letters or mouse pointers are easier to use and less subject to errors.

Note, however, that you could easily replace menu/2 with any other kind of menuing routine that you care to implement. The important thing is that you specify what the menu choices are to be, and menu/2 takes care of the rest of the work. Thus, menu/2 establishes an important conceptual boundary between deciding what is to be *on* the menu, and deciding how to *implement* the menu. Few other languages let you make such a clean distinction.

Exercise 5.5.1

Get menu/2 working on your computer and verify that it works correctly.

Exercise 5.5.2

Note that menu/2 uses a recursive loop to deal with invalid choices. Rewrite it to use a repeat loop instead.

Exercise 5.5.3

Rewrite menu/2 so that the user makes a choice by typing, not a number, but the first letter of the word to be chosen.

5.6. READING FILES WITH get_byte

When we move from reading the keyboard to reading files, we have two new concerns:

- Are we going to get every byte of the file intact and unchanged?

- What is going to happen at end of file?

Here, unfortunately, various implementations of Prolog part ways. In Arity Prolog, get0 simply fails at end of file, while in most other Prologs it returns code −1. In ALS Prolog, get0 skips all bytes with value 0 or 13; in Cogent (Amzi) Prolog, get0 treats value 26 as an end-of-file mark; in other Prologs, get0 preserves all bytes intact.

To simplify matters, we will use the ISO Prolog predicate get_byte/1, which reads each byte as a numeric code and returns −1 at end of file. (The difference between get_byte and get_code is that get_byte is guaranteed not to do any special handling of end-of-line marks, end-of-file marks, or unprintable codes.) If get_byte is not built into your Prolog, you will have to define it. In most Prologs, this definition suffices,

```
get_byte(C) :- get0(C).
```

because get0 and get_byte are the same thing. In Arity Prolog, use this definition instead:

```
% File MENU.PL
% A menu generator in Prolog

% menu(+Menu,-Result)
%  Displays a menu of up to 9 items and returns the user's choice.
%  Menu is a list of the form [item(Message,Value),item(Message,Value)...]
%  where each Message is to be displayed and Value is to be returned
%  as Result if the user chooses that item.

menu(Menu,Result) :- menu_display(Menu,49,Last),
                     menu_choose(Menu,49,Last,Result),
                     nl.

% Display all the messages and simultaneously count them.
% The count starts at 49 (ASCII code for '1').

menu_display([],SoFar,Last) :-
   !,
   % not an item, so don't use this number
   Last is SoFar - 1.

menu_display([item(Message,_)|Tail],SoFar,Last) :-
   put(32),
   put(32),
   put(SoFar),        % appropriate digit
   put(32),           % blank
   write(Message),
   nl,
   Next is SoFar + 1,
   menu_display(Tail,Next,Last).

% Get the user's choice. If invalid, make him/her try again.

menu_choose(Menu,First,Last,Result) :-
   write('Your choice ('),
   put(First),
   write(' to '),
   put(Last),
   write('): '),
   get(Char),
   menu_choose_aux(Menu,First,Last,Result,Char).
```

Figure 5.2   A menu-generating procedure (continued on next page).

```
menu_choose_aux(Menu,First,Last,Result,Char) :-
    Char >= First,
    Char =< Last,
    !,
    menu_select(Menu,First,Char,Result).

menu_choose_aux(Menu,First,Last,Result,_) :-
    put(7),             % beep
    put(13),            % return to beginning of line
    menu_choose(Menu,First,Last,Result).

% Find the appropriate item to return for Char

menu_select([item(_,Result)|_],First,First,Result) :- !.

menu_select([_|Tail],First,Char,Result) :-
    NewFirst is First+1,
    menu_select(Tail,NewFirst,Char,Result).


% Demonstrate the whole thing

demo :- menu([item('Georgia',ga),
              item('Florida',fl),
              item('Hawaii',hi)],Which),
        write('You chose: '),
        write(Which),
        nl.


% End of MENU.PL
```

Figure 5.2 (Continued).

```
get_byte(C) :- get0(C), !.
get_byte(-1).
```

Experimentation may be needed to determine how to best define `get_byte` in your Prolog.[3]

Exercise 5.6.1

> Get `get_byte` working on your computer. Ensure that it works correctly not only when reading from the keyboard, but also when reading a file using `see`.

Exercise 5.6.2

> On your computer, does `get_byte` (as you have defined it) let you repeatedly attempt to read past the same end of file, or does it give a runtime error if you bump into the same end-of-file mark more than once?

5.7. FILE HANDLES (STREAM IDENTIFIERS)

In the rest of this chapter, we will perform all file input by redirecting standard input with `see`. We do this reluctantly; it's portable but risky. In particular, if the program crashes while input is redirected, you may not be able to type any further commands into the Prolog system.

Almost every Prolog implementation provides a way to access files through HANDLES (STREAM IDENTIFIERS). For example,

```
read(H,X)
```

usually means "Read a term into X from the file whose handle is H." The handle is a value that is given to you when you open the file.

Unfortunately, the syntax for accessing files in this way is widely variable. The proposed ISO system is described in Appendix A; the actual syntax used in Quintus Prolog and SWI Prolog looks like this:[4]

```
test :- open('myfile1.txt',read,File1),
        read(File1,Term),
        close(File1),
        open('myfile2.txt',write,File2),
        write(File2,Term),
        close(File2).
```

The idea is that the `open` predicate opens a file for either reading or writing and instantiates `File1` to its handle. You then give `File1` as an argument of all subsequent predicates that use the file.

---

[3]In Cogent Prolog 2.0, to read all the bytes of a file transparently, you will have to open it as binary and access it by file handle (see the next section and your manual). As far as we can determine, users of ALS Prolog 1.2 are simply out of luck, unless they want to link in a subroutine written in C.

[4]For an Arity Prolog example, see Appendix B.

Exercise 5.7.1

Adapt the example just given so that it works on your computer (or demonstrate that it already works as is).

Exercise 5.7.2

Adapt the predicates in READSTR.PL to take an extra argument for the file handle, and get them working on your computer. Notice that you can add the new predicates to READSTR.PL without conflict, because they have different arities than the old ones.

5.8. FIXED-LENGTH FIELDS

Many data files in the business world consist of fixed-length fields; Figure 5.3 shows an example. Each line is called a RECORD. The fields may or may not consist of characters, and records may or may not end with end-of-line marks. That is, the file may or may not be a text file.

Reading a fixed-length field is simple: start with the number of bytes to be read, and count down to 0, like this:

```
% read_bytes(+N,-String)                       %%% preliminary version
%  Reads N bytes into String.

read_bytes(0,[]) :- !.

read_bytes(N,[C|Rest]) :-
    get_byte(C),
    NextN is N-1,
    read_bytes(NextN,Rest).
```

Notice that in Prolog, we often count down when an ordinary programming language would count up (for i:=1 to N or the like). That lets us compare the loop variable to 0 (a constant) rather than comparing to N (which would have to be another parameter supplied at runtime).

The version of **read_bytes** that we'll actually use is more complicated and is shown in Figure 5.4. It uses one character of lookahead to check for an unexpected

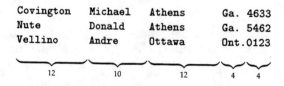

Figure 5.3   File FIXEDLEN.DAT, a data file with fixed-length fields. Each line may be followed by a 1- or 2-byte end-of-line mark, depending on the operating system and the file format.

end-of-file mark. In Figure 5.4 we also define `skip_bytes`, which skips a specified number of bytes without storing them in a list.

Most Prologs also include a `seek` command to jump to a particular position in a random-access file, but we do not use it here because of lack of standardization. Even the ISO standard makes the details of this operation up to the implementor.

Exercise 5.8.1

Get `read_bytes` and `skip_bytes` working on your computer. Demonstrate that they work by using them to read FIXEDLEN.DAT.

Exercise 5.8.2

On your computer, what does `read_bytes` do if you repeatedly try to read past the end of the file?

Exercise 5.8.3

Why is '?- `skip_bytes(80).`' faster than '?- `read_bytes(80,_).`'?

Exercise 5.8.4

Define a predicate `read_record/1` that will read FIXEDLEN.DAT one record at a time, returning each record as a Prolog term, like this:

```
?- see('fixedlen.dat'), read_record(A), read_record(B), seen.
A = record('Covington   ','Michael   ','Athens      ','Ga. ',4633)
B = record('Nute        ','Donald    ','Athens      ','Ga. ',5462)
```

You will have to use `read_bytes` to read the individual fields as strings, and then use `name` (or `atom_codes` and `number_codes`) to convert the strings to atoms or numbers as appropriate. Be sure you don't forget the end-of-line mark, which will be either 1 or 2 bytes long depending on the operating system.

Exercise 5.8.5

Is `'Athens    '` the same term as `'Athens'`? Explain.

Exercise 5.8.6

Modify `read_record` to discard blanks at the beginning and end of each field, so that you get `'Athens'` (etc.) without unnecessary blanks. Call your new procedure `read_record_1`.

Exercise 5.8.7

Modify `read_bytes` so that it if hits the end of the file, it returns the atom `end_of_file` instead of returning a string. Call your new procedure `read_bytes_1`.

Exercise 5.8.8

Using `read_bytes_1`, modify `read_record` so that it, too, returns `end_of_file` if it hits the end of the file. Call your new procedure `read_record_2`.

```
% File READBYTE.PL
% Reads fixed-length fields from files.

% Insert appropriate definition of get_byte here:
get_byte(C) :- get0(C).

% read_bytes(+N,-String)
%  Reads the next N bytes from current input, as a list of ASCII codes.
%  Stops if end of file is encountered prematurely.

read_bytes(N,String) :-
  get_byte(C),
  read_bytes_aux(C,N,String).

read_bytes_aux(-1,_,[]) :- !.      % end of file, so stop

read_bytes_aux(C,1,[C]) :- !.      % no more bytes to read, so stop

read_bytes_aux(C,N,[C|Rest]) :-    % keep going
  get_byte(NextC),
  NextN is N-1,
  read_bytes_aux(NextC,NextN,Rest).

% skip_bytes(+N)
%  Skips the next N bytes on standard input

skip_bytes(0) :- !.                % special case

skip_bytes(N) :-                   % ordinary case
  N > 0,
  get_byte(C),
  skip_bytes_aux(C,N).

skip_bytes_aux(-1,_) :- !.         % end of file, so stop

skip_bytes_aux(_,N) :-             % keep going
  NextN is N-1,
  skip_bytes(NextN).


% Demonstration, should print [65,116,104,101,110,115,32,32,32,32,32,32]

demo :- see('fixedlen.dat'),
        skip_bytes(22),
        read_bytes(12,String),
        seen,
        write(String), nl.
```

Figure 5.4 Routines for reading fixed-length fields.

5.9. NOW WHAT DO YOU DO WITH THE DATA?

Now that you can read data files from Prolog, what do you do with them? Depending on the purpose of your Prolog program, there are three main options:

- Read the file one record at a time and process each record somehow.

  This is a suitable approach if the purpose of your program is to work through the whole file and compute something from it.

- Read each record and convert it into a Prolog fact, which is then asserted into the knowledge base.

  This is a practical approach if you want to use the file to answer queries, and the file (or the portion of it you are interested in) is not excessively large. (The built-in predicate `statistics` will tell you how much memory is available in your Prolog implementation.)

- Search the whole file, on disk, when you need information from it.

  This is the slowest option, but sometimes the only practical one if the file is gigantic. Fortunately, most large database files can be searched in ways that are faster than a pure sequential search — each record contains pointers to other records, or there is a hashing algorithm, or both.

The structure of database files is outside the scope of this book, but we want you to be aware that there are many different ways to use data within a Prolog program.

Exercise 5.9.1

Drawing upon your answers to all the exercises in the previous section, define a predicate `record/6` that can be queried as if it were a set of Prolog facts, but which actually works by opening FIXEDLEN.DAT and finding the first record that matches your query. For example, if you type

```
?- record(Name,FirstName,'Athens',State,Num).
```

the computer should open FIXEDLEN.DAT, start reading, and eventually yield the answer:

```
Name='Covington' FirstName='Michael' State='Ga.' Num=4633
```

To simplify matters, do not look for alternative solutions; use only the first record that matches the query.

5.10. COMMA-DELIMITED FIELDS

Figure 5.5 shows another data format that is popular for transferring data between business software packages: COMMA-DELIMITED FIELDS, i.e., text with the fields separated by commas. Commonly, although not always, alphabetic fields are enclosed in quotes so that commas within them will not be taken as separators.

Reading comma-delimited fields in Prolog is straightforward. The key is to implement a procedure called `read_until` that accepts bytes up to and including a

```
4633,"Covington","M","A","Athens","Georgia"
5462,"Nute","D","E","Athens","Georgia"
123,"Vellino","A",,"Ottawa","Ontario"
```

Figure 5.5   File COMMADEL.DAT, a data file with comma-delimited fields.

specific code (or end of file or end of line, whichever comes first). Then, to read a comma-delimited field, simply `read_until` a comma.

The quotes complicate the problem slightly. The actual algorithm is to read the first character of the field, and then, if it is not a quote, `read_until` a comma. However, if the field begins with a quote, the computer must `read_until` the closing quote (thereby obtaining the data), then `read_until` the comma (to discard it). Figure 5.6 shows the complete implementation.

Exercise 5.10.1

Get `read_cdf` working on your computer. Show that it can read COMMADEL.DAT field-by-field.

Exercise 5.10.2

Reimplement `read_record` from two sections back, but this time make it use `read_cdf` to read COMMADEL.DAT. Call it `read_cdf_record`.

5.11. BINARY NUMBERS

Not all data files consist of printable characters. Some of the fields in any data file are likely to be binary numbers. That is, the number 36, for instance, is likely to be represented not as the bytes for the characters '3' and '6', but as the binary number 36 (100100).

Small integers are often stored in 16 bits (two bytes). For example, the number 1993 is, in binary, 0000011111001001. That won't fit into one byte, so it's split across two: 00000111 11001001. The Prolog program's job is to read these two bytes (which individually have values of 7 and 201 respectively) and put them together: $(7 \times 256) + 201 = 1993$. In effect, we're treating the bytes as base-256 digits.

There are three complications. First, on IBM PC compatible machines, the bytes are stored in the opposite of the order you might expect: The less significant byte comes first. (Sun Sparcstations put the more significant byte first.) Second, negative numbers are represented in twos-complement notation, so if you get 65535, you should convert it to -1; in fact, any value greater than 32767 actually represents a negative number. Third, all these calculations assume that the Prolog system's arithmetic is not limited to 16 bits per integer. Virtually all Prolog systems automatically switch to floating-point arithmetic when the available integers are not big enough, so we do not expect a problem here. The code for reading signed and unsigned 16-bit integers is shown in Figure 5.7.

```
% File READCDF.PL
% Reading comma-delimited fields from a file

% Insert suitable definition of get_byte here
get_byte(C) :- get0(C).


% read_until(+Target,-String)
% Reads characters until a specific character is found,
% or end of line, or end of file.

read_until(Target,String) :-
   get_byte(C),
   read_until_aux(C,Target,String).

read_until_aux(-1,_,[]) :- !.      % end of file, so stop
read_until_aux(13,_,[]) :- !.      % end of line (DOS)
read_until_aux(10,_,[]) :- !.      % end of line (UNIX)

read_until_aux(T,T,[])  :- !.      % found the target, so stop

read_until_aux(C,T,[C|Rest]) :-    % keep going
   read_until(T,Rest).




% read_cdf(-String)
% Reads a comma-delimited field.

read_cdf(String) :-
   get_byte(FirstChar),            % look at first character
   read_cdf_aux(FirstChar,String).

read_cdf_aux(34,String) :-         % field begins with "
   !,
   read_until(34,String),          % read until next "
   read_until(44,_).               % consume the following comma

read_cdf_aux(C,String) :-          % field does not begin with "
   read_until_aux(C,44,String).    % (just in case C is -1 or 10...)
```

Figure 5.6   Routines to read comma-delimited fields.

```
% File READI16.PL
% Routines to read 16-bit binary integers from a file

% Assumes less significant byte comes first (as on PC's, not Sparcstations).
% If this is not the case, swap Lo and Hi in read_u16/1.


:- ensure_loaded('readbyte.pl').  % or use reconsult if necessary


% read_u16(-Integer)
%  Reads 2 bytes as a 16-bit unsigned integer, LSB first.

read_u16(I) :-              % 16-bit unsigned integer
   read_bytes(2,[Lo,Hi]),
   I is Hi*256 + Lo.




% read_i16(-Integer)
%  Reads 2 bytes as a 16-bit signed integer, LSB first.

read_i16(I) :-             % 16-bit signed integer
  read_u16(U),
  u16_to_i16(U,I).




% u16_to_i16(+U,-I)
%  Converts 16-bit unsigned to signed integer.

u16_to_i16(U,I) :- U > 32767, !, I is U - 65536.

u16_to_i16(U,U).
```

Figure 5.7   Routines for reading 16-bit binary integers.

Even floating-point numbers can be stored in binary, and a huge variety of formats is used. We will look at IEEE 64-bit format, a representation recommended by the Institute of Electrical and Electronic Engineers. In IEEE 64-bit format, a floating-point number consists of:

- One bit to denote sign (1 for negative, 0 for positive);

- 11 bits for the exponent, biased by adding 1023;

- 56 bits for the mantissa, without its first digit (which is always 1).

The MANTISSA and EXPONENT are the parts of a number written in scientific notation. For example, in the number 3.14×10^{23}, 3.14 is the mantissa and 23 is the exponent. Naturally, IEEE 64-bit format is binary, not decimal.

The first digit of the mantissa is always 1 because floating-point numbers are *normalized*. To understand normalization, think about how numbers are written in scientific notation. We never write 0.023×10^3 — instead, we write 2.3×10^1. That is, we shift the mantissa so that its first digit is nonzero and adjust the exponent accordingly. That's called NORMALIZATION. Now in binary, if the first digit is not 0, then the first digit is necessarily 1. That's why the first digit of the mantissa of a normalized binary floating-point number can be omitted.

Finally, the exponent is normalized by adding 1023 so that the available range will be -1023 to $+1024$ rather than 0 to 2047.

If we can evaluate the sign, the mantissa, and the exponent, the value of the floating-point number is given by the formula:

$$Value = -1^{Sign} \times (1 + Mantissa) \times 2^{Exponent - 1023}$$

Recall that *Sign* is either 1 or 0.

The evaluation is clumsy because the boundaries between sign and exponent, and between exponent and mantissa, fall within rather than between the bytes. Fortunately, we can pick the bytes apart using simple arithmetic: if B is the value of an 8-bit byte, then B `//` 128 is its first bit and B `mod` 128 is the value of its remaining bits. In the same way, we can split a byte in half by dividing by 16.

There are two special cases:

- If the mantissa and exponent are all zeroes, then the number is taken to be exactly 0.0 (not 1×2^{-1023}, which is what the formula gives and which would otherwise be the smallest representable number). This gets around the problem that the mantissa of 0 never begins with 1, even after normalization.

- If all 11 bits of the exponent are 1, the number is interpreted as "not a number" ("NaN"), i.e., a number with an unknown or uncomputable value. (There is a further distinction between NaN and "infinity," which we will ignore here.)

One last subtlety: The bytes are stored in reverse order (least significant first); that is, they are read in the opposite of the order in which you would write a number in binary. This affects only the order of the bytes themselves, not the order of the bits within the bytes.

Figure 5.8 contains the actual code to read IEEE 64-bit floating-point numbers. It is not elegant, but it shows that Prolog has the power to handle unfamiliar data formats, even very exotic ones. You do not have to have 64-bit arithmetic to run this code; it works in any floating-point arithmetic system.

IEEE and other floating-point number formats are described concisely by Kain (1989:456-460). Arity Prolog has a large library of built-in predicates for reading binary numbers; other Prologs may also have libraries to handle similar tasks.

Exercise 5.11.1

Get `read_i16` and `read_u16` working on your computer. Test them by reading the byte codes of the characters '!!', which should decode as 8224 (the same whether signed or unsigned).

Exercise 5.11.2   (small project)

Using a C or Pascal program, write some 16-bit binary integers to a file, then read them back in using a Prolog program. (To write binary integers in C, use `fwrite` with an integer argument; in Pascal, create a `file of integer`.)

Exercise 5.11.3

Get `read_f64` working on your computer. Test it by reading the byte codes of the characters '!!!ABCDE', which should decode as approximately 4.899×10^{25}.

Exercise 5.11.4   (small project)

If you have access to a C or Pascal compiler that uses IEEE floating-point representation, then do the same thing as in Exercise 5.11.2, but with floating-point numbers.

Exercise 5.11.5

Modify `read_u16`, `read_i16`, and `read_f64` so that each of them returns the atom `end_of_file` if the end of the file is encountered where data is expected.

5.12. GRAND FINALE: READING A LOTUS SPREADSHEET

Figure 5.9 shows a Prolog program that reads spreadsheets in Lotus .WKS format. Because so much information in the business world is stored in spreadsheets, or is easily imported into them, a program like this can greatly extend the usefulness of Prolog.

Walden (1986) gives a full description of .WKS format, which is the file format used by early versions of Lotus 1-2-3. More recent spreadsheet programs can still use .WKS format if you tell them to, although it is no longer the default.

The spreadsheet file consists of a series of FIELDS (RECORDS), each of which comprises:

• A 16-bit OPCODE (operation code) indicating the type of field;

• A 16-bit number giving the length of the field;

• The contents of the field, which depend on its type.

```
% File READF64.PL
% Routine to read IEEE 64-bit binary numbers from a file

:- ensure_loaded('readbyte.pl').  % or use reconsult if necessary


% read_f64(-Float)
%  Reads 8 bytes as an IEEE 64-bit floating-point number.

read_f64(Result) :-
  read_bytes(8,[B0,B1,B2,B3,B4,B5,B6,B7]),
  Sign is B7 // 128,              % 1 bit for sign
  B7L is B7 mod 128,             % first 7 bits of exponent
  B6H is B6 // 16,               % last 4 bits of exponent
  B6L is B6 mod 16,              % first 4 bits of mantissa
  read_f64_aux(B0,B1,B2,B3,B4,B5,B6L,B6H,B7L,Sign,Result).

read_f64_aux(0,0,0,0,0,0,0,0,0,_, 0.0) :- !.

read_f64_aux(_,_,_,_,_,_,_,15,127,_, not_a_number) :- !.

read_f64_aux(B0,B1,B2,B3,B4,B5,B6L,B6H,B7L,Sign, Result) :-
  Exponent is B7L*16 + B6H - 1023,
  Mantissa is
    ((((((B0/256+B1)/256+B2)/256+B3)/256+B4)/256+B5)/256+B6L)/16 + 1,
  power(-1,Sign,S),
  power(2,Exponent,E),
  Result is S * Mantissa * E.


% power(X,N,Result)
%  Finds the Nth power of X (for integer N).  Needed because some
%  Prologs still don't have exponentiation in the 'is' predicate.

power(_,0,1) :- !.

power(X,E,Result) :-
  E > 0,
  !,
  EE is E-1,
  power(X,EE,R),
  Result is R*X.

power(X,E,Result) :-
  % E < 0,
  EE is E+1,
  power(X,EE,R),
  Result is R/X.
```

Figure 5.8 Procedure to read IEEE 64-bit floating-point numbers.

The bulk of the fields in an ordinary spreadsheet are NON-DATA FIELDS — that is, they contain information about how to print or display the spreadsheet. In order to preserve all defaults, a full set of these is saved with even the smallest spreadsheet. Accordingly, we can ignore nearly all the opcodes. The opcodes that are significant are:

0 Beginning of file

1 End of file

13 Integer

14 Floating-point constant

15 Text constant ("label")

16 Formula with stored floating-point value

Although our program does not try to decode formulas, it would be quite possible to do so, producing expressions that could be evaluated using is. We content ourselves with retrieving the floating-point value that is stored along with each formula.

Like all the examples in this chapter, LOTUS.PL reads from standard input. Naturally, in any practical application, it should be adapted to read from a file identified by a handle.

Exercise 5.12.1

Get LOTUS.PL working on your computer. Write a procedure, dump_spreadsheet, which reads an entire spreadsheet file and writes out the contents of each field.

(The program files accompanying this book include a spreadsheet file, SAMPLE.WKS, which you can use for testing. Be sure that if you transfer SAMPLE.WKS from one computer to another, it is transferred in binary form.)

Exercise 5.12.2

Modify LOTUS.PL to complain if the first field of the spreadsheet is not a beginning-of-file code. (That situation would indicate that the file being read is probably not really a spreadsheet, at least not one in .WKS format.)

Exercise 5.12.3

Modify LOTUS.PL to return end_of_file if it encounters an unexpected end of file. (This will depend on having previously made similar modifications to read_bytes, read_u16, etc.)

Exercise 5.12.4   (term project)

Modify LOTUS.PL to decode the formulas stored in the spreadsheet. For a description of the data format, see Walden (1986).

```
% File LOTUS.PL
% Reads a Lotus .WKS spreadsheet, field by field.

:- ensure_loaded('readbyte.pl').   % or use reconsult if necessary
:- ensure_loaded('readi16.pl').    % or use reconsult if necessary
:- ensure_loaded('readf64.pl').    % or use reconsult if necessary

% Insert definition of atom_codes here if not built in
atom_codes(Atom,Codes) :- name(Atom,Codes).

% read_significant_field(-Field)
%  Reads a field from the spreadsheet (like read_field below),
%  but skips non-data fields.

read_significant_field(Result) :-   % like read_field, skips non-data
   repeat,
     read_field(R),
     \+ R == non_data_field,
   !,
   Result = R.

% read_field(-Field)
%  Reads a field from the spreadsheet, returning one of the following:
%
%  beginning_of_file           -- Lotus beginning-of-file code
%  end_of_file                 -- Lotus end-of-file code
%  cell(Col,Row,integer,Value) -- An integer. Col and Row numbered from 0.
%  cell(Col,Row,float,Value)   -- A floating-point number.
%  cell(Col,Row,formula,Value) -- The numerical value of a formula.
%  cell(Col,Row,text,Value)    -- A text field (as a Prolog atom).
%  non_data_field              -- Anything else (print formats, etc.).

read_field(Result) :-
   read_u16(Opcode),
   read_field_aux(Opcode,Result).

read_field_aux(0,beginning_of_file) :-
   !,
   read_u16(Length),
   skip_bytes(Length).

read_field_aux(1,end_of_file) :-
   !.
   % no need to read the trivial bytes that follow
```

Figure 5.9   Routines to read a spreadsheet in .WKS format (continued on next page).

```
read_field_aux(13,cell(Col,Row,integer,Value)) :-
    !,
    skip_bytes(3),      % length and format information
    read_u16(Col),
    read_u16(Row),
    read_i16(Value).

read_field_aux(14,cell(Col,Row,float,Value)) :-
    !,
    skip_bytes(3),      % length and format information
    read_u16(Col),
    read_u16(Row),
    read_f64(Value).

read_field_aux(15,cell(Col,Row,text,Value)) :-
    !,
    read_u16(Length),
    skip_bytes(1),      % format code
    read_u16(Col),
    read_u16(Row),
    Rest is Length - 7,
    skip_bytes(1),               % alignment code at beg. of string
    read_bytes(Rest,String),
    atom_codes(Value,String),
    skip_bytes(1).               % final zero byte at end of string

read_field_aux(16,cell(Col,Row,formula,Value)) :-
    !,
    skip_bytes(3),      % length and format information
    read_u16(Col),
    read_u16(Row),
    read_f64(Value),   % numeric value of formula
    read_u16(LengthOfRest),
    skip_bytes(LengthOfRest).  % don't try to decode formula itself

read_field_aux(_,non_data_field) :-
    read_u16(Length),
    skip_bytes(Length).


% Demonstration

wksdemo :- see('sample.wks'),
           repeat,
             read_significant_field(F), writeq(F), nl,
           F == end_of_file,
           !,
           seen.
```

Figure 5.9 (Continued).

Chapter 6

Prolog as Its Own Metalanguage

6.1. LANGUAGE AND METALANGUAGE

A METALANGUAGE is a language used to describe another language. Throughout this book we are describing Prolog in English; that is, we are using English as a metalanguage for Prolog. We could use English or any human language as a metalanguage for any programming language. Some programming languages, such as ALGOL, have special metalanguages in which their official descriptions are written.

Prolog is almost unique, however, in the extent to which it can serve as its own metalanguage. This manifests itself in a number of features:

- A program can create new goals by computation and then execute them. That is, you can use Prolog to describe how to construct Prolog goals.

- A program can examine itself (using `clause`) and modify itself (using `assert` and `retract`).

- By declaring operators, a program can even change the syntax of the Prolog language itself.

- A Prolog program can extend and modify the inference engine that controls program execution. Thus, the language can change itself in ways that go beyond superficial syntax.

These capabilities enable Prolog to do things that are completely foreign to most programming languages. Crucially, Prolog blurs the distinction between program and data. In most programming languages, you have to distinguish very clearly between decisions that you make when writing the program and decisions that the computer makes when running the program. For instance, all the arithmetic expressions in a BASIC or Pascal program are written by the programmer in advance, though the program may decide, at run time, which one of them to use. In Prolog, the program can extend and modify itself as it runs. Because of this, rank beginners often have an easier time learning Prolog than people who have been programming in other languages and have learned, slowly and painfully, that computers don't work this way.

We have already used the metalinguistic features of Prolog for a few special purposes. We briefly demonstrated the use of `call`, and LEARNER.PL, back in Chapter 2, used `assert` to modify itself. In this chapter we will develop more substantial extensions to the inference engine and syntax of Prolog.

Exercise 6.1.1

Can any language (human or artificial) serve as a metalanguage for any other language? If not, what are the limitations?

6.2. COLLECTING ALTERNATIVE SOLUTIONS INTO A LIST

Consider the small knowledge base:

```
father(michael,cathy).
father(charles_gordon,michael).
father(jim,melody).
```

We can ask Prolog to display the names of all the fathers by issuing a query such as:

```
?- father(X,_), write(X), nl, fail.
```

That is: Find an X for which `father(X,_)` succeeds, print it, and backtrack to find another one.

But what if, instead of *displaying* the names, we want to *process* them further as a list? We are in a dilemma. In order to get all the names, the program must backtrack. But in order to construct the list, it must use recursion, passing the partially constructed list as an argument from one iteration to the next — which a backtracking program cannot do.

One possibility would be to use `assert` and `retract` to implement roughly the following algorithm:

1. Backtrack through all solutions of `father(X,_)`, storing each value of X in a separate fact in the knowledge base;

2. After all solutions have been tried, execute a recursive loop that retracts all the stored clauses and gathers the information into a list.

Fortunately, we don't have to go through all this. The built-in predicate `findall` will gather the solutions to a query into a list without needing to perform asserts and retracts.[1] Here's an example:

---

[1] If your Prolog lacks `findall`, define it: `findall(V,Goal,L) :- bagof(V,Goal^Goal,L).`

```
?- findall(X,father(X,_),L).
L = [michael,charles_gordon,jim]
```

More generally, a query of the form

```
?- findall(Variable,Goal,List).
```

will instantiate List to the list of all instantiations of Variable that correspond to solutions of Goal. You can then process this list any way you want to.

The first argument of findall need not be a variable; it can be any term with variables in it. The third argument will then be a list of instantiations of the first argument, each one corresponding to a solution of the goal. For example:

```
?- findall(Parent+Child,father(Parent,Child),L).
L = [michael+cathy,charles_gordon+michael,jim+melody]
```

Here the plus sign (+) is, of course, simply a functor written between its arguments.

Exercise 6.2.1

Given the knowledge base
```
employee('John Finnegan','secretary',9500.00).
employee('Robert Marks','administrative assistant',12000.00).
employee('Bill Knudsen','clerk-typist',8250.00).
employee('Mary Jones','section manager',32000.00).
employee('Alice Brewster','c.e.o.',1250000.00).
```
what query (using findall) gives a list of all the employees' names (and nothing else)?

Exercise 6.2.2

Using the same knowledge base as in the previous exercise, define a procedure named average_salary(X) which will unify X with the average salary. To do this, first use findall to collect all the salaries into a list; then work through the list recursively, counting and summing the elements.

Exercise 6.2.3

Using the same knowledge base as in Exercise 6.2.1, show how to use findall to construct the following list:
```
[['John Finnegan',9500.00],
 ['Robert Marks',12000.00],
 ['Bill Knudsen',8250.00],
 ['Mary Jones',32000.00],
 ['Alice Brewster',1250000.00]]
```

Exercise 6.2.4

Do the same thing as in the previous exercise, but this time collect into the list only the employees whose salaries are above $10,000.
Hint: Use a compound goal as the second argument of findall.

6.3. USING bagof AND setof

A BAG is a mathematical object like a set except that the same element can occur in it more than once. Obviously, findall creates a bag, not a set, because the same solution can appear in it more than once.   Likewise, bagof creates a bag in the form of a list containing all the solutions to a query; setof does the same thing except that the list is sorted into alphabetical order and duplicates are removed. The sorting operation takes extra time, but it can be worthwhile if it saves duplication of subsequent work.

The big difference between bagof and setof on the one hand, and findall on the other, concerns the way they handle uninstantiated variables in Goal that do not occur in X. As you might expect, findall treats them as uninstantiated on every pass. Thus,

```
?- findall(X,parent(X,Y),L).
```

means "Find everyone who is the parent of anybody" — Y need not have the same value for each parent. However,

```
?- bagof(X,parent(X,Y),L).
```

means "Find all the values of X that go with some *particular* value of Y." Other values of Y will produce alternative solutions to bagof, not additional entries in the same list. Here's an example:

```
parent(michael,cathy).
parent(melody,cathy).
parent(greg,stephanie).
parent(crystal,stephanie).

?- findall(X,parent(X,Y),L).
X = _0001, Y = _0002, L=[michael,melody,greg,crystal]

?- bagof(X,parent(X,Y),L).
X = _0001, Y = cathy, L = [michael,melody] ;
X = _0001, Y = stephanie, L = [greg,crystal]

?- setof(X,parent(X,Y),L).
X = _0001, Y = cathy, L = [melody,michael] ;
X = _0001, Y = stephanie, L = [crystal,greg]
```

Of course setof is just like bagof except that it sorts the list and removes duplicates (if any).

In the terminology of formal logic, findall treats Y as EXISTENTIALLY QUANTI-FIED — that is, it looks for solutions that need not all involve the same value of Y — while setof and bagof treat Y as something for which you want to find a specific value.

There is another option. You can do this:

```
?- bagof(X,Y^parent(X,Y),L).
X = _0001, Y = _0002, L = [michael,melody,greg,crystal]
```

Prefixing Y^ to the goal indicates that Y is to be treated as existentially quantified within it.

More generally, if the second argument of setof or bagof is not Goal but rather Term^Goal, then all the variables that occur in Term are treated as existentially quantified in Goal.[2] As an extreme case, if you write bagof(V,Goal^Goal,L) then all the variables in Goal will be existentially quantified and bagof will work exactly like findall.

Finally, a word of warning: findall, bagof, and setof are relatively costly, time-consuming operations. Don't use them unless you actually need a list of solutions; first, think about whether your problem could be solved by backtracking through alternative solutions in the conventional manner.

Exercise 6.3.1

Go back to FAMILY.PL (Chapter 1), add a definition of ancestor, and show how to use setof or bagof (not findall) to construct:

1. A list of all the ancestors of Cathy, in the order in which they are found;

2. A list of all the ancestors of Cathy, in alphabetical order;

3. A list of terms of the form ancestor(X,Y) where X and Y are instantiated to an ancestor and a descendant, and have all possible values. That is: [ancestor(charles, charles_gordon),ancestor(charles_gordon,michael)...] (not necessarily in that order).

4. A list of people who are ancestors (without specifying who they are ancestors of).

6.4. FINDING THE SMALLEST, LARGEST, OR "BEST" SOLUTION

Quite often, you'll want to find the "best" of many alternative solutions to a query. "Best" means different things in different situations, of course, but the underlying idea is that of all the possible solutions, you want the one that surpasses all the others according to some criterion. There are three main approaches:

- Use setof and exploit the built-in sorting process so that the "best" solution comes out at the beginning (or perhaps the end) of the list;

- Use bagof or setof and then work through the list to pick out the solution you want; or

- Search for the "best" solution directly, comparing each alternative against all the others.

For concreteness, let's work with the following rather boring knowledge base:

---

[2]In some versions of Cogent Prolog and LPA Prolog, Term can only be a variable; all the other Prologs that we have tried allow it to be any term containing variables.

```
age(cathy,8).
age(sharon,4).
age(aaron,3).
age(stephanie,7).
age(danielle,4).
```

Which child is the youngest? We'll try the first and third strategies, leaving the second one as an exercise.

It's easy to make `setof` give us the age of the youngest child. Consider these queries:

```
?- setof(A,N^age(N,A),L).
L = [3,4,7,8]
```

```
?- setof(A,N^age(N,A),[Youngest|_]).
Youngest = 3
```

The first query retrieves a sorted list of the children's ages; the second query retrieves only the first element of that list. So far so good.

Getting the name of the youngest child involves some subtlety. Recall that the first argument of `setof`, `bagof`, or `findall` need not be a variable; it can be a term containing variables. In particular, we can get a list of children's names together with their ages in any of the following ways (among others):

```
?- setof([A,N],N^age(N,A),L).
L = [[3,aaron],[4,sharon],[4,danielle],[7,sharon],[8,cathy]]
```

```
?- setof(f(A,N),N^age(N,A),L).
L = [f(3,aaron),f(4,sharon),f(4,danielle),f(7,sharon),f(8,cathy)]
```

```
?- setof(A+N,N^age(N,A),L).
L = [3+aaron,4+sharon,4+danielle,7+sharon,8+cathy]
```

In the first query we ask for each solution to be expressed as a 2-element list containing `A` and `N`; in the second query we ask for a term `f(A,N)`; and in the third query we ask for a term `A+N`.

Notice why `3+aaron` comes out as the first element. When `setof` compares two terms to decide which one should come first, it looks first at the principal functor, and then at the arguments beginning with the first. Numbers are compared by numeric value, and atoms are compared by alphabetical order. Accordingly, since all the terms in the list have the same functor (+), and all have numbers as the first argument, the one with the smallest number comes out first.

You don't have to use `setof`. Here is a purely logical query that solves the same problem:

```
?- age(Youngest,Age1), \+ (age(_,Age2), Age2 < Age1).
Youngest = aaron
```

Think for a moment about how the backtracking works. Prolog will try every possible solution for `age(Youngest,Age1)` until it gets one for which it can't find a younger child. That means that every entry in the knowledge base is compared with all of the others; if there are N children, there are N^2 comparisons.

Is this inefficient? Maybe; `setof` can perform its sorting with only $N \log_2 N$ comparisons. However, if N is fairly small, it's probably faster to do more comparisons and avoid constructing lists, because list construction is a fairly slow and expensive operation.

Exercise 6.4.1

Show how to use `setof` to find out which child's name comes first in alphabetical order.

Exercise 6.4.2

How would you find out which child's name comes `last` in alphabetical order?

Exercise 6.4.3

What would be the result of this query? Predict the result before trying it.

```
?- setof(N+A,N^age(N,A),L).
```

Exercise 6.4.4

Define a predicate `find_six(X)` that will instantiate `X` to the name of the child whose age is closest to 6.
Hint: Let the second argument of `setof` be a compound goal such as `(age(N,A), Diff is abs(6-A))`, then sort on `Diff`.

Exercise 6.4.5

Rewrite `find_six` so that instead of using `setof`, it uses a purely logical query. Call it `logical_find_six`.

Exercise 6.4.6   (small project)

On your Prolog system, compare the time taken to find the youngest child by using `setof` to the time taken by using a purely logical query. Try larger knowledge bases. How large does the knowledge base need to be in order for `setof` to be the faster technique?

6.5. INTENSIONAL AND EXTENSIONAL QUERIES

We know how to state, in Prolog, facts about individuals and also generalizations:

```
dog(fido).              "Fido is a dog."
animal(X) :- dog(X).    "Dogs are animals."
```

We also know how to ask questions about individuals:

```
?- dog(fido).           "Is Fido a dog?"
```

How can we ask a question such as "Are dogs animals?" There are two things this question might mean:

(1) Is there a rule or set of rules by means of which all dogs can be proven to be animals?

(2) Regardless of what the rules say, is it the case that all of the dogs actually listed in the knowledge base are in fact animals?

We can call (1) and (2) the INTENSIONAL and EXTENSIONAL interpretations, respectively, of the question "Are dogs animals?" Of these, (1) is primarily a question about the contents of the rule set, whereas (2) asks Prolog to make a generalization about a set of known individuals. Of course, if (1) is true, (2) will always be true also, though the converse is not the case.

We will pursue (2) here. Intuitively, we want to say that "All dogs are animals" is true if (a) there is at least one dog in the knowledge base, and (b) there is no dog in the knowledge base that is not an animal. We insist that there must be at least one dog in the knowledge base so that, for instance, "Snails are monkeys" does not come out true merely because there are no snails in the knowledge base.

We want to define a predicate `for_all(GoalA,GoalB)` that succeeds if all of the instantiations that make `GoalA` true also make `GoalB` true. For the results to be meaningful, `GoalA` and `GoalB` must of course share at least one variable. We could then ask "Are dogs animals?" with the query:

```
?- for_all(dog(X),animal(X)).
```

One way to define `for_all` is as follows:

```
% for_all(GoalA,GoalB)
% Succeeds if all solutions for GoalA also satisfy GoalB,
% and there is at least one solution for both goals.

for_all(GoalA,GoalB) :-
    \+ (call(GoalA), \+ call(GoalB)),        % 1
    call(GoalA),                             % 2
    !.                                       % 3
```

The nested negations in line 1 may be confusing. Line 1 fails if the compound goal

```
(call(GoalA), \+ call(GoalB))
```

succeeds, and vice versa. This compound goal, in turn, succeeds if there is a way to make `GoalA` succeed (instantiating some variables shared with `GoalB` in the process) such that `GoalB` then fails. If we find a dog that is not an animal, the compound goal succeeds and line 1 fails. Otherwise, line 1 succeeds.

If line 1 succeeds, line 2 then checks that there was indeed at least one dog in the knowledge base. We cannot reverse the order of lines 1 and 2 because line 2 instantiates some variables that must be uninstantiated in line 1. The cut in line 3 ensures that we do not generate spurious alternatives by making line 2 succeed in different ways.

Exercise 6.5.1

Given the knowledge base

```
dog(fido).
dog(rover).
dog(X) :- bulldog(X).

bulldog(bucephalus).

animal(X) :- dog(X).
animal(felix).
```

is it true that all dogs are animals? That all animals are dogs? That all bulldogs are animals? That all dogs are bulldogs? Give the query (using `for_all`) that you would use to make each of these tests.

6.6. OPERATOR DEFINITIONS

Most Prolog functors are written immediately in front of a parenthesized argument list: `functor(arg1,arg2)`. Functors that can be written in other positions are called OPERATORS. For example, the structure `+(2,3)` can be written `2+3` because its functor, +, is an infix operator.

Do not confuse operators with operations. Some operators denote arithmetic operations (+ - * /), but other operators serve entirely different purposes. In fact, any Prolog functor can be declared to be an operator, and doing this changes only its syntax, not its meaning.

To create an operator, you must specify the operator's POSITION, PRECEDENCE, and ASSOCIATIVITY. Let's deal with position first. An INFIX operator comes between its two arguments, like + in 2+3; a PREFIX operator comes before its one argument, without parentheses, like \+ in `\+ dog(felix)`; and a POSTFIX operator comes after its one argument.

Precedence determines how expressions are interpreted when there are no parentheses to show how to group them. For example, 2+3*4 is interpreted as 2+(3*4), not (2+3)*4, because + has higher precedence than *. The operator with lower precedence applies to a smaller part of the expression. Precedences are expressed as numbers between 1 and 1200 (between 1 and 256 in some older implementations). Table 6.1 shows the usual set of built-in operators.

Associativity determines what happens when several operators of the same precedence occur in succession without parentheses: should 2+3+4 be interpreted as (2+3)+4 (left-associative), or as 2+(3+4) (right-associative), or simply disallowed?

Position and associativity are specified by the symbols `fx`, `fy`, `xf`, `yf`, `xfx`, `xfy`, and `yfx` (Table 6.2). Here f stands for the position of the operator itself; x stands for an argument that does not allow associativity; and y stands for an associative argument. Thus, `fx` designates a prefix operator with one argument and no associativity; `yfx` designates an infix operator that is associative on the left but not the right.

A complete operator definition looks like this:

```
?- op(100,xfx,is_father_of).
```

This query tells Prolog to allow the functor `is_father_of` to be written between its arguments, with a precedence of 100 and no associativity. After executing this query, Prolog will accept facts and rules such as:

TABLE 6.1   COMMONLY PREDEFINED PROLOG OPERATORS.

For the official ISO set, see Appendix A.

Priority	Specifier	Operators
1200	xfx	:- -->
1200	fx	:- ?-
1100	xfy	;
1050	xfy	->
1000	xfy	,
900	fy	\+ (or, in some Prologs, **not**)
700	xfx	= \= == \== @< @=< @> @>= is =:= =\= < =< > >= =..
500	yfx	+ -
400	yfx	* / // mod
200	xfy	^
200	fy	-

TABLE 6.2   OPERATOR SYNTAX SPECIFIERS.

Specifier	Meaning
fx	Prefix, not associative
fy	Prefix, right-associative (like \+)
xf	Postfix, not associative
yf	Postfix, left-associative
xfx	Infix, not associative (like =)
xfy	Infix, right-associative (like the comma in compound goals)
yfx	Infix, left-associative (like +)

```
michael is_father_of cathy.
X is_father_of Y  :-  male(X), parent(X,Y).
```

and queries such as:

```
?- X is_father_of cathy.
X = michael
yes
```

Notice that the op declaration is a query, not a fact. If you include it as a line in your program, it must begin with ':-', like this:

```
:- op(100,xfx,is_father_of).
```

Then it will affect the reading of all subsequent facts, rules, and embedded queries as the Prolog system consults your program. In fact, it will affect all input and output performed by read, write, consult, and any other procedures that recognize Prolog syntax. In virtually all Prologs, the op declaration will stay in effect until the end of your Prolog session, although the ISO standard does not require this. Naturally, you can also execute an op declaration as a subgoal within one of your procedures, if you wish.

Finally, note that operators composed entirely of the special characters

$$\# \; \$ \; \& \; * \; + \; - \; . \; / \; : \; < \; = \; > \; ? \; @ \; \char94 \; \char126 \; \backslash$$

have some special properties. First, unlike most other atoms that contain nonal-phanumeric characters, they need not be written in quotes. Second, they need not be separated from their arguments by spaces (unless, of course, their arguments also consist of those special characters). For example, X>=Y is equivalent to X >= Y because > and = are special characters, but Xmod3 is not equivalent to X mod 3.

Like any other functor, an operator can have different meanings in different contexts. For example, / denotes division in arithmetic expressions, but in the argument of abolish elsewhere it joins the functor and arity of a predicate that is being referred to (e.g., abolish(fff/2)), and you could use it for still other purposes anywhere you wish.

Exercise 6.6.1

Construct an appropriate op declaration so that
likes(kermit,piggy).
can be written
kermit likes piggy.
Demonstrate that your op declaration affects the behavior of write.

Exercise 6.6.2

In op declarations, why isn't yfy a possible specifier of precedence and position?

Exercise 6.6.3

By redefining built-in operators, make Prolog arithmetic expressions obey the "right-to-left rule" of the programming language APL. That is, change the syntax of +, -, *, and / so that all of them have the same precedence and expressions are evaluated from right to left; for example, 2+3*4+5/6-7 should be interpreted as 2+(3*(4+(5/(6-7)))). To verify that your redefinitions have had the desired effect, try the following queries:
?- X is 2*3+4.   (should give 14, not 10)
?- X is 1.0/2.5-6.5.   (should give -0.25, not -6.1)

6.7. GIVING MEANING TO OPERATORS

Operator definitions define only the syntax of the operators. The meaning, or se-mantics, of an operator is up to the programmer.

In the past, some Prologs have used the ampersand (&) rather than the comma to join elements of compound goals. This has the great advantage that compound goals do not look like argument lists; the query

?- call(p(a) & q(a) & r(a)).

clearly invokes call with only one argument. In ordinary Prolog, we have to use extra parentheses to get the same effect, like this:

?- call((p(a), q(a), r(a))).

because, without the extra parentheses, `call` would be taken as having three arguments.

We can define the ampersand to work this way even in ordinary Prolog. First, let's define its syntax. We want `&` to be an infix operator with slightly lower precedence than the comma, so that `f(a&b,c)` will mean `f((a&b),c)`, not `f(a&(b,c))`. Further, as we will see shortly, `&` should be right-associative. In most Prologs, then, the appropriate operator definition is:

```
:- op(950,xfy,&).
```

Next we need to tell Prolog how to solve a goal that contains ampersands. Obviously, `GoalA & GoalB` should succeed if `GoalA` succeeds and then `GoalB` succeeds with the same instantiations. That is:

```
GoalA & GoalB  :-  call(GoalA), call(GoalB).
```

This is just an ordinary Prolog rule. It could equally well be written as:

```
'&'(GoalA,GoalB) :- call(GoalA), call(GoalB).
```

Because `&` is right-associative, this rule can in fact handle an unlimited number of goals joined by ampersands. Suppose we issue the query:

```
?- write(one) & write(two) & write(three).
```

Because of the right-associativity, this goal is equivalent to:

```
?- write(one) & (write(two) & write(three)).
```

This unifies with the head of the rule defining `&`, with the instantiations:

```
GoalA = write(one)
GoalB = (write(two) & write(three))
```

The new goals are `call(GoalA)`, which is satisfied by writing `one` on the screen, and `call(GoalB)`, which invokes the rule for `&` recursively. File AMPERS.PL (Figure 6.1) illustrates the whole thing.

Exercise 6.7.1

Show how to define the operators **and** and **or** to mean "and" and "or" respectively, so that you will be able to write clauses like this:

```
green(X) :- (plant(X) and photosynthetic(X)) or frog(X).
```

Demonstrate that your solution works correctly.

Exercise 6.7.2

What happens if there is a cut in one of the subgoals that are joined by ampersands in AMPERS.PL? Why?

```
% File AMPERS.PL
% How to make the ampersand mean "and" in Prolog

% Syntax of &
:- op(950,xfy,&).

% Semantics of &
GoalA & GoalB :- call(GoalA), call(GoalB).

% Demonstration knowledge base

parent(michael,cathy).
parent(melody,cathy).
parent(charles_gordon,michael).
parent(hazel,michael).
parent(jim,melody).
parent(eleanor,melody).

grandparent(X,Y) :- parent(Z,Y) & parent(X,Z).
only_child(X) :- parent(P,X) & \+ (parent(P,Z) & Z\==X).

test :- only_child(C), write(C), write(' is an only child'), nl.
```

Figure 6.1   Example of defining an operator as a Prolog predicate.

6.8. PROLOG IN PROLOG

Our definition of & suggests a strategy for rewriting Prolog's whole inference engine in Prolog and thus developing a customized version of the language. Recall that the predicate clause(Head,Body) can retrieve any of the clauses in the knowledge base, or at least any that are declared dynamic;[3] it does this by trying to unify Head with the head of a clause and Body with the body of that clause (or with true if the clause is a fact). Alternative clauses are obtained as multiple solutions to clause upon backtracking.

The body of a rule is usually a compound goal, that is, a structure held together by right-associative commas that work just like the ampersands above. Thus, given the rule:

```
f(X) :- g(X), h(X), i(X), j(X).
```

the query

```
?- clause(f(abc),Body).
```

will instantiate Body to:

```
g(abc), h(abc), i(abc), j(abc)
```

---

[3]Some Prologs lack this restriction.

```
% File INTERP.PL
% Metainterpreter for Prolog

% interpret(+Goal)
%  Executes Goal.

interpret(true) :- !.

interpret((GoalA,GoalB)) :- !,
                           interpret(GoalA),
                           interpret(GoalB).

interpret(Goal) :-  clause(Goal,Body),
                    interpret(Body).


% Test knowledge base  (note the dynamic declarations!)

:- dynamic(parent/2).
parent(michael,cathy).
parent(melody,cathy).
parent(charles_gordon,michael).
parent(hazel,michael).
parent(jim,melody).
parent(eleanor,melody).

:- dynamic(grandparent/2).
grandparent(X,Y) :- parent(Z,Y), parent(X,Z).

test :- interpret(grandparent(A,B)), write([A,B]), nl, fail.
                                     % prints out all solutions
```

Figure 6.2   The Prolog inference engine expressed in Prolog.

which is equivalent to:

g(abc), (h(abc), (i(abc), j(abc)))

To execute this goal, we work through it in the same manner as with the ampersands in AMPERS.PL. We can define interpret (which takes a goal as an argument and executes it) as shown in Figure 6.2. Then, to use interpret, we simply type, for example,

?- interpret(grandparent(X,Y)). instead of ?- grandparent(X,Y).

This algorithm is from Clocksin and Mellish (1984:177). The cuts are green: They save steps but do not affect the logic of the program. Notice that call is not used; every successful goal ends up as an invocation of interpret(true).

This is a METAINTERPRETER or METACIRCULAR INTERPRETER for Prolog. It is, of course, slower than the original Prolog interpreter under which it runs, but the speed difference is not dramatic because the original interpreter is still doing nearly all the work. More importantly, it does not recognize built-in predicates because there are no clauses for them, and it offers no straightforward way to perform cuts. These features can, of course, be added by writing a more complex metainterpreter.

Metainterpreters are useful because they can be modified to interpret languages other than the Prolog in which they are written. With minor changes, we could make our metainterpreter use ampersands rather than commas to form compound goals, or even change its inference strategy entirely, for example by making it try to solve each goal using facts before trying any rules. Even when interpreting straight Prolog, a metainterpreter can keep records of the steps of the computation, assist with debugging, and even check for loops.

Exercise 6.8.1

On your Prolog system, does `clause` have access to all clauses or only the ones that are declared dynamic? Experiment to find out.

Exercise 6.8.2

Get `interpret` working on your machine. Demonstrate that it correctly performs the computations used in FAMILY.PL (Chapter 1).

Exercise 6.8.3

Add clauses to `interpret` to handle negation (\+) and equality (=). Using these extensions, add the definition of "sibling" to FAMILY.PL and show that `interpret` processes it correctly.

Exercise 6.8.4

Extend `interpret` to handle ordinary built-in predicates (e.g., `write`) by trying to execute each subgoal via `call` if no clauses for it can be found. Show that queries such as
```
?- interpret( (father(X,cathy), write(X)) ).
```
are handled correctly. What happens to cuts? Why?

6.9. EXTENDING THE INFERENCE ENGINE

Another, less radical, way to extend Prolog is to add another inference strategy on top of the existing inference engine. Such a system does not require a metainterpreter. It processes a goal by trying to execute it with `call` and then trying another strategy if `call` did not work. Thus, conventional Prolog goals are processed in the normal way, and other types of goals can be processed as well.

For a concrete example, consider how to express, in Prolog, the fact that all dogs are canines and all canines are dogs. If we use two rules,
```
canine(X) :- dog(X).
dog(X) :- canine(X).
```

we will get loops because each rule will call the other. A different inference strategy is needed.

First we need to record the fact that `canine(X)` and `dog(X)` stand in a biconditional relation. We could use a predicate called `bicond` and put the following fact in the knowledge base:

```
bicond(canine(X),dog(X)).
```

A more elegant approach is possible. Instead of `bicond`, let's call the predicate '`-:-`' (an operator similar to '`:-`', but symmetrical). For this we need the operator definition:

```
:- op(950,xfx,'-:-').
```

We can then relate `canine` and `dog` with the fact:

```
canine(X) -:- dog(X).
```

We will call this a BICONDITIONAL RULE. Neither side of it can be a compound goal.

File BICOND.PL (Figure 6.3) defines a predicate `prove` which is like `call` except that it can also use biconditional rules. Its strategy is as follows: First see if the goal can be satisfied with `call`. If not, see if it matches one side of a biconditional rule, and if so, call the other side of that rule.

To see that we get the correct results, consider the following knowledge base and queries:

```
dog(fido).
canine(rolf).
dog(X) -:- canine(X).

?- dog(X).
X = fido

?- canine(X).
X = rolf

?- prove(dog(X)).
X = fido ;
X = rolf

?- prove(canine(X)).
X = rolf ;
X = fido
```

Queries with `prove` recognize biconditionals, while ordinary queries do not. Biconditionals do not cause loops because `prove` does not call itself.

Unfortunately, `prove` has its limitations. Because it is not recursive, it does not recognize that biconditionality is transitive. The knowledge base

```
f(X) -:- g(X).
g(X) -:- h(X).
```

```
% File BICOND.PL
% Inference engine for biconditionals in Prolog

% The -:- operator joins the two sides of a biconditional rule.

:- op(950,xfx,'-:-').


% Inference engine for biconditionals

prove(Goal)   :-  call(Goal).

prove(GoalA) :-   (GoalA -:- GoalB),
                   call(GoalB).

prove(GoalB) :-   (GoalA -:- GoalB),
                   call(GoalA).


% Sample knowledge base

dog(fido).
canine(rolf).
dog(X) -:- canine(X).

test :- prove(dog(X)), write(X), nl, fail.
                            % prints all solutions
```

Figure 6.3   A rudimentary inference engine for biconditionals.

does not enable the computer to infer `f(fido)` from `h(fido)`. If we make `prove` recursive in the straightforward way — so that it invokes itself instead of invoking `call` — we get transitivity, but we also reintroduce loops. A more sophisticated version of `prove` might keep a record of the biconditional rules that it has used so that it can chain rules together without using the same rule more than once.

Exercise 6.9.1

Implement an inference engine that can handle symmetric 2-place predicates (those whose arguments can be interchanged) without looping. Put the functor `symmetric` in front of each fact that is to have the symmetric property, and let `symmetric` be a prefix operator. For example:

```
symmetric married(john,mary).
symmetric married(melody,michael).

?- prove(married(mary,john)).
yes

?- prove(married(john,mary)).
yes

?- prove(married(michael,Who)).
Who = melody

?- prove(married(abc,xyz)).
no
```

6.10. PERSONALIZING THE USER INTERFACE

Not only the inference engine, but also the top-level user interface of Prolog can be customized. In the typical Prolog top level, the computer types:

```
?-
```

and the user replies by typing a query. Some Prologs also let the user type rules and facts which are added to the knowledge base.

File TOPLEVEL.PL (Figure 6.4) defines a top level whose dialogues with the user look like this:

```
Type a query:              father(X,cathy).
Solution found:            father(michael,cathy)
Look for another? (Y/N): n

Type a query:              father(joe,cathy).
No (more) solutions

Type a query:              parent(X,Y).
Solution found:            parent(michael,cathy)
Look for another? (Y/N): y
```

```
% File TOPLEVEL.PL
% A customized user interface for Prolog

% top_level
%  Starts the user interface.

top_level :-   repeat,
               nl,
               write('Type a query:            '),
               read(Goal),
               find_solutions(Goal),
               fail.


% find_solutions(+Goal)
% Satisfies Goal, displays it with instantiations,
%  and optionally backtracks to find another solution.

find_solutions(Goal) :-
   call(Goal),
   write('Solution found:         '),
   write(Goal),
   nl,
   write('Look for another? (Y/N): '),
   get(Char), nl,
   (Char = 78 ; Char = 110),    % N or n
   !.

find_solutions(_) :-
   write('No (more) solutions'),
   nl.


% Demonstration knowledge base

father(michael,cathy).
mother(melody,cathy).
parent(X,Y) :- father(X,Y).
parent(X,Y) :- mother(X,Y).
```

Figure 6.4 A user-friendly top level for Prolog.

```
Solution found:            parent(melody,cathy)
Look for another? (Y/N): y
No (more) solutions
```

This is just like the usual Prolog top level except that the messages are much more explicit, and answers are reported by displaying the query with the variable values filled in. All Prolog queries are acceptable — not only queries about the knowledge base but also calls to built-in predicates such as consult.

The code defining this top level is only 18 lines long. The procedure `top_level` is an endless `repeat–fail` loop that accepts queries from the keyboard and passes them to `find_solutions`. (Note by the way that the name `top_level` has no special significance. This procedure becomes the top level of the Prolog environment when you start it by typing '?- `top_level`.')

The procedure `find_solutions` has two clauses. The first clause finds a solution, prints it, and asks the user whether to look for others. If the user types N or n (for "no"), `find_solutions` executes a cut, and control returns to `top_level`. Otherwise, `find_solutions` backtracks. If no further solutions can be found and the cut has not been executed, control passes to the second clause and the message "No (more) solutions" is displayed.

How do you get out of `top_level`? Simple: type '`halt`.' to leave Prolog, just as if you were using the ordinary top level.

A customized top level can make Prolog much more user-friendly. We have found it useful to introduce beginners to Prolog with a menu-driven user interface that lets them display the knowledge base, add or remove clauses, and execute queries. In this way the use of a file editor is avoided. Moreover, a customized top level can be combined with an enhanced inference engine to turn Prolog into a powerful knowledge engineering system.

Exercise 6.10.1

> Get `top_level` working on your computer. Then modify it so that it uses `setof` to obtain and display all the solutions at once, rather than asking the user whether to backtrack. Call the modified version `top_level_2`.

6.11. BIBLIOGRAPHICAL NOTES

Sterling and Shapiro (1994) and O'Keefe (1990) explore the use of Prolog as its own metalanguage in considerable detail. O'Keefe gives metainterpreters that handle cuts correctly (as well as critiques of a lot of simple metainterpreters).

Marcus (1986:213-220) shows how to extend Prolog, via operator definitions, to comprise a user-friendly database language. Although not adequate for full natural language processing, suitable operator definitions can make Prolog look a great deal more like English.

Chapter 7

Advanced Techniques

7.1. STRUCTURES AS TREES

So far, we've looked at Prolog structures purely in terms of their written representation; for example, we think of `f(a,b)` as something written with an `f`, a pair of parentheses, an `a`, a comma, and a `b`.

Now let's distinguish the written representation from the structure itself. The commas and parentheses are not really parts of the structure; they are just notations to show how the parts fit together. A Prolog structure is really, on a deeper level, a tree-like object. For example, the structure `f(g(h,i),j(k,l))` can be represented by this diagram:

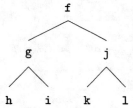

The crucial concept here is that the structure expresses a relation between a functor and a series of arguments. Tree diagrams like this one are very handy for figuring out whether two structures will unify, and, if so, what the result will be.

Prolog clauses and goals are structures, too. The clause

```
a :- b, c, d.
```

173

is really

```
a :- (b, (c, d)).
```

or rather:

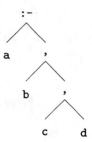

Knowing this structure is crucial if you want to write a Prolog program that processes other Prolog programs.

Notice that here the comma is a functor, not just a notational device. Recall that there are three uses for commas in Prolog:

- As an infix operator that means "and," for joining goals together (as in the clause `a :- b, c, d` above);

- As an argument separator in structures (as in `f(a,b,c)`);

- As an element separator in lists (as in `[a,b,c]`).

The first kind of comma is a functor; the latter two kinds are not and do not show up in tree diagrams.

Exercise 7.1.1

Draw tree diagrams of the following structures:
`asdf(a1,a2,a3,a4)`   `g(x(y,z,w),q(p,r(e(f))))`   `2+3*4+5`
Hint: Recall that + and * are functors that are written between their arguments.

Exercise 7.1.2

Draw tree diagrams of the following two structures and then of the structure formed by unifying them:
`a(b,X,c(d,X,e))`   `a(Y,p,c(d,Z,e))`

Exercise 7.1.3

Demonstrate all three uses of commas in a single Prolog clause. Label each of the commas to indicate its function.

Exercise 7.1.4   (project)

Define a predicate `display_tree` that will display any Prolog structure as a tree diagram. (How you display the tree will depend on what tools are available to you; you can use either graphics or typewritten characters.)

7.2. LISTS AS STRUCTURES

Lists are structures, too. Specifically, a list is a tree that branches only on the right, like this:

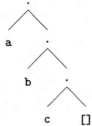

In functor-argument notation, this structure would be written .(a,.(b,.(c,[]))), but we normally write [a,b,c] instead.   The two are equivalent; they are two notations for the same thing. Note some further equivalences:

```
.(a,[])              =     [a]
.(a,.(b,.(c,[])))    =     [a,b,c]
.(a,b)               =     [a|b]        % an improper list
.(a,.(b,.(c,d)))     =     [a,b,c|d]    % another improper list
```

Every nonempty list has the dot (.) as its principal functor. Note however that the empty list [] is not a structure and does not contain the dot functor.

Now look again at how lists branch. Each dot functor has two arguments: Its first argument is *one element*, and its second argument is *another list*. That is:

Every list consists of an element plus another list or [].

This is the concept that makes a list what it is. If the whole thing does not end in [] it is called an IMPROPER LIST (like a dotted pair in Lisp).

The big advantage of lists over multiargument structures is that you can process a list without knowing how many elements it has. Any nonempty list will unify with .(X,Y) (more commonly written [X|Y]), regardless of the number of elements. You can process the element X and then recursively pick apart the list Y the same way you did the original list.

List-like structures can be constructed with any two-argument functor; for example, f(a,f(b,f(c,[]))) is a list-like structure whose principal functor happens to be f rather than the dot. Infix operators are particularly useful for this purpose. For example, if you are accumulating a sequence of numbers that will eventually be summed, it may be desirable to link them together with the functor + rather than the usual list structure, thus:

```
1+2
(1+2)+3          or simply    1+2+3
((1+2)+3)+4)     or simply    1+2+3+4
```

When you've constructed the whole sequence, you can find the sum by putting the sequence on the right-hand side of is.

Notice that because + is left-associative, this particular list is a tree that branches on the left rather than on the right. Nonetheless, you can pick off one element at a time, just as you would with a list: 2+3+4+5 unifies with X+Y to give X=2+3+4 and Y=5.

Exercise 7.2.1

Draw tree diagrams of each of the following terms:

   [a,b,c,d]   [a,b,c|d]   f(a,f(b,f(c,d)))   a+b+c+d

Exercise 7.2.2

Demonstrate, using the computer, that [a,b] = .(a,.(b,[])).

Exercise 7.2.3

What is the result of the following query? Explain.

   ?- [a,b,c] =.. What.

Exercise 7.2.4

What is the most concise way of writing [x,y|[]]?

Exercise 7.2.5

Write .(.(a,.(b,[])),.(c,[])) in ordinary list notation (with square brackets and commas) and draw a tree diagram of it.

Exercise 7.2.6

Define a predicate `improper_list/1` that will succeed if its argument is an improper list, and fail otherwise.

7.3. HOW TO SEARCH OR PROCESS ANY STRUCTURE

Sometimes you'll need to write a procedure that accepts any Prolog term whatsoever, and searches or processes it in some way, looking at every functor and argument throughout. This isn't hard to do. The basic strategy is:

- If the term is an atom, number, or variable, use it as it is; there's no need to take it apart further.

- If the term is a structure, then:

  Convert it into a list using '=..';

  Recursively process all the elements of the list, creating a new list;

  Convert the resulting list back into a structure, again using '=..'.

Recall that '=..' converts any structure into a list consisting of its functor and arguments, e.g., f(a,b) =.. [f,a,b]. This works even for lists, because a list is merely a term with the dot as its principal functor, and '=..' recognizes it as such.

File REWRITE.PL (Figure 7.1) shows how to search any term and make a copy of it in which every occurrence of a within it is changed to b, like this:

```
?- rewrite_term(f(a,[b,a(X),d]),What).
What = f(b,[b,b(X),d])
```

This is, of course, an oversimplified example; in real life there's not much point to changing every a to b, but you could use a procedure like this as the basis of a Prolog macro system, to implement extensions to the Prolog language.

Exercise 7.3.1

Modify `rewrite_term` so that it changes a's to b's only when the a's are atoms, not functors. (Simple.)

Exercise 7.3.2

Define a predicate `count_a/2` that will simply search for occurrences of a (as atom or functor) in any term and report how many it found, thus:

```
?- count_a(f(a,[b,a(X),d]),What).
What = 2
```

Note that you don't have to make a copy of the term — just keep a count of a's.

Exercise 7.3.3   (small project)

Develop an alternative version of `rewrite_term` that uses `functor/3` and `arg/3` instead of '=..'. On your system, is it faster or slower than the original?

7.4. INTERNAL REPRESENTATION OF DATA

Prolog handles all memory management dynamically. That is, it doesn't set aside space for all the constants and variables at the beginning of the program; instead, it allocates space as needed while the program runs. That allows you to create large objects, such as lists, without declaring them in advance. But it also means that there is no way to predict what memory location a particular item will occupy, and it is not possible to associate data items with fixed addresses as is done in conventional languages. Instead, all memory access is done through POINTERS, which are memory locations that store the addresses of other memory locations.

Every Prolog structure is a network of CONS CELLS, so named because of the function CONS ("construct") that creates cons cells in Lisp. Each cons cell contains a pointer to the functor, plus pointers to each of the arguments (Figure 7.2). Atoms reside in the SYMBOL TABLE; variables and numbers are represented by special codes in the cell itself.

Crucially, if the same atom occurs in more than one place, only one copy of it need exist because many pointers can point to it. Thus, a program that contains the term

```
asdfasdf(asdfasdf,asdfasdf,asdfasdf,asdfasdf,asdfasdf,asdfasdf)
```

actually contains only one copy of `asdfasdf`.

Lists are a special case. If the dot functor worked as we described it in the previous section, the internal representation of the list [a,b,c] would be as shown in Figure 7.3(a). In fact, however, most Prolog implementations treat lists specially

```
% File REWRITE.PL
% Example of searching an arbitrary term using =..


% rewrite(X,Y)
%  Tells rewrite_term what to rewrite.

rewrite(a,b) :- !.    % change all a to b
rewrite(X,X).         % leave everything else alone


% rewrite_term(+Term1,-Term2)
%  Copies Term1 changing every atom or functor 'a' to 'b'
%  (using rewrite/2 above).

rewrite_term(X,X) :-
   var(X),            % don't alter uninstantiated variables
   !.

rewrite_term(X,Y) :-
   atomic(X),         % 'atomic' means atom or number
   !,
   rewrite(X,Y).

rewrite_term(X,Y) :-
   X =.. XList,                % convert structures to lists
   rewrite_aux(XList,YList),   % process them
   Y =.. YList.                % convert back to structures

rewrite_aux([],[]).

rewrite_aux([First|Rest],[NewFirst|NewRest]) :-
   rewrite_term(First,NewFirst),   % note recursion here
   rewrite_aux(Rest,NewRest).
```

Figure 7.1   Example of searching an arbitrary term.

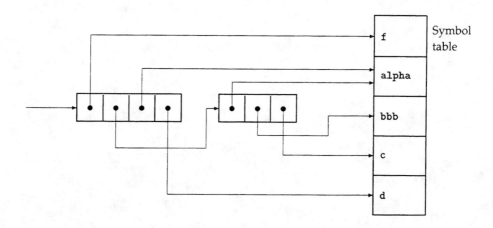

Figure 7.2 Internal representation of the term `f(alpha(bbb,c),alpha,d)`.

and omit the pointers to the dot functor, so that they actually use the more compact representation in Figure 7.3(b). The unifier knows about the dot functor and regenerates it whenever needed so that, as far as the programmer is concerned, it always seems to be there, except that it doesn't take up any space. Each cell contains a TAG (not shown) that indicates whether it is a structure or a list element; tags keep Figure 7.3(b) from being interpreted as `a(b(c(d,[])))`.

Either way, the distinctive thing about lists is that the cons cells are arranged in a linear chain. Only the first element of the list can be accessed in a single step. All subsequent elements are found by following a chain of pointers, a process known as "CDRing down the list" (again, CDR, pronounced "could-er," is the name of a Lisp function). It thus takes five times as long to reach the fifth element of the list as to reach the first element. This leads to a programming maxim:

Work on lists at the beginning, not at the end.

It is also a good idea to "avoid consing," i.e., avoid creating new lists and structures unnecessarily. Allocating new cons cells requires time as well as memory. Rather than transforming `[a,b,c,d]` into `[a,b,c]`, unify `[a,b,c,d]` with `[X,Y,Z|_]`, if that will do the same job, or store the list elements in the opposite order.

As a Prolog program runs, it allocates many cons cells, which are obtained from an unused memory area known as the HEAP or GLOBAL STACK. Just as frequently, it releases cons cells that are no longer needed. Periodically, it must perform GARBAGE COLLECTION and gather up the unused cons cells, returning them to the heap for future use. In Prolog, unlike Lisp, some garbage collection can be performed upon exit from each procedure, since its variable instantiations no longer exist. Some

(a) Full representation:

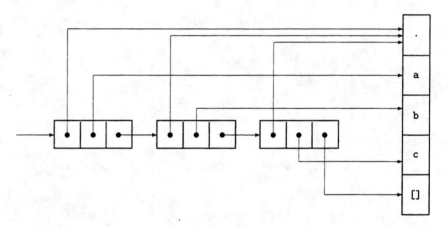

(b) Compact representation:

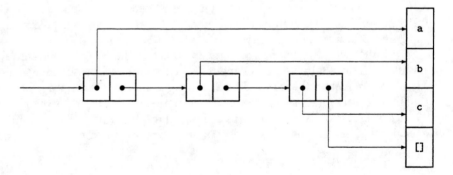

Figure 7.3   Internal representation of the list [a,b,c].

implementations take advantage of this fact, and some wait until the heap is empty before performing any garbage collection. In many Prologs, the built-in predicate gc performs garbage collection when you call it.

Exercise 7.4.1

Sketch the internal representations of each of the following structures:

a(b,c,d)   a(b(c),d(e))   asdfasdf(asdfasdf,asdfasdf)

Exercise 7.4.2

Which takes up more space, [a,b,c] or a+b+c+[]? Or are they the same size? Explain.

Exercise 7.4.3

Assuming that each pointer occupies 4 bytes, how much space is saved by representing [a,b,c,d,e,f] the compact way instead of the original way?

Exercise 7.4.4

Think about the circumstances under which atoms get added to the symbol table. Clearly, atoms that occur in the program itself are placed in the symbol table when the program is initially consulted or compiled. Some predicates, such as read, can introduce new atoms at run time. What other predicates can do this?

7.5. SIMULATING ARRAYS IN PROLOG

Lists in Prolog or Lisp are quite different from arrays in other languages, because all the elements of an array have locations known in advance, and any element of an array can be reached as quickly as any other.

Prolog has no arrays, but it has two reasonable substitutes. Instead of using an array as a lookup table, you can use a set of facts, as in this table of prime numbers:

```
nthprime(1,2).
nthprime(2,3).
nthprime(3,5).
nthprime(4,7).
nthprime(5,11).
nthprime(6,13).
   ⋮
```

These table entries can be looked up very quickly. Of course it isn't easy to add or change entries in this kind of table, though it's perfectly possible.

Another way to simulate an array is to use a functor with many arguments and access the arguments individually using arg. For example, given the structure

```
primes(2,3,5,7,9,11,13,17,19,23,29)
```

you can pick out individual elements like this:

```
?- arg(1,primes(2,3,5,7,9,11,13,17,19,23,29),What).
What = 2
```

```
?- arg(5,primes(2,3,5,7,9,11,13,17,19,23,29),What).
What = 9
```

In effect, you are using the argument positions of a cons cell as if they were an array of pointers. Remember that a two-dimensional array is equivalent to a one-dimensional array of one-dimensional arrays, and so on for higher dimensions.

Finally, notice that even if Prolog did have arrays, you still wouldn't be able to swap or rearrange the elements of an array in place (without making a copy of the array) because Prolog lacks a destructive assignment statement (that is, Prolog doesn't let you change the value of a variable that is already instantiated). Thus, some array-based algorithms cannot be implemented directly in Prolog, although they can of course be simulated using extra copying operations or different data structures.

Exercise 7.5.1

Suggest at least two good ways to represent a $3 \times 3 \times 3$ array of numbers in Prolog.

Exercise 7.5.2   (project)

Implement matrix multiplication in Prolog. Finding the best way to do this will require considerable thought.

7.6. DIFFERENCE LISTS

A DIFFERENCE LIST is a list whose tail can be accessed without CDRing down the list. This is achieved by keeping a copy of the tail outside the list. Thus,

```
difflist([a,b,c|Tail],Tail)
```

is a difference list with the members a, b, and c. Crucially, terms that occur in both the head and the tail do not count; the above list will continue to represent the sequence $\langle a, b, c \rangle$ no matter what value Tail is instantiated to. That's why it's called a *difference* list: Its contents are the *difference* between the whole list and the tail.

Before we put difference lists to use, let's develop a better notation for them. Any two-argument functor can be substituted for difflist/2. An infix operator would be particularly convenient. In fact, we can use the infix operator / (the same operator that denotes division in arithmetic expressions).[1] The practice of "overloading" an operator — that is, giving it multiple meanings in different contexts — is perfectly legitimate. In fact, / already has two meanings: it denotes division in arithmetic expressions, and it joins a functor to an arity in queries such as abolish(parent/2).

We will thus write the difference list $\langle a, b, c \rangle$ as:

---

[1]In the Prolog literature, it is common to define \ as an infix operator for this purpose; using / saves us an op declaration. Pereira and Shieber (1987), thinking along similar lines, use the minus sign (−).

```
[a,b,c|Tail]/Tail
```

Difference lists can be concatenated in constant time, regardless of their length. Recall that append (Chapter 3) has to CDR all the way down the first list before it can join it to the second. This is not the case with append_dl, which appends difference lists in a single step with just one clause:

```
append_dl(X/Y, Y/Z, X/Z).
```

It may take some thought to see how this works. To begin with, the tail of the first list and the head of the second list must be unifiable. This is usually no problem because the tail of the first list is uninstantiated. Consider the query:

```
?- append_dl([a,b|A]/A, [c,d|C]/C, Result).
```

This sets up, in succession, the following instantiations:

```
X = [a,b|A]
Y = A = [c,d|C]
Z = C
Result = X/Z = [a,b|A]/C = [a,b,c,d|C]/C
```

The very last step is crucial: By instantiating A, the heretofore uninstantiated tail of the first list, we add elements to the list itself. Notice, by the way, that although the result has an uninstantiated tail, the first list no longer does. Accordingly, you cannot use the same list as the first argument of append_dl more than once in the same clause.

Difference lists are powerful but counterintuitive. They appear most often in procedures that were first implemented with conventional lists and then carefully rewritten for efficiency. Sterling and Shapiro (1994) use difference lists extensively and discuss them at length.

Exercise 7.6.1

Define a predicate app3_dl that concatenates three difference lists:
```
?- app3_dl([a,b|X]/X,[c,d|Y]/Y,[e,f|Z]/Z,What).
What = [a,b,c,d,e,f|Z]/Z
```
What are the values of X and Y after performing the concatenation?

7.7. QUICKSORT

It is often necessary to put the elements of a list into numeric or alphabetical order. Most programmers are familiar with sorting algorithms that swap elements of arrays in place — something that is impossible in Prolog. The most efficient way to sort a list is usually to call a built-in machine-language routine that can perform an array-based sort on Prolog list elements without doing any consing. Several Prologs provide a built-in predicate, sort/2, that does this.

One sorting algorithm that lends itself well to implementation in Prolog is C. A. R. Hoare's famous Quicksort (Hoare 1962), which was the first recursive algorithm to make an impact on everyday business data processing. The idea behind Quicksort is this:

1. Pick an arbitrary element of the list (e.g., the first). Call it `Pivot`.

2. Divide the remaining elements into two lists: elements that should come before `Pivot` and elements that should come after it. Call these `Before` and `After` respectively.

3. Recursively sort `Before`, giving `SortedBefore`, and `After`, giving `SortedAfter`.

4. Concatenate `SortedBefore` + `Pivot` + `SortedAfter` to get the result.

This algorithm has no simple nonrecursive counterpart. It takes time proportional to $N \log_2 N$ if the elements are initially in random order, or proportional to N^2 if they are initially in an order that prevents the partitioning step (Step 2) from working effectively.

File QSORT.PL (Figure 7.4) gives several Prolog implementations of Quicksort: a straightforward implementation that uses `append`, an implementation with difference lists, and an implementation with what has been called "stacks." The original Quicksort uses `append`, which is excessively slow in some implementations; the latter two Quicksorts get by without `append`.

The published literature on Quicksort is immense; for a thorough treatment, see Knuth (1973:113–123). Many tricks have been developed to keep Quicksort from becoming too inefficient when the elements are already almost in order; a simple one is to use the median of three elements as the pivot.

You'll notice that Quicksort uses the comparison operator `@<` to compare terms for alphabetical order. All our sorting algorithms will do this. Of course, if you are only sorting numbers, you can use `<` to compare terms numerically, and if you are sorting specialized data structures of some kind, you may need to write your own comparison predicate.

Exercise 7.7.1

Look closely at `dlqsort` and `iqsort`. Are these the same algorithm? Explain, in detail, how they correspond and what the differences are. What effect would you expect the differences to have on performance?

Exercise 7.7.2

Some textbooks say that Quicksort takes time proportional to $N \log_{10} N$ or $N \ln N$ rather than $N \log_2 N$. Are they right? Explain.

Exercise 7.7.3

Modify Quicksort so that it removes duplicates in the list being sorted. That is, after sorting, `[a,b,r,a,c,a,d,a,b,r,a]` should come out as `[a,b,c,d,r]`, not as `[a,a,a,a,a,b,b,c,d,r,r]`.

```
% File QSORT.PL
% Several versions of Quicksort

% For maximum portability, this code includes some cuts that are
% unnecessary in implementations that have first-argument indexing.

% partition(+List,+Pivot,-Before,-After)
%   Divides List into two lists, one
%   containing elements that should
%   come before Pivot, the other containing
%   elements that should come after it.
%   Used in all versions of Quicksort.

partition([X|Tail],Pivot,[X|Before],After) :-    % X precedes Pivot
   X @< Pivot,
   !,
   partition(Tail,Pivot,Before,After).

partition([X|Tail],Pivot,Before,[X|After]) :-    % X follows Pivot
   !,
   partition(Tail,Pivot,Before,After).

partition([],_,[],[]).                           % Empty list


% Original Quicksort algorithm
% (Sterling and Shapiro, 1994:70; Clocksin and Mellish 1984:157)

quicksort([X|Tail],Result) :-
   !,
   partition(Tail,X,Before,After),
   quicksort(Before,SortedBefore),
   quicksort(After,SortedAfter),
   append(SortedBefore,[X|SortedAfter],Result).

quicksort([],[]).

% Delete next 2 lines if append/3 is built in
append([],X,X).
append([X|Tail],Y,[X|Z]) :- append(Tail,Y,Z).
```

Figure 7.4   Quicksort in Prolog (continued on next page).

```prolog
% Quicksort with difference lists
%   (Sterling and Shapiro 1994:289)

dlqsort(List,Result) :- quicksort_dl(List,Result/[]).

quicksort_dl([X|Tail],Result/ResultTail) :-
   !,
   partition(Tail,X,Before,After),
   quicksort_dl(Before,Result/[X|Z]),
   quicksort_dl(After,Z/ResultTail).

quicksort_dl([],X/X).


% Improved Quicksort using "stacks"
%   (separate variables for the tail of the list)
%   (Kluzniak and Szpakowicz 1985; Clocksin and Mellish 1984:157)

iqsort(List,Result) :- iqsort_aux(List,[],Result).

iqsort_aux([X|Tail],Stack,Result) :-
   !,
   partition(Tail,X,Before,After),
   iqsort_aux(After,Stack,NewStack),
   iqsort_aux(Before,[X|NewStack],Result).

iqsort_aux([],Stack,Stack).


% Demonstration predicates

test1 :- quicksort([7,0,6,5,4,9,4,6,3,3],What), write(What).
test2 :- dlqsort([7,0,6,5,4,9,4,6,3,3],What),   write(What).
test3 :- iqsort([7,0,6,5,4,9,4,6,3,3],What),    write(What).


% End of QSORT.PL
```

Figure 7.4 (Continued).

7.8. EFFICIENCY OF SORTING ALGORITHMS

Table 7.1 compares the performance of Quicksort and some other sorting algorithms. Perhaps the most obvious fact is that the performance of Quicksort really deteriorates if the elements of the list are already almost in sequence. This is due to our particular partitioning strategy, using the first element as the pivot, and could be corrected by partitioning differently.

Further, the "improved" Quicksort and the difference-list Quicksort are not noticeably better than the original one. That's partly because Quintus Prolog handles **append** very efficiently. (In fact, in the version we used, **append** was built-in, but a user-defined version of **append** was nearly as fast.) By contrast, in an early version of Arity Prolog, we found as much as a factor-of-8 speed difference between the original Quicksort and the "improved" one.

What this shows is that optimizations can be implementation-dependent. Quintus Prolog is based on a set of algorithms and data structures called the Warren Abstract Machine (Aït-Kaci 1991); Arity Prolog is not. Tricks for improving performance in one of them do not necessarily work in the other. This does not lead to the conclusion that either Arity or Quintus is better than the other; they're just different. On the other hand, any change that reduces the number of steps in the algorithm will be beneficial on any computer, regardless of details of implementation.

Exercise 7.8.1

Modify Quicksort by changing the partitioning algorithm so that its performance does not deteriorate so much if the list is already almost sorted. Demonstrate that your version is faster (on such a list) than the original.

Exercise 7.8.2

The algorithms in QSORT.PL include some cuts that are not necessary in Prolog implementations that have first-argument indexing. Remove the unnecessary cuts. How should this affect performance?

Exercise 7.8.3

Classify the sorting algorithms in Table 7.1 into those that sort an N-element list in time approximately proportional to N^2, those that take time approximately proportional to $N \log_2 N$, and those that fit into neither category.
Hint: Whenever N is multiplied by 10, N^2 increases by a factor of 100, but $N \log_2 N$ increases by a factor of about 33.

Exercise 7.8.4

Judging from their performance, which of the algorithms in Table 7.1 are essentially varieties of Quicksort, and which ones are fundamentally different?

Exercise 7.8.5

In Table 7.1, what evidence is there that the built-in **sort** predicate uses different sorting algorithms for lists of different lengths? (Look especially at memory usage.)

TABLE 7.1 TIME AND MEMORY NEEDED TO SORT LISTS OF VARIOUS LENGTHS.

Quintus Prolog 3.1, compiled, on a Sparcstation 1+ computer.

Algorithm	Elements in random order	Elements already almost sorted	Elements initially almost backward
Built-In Sort Predicate			
10 elements	0.95 ms (0.2 KB)	0.85 ms (0.2 KB)	0.85 ms (0.2 KB)
100 elements	14.5 ms (3.6 KB)	8.34 ms (1.7 KB)	1.33 ms (14 KB)
1000 elements	142 ms (35 KB)	58.3 ms (9.5 KB)	58.3 ms (11 KB)
Original Quicksort			
10 elements	0.78 ms (0.4 KB)	1.18 ms (0.5 KB)	1.15 ms (0.7 KB)
100 elements	20.3 ms (10 KB)	106 ms (40 KB)	43.7 ms (29 KB)
1000 elements	945 ms (387 KB)	10747 ms (3918 KB)	1243 ms (635 KB)
Difference-List Quicksort			
10 elements	0.83 ms (0.5 KB)	1.28 ms (0.7 KB)	1.15 ms (0.7 KB)
100 elements	20.8 ms (10 KB)	109 ms (42 KB)	42.0 ms (19 KB)
1000 elements	950 ms (380 KB)	10617 ms (3934 KB)	1212 ms (499 KB)
"Improved" Quicksort			
10 elements	0.73 ms (0.3 KB)	1.20 ms (0.4 KB)	1.15 ms (0.4 KB)
100 elements	19.8 ms (7.5 KB)	107 ms (39 KB)	41.0 ms (17 KB)
1000 elements	943 ms (357 KB)	10760 ms (3910 KB)	1208 ms (476 KB)
Mergesort			
10 elements	1.53 ms (1.2 KB)	1.55 ms (1.1 KB)	1.58 ms (1.1 KB)
100 elements	28.5 ms (20 KB)	29.0 ms (18 KB)	29.7 ms (22 KB)
1000 elements	406 ms (269 KB)	412 ms (242 KB)	440 ms (291 KB)
Treesort			
10 elements	0.88 ms (0.6 KB)	1.43 ms (0.9 KB)	1.35 ms (0.9 KB)
100 elements	24.0 ms (16 KB)	129 ms (80 KB)	48.2 ms (35 KB)
1000 elements	1132 ms (721 KB)	12739 ms (7829 KB)	1445 ms (960 KB)

Exercise 7.8.6   (small project)

> Find out how to access the system clock on your computer and conduct some timings of your own. Replicate as much of Table 7.1 as you can.

7.9. MERGESORT

A faster sorting algorithm is based on the operation of *merging* (combining) two lists that are already sorted. Clearly, a pair of lists such as

```
[0,1,3,5,6,7,9]
[2,4,6,8]
```

can be combined into one sorted list by picking off, one at a time, the first element of one list or the other, depending on which should come first: first 0, then 1 (still from the first list), then 2 (from the second list), then 3 (from the first list), and so on. You never have to look past the first element of either list. Here's a merging algorithm in Prolog:

```
% merge(+List1,+List2,-Result)
%   Combines two sorted lists into a sorted list.

merge([First1|Rest1],[First2|Rest2],[First1|Rest]) :-
  First1 @< First2,
  !,
  merge(Rest1,[First2|Rest2],Rest).

merge([First1|Rest1],[First2|Rest2],[First2|Rest]) :-
  \+ First1 @< First2,
  !,
  merge([First1|Rest1],Rest2,Rest).

merge(X,[],X).

merge([],X,X).
```

To use `merge` as the core of a sorting algorithm, we'll sort in the following way:

- Partition the original list into two smaller lists.

- Recursively sort the two lists.

- Finally, merge them back together.

The recursion is not endless because the middle step can be omitted when a list has fewer than two elements. Here's the implementation:

```
% msort(+List1,-List2)
%   Sorts List1 giving List2 using mergesort.
```

```
msort([First,Second|Rest],Result) :-   % list has at least 2 elements
   !,
   partition([First,Second|Rest],L1,L2),
   msort(L1,SL1),
   msort(L2,SL2),
   merge(SL1,SL2,Result).


msort(List,List).                      % list has 0 or 1 element
```

Finally, we have to tackle the job of partitioning a list into two. One simple way to do this is to put alternate elements into the two partitions, so that [0,1,2,3,4,5] gets split into [0,2,4] and [1,3,5]:

```
% partition(+List,-List1,-List2)
%   splits List in two the simplest way,
%   by putting alternate members in different lists


partition([First,Second|Rest],[First|F],[Second|S]) :-  % >= 2 elements
   !,
   partition(Rest,F,S).


partition(List,List,[]).                                % 0 or 1 element
```

Table 7.1 shows that mergesort is fast, and, unlike Quicksort, its efficiency does not suffer if the list is already almost sorted or almost backward.

Exercise 7.9.1

Modify **merge** so that it removes duplicates from the lists that it creates. Call your version **merge_rd**. To demonstrate that it works, try the query:
```
?- merge_rd([a,a,c,c],[b,b],What).
What = [a,b,c]
```
Do not use **remove_duplicates** or **member**. Traverse each list only once.

Exercise 7.9.2

Get **msort** working on your computer and modify it to use **merge_rd**. Call your version **msort_rd**.

Exercise 7.9.3

If your Prolog correctly implements the if-then operator (Chapter 4, Section 4.7), use it to combine the first two clauses of **merge** into one, thereby speeding up the algorithm.

Exercise 7.9.4   (small project)

Devise a better partitioning algorithm for mergesort. Your goal should be to preserve (some or all) ordered subsequences that already exist, so that mergesort will proceed much faster if the list is already almost sorted. For example, in the list [5,4,9,0,1,2,3,7,0,6], the sequence [0,1,2,3,7] should not be broken up, since **merge** can handle it directly.

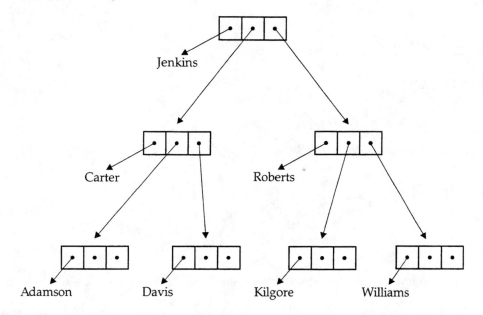

Figure 7.5   A binary tree. Each cell contains a pointer to a name (or other data) together with pointers to cells that alphabetically precede and follow it.

You do not have to preserve all such sequences; instead, experiment with techniques to increase the probability of preserving them.

7.10. BINARY TREES

So far we've been assuming that you'll store items in a list in the wrong order, then sort the list. If you want to keep a set of items sorted all the time, a list isn't the best structure in which to store it. Instead, you should use a BINARY TREE.

Figure 7.5 shows the general idea. Unlike a list, a binary tree associates each element with pointers to two subordinate trees, not just one. What's more, you can find any element very quickly by using alphabetical order, as follows:

- Start at the top.

- If the item you want should come *before* the item you're currently looking at, then follow the *left* pointer.

- If the item you want should come *after* the item you're currently looking at, then follow the *right* pointer.

On the average, it takes only $\log_2 N$ steps to find any element of an N-element tree this way. By contrast, finding any element of an N-element list takes, on the average, $N/2$ steps.

We can represent a binary tree in Prolog as a structure of the type

```
tree(tree(tree(empty,
               'Adamson',
               empty),
          'Carter',
          tree(empty,
               'Davis',
               empty)),
     'Jenkins',
     tree(tree(empty,
               'Kilgore',
               empty),
          'Roberts',
          tree(empty,
               'Williams',
               empty)))
```

Figure 7.6   A Prolog term representing Figure 7.5.

```
tree(Element,Left,Right)
```

where `Element` is an element and `Left` and `Right` are additional trees. We will use the atom `empty` to designate an empty tree (one with no elements and no pointers). Figure 7.6 shows what the tree in Figure 7.5 looks like when encoded this way. Notice that Figure 7.5 is not a full tree diagram of this structure (such as we were drawing in Section 7.1), but the essential relationships are preserved.

To insert an element into a tree, you use alphabetic order to search for the place where it ought to go and put it there:

```
% insert(+NewItem,-Tree,+NewTree)
%   Inserts an item into a binary tree.

insert(NewItem,empty,tree(NewItem,empty,empty)) :- !.

insert(NewItem,tree(Element,Left,Right),tree(Element,NewLeft,Right)) :-
   NewItem @< Element,
   !,
   insert(NewItem,Left,NewLeft).

insert(NewItem,tree(Element,Left,Right),tree(Element,Left,NewRight)) :-
   insert(NewItem,Right,NewRight).
```

If the elements to be inserted are initially in random order, the tree remains well balanced — that is, the chances are about equal of branching to the left or to the right in any particular case. If the elements are inserted predominantly in ascending or descending order, the tree becomes unbalanced and list-like (Figure 7.7).

Trees can be searched quickly because the process of finding an element is like that of inserting it, except that we stop when we find a node whose element

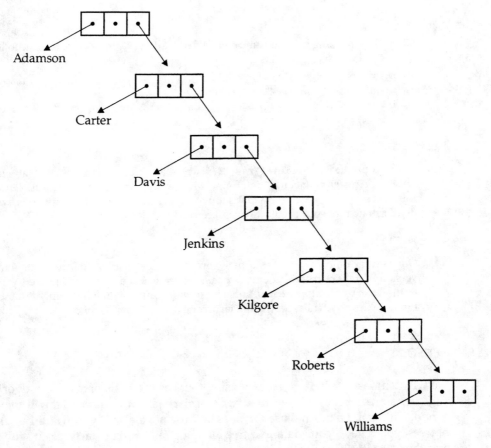

Figure 7.7   An unbalanced binary tree, containing the same data as in Figure 7.5 but inserted in a different order.

matches the one we are looking for. On the average, in a tree with N nodes, the number of nodes that must be examined to find a particular element is proportional to $\log_2 N$ if the tree is well balanced, or proportional to N if the tree is severely unbalanced. Of course, nodes can have other arguments containing information associated with the key element; in this case, the binary tree becomes the core of a fast information-retrieval system.

Many strategies have been developed for keeping trees balanced as they are built. For a survey, see Wirth (1986:196-268).

Exercise 7.10.1

Get `insert` working on your computer. What tree do you get by executing the following query? Draw a diagram of it.

```
?- insert(nute,empty,Tree1),
   insert(covington,Tree1,Tree2),
   insert(vellino,Tree2,Tree3),
   write(Tree3), nl.
```

Exercise 7.10.2

Define a predicate `retrieve(Tree,Element)` that succeeds if `Element` is an element of `Tree`. At each branching, determine whether `Element` should be in the left or the right subtree, and search only that subtree. Using the tree from the previous exercise, demonstrate that your predicate works correctly.

Exercise 7.10.3

Our version of `insert` makes a new copy of at least part of the tree. Implement a version of `insert` in which empty positions are marked by uninstantiated variables (rather than by the atom `empty`), and new subtrees can be added by simply instantiating the variables. (What list processing technique does this correspond to?)

7.11. TREESORT

We will demonstrate binary trees by using them as the basis of a sorting algorithm: we'll transform a list into a tree, then transform it back into a list, and it will come out sorted. This is not a normal use for trees because normally, if you want the benefits of trees, you'd keep your data in a tree all along rather than starting out with a list and then transforming it. But it does make a good demonstration of the power of binary trees.

The algorithm is shown in file TREESORT.PL (Figure 7.8). Table 7.1 shows that its performance is comparable to Quicksort, and, indeed, it is essentially a Quicksort with much of the recursion expressed in the data structure, not just in the procedures. We emphasize that TREESORT.PL was written for readability, not efficiency; it could probably be speeded up a few percent without difficulty.

The algorithm to convert a list into a tree is simple: CDR down the list and call `insert` once for each element. To turn the tree back into a list, retrieve the elements in right–left order and build the list tail first, starting with the last element and adding the others in front of it. This is done as follows:

```
% File TREESORT.PL
% Sorting a list by converting it into
% a binary tree, then back into a list


% treesort(+List,-NewList)
%   Sorts List giving NewList.

treesort(List,NewList) :-
   list_to_tree(List,Tree),
   tree_to_list(Tree,NewList).



% insert(+NewItem,-Tree,+NewTree)
%   Inserts an item into a binary tree.

insert(NewItem,empty,tree(NewItem,empty,empty)) :- !.

insert(NewItem,tree(Element,Left,Right),tree(Element,NewLeft,Right)) :-
   NewItem @< Element,
   !,
   insert(NewItem,Left,NewLeft).

insert(NewItem,tree(Element,Left,Right),tree(Element,Left,NewRight)) :-
   insert(NewItem,Right,NewRight).



% insert_list(+List,+Tree,-NewTree)
%   Inserts all elements of List into Tree giving NewTree.

insert_list([Head|Tail],Tree,NewTree) :-
   !,
   insert(Head,Tree,MiddleTree),
   insert_list(Tail,MiddleTree,NewTree).

insert_list([],Tree,Tree).
```

Figure 7.8   A sorting algorithm based on binary trees (continued on next page).

```
% list_to_tree(+List,-Tree)
%  inserts all elements of List into an initially empty tree.

list_to_tree(List,Tree) :- insert_list(List,empty,Tree).



% tree_to_list(+Tree,-List)
%  places all elements of Tree into List in sorted order.

tree_to_list(Tree,List) :-
   tree_to_list_aux(Tree,[],List).

tree_to_list_aux(empty,List,List).

tree_to_list_aux(tree(Item,Left,Right),OldList,NewList) :-
   tree_to_list_aux(Right,OldList,List1),
   tree_to_list_aux(Left,[Item|List1],NewList).



% Demonstration predicate

test :- treesort([7,0,6,5,4,9,4,6,3,3],What), write(What).


% End of TREESORT.PL
```

Figure 7.8 (Continued).

1. Recursively extract all the elements in the right subtree and add them to the list.

2. Add the element in the top node to the list.

3. Recursively extract all the elements in the left subtree, and add them to the list.

This is implemented in the predicate `tree_to_list` in TREESORT.PL.

Much time can be saved by avoiding the use of lists altogether. If all you want to do is write out the elements of a tree in sorted order, without actually converting them back into a list, you can just traverse the tree, like this:

```
% write_sorted(+Tree)
%   prints out the elements of Tree in sorted order

write_sorted(empty) :- !.

write_sorted(tree(Element,Left,Right)) :-
    write_sorted(Left),
    write(Element), write(' '),
    write_sorted(Right).
```

Trees are a good alternative to lists in situations where the data must be searched quickly or retrieved in a particular order.

Exercise 7.11.1

Get `treesort` working on your computer and modify it to eliminate duplicates in the list being sorted. Call your version `treesort_rd`.

Exercise 7.11.2

In TREESORT.PL, why does `tree_to_list_aux` traverse `Right` before traversing `Left`?

7.12. CUSTOMIZED ARITHMETIC: A REPLACEMENT FOR `is`

There is no easy way to extend the syntax of expressions that can be evaluated by `is`. If your Prolog doesn't have `exp()` or `log2()` or `arcsec()`, or whatever you need, you're seemingly out of luck.

Accordingly, here we work around the problem by writing an extensible replacement for `is`. We'll call it `:=` in honor of the Pascal assignment statement,[2] although it is in fact an expression evaluator like `is`.

Prolog operator priorities make it easy to split up expressions in the desired way. Recall that, for instance, `2*3+4/5` will unify with `X+Y` because `+` has higher priority than any other operator within it and is therefore the principal functor. So:

---

[2]The Pascal assignment operator `:=` is the same as in the earlier language ALGOL. Computer folklore says that the choice of `:=` for ALGOL was the result of a typesetting error: The author of an early document instructed the typesetter to set $\Leftarrow$ (to symbolize copying from right to left) everywhere he had typed `:=`, and the instruction was ignored. This is not confirmed; `:=` already meant "is defined as" in mathematical papers.

- To evaluate X+Y (where X and Y are expressions), first evaluate X and Y, then add the results.

- To evaluate X*Y (where X and Y are expressions), first evaluate X and Y, then multiply the results.

It's obvious how to fill in -, /, and other arithmetic operations. Moreover,

- To evaluate a plain number, just leave it alone.

File ARITH.PL (Figure 7.9) shows the whole thing. We implement +, -, *, /, and rec() (which means "reciprocal" and is put there to show that we can make up our own evaluable functors). You could, of course, add any other functors that you wish. [Algorithms for computing sines, cosines, and many other mathematical functions are given by Abramowitz and Stegun (1964).] Note however that := may run considerably slower than is because some Prologs (Quintus, for instance) compile is-queries into basic arithmetic operations on the computer, while the only thing the compiler can do with a query to := is make a call to the procedure you have defined.

Exercise 7.12.1

Get ':=' working on your computer. Compare the time taken to execute the two goals X is 2+3/4 and Y := 2+3/4. To get a meaningful comparison, you will have to construct a loop that performs the computation perhaps 100 to 1000 times.

Exercise 7.12.2

Modify the definition of := so that first-argument indexing can speed up the choice of clauses.
Hint: the query Result := Expression could call a predicate such as eval(Expression, Result), which could index on the principal functor of Expression.

7.13. SOLVING EQUATIONS NUMERICALLY

We also lamented in Chapter 3 that Prolog cannot solve for numerical unknowns in equations; for example, the query

```
?- X+1 is 1/X.        % wrong!
```

does not work. Clearly, the reason Prolog can't solve such queries is that it can't exhaustively search the whole set of real numbers.

However, *heuristic* searching for numbers is quite feasible, and techniques for doing it are at least as old as Sir Isaac Newton. In this section we'll develop a numerical equation solver that will answer queries such as these:

```
?- solve( X + 1 = 1 / X ).
X = 0.618034
```

```
?- solve( X = cos(X) ).
X = 0.739085
```

```
% File ARITH.PL
% A homemade substitute for 'is'

% Result := Expression
%  Evaluates expressions in much the same way as 'is'.
%  Evaluable functors are + - * / and rec() (reciprocal).

:- op(700,xfx,:=).

Result := X + Y   :-   !,
                       Xvalue := X,
                       Yvalue := Y,
                       Result is Xvalue + Yvalue.

Result := X - Y   :-   !,
                       Xvalue := X,
                       Yvalue := Y,
                       Result is Xvalue - Yvalue.

Result := X * Y   :-   !,
                       Xvalue := X,
                       Yvalue := Y,
                       Result is Xvalue * Yvalue.

Result := X / Y   :-   !,
                       Xvalue := X,
                       Yvalue := Y,
                       Result is Xvalue / Yvalue.

Result := rec(X)  :-   !,
                       Xvalue := X,
                       Result is 1 / Xvalue.

Term    := Term   :-   !,
                       number(Term).

_       := Term   :-   write('Error, can''t evaluate '), write(Term), nl,
                       !, fail.
```

Figure 7.9 An expression evaluator in Prolog.

To solve *Left* = *Right*:

function *Dif*(*X*) = *Left* − *Right*
where *X* occurs in *Left* and/or in *Right*;

procedure *Solve*:
  begin
    Guess1 := 1;
    Guess2 := 2;
    repeat
      Slope := (*Dif*(*Guess2*) − *Dif*(*Guess1*))/(*Guess2* − *Guess1*);
      Guess1 := *Guess2*;
      Guess2 := *Guess2* − (*Dif*(*Guess2*)/*Slope*)
    until *Guess2* is sufficiently close to *Guess1*;
    result is *Guess2*
  end.

Figure 7.10   The secant method, expressed in Pascal-like pseudocode.

Crucially, this is a *numerical* solver, not an *analytic* one. That is, it does not solve by manipulating the equation itself (except for one minor change which we'll get to); instead, it takes the equation, as given, and searches heuristically for the number that will satisfy it.[3]

The technique that we'll use is called the *secant method*. Given an equation *Left* = *Right*, we'll define a function

$$Dif(X) = Left - Right$$

where *X* is a variable that appears in *Left*, *Right*, or both. Now, instead of trying to make *Left* = *Right*, we'll be trying to make *Dif*(*X*) = 0.

We'll do this by taking two guesses at the value of *X* and comparing the corresponding values of *Dif*(*X*). One of them will be closer to zero than the other. Not only that, but the amount of difference between them will tell us how much farther to change *X* in order to get *Dif*(*X*) even closer to zero. Figure 7.10 shows the whole algorithm in Pascal-like pseudocode.

Figure 7.11 shows how this algorithm is implemented in Prolog. First, `free_in` searches the equation to find a variable to solve for. Then `define_dif` creates and asserts a clause to compute *Dif*(*X*). Finally, `solve_for` conducts the search itself.

The secant method works surprisingly well but isn't infallible. It can fail in three major ways. First, it may try two values of *X* that give the same *Dif*(*X*); when this happens, it can't tell what to do next, and the program crashes with a division by zero. That's why

```
?- solve(X*X = X*3).
```

---

[3]Sterling and Shapiro (1994) give an analytic equation solver in Prolog, with references to the literature.

fails or terminates abnormally. Second, it may simply fail to converge in a reasonable number of iterations; that's why

```
?- solve(sin(X) = 0.001).
```

never finds a solution (at least on our computer; yours may be different). Last, the secant method may jump over excessively large portions of the sine curve or similar periodic functions, so that even when it ultimately solves a problem, the solution is not the one with X nearest zero. That's why you get

```
?- solve(sin(X) = 0.01).
X = 213.6383
```

when you might have expected **X** (in radians) to be very close to 0.01. All of these failures can often be prevented by choosing different initial guesses for **X**, instead of always using 1 and 2.

We chose the secant method only because of its simplicity. For information on other, better, numerical methods for solving equations, see Hamming (1971) and Press, Flannery, Teukolsky, and Vetterling (1986).

Exercise 7.13.1

Get SOLVER.PL working on your computer and use it to solve Kepler's equation, $E - 0.01 \sin E = 2.5$. What solution do you get?

Exercise 7.13.2

What happens when you try to solve $X = X + 1$ using SOLVER.PL?

Exercise 7.13.3   (project)

Implement a better numerical equation solver. This could be anything from a minor improvement to SOLVER.PL all the way to a program that uses considerable intelligence to select the best of several methods.

7.14. BIBLIOGRAPHICAL NOTES

This is the chapter in which our narrow view of Prolog suddenly opens out onto the wide world of symbolic computing, and it is not possible to provide a narrowly focused bibliography.

The best general references on Prolog algorithms are Sterling and Shapiro (1994) and O'Keefe (1990), and the ongoing series of logic programming books published by MIT Press. On the implementation of Prolog, see Maier and Warren (1988), Aït-Kaci (1991), and Boizumault (1993).

```prolog
% File SOLVER.PL
% Numerical equation solver (Covington 1989)


% solve(+(Left=Right))
%   Left=Right is an arithmetic equation containing an uninstantiated
%   variable.  On exit, that variable is instantiated to a solution.

solve(Left=Right) :-
   free_in(Left=Right,X),
   !,                           % accept only one answer from free_in
   define_dif(X,Left=Right),
   solve_for(X).


% free_in(+Term,-Variable)
%   Variable occurs in Term and is uninstantiated.

free_in(X,X) :- % An atomic term
    var(X).

free_in(Term,X) :- % A complex term
    Term \== [[]],
    Term =.. [_,Arg|Args],
    (free_in(Arg,X) ; free_in(Args,X)).


% define_dif(-X,+(Left=Right))
%   Defines a predicate to compute Left-Right given X.
%   Here X is uninstantiated but occurs in Left=Right.

define_dif(X,Left=Right) :-
   abolish(dif,2),
   assert((dif(X,Dif) :- Dif is Left-Right)).


% solve_for(-Variable)
%   Sets up arguments and calls solve_aux (below).

solve_for(Variable) :-
   dif(1,Dif1),
   solve_aux(Variable,1,Dif1,2,1).
```

Figure 7.11 A numerical equation solver (continued on next page).

```
% solve_aux(-Variable,+Guess1,+Dif1,+Guess2,+Iteration)
% Uses the secant method to solve for Variable (see text).
% Other arguments:
% Guess1     -- Previous estimated value.
% Dif1     -- What 'dif' gave with Guess1.
% Guess2     -- A better estimate.
% Iteration -- Count of tries taken.

solve_aux(_,_,_,_,100) :-
   !,
   write('[Gave up at 100th iteration]'),nl,
   fail.

solve_aux(Guess2,Guess1,_,Guess2,_) :-
   close_enough(Guess1,Guess2),
   !,
   write('[Found a satisfactory solution]'),nl.

solve_aux(Variable,Guess1,Dif1,Guess2,Iteration) :-
   write([Guess2]),nl,
   dif(Guess2,Dif2),
   Slope is (Dif2-Dif1) / (Guess2-Guess1),
   Guess3 is Guess2 - (Dif2/Slope),
   NewIteration is Iteration + 1,
   solve_aux(Variable,Guess2,Dif2,Guess3,NewIteration).


% close_enough(+X,+Y)
% True if X and Y are the same number to within a factor of 1.000001.

close_enough(X,Y) :-  Quot is X/Y, Quot > 0.999999, Quot < 1.000001.


% Demonstration predicate

test :- solve(X=1+1/X), write(X), nl.


% End of SOLVER.PL
```

Figure 7.11 (Continued).

Part II

Artificial Intelligence Applications

Chapter 8

Artificial Intelligence
and the Search for Solutions

8.1. ARTIFICIAL INTELLIGENCE, PUZZLES, AND PROLOG

Prolog is a product of artificial intelligence research. Its creation and continued development are motivated by the need for a powerful programming language well suited to symbolic processing. This kind of computing — so different in many ways from numerical computing — is what artificial intelligence is all about.

Artificial intelligence (AI) has come to the attention of most people only in the last few years because of the coverage it has received in the popular press, but it is not really a new concept. Researchers like John McCarthy at Stanford University, Marvin Minsky at M.I.T., and Herbert Simon at Carnegie-Mellon University were creating this field as early as the 1950's. The recent enthusiasm for artificial intelligence has been fueled by the appearance of a new technology based on this research. This new technology includes expert systems, natural language interfaces, and new programming tools such as Prolog.

To understand the purpose and power of Prolog, we must examine how it is applied to some of the classic problems in AI. But first, what is AI? We will look at some of the fundamental goals that have been suggested for artificial intelligence research. Then we will look at some classic AI problems, including programs that can play games and solve puzzles. We will continue our discussion of AI topics in the next four chapters, looking at expert systems, automated reasoning, and natural language processing.

The most controversial goal that has been suggested for AI is to build thinking machines. According to the "hard" AI researcher, artificial intelligence is exactly what its name implies: the attempt to build intelligent artifacts. One of the most important lessons of artificial intelligence research is that we know very little about what "intelligence" really is. The more we tinker with our computers, the more we are impressed with how easily our minds perform complex tasks even though we can't begin to explain how we are able to do these things.

Alan Turing, the noted British mathematician, proposed the famous "Turing test" for machine intelligence. He proposed that a machine was intelligent if a person communicating with it, perhaps over a teletype so that he couldn't see it, couldn't tell that he was communicating with a machine rather than another human being. But Turing's test doesn't tell us what intelligence is. It proposes an independent criterion for deciding whether a machine has intelligence, whatever it is. Turing predicted that some machine would pass his test by the year 2000. Most people working in AI agree that no machine will pass Turing's test by 2000, and perhaps no machine will ever pass it.

Some critics argue that it is impossible for a machine to be intelligent in the way that humans are intelligent. At best, these arguments show that none of the machines we have or envision now are humanly intelligent. They really do not show that such a machine is impossible. Until we can say just what intelligence is, it's difficult to see how anyone could prove that machine intelligence is either possible or impossible.

Not every scientist whose work falls within the vague realm of AI is trying to build an intelligent machine. What other goals are there for AI?

One possible goal is to build machines that do things a human needs intelligence to do. We aren't trying to build machines that are intelligent, but only to build machines that simulate intelligence. For example, whatever intelligence is, it is needed to play chess or to prove theorems in mathematics. Let's see if we can build computers that simulate intelligence by performing these tasks as well as a human can.

This criterion does not separate what we have come to call artificial intelligence from many other things. Pocket calculators and even thermostats perform tasks that a human needs intelligence to perform, but we probably wouldn't say that these devices simulate intelligence. They certainly aren't usually included in lists of great successes in AI research. On the other hand, AI is concerned with things like vision and hearing. Do humans require intelligence to see and hear? Very primitive animals can do these things as well as or better than we can.

Part of our problem is that we are once again running into the question, What is intelligence? If we set this question aside and just try to build machines that simulate intelligence, we may also end up taking the machine as the definition of intelligence. Something like this has happened with IQ tests already: some people propose that intelligence as whatever it is the IQ test measures. Even if we avoid this pitfall, it may only be an illusion to think that it is easier to simulate intelligence than to build a truly intelligent machine. If we are not sure what intelligence is, it is no easier to recognize simulated intelligence than real intelligence in a machine.

The AI scientist must therefore try to reach a better understanding of what intelligence is. He differs from other investigators interested in this same problem mainly because his primary research tool is the computer. This, then, is a third possible goal for AI research: to investigate intelligence by means of computers.

Perhaps we should stretch our boundaries a bit. Human intelligence may include many things like reasoning, learning, problem solving, rule following, language understanding, and much more. Further, these are only part of what many AI researchers are investigating. For example, perception and memory, with its attendant failures of forgetting, are among the topics explored by some AI scientists. Yet we might hesitate to call these processes intelligent, although we might agree that they somehow contribute to intelligence. The whole range of human mental activities and abilities are called *cognitive* processes. One goal of AI research, then, is to use computers to help us better understand these processes.

On this view of artificial intelligence, AI research begins not with computers but with humans. Scientists from different disciplines, including psychology, linguistics, and philosophy, have been studying cognitive processes since long before computers became commonplace. When these cognitive scientists begin to use computers to help them construct and test their theories of human cognition, they become AI scientists.

Using computers in this way has certain advantages over other methods of investigation. Unlike abstract theories, computer programs either run or they don't; when they run, they give definite outputs for specific inputs. We might think of the computer as a kind of cognitive wind tunnel. We have a theory about how humans perform some cognitive process, analogous to a theory about how a wing lifts an airplane. We build a program based on our theory just as an aeronautical engineer builds a model wing based on his theory. We run the program on our computer as the aeronautical engineer tries out his model wing in the wind tunnel. We see how it runs and use what we learn to improve our theory.

Suppose we devise a theory about human cognition and then embody the theory in a program. When we run the program, it gives results that agree with our observations of real, living humans. Does this mean that the theory we used to build the program was correct? Unfortunately, no. The theory and the program may get the same results a human gets, but do it in a very different way than a human does. For example, a pocket calculator does arithmetic by converting to binary numbers whereas a human being works directly with decimal numbers. So although computer modeling can help us find flaws in our theories, it can never finally confirm them.

AI represents a new technology as well as an area of basic research. Technological spinoffs of AI include new programming languages and techniques that can be used for many different purposes. Prolog is one of these. Besides scientists who do what we might call basic AI research, we should also talk about a group that we could call AI technicians. These are people whose goal is to find ways to solve real, everyday problems using computers. What distinguishes them from other programmers and software designers is that they use the tools that have been developed through AI research.

Some AI practitioners not only use existing AI techniques but also try to develop new techniques for using computers to solve problems. How do we distinguish these researchers from computer scientists generally? We will base the distinction on the kinds of problems AI scientists are trying to solve. Humans do many different kinds of things, and they are good at explaining exactly how they do some of them. Examples are adding a column of numbers or alphabetizing a list of words. Humans have great difficulty explaining how they do other things, such as understanding a sentence or riding a bicycle. We have good theories about arithmetic, but our theories about understanding language are primitive by comparison. Some AI researchers would describe what they do as trying to find ways to get computers to do the things that humans can do without being able to say exactly how they do them.

We have four possible goals that an AI researcher might pursue: building intelligent machines, building machines that simulate intelligence, using computers to better understand intelligence, and finding ways to get a computer to do things that humans do but can't explain how they do. Of course, these are not exclusive goals and a particular AI scientist might be chasing all of these goals at once. Nor does this list exhaust the goals of artificial intelligence. Different AI researchers might give quite different accounts of what they are doing. None of this gives us a tight definition of artificial intelligence, but we hope it provides some understanding of what some of us working in AI think we are about.

Humans love games and puzzles. Even simple games and puzzles often require considerable intelligence. Since the early days of AI, researchers have been intrigued with the possibility of a machine that could play a really complex game like chess as well as any human could. Many of us have met chess programs that play better than we do.

The original hope was that in developing game playing programs we might learn something crucial about the nature of intelligence. Unfortunately, it is often difficult to apply much of what we learn from one program directly to another program. But some things have become clear through this and other kinds of research, including efforts to build automated theorem provers.

Let's look at what is involved in playing a game or solving a puzzle. There is something that is manipulated. This may be a board and pieces, letters and words, or even our own bodies. There is some initial configuration in which the things to be manipulated are placed. There is a set of rules determining how these things may be manipulated during the game. There is a specification of a situation which, if achieved, constitutes success. All of these factors define the game or puzzle.

Besides the defining rules, there may be rules of strategy associated with a game. These rules recommend specific choices from among the legal moves we can make in different situations during the game. Because they are only advisory, we can violate these rules and still play the game.

To write a program that can play a game or solve a puzzle, we will need to find a way to represent the initial situation, the rules for making legal moves, and the definition of a winning situation. Most of us know how to play tic-tac-toe. We know how to draw the grid and how to make the moves. We know what constitutes a win. However, it is not obvious how best to represent all this knowledge in a program. This problem of knowledge representation is one of the most common problems in all AI efforts.

Different ways of representing knowledge may make solving a problem more or less difficult. (Consider, for instance, trying to do long division using Roman numerals.) All of us have tangled with a frustrating problem at some time, then suddenly seen a new way of looking at the problem that makes its solution simple. The way we choose to represent the knowledge needed to play a game can make the task of writing a program that plays the game difficult or easy.

We will limit our attention to puzzles and other problems that can be solved by a single person. These are easier to understand and analyze than competitive games where we must take into account the moves of another person. Some of the puzzles we will discuss are not just for entertainment; they represent practical problems.

Once we develop a good representation of the situations that can arise in a puzzle, define the initial situation and the legal moves that can be made, and characterize the criteria for success, we should be able to use the method of exhaustive search to solve the puzzle. That is, we can try all possible sequences of moves until we find one that solves the puzzle. To be exhaustive, the procedure for generating sequences of moves must eventually generate every sequence of moves that could possibly be made. If there is a solution to the puzzle, exhaustive search must eventually find it.

We will use the method of exhaustive search to solve a maze, to solve the missionaries and cannibals puzzle, to solve a peg-board puzzle, to color a map, to search a molecular structure for specified substructures, and to make flight connections. We will also look at some faster methods for searching for solutions that are *not* exhaustive. Finally, we will develop routines for conducting forward-chaining and breadth-first inference within Prolog as alternatives to Prolog's normal mode of depth-first backward-chaining inference.

8.2. THROUGH THE MAZE

Our first puzzle is a simple maze. The object, of course, is to find a path through the maze from the start to the finish. First, we must represent the maze in a form Prolog can use. The maze was constructed on a piece of graph paper. It is six squares wide and six squares high. We begin by numbering these squares (Figure 8.1).

Treating `start` and `finish` as positions in the maze, we have a total of 38 positions. From each of these we can move to certain other positions. If we can move from one position to another, we will say that these two positions are connected. We enter a single fact in the definition of the predicate `connect/2` for each pair of connected locations. Then we define a `connected_to` predicate using the predicate connect:

```
connect(start,2).
connect(1,7).
connect(2,8).
...
connect(32,finish).
connected_to(A,B) :- connect(A,B).
connected_to(A,B) :- connect(B,A).
```

A path through the maze is a list of positions with `start` at one end of the list and `finish` at the other, such that every position in the list is connected to the

START

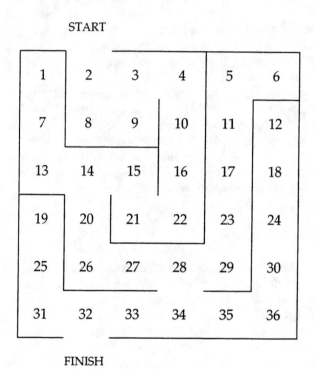

FINISH

Figure 8.1   A simple maze with locations within the maze numbered.

positions before and after it. Initially, our path contains the single point `start` which we place into a list. From this initial path, we want to generate a complete path from `start` to `finish`. Once a solution is found, we want our program to display it for us.

```
solve_maze :- path([start],Solution), write(Solution).
```

The procedure `path` will find a solution to the maze puzzle. Of course, when we reach `finish` we have a solution and our search is ended.

```
path([finish|RestOfPath],[finish|RestOfPath]).
```

At each intermediate step in our search for a solution to the maze, we have a list of the positions we have already visited. The first member of this list is our current position. We proceed by looking for a new position that we can reach from our current position. This new position must be connected to our current position. We don't want to move around in a circle or back and forth between the same positions, so our new position will also have to be a point that isn't already in the path we are building.

```
path([CurrentLocation|RestOfPath],Solution) :-
        connected_to(CurrentLocation,NextLocation),
        \+ member(NextLocation,RestOfPath),
        path([NextLocation,CurrentLocation|RestOfPath],Solution).
```

If the procedure `path` reaches a point where it cannot find a new position, Prolog will backtrack. Positions will be dropped off the front of the path we have built until we reach a point where a new position can be reached. Then the search will move forward again until we reach `finish` or another dead end. Since the maze has a solution, Prolog will eventually find it if we have defined our procedure correctly. The complete program is called MAZE.PL.

Exercise 8.2.1

Construct a maze that has more than one solution, i.e., more than one path through the maze. Define a procedure `shortest_path` that finds a shortest solution to the maze.

Exercise 8.2.2

How would you represent a three-dimensional maze constructed in a $4 \times 4 \times 4$ grid? How would you modify `solve_maze` to find a path through this three-dimensional maze?

8.2.1. Listing of MAZE.PL

```
% MAZE.PL
% A program that finds a path through a maze.

solve_maze :- path([start],Solution), write(Solution).

path([finish|RestOfPath],[finish|RestOfPath]).
path([CurrentLocation|RestOfPath],Solution) :-
```

```
        connected_to(CurrentLocation,NextLocation),
        \+ member(NextLocation,RestOfPath),
        path([NextLocation,CurrentLocation|RestOfPath],Solution).

connected_to(Location1,Location2) :- connect(Location1,Location2).
connected_to(Location1,Location2) :- connect(Location2,Location1).

member(X,[X|_]).
member(X,[_|Y]) :-
        member(X,Y).
```

8.2.2. Listing of MAZE1.PL (Connectivity Table)

```
% MAZE1.PL
% Connectivity table for the maze in Figure 8.1

connect(start,2).          connect(1,7).
connect(2,8).              connect(3,4).
connect(3,9).              connect(4,10).
connect(5,11).             connect(5,6).
connect(7,13).             connect(8,9).
connect(10,16).            connect(11,17).
connect(12,18).            connect(13,14).
connect(14,15).            connect(14,20).
connect(15,21).            connect(16,22).
connect(17,23).            connect(18,24).
connect(19,25).            connect(20,26).
connect(21,22).            connect(23,29).
connect(24,30).            connect(25,31).
connect(26,27).            connect(27,28).
connect(28,29).            connect(28,34).
connect(30,36).            connect(31,32).
connect(32,33).            connect(33,34).
connect(34,35).            connect(35,36).
connect(32,finish).
```

8.3. MISSIONARIES AND CANNIBALS

Our second puzzle is the familiar plight of the missionaries and the cannibals. Three missionaries and three cannibals must cross a river, but the only available boat will hold only two people at a time. There is no bridge, the river cannot be swum, and the boat cannot cross the river without someone in it. The cannibals will eat any missionaries they outnumber on either side of the bank. The problem is to get everyone across the river with all of the missionaries uneaten.

As with the maze puzzle, we begin by deciding how we will represent the problem in Prolog. We designate one bank of the river the left bank and the other the right bank, and we assume that initially the boat, all of the missionaries, and all of the cannibals are on the left bank. At any stage of the process of ferrying the missionaries and the cannibals across the river, we will have some missionaries on the left bank of the river and some on the right bank, some of the cannibals on the left bank of the river and some on the right bank, and the boat will be on either the left or the right bank. We can represent this information with a structure that tells us how many missionaries are on the left bank, how many cannibals are on the left bank, and the location of the boat: `state(M,C,B)`. Here the variables M and C can take values from 0 to 3 and the variable B can take values 1 (left bank) or r (right bank).

The structure `state(3,3,1)` represents the situation at the beginning of the puzzle, and the structure `state(0,0,r)` represents the situation we want to achieve. A solution to the puzzle will be a list of situations with `state(3,3,1)` at one end of the list and `state(0,0,r)` at the other end. Since the program produces a list of states in the reverse order that they occur, we have the program reverse the solution before displaying it.

```
cannibal :- solve_cannibal([state(3,3,1)],Solution),
            reverse(Solution,[],OrderedSolution),
            show_states(OrderedSolution).

solve_cannibal([state(0,0,r)|PriorStates],
               [state(0,0,r)|PriorStates]).
```

Any two successive states in the solution will have to satisfy several conditions. First, the boat will be on opposite sides of the river in the two states. That is, nobody crosses the river without the boat. Second, the cannibals will never outnumber the missionaries on either side of the river. Third, each of the states could be produced from the other by sending a boat-load of missionaries and cannibals across the river in the appropriate direction.

We solve the puzzle in much the same way that we solved the maze problem, except that at each stage in our search for a solution the restrictions placed on the next move are more complicated. We want Prolog to explore all possible combinations of trips across the river until it finds one that works. At any point in this process, we will have a list of states that resulted from the trips that have been made so far. The first member of this list is the current state. We want Prolog to look for a next state that can be reached from the current state. The next state must be the result of a legal boat trip beginning from the current state, must not endanger any missionaries, and must be a state that did not occur earlier in our list. This last requirement prevents Prolog from moving the same people back and forth across the river without ever making any progress. To accomplish this, we add two clauses to our definition of `solve_cannibal`, one for when the boat is on the left bank and one for when the boat is on the right bank.

```
solve_cannibal([state(M1,C1,1)|PriorStates],Solution) :-
      member([M,C],[[0,1],[1,0],[1,1],[0,2],[2,0]]),
                                            % Condition 1
      M1 >= M,                              % Condition 2
      C1 >= C,                              % Condition 3
      M2 is M1 - M,                         % Condition 4
      C2 is C1 - C,                         % Condition 5
```

```
        member([M2,C2],[[3,_],[0,_],[N,N]]),      % Condition 6
        \+ member(state(M2,C2,r),PriorStates),    % Condition 7
        solve_cannibal([state(M2,C2,r),state(M1,C1,1)|PriorStates],
                       Solution).
solve_cannibal([state(M1,C1,r)|PriorStates],Solution) :-
        member([M,C],[[0,1],[1,0],[1,1],[0,2],[2,0]]),
        3 - M1 >= M,
        3 - C1 >= C,
        M2 is M1 + M,
        C2 is C1 + C,
        member([M2,C2],[[3,_],[0,_],[N,N]]),
        \+ member(state(M2,C2,1),PriorStates),
        solve_cannibal([state(M2,C2,1),state(M1,C1,r)|PriorStates],
                       Solution).
```

To understand the program, we must understand the conditions in the first clause above. Condition 1 specifies that the boat carries at least one and at most two individuals across the river on the next trip. Conditions 2 and 3 ensure that no more missionaries and cannibals enter the boat than are presently on the left bank of the river. Conditions 4 and 5 determine how many missionaries and cannibals will be on the left bank of the river after the next trip. Condition 6 checks to see that the missionaries are all safe after the trip. A state is safe if all the missionaries are on the same bank (and thus cannot be outnumbered) or if there is an equal number of missionaries and cannibals on the left bank (and thus also an equal number on the right bank). Finally, condition 7 guarantees that the program does not return to a previous state. If `solve_cannibal` reaches a point where it cannot find a safe trip that will produce a situation it hasn't already tried, Prolog backtracks to a point where a new situation is available. Then the search moves forward again.

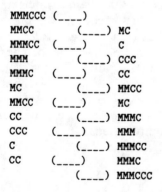

```
MMMCCC  (____)
MMCC            (____)  MC
MMMCC   (____)          C
MMM             (____)  CCC
MMMC    (____)          CC
MC              (____)  MMCC
MMCC    (____)          MC
CC              (____)  MMMC
CCC     (____)          MMM
C               (____)  MMMCC
CC      (____)          MMMC
                (____)  MMMCCC
```

Figure 8.2 A solution to the missionaries and cannibals puzzle.

We display the solution to our puzzle with a little pizzazz by constructing a series of pictures. This involves reversing the solution list so that the solutions are displayed in the order generated. The predicate `show_states` and its auxiliaries do this, drawing pictures with ordinary ASCII characters as shown in Figure 8.2.

Exercise 8.3.1

Another version of the missionaries and cannibals puzzle assumes that the missionaries are safe from the cannibals, but that the cannibals are in danger of conversion if they are ever outnumbered by the missionaries. What changes in CANNIBAL.PL will protect the cannibals from the missionaries?

Exercise 8.3.2

A farmer needs to transport a fox, a goose, and a bag of grain across a small stream. He can carry only one item at a time. Given the opportunity, the fox will eat the goose and the goose will eat the grain. Write a Prolog program that finds and displays a solution to this puzzle. The program should be invoked by the query ?- `farmer`.

Exercise 8.3.3

With an unlimited water supply, a 5 gallon bucket, and a 3 gallon bucket, you need to measure out exactly one gallon of water. Write a Prolog program to find a way to do this. The program should be invoked by the query ?- `buckets`.

8.3.1. Listing of CANNIBAL.PL

```
% CANNIBAL.PL
% This program solves the cannibals and missionaries puzzle.

cannibal :-
        solve_cannibal([state(3,3,1)],Solution),
        reverse(Solution,[],OrderedSolution),
        show_states(OrderedSolution).

%
% solve_cannibal(+Sofar,-Solution)
%    searches for a Solution to the cannibals and missionaries
%    puzzle that extends the sequence of states in Sofar.
%

solve_cannibal([state(0,0,r)|PriorStates],
               [state(0,0,r)|PriorStates]).
solve_cannibal([state(M1,C1,1)|PriorStates],Solution) :-
        member([M,C],[[0,1],[1,0],[1,1],[0,2],[2,0]]),
            % One or two persons cross the river.
        M1 >= M,C1 >= C,
            % The number of persons crossing the river is
            % limited to the number on the left bank.
        M2 is M1 - M, C2 is C1 - C,
            % The number of persons remaining on the left bank
            % is decreased by the number that cross the river.
        member([M2,C2],[[3,_],[0,_],[N,N]]),
            % The missionaries are not outnumbered on either
```

```
                % bank after the crossing.
            \+ member(state(M2,C2,r),PriorStates),
                % No earlier state is repeated.
            solve_cannibal([state(M2,C2,r),state(M1,C1,l)|PriorStates],Solution).
    solve_cannibal([state(M1,C1,r)|PriorStates],Solution) :-
            member([M,C],[[0,1],[1,0],[1,1],[0,2],[2,0]]),
                % One or two persons cross the river.
            3 - M1 >= M, 3 - C1 >= C,
                % The number of persons crossing the river is
                % limited to the number on the right bank.
            M2 is M1 + M, C2 is C1 + C,
                % The number of persons remaining on the right bank
                % is decreased by the number that cross the river.
            member([M2,C2],[[3,_],[0,_],[N,N]]),
                % The missionaries are not outnumbered on either
                % bank after the crossing.
            \+ member(state(M2,C2,l),PriorStates),
                % No earlier state is repeated.
            solve_cannibal([state(M2,C2,l),state(M1,C1,r)
                    |PriorStates],Solution).

show_states([]).
show_states([state(M,C,Location)|LaterStates]) :-
            write_n_times('M',M),
            write_n_times('C',C),
            N is 6 - M - C,
            write_n_times(' ',N),
            draw_boat(Location),
            MM is 3 - M,
            CC is 3 - C,
            write_n_times('M',MM),
            write_n_times('C',CC),
            nl,
            show_states(LaterStates).

write_n_times(_,0) :- !.
write_n_times(Item,N) :-
            write(Item),
            M is N - 1,
            write_n_times(Item,M).

draw_boat(l) :- write(' (____)      ').
draw_boat(r) :- write('      (____) ').

member(X,[X|_]).
member(X,[_|Y]) :- member(X,Y).

reverse([],List,List).
reverse([X|Tail],SoFar,List) :-
            reverse(Tail,[X|SoFar],List).
```

8.4. THE TRIANGLE PUZZLE

The triangle puzzle, also called the Christmas tree puzzle, is played with fifteen pegs and a board. The board has fifteen holes drilled in it in a triangular pattern like this:

```
        o
       o o
      o o o
     o o o o
    o o o o o
```

Initially, there is a peg in each hole. The player removes one peg, then proceeds to jump one peg over another, each time removing the peg that has been jumped. A jump must always be in a straight line, and only one peg can be jumped at a time. The object of the game is to finish with only one peg in the board.

A solution to the puzzle is represented by a sequence of boards, with fourteen pegs in the initial board and one peg in the final board. For each pair of adjacent boards in the solution, we must be able to produce the latter member of the pair from the earlier by a legal jump.

Our program has at the top level a procedure triangle(N) that removes the Nth peg from the triangle, calls the procedure solve_triangle that actually finds the solution, reverses the solution and displays it one triangle at a time.

```
triangle(N) :- remove_peg(N,StartingTriangle),
               solve_triangle(14,[StartingTriangle],Solution),
               reverse(Solution,[],OrderedSolution),
               nl,nl,
               show_triangles(OrderedSolution).
```

The procedure solve_triangle uses a number as its first argument to keep track of how many pegs are in the current triangle. This makes checking for success easy: a solution to the puzzle has been reached if there is one peg left. If there are more pegs left, solve_triangle finds a triangle that can be produced from the current triangle by a legal jump and adds it to the list of triangles. The procedure prints the number of triangles left in the new triangle so we have something to watch while the search proceeds. Then it recurses.

```
solve_triangle(1,Solution,Solution).
solve_triangle(Count,[CurrentTriangle|PriorTriangles],Solution):-
        jump(CurrentTriangle,NextTriangle),
        NewCount is Count - 1,
        write(NewCount),sp,
        solve_triangle(NewCount,
                [NextTriangle,CurrentTriangle|PriorTriangles],
                Solution).
```

Notice that solve_triangle doesn't check to see if we have returned to a previous position. In the maze or the missionaries and cannibals puzzle we had to do this, but each jump in the triangle puzzle eliminates a peg and produces a position that we could not have reached earlier.

Before we can use `triangle_solver`, we need a way to compute the triangles that result from making a legal jump in the current triangle. There are many ways to do this, but one of the most elegant was suggested by Richard O'Keefe of the Royal Melbourne Institute of Technology in an electronic mail discussion of the triangle puzzle. First, we represent each triangle with a list of fifteen holes where each hole is represented by a variable:

```
        [A,
        B,C,
       D,E,F,
      G,H,I,J,
     K,L,M,N,P]
```

Representing a jump as a transformation from one triangle to another, we see that only three holes in a triangle are affected by any jump. The remaining holes remain empty or occupied — just as they were prior to the jump. Using 1 to represent a peg and 0 to represent an empty hole, we can define a binary predicate `jump` by a set of clauses like the following:

```
jump(triangle(1,
             1,C,
            0,E,F,
           G,H,I,J,
          K,L,M,N,P),
     triangle(0,
             0,C,
            1,E,F,
           G,H,I,J,
          K,L,M,N,P)).
```

We need one such clause for each possible jump. All that remains is to define a procedure that removes the initial peg and routines for displaying the finished solution.

Exercise 8.4.1

A variation on the triangle puzzle is to remove all but one peg, but to leave the last peg in the hole that was empty at the beginning of the puzzle. Define a predicate called `my_triangle` that looks for a solution like this. Is there a solution to this problem?

Exercise 8.4.2

Another variation of the triangle puzzle is to leave 8 pegs on the board with no legal jump left. Write a predicate called `triangle8` that looks for such a solution. Does it succeed?

Exercise 8.4.3

Analyze the solution you get to the query `?- triangle(1)`. You will see that the moves come in a certain order. Reorder the clauses in the definition of jump so the moves in this solution are at the top of the definition of jump. What effect does this have on the time it takes to find a solution to `?- triangle(1)`? Do you get the same solution? Explain what you observe.

Exercise 8.4.4

Define a predicate `triangle10/1`, together with all the auxiliary predicates needed, to search for a solution for the triangle puzzle with ten pegs in this arrangement:

Is there a solution for the ten-peg triangle puzzle?

8.4.1. Listing of TRIANGLE.PL

```
% TRIANGLE.PL
% This program solves the triangle puzzle.

%
% triangle(+N)
%   Finds and displays a solution to the triangle problem
%   where the Nth peg is removed first.
%

triangle(N) :-
     remove_peg(N,StartingTriangle),
     solve_triangle(14,[StartingTriangle],Solution),
     reverse(Solution,[],OrderedSolution),
     nl,nl,
     show_triangles(OrderedSolution).

%
% solve_triangle(+N,+Sofar,-Solution)
%   Searches for a solution to the triangle problem from a
%   position with N pegs arranged in the pattern Sofar.
%

solve_triangle(1,Solution,Solution).
solve_triangle(Count,[CurrentTriangle|PriorTriangles],Solution):-
     jump(CurrentTriangle,NextTriangle),
     NewCount is Count - 1,
     write(NewCount), nl,
     solve_triangle(NewCount,
                    [NextTriangle,CurrentTriangle|PriorTriangles],
                    Solution).

%
% remove_peg(+N,-Triangle)
```

```
%    Produces a Triangle with an empty Nth hole and pegs
%    in all other holes.
%

remove_peg(1,triangle(0,1,1,1,1,1,1,1,1,1,1,1,1,1,1)).
remove_peg(2,triangle(1,0,1,1,1,1,1,1,1,1,1,1,1,1,1)).
remove_peg(3,triangle(1,1,0,1,1,1,1,1,1,1,1,1,1,1,1)).
remove_peg(4,triangle(1,1,1,0,1,1,1,1,1,1,1,1,1,1,1)).
remove_peg(5,triangle(1,1,1,1,0,1,1,1,1,1,1,1,1,1,1)).
remove_peg(6,triangle(1,1,1,1,1,0,1,1,1,1,1,1,1,1,1)).
remove_peg(7,triangle(1,1,1,1,1,1,0,1,1,1,1,1,1,1,1)).
remove_peg(8,triangle(1,1,1,1,1,1,1,0,1,1,1,1,1,1,1)).
remove_peg(9,triangle(1,1,1,1,1,1,1,1,0,1,1,1,1,1,1)).
remove_peg(10,triangle(1,1,1,1,1,1,1,1,1,0,1,1,1,1,1)).
remove_peg(11,triangle(1,1,1,1,1,1,1,1,1,1,0,1,1,1,1)).
remove_peg(12,triangle(1,1,1,1,1,1,1,1,1,1,1,0,1,1,1)).
remove_peg(13,triangle(1,1,1,1,1,1,1,1,1,1,1,1,0,1,1)).
remove_peg(14,triangle(1,1,1,1,1,1,1,1,1,1,1,1,1,0,1)).
remove_peg(15,triangle(1,1,1,1,1,1,1,1,1,1,1,1,1,1,0)).


%
% jump(+CurrentTriangle,-NextTriangle)
%    Finds a NextTriangle that can be produced from
%    CurrentTriangle by a legal jump. To save space,
%    all but the first clause are displayed in linear
%    format.
%

jump(triangle(1,
            1,C,
           0,E,F,
          G,H,I,J,
         K,L,M,N,P),
      triangle(0,
            0,C,
           1,E,F,
          G,H,I,J,
         K,L,M,N,P)).
jump(triangle(1,B,1,D,E,0,G,H,I,J,K,L,M,N,P),
     triangle(0,B,0,D,E,1,G,H,I,J,K,L,M,N,P)).
jump(triangle(A,1,C,1,E,F,0,H,I,J,K,L,M,N,P),
     triangle(A,0,C,0,E,F,1,H,I,J,K,L,M,N,P)).
jump(triangle(A,1,C,D,1,F,G,H,0,J,K,L,M,N,P),
     triangle(A,0,C,D,0,F,G,H,1,J,K,L,M,N,P)).
jump(triangle(A,B,1,D,1,F,G,0,I,J,K,L,M,N,P),
     triangle(A,B,0,D,0,F,G,1,I,J,K,L,M,N,P)).
jump(triangle(A,B,1,D,E,1,G,H,I,0,K,L,M,N,P),
     triangle(A,B,0,D,E,0,G,H,I,1,K,L,M,N,P)).
jump(triangle(0,1,C,1,E,F,G,H,I,J,K,L,M,N,P),
     triangle(1,0,C,0,E,F,G,H,I,J,K,L,M,N,P)).
jump(triangle(A,B,C,1,1,0,G,H,I,J,K,L,M,N,P),
```

```
            triangle(A,B,C,0,0,1,G,H,I,J,K,L,M,N,P)).
jump(triangle(A,B,C,1,E,F,G,1,I,J,K,L,0,N,P),
     triangle(A,B,C,0,E,F,G,0,I,J,K,L,1,N,P)).
jump(triangle(A,B,C,1,E,F,1,H,I,J,0,L,M,N,P),
     triangle(A,B,C,0,E,F,0,H,I,J,1,L,M,N,P)).
jump(triangle(A,B,C,D,1,F,G,1,I,J,K,0,M,N,P),
     triangle(A,B,C,D,0,F,G,0,I,J,K,1,M,N,P)).
jump(triangle(A,B,C,D,1,F,G,H,1,J,K,L,M,0,P),
     triangle(A,B,C,D,0,F,G,H,0,J,K,L,M,1,P)).
jump(triangle(0,B,1,D,E,1,G,H,I,J,K,L,M,N,P),
     triangle(1,B,0,D,E,0,G,H,I,J,K,L,M,N,P)).
jump(triangle(A,B,C,0,1,1,G,H,I,J,K,L,M,N,P),
     triangle(A,B,C,1,0,0,G,H,I,J,K,L,M,N,P)).
jump(triangle(A,B,C,D,E,1,G,H,1,J,K,L,0,N,P),
     triangle(A,B,C,D,E,0,G,H,0,J,K,L,1,N,P)).
jump(triangle(A,B,C,D,E,1,G,H,I,1,K,L,M,N,0),
     triangle(A,B,C,D,E,0,G,H,I,0,K,L,M,N,1)).
jump(triangle(A,0,C,1,E,F,1,H,I,J,K,L,M,N,P),
     triangle(A,1,C,0,E,F,0,H,I,J,K,L,M,N,P)).
jump(triangle(A,B,C,D,E,F,1,1,0,J,K,L,M,N,P),
     triangle(A,B,C,D,E,F,0,0,1,J,K,L,M,N,P)).
jump(triangle(A,B,0,D,1,F,G,1,I,J,K,L,M,N,P),
     triangle(A,B,1,D,0,F,G,0,I,J,K,L,M,N,P)).
jump(triangle(A,B,C,D,E,F,G,1,1,0,K,L,M,N,P),
     triangle(A,B,C,D,E,F,G,0,0,1,K,L,M,N,P)).
jump(triangle(A,0,C,D,1,F,G,H,1,J,K,L,M,N,P),
     triangle(A,1,C,D,0,F,G,H,0,J,K,L,M,N,P)).
jump(triangle(A,B,C,D,E,F,0,1,1,J,K,L,M,N,P),
     triangle(A,B,C,D,E,F,1,0,0,J,K,L,M,N,P)).
jump(triangle(A,B,0,D,E,1,G,H,I,1,K,L,M,N,P),
     triangle(A,B,1,D,E,0,G,H,I,0,K,L,M,N,P)).
jump(triangle(A,B,C,D,E,F,G,0,1,1,K,L,M,N,P),
     triangle(A,B,C,D,E,F,G,1,0,0,K,L,M,N,P)).
jump(triangle(A,B,C,0,E,F,1,H,I,J,1,L,M,N,P),
     triangle(A,B,C,1,E,F,0,H,I,J,0,L,M,N,P)).
jump(triangle(A,B,C,D,E,F,G,H,I,J,1,1,0,N,P),
     triangle(A,B,C,D,E,F,G,H,I,J,0,0,1,N,P)).
jump(triangle(A,B,C,D,0,F,G,1,I,J,K,1,M,N,P),
     triangle(A,B,C,D,1,F,G,0,I,J,K,0,M,N,P)).
jump(triangle(A,B,C,D,E,F,G,H,I,J,K,1,1,0,P),
     triangle(A,B,C,D,E,F,G,H,I,J,K,0,0,1,P)).
jump(triangle(A,B,C,D,E,F,G,H,I,J,0,1,1,N,P),
     triangle(A,B,C,D,E,F,G,H,I,J,1,0,0,N,P)).
jump(triangle(A,B,C,0,E,F,G,1,I,J,K,L,1,N,P),
     triangle(A,B,C,1,E,F,G,0,I,J,K,L,0,N,P)).
jump(triangle(A,B,C,D,E,0,G,H,1,J,K,L,1,N,P),
     triangle(A,B,C,D,E,1,G,H,0,J,K,L,0,N,P)).
jump(triangle(A,B,C,D,E,F,G,H,I,J,K,L,1,1,0),
     triangle(A,B,C,D,E,F,G,H,I,J,K,L,0,0,1)).
jump(triangle(A,B,C,D,E,F,G,H,I,J,K,0,1,1,P),
     triangle(A,B,C,D,E,F,G,H,I,J,K,1,0,0,P)).
```

```
jump(triangle(A,B,C,D,0,F,G,H,1,J,K,L,M,1,P),
    triangle(A,B,C,D,1,F,G,H,0,J,K,L,M,0,P)).
jump(triangle(A,B,C,D,E,F,G,H,I,J,K,L,0,1,1),
    triangle(A,B,C,D,E,F,G,H,I,J,K,L,1,0,0)).
jump(triangle(A,B,C,D,E,0,G,H,I,1,K,L,M,N,1),
    triangle(A,B,C,D,E,1,G,H,I,0,K,L,M,N,0)).

%
% Procedure to display a solution.
%

show_triangles([]) :- !.
show_triangles([
    triangle(A,
            B,C,
           D,E,F,
          G,H,I,J,
         K,L,M,N,P)|LaterTriangles]) :-
    sp(4),write(A),nl,
    sp(3),write(B),sp(1),write(C),nl,
    sp(2),write(D),sp(1),write(E),sp(1),write(F),nl,
    sp(1),write(G),sp(1),write(H),sp(1),write(I),sp(1),write(J),nl,
    write(K),sp(1),write(L),sp(1),write(M),sp(1),
        write(N),sp(1),write(P),nl,
    write('Press any key to continue. '),
    get0(_),
    nl,nl,
    show_triangles(LaterTriangles).

sp(0).
sp(N) :- write(' '),
        M is N - 1,
        sp(M).
```

8.5. COLORING A MAP

Assigning colors to the countries on a map so no two adjacent countries have the same color is easy in Prolog. We define a tail-recursive map coloring routine that takes a list of country-color pairs representing color assignments that have already been made as input and returns a list of color-country pairs that includes all the countries on the map. This routine checks first to see if any countries remain to be colored. If so, it assigns it a color that is not prohibited by previous color assignments, adds this new country-color pair to the list, and calls itself recursively. Otherwise, the current list of color assignments is complete.

```
color_map(List,Solution) :- remaining(Country,List),
                            color(Hue),
                            \+ prohibited(Country,Hue,List),
                            write(Country),
```

```
                              nl,
                              color_map([[Country,Hue]|List],Solution).
color_map(Solution,Solution).
```

We have added the **write** command so we can watch what the routine is doing as it searches for a solution.

Given the current list of countries and their assigned colors, we cannot assign a color to a new country if one of its neighbors is on the list and already has that color:

```
prohibited(Country,Hue,List)  :-  borders(Country,Neighbor),
                                  member([Neighbor,Hue],List).
```

It can be proven mathematically that we will never need more than four colors for any map. So we store four colors in clauses for the predicate **color/1**. We have selected the colors red, blue, green, and yellow.

The predicate **prohibited/3** calls the predicate **borders/2**. We list each pair of neighboring countries using the predicate **beside/2**. Then we use **beside** to define **borders**.

```
borders(Country,Neighbor)  :-  beside(Country,Neighbor).
borders(Country,Neighbor)  :-  beside(Neighbor,Country).
```

We call the main predicate **map**. Used as a query, this predicate calls **color_map** with an initially empty list of country-color pairs. When **color_map** returns a complete coloring scheme for the map, it is displayed using the **writeln/1** routine.

```
map :- color_map([],Solution),
       writeln(Solution).
```

Finally, we need a representation of the map itself. This is a series of clauses for the predicates **country** and **beside**. In the listing MAP.PL, we have included geographical data for South America.

Exercise 8.5.1

Develop a listing similar to SAMERICA.PL called AFRICA.PL that provides geographical data on Africa to be used with MAP.PL. Run MAP.PL with AFRICA.PL to see the results.

Exercise 8.5.2

Could you color a map of either South America or Africa using only three colors? Explain. How could you modify MAP.PL to get Prolog to answer this question for you?

Exercise 8.5.3

Consider a three-dimensional assembly without any spaces inside such a Chinese puzzle cube. It can be proven that the parts of such an assembly can be painted in four different colors so that no two parts that come into contact with each other are the same color. How would you modify **map/0** to color such an assembly? How would you represent the assembly for the purposes of your program?

8.5.1. Listing of MAP.PL

```
% MAP.PL
%   A program for coloring maps.


%
% map
%   Finds and displays an assignment of colors to the regions
%   on a map so no adjacent regions are the same color.
%


map :- color_map([],Solution), writeln(Solution).


%
% color_map(+Sofar,-Solution)
%   Searches for a legitimate assignment Solution of colors for
%   regions on a map that includes the partial assignment Sofar.
%


color_map(Sofar,Solution) :-
     country(Country),
     \+ member([Country,_],Sofar),
     color(Hue),
     \+ prohibited(Country,Hue,Sofar),
     write(Country),nl,
     color_map([[Country,Hue]|Sofar],Solution).
color_map(Solution,Solution).



%
% prohibited(+Country,-Hue,+Sofar)
%   Country cannot be colored Hue if any region adjacent to
%   Country is already assigned Hue in Sofar.
%


prohibited(Country,Hue,Sofar) :-
     borders(Country,Neighbor),
     member([Neighbor,Hue],Sofar).


%
% borders(+Country,-Neighbor)
%   Succeeds if Country and Neighbor share a border.
%


borders(Country,Neighbor) :- beside(Country,Neighbor).
borders(Country,Neighbor) :- beside(Neighbor,Country).

writeln([]).
writeln([X|Y]) :-
     write(X), nl,
```

```
    writeln(Y).
```

% Only four colors are ever needed

```
color(red).
color(blue).
color(green).
color(yellow).
```

```
member(X,[X|_]).
member(X,[_|Y]) :-
    member(X,Y).
```

8.5.2. Listing of SAMERICA.PL (Data for MAP.PL)

```
% SAMERICA.PL
%   Geographical data for South America to be used
%   with MAP.PL.
```

```
country(antilles).       country(argentina).
country(bolivia).        country(brazil).
country(colombia).       country(chile).
country(ecuador).        country(french_guiana).
country(guyana).         country(paraguay).
country(peru).           country(suriname).
country(uruguay).        country(venezuela).
```

```
beside(antilles,venezuela).     beside(argentina,bolivia).
beside(argentina,brazil).       beside(argentina,chile).
beside(argentina,paraguay).     beside(argentina,uruguay).
beside(bolivia,brazil).         beside(bolivia,chile).
beside(bolivia,paraguay).       beside(bolivia,peru).
beside(brazil,colombia).        beside(brazil,french_guiana).
beside(brazil,guyana).          beside(brazil,paraguay).
beside(brazil,peru).            beside(brazil,suriname).
beside(brazil,uruguay).         beside(brazil,venezuela).
beside(chile,peru).             beside(colombia,ecuador).
beside(colombia,peru).          beside(colombia,venezuela).
beside(ecuador,peru).           beside(french_guiana,suriname).
beside(guyana,suriname).        beside(guyana,venezuela).
```

8.6. EXAMINING MOLECULES

We can think of a molecular structure diagram as a graph, i.e., a set of connected points. A graph can be represented as a connectivity table that tells us which nodes in the graph are connected to each other. We can represent a connectivity table in Prolog as a set of facts using a single two-place predicate. A maze can also be thought of as a graph, and we used this technique to represent a maze earlier in this chapter.

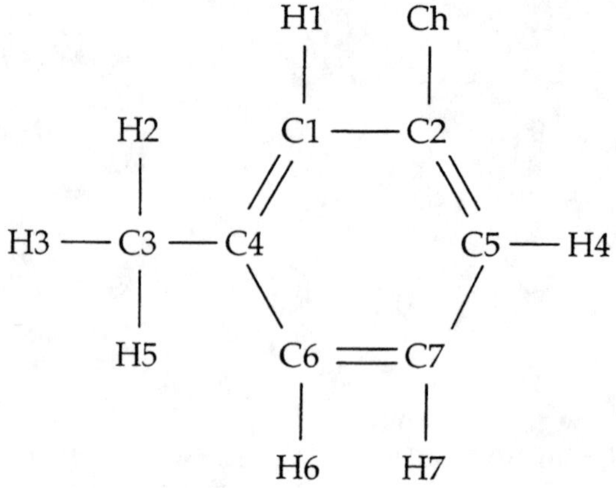

Figure 8.3   Molecular diagram for 3-chloro-toluene.

As we have seen, Prolog is a good tool for solving mazes. Solving a maze amounts to finding a subgraph within a graph. Prolog is just as good at finding other kinds of subgraphs as it is at solving mazes. Searching a molecule for particular substructures is a not very special case of finding subgraphs in a graph. Prolog is a very good tool for what we might call molecular query, illustrated in the program CHEM.PL.

Rather than use bare connectivity tables to represent the structure of a molecule, we will let the connectivity tables store other information about the molecule as well. In a molecular structure diagram, each node in the graph represents an atom of a particular element, so what we want is a *labeled* graph where each node is labeled by the name of an element. Consider the organic compound 3-chloro-toluene, which has the structure shown in Figure 8.3. The molecule contains seven carbon atoms and seven hydrogen atoms, plus a single chlorine atom. A single line in the structural diagram indicates that the two atoms are connected by a single bond (one shared electron); a double line indicates a double bond (two shared electrons). (We use Ch for the chlorine atom instead of the usual Cl because Cl is so easy to confuse with the carbon atom C1.) We represent this molecule by recording information about each atom in clauses for the predicate `atom_specs/3`:

```
% 3CTOLUEN.PL
%    A molecular structure example.

atom_specs(h1,hydrogen,[c1]).
atom_specs(h2,hydrogen,[c3]).
atom_specs(h3,hydrogen,[c3]).
atom_specs(h4,hydrogen,[c5]).
atom_specs(h5,hydrogen,[c3]).
atom_specs(h6,hydrogen,[c6]).
atom_specs(h7,hydrogen,[c7]).
```

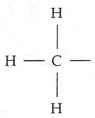

Figure 8.4   Structure of a methyl group.

```
atom_specs(c1,carbon,[c2,c4,h1]).
atom_specs(c2,carbon,[c1,c5,ch]).
atom_specs(c3,carbon,[c4,h2,h3,h5]).
atom_specs(c4,carbon,[c1,c3,c6]).
atom_specs(c5,carbon,[c2,c7,h4]).
atom_specs(c6,carbon,[c4,c7,h6]).
atom_specs(c7,carbon,[c5,c6,h7]).
atom_specs(ch,chlorine,[c2]).
```

The first argument for `atom_specs` is the name of an atom, the second is the element type for the atom, and the third is a list of other atoms to which the first atom is bonded (the connectivity information). Some information is represented in this list of clauses more than once. For example, we can infer from either

```
atom_specs(c1,carbon,[c2,c4,h1]).
```

or

```
atom_specs(c2,carbon,[c1,c5,ch]).
```

that the two carbon atoms C1 and C2 are bonded to each other. This repetition makes it easier to write routines that find substructures in the molecule. We do not explicitly record information about which of the chemical bonds in the molecule are single or double. With enough information about chemistry, Prolog should be able to deduce this.

We define predicates that tell us whether two atoms are bonded to each other and whether an atom is an atom of a certain element.

```
bonded(A1,A2) :- atom_specs(A1,_,Neighbors),
                 member(A2,Neighbors).
```

```
element(A1,Element) :- atom_specs(A1,Element,_).
```

Next we define some molecular structure query predicates. We begin with a very easy one. A methyl group is a substructure with one carbon atom and three hydrogen atoms arranged as in Figure 8.4. We identify a methyl group by looking for its single carbon atom since that is the only atom in the group that can combine with other parts of the molecule.

$$H \longrightarrow O \longrightarrow$$

Figure 8.5   Structure of a hydroxyl group.

```
methyl(C) :- element(C,carbon),
             bonded(C,H1), element(H1,hydrogen),
             bonded(C,H2), element(H2,hydrogen),
             H1 \== H2,
             bonded(C,H3), element(H3,hydrogen),
             H3 \== H1, H3 \== H2.
```

A more complicated structure is a six-membered ring of carbon atoms. We find these with the following procedure.

```
six_membered_carbon_ring([A1,A2,A3,A4,A5,A6]) :-
     element(A1,carbon), bonded(A1,A2),
     element(A2,carbon), bonded(A2,A3), A1 \== A3,
     element(A3,carbon), bonded(A3,A4),
          \+ member(A4,[A1,A2,A3]),
     element(A4,carbon), bonded(A4,A5),
          \+ member(A5,[A1,A2,A3,A4]),
     element(A5,carbon), bonded(A5,A6),
     element(A6,carbon), bonded(A6,A1),
          \+ member(A6,[A1,A2,A3,A4,A5]).
```

This is not a very efficient procedure, but it gives us correct answers and is easy to understand. There are several tests to make sure the ring does not loop back on itself. We might eliminate or simplify some of these tests if we incorporate more chemistry into our procedure. For example, if we know that three-membered carbon rings are impossible, we could simplify the procedure by leaving out tests for combinations that could only occur if the procedure found a three-membered carbon ring.

We might want to know if there is a methylated six-membered ring of carbon atoms within a molecule. To find these for us, the predicate `meth_carbon_ring/1` is defined using previously defined predicates.

```
meth_carbon_ring([C|Ring]) :- six_membered_carbon_ring(Ring),
                              member(A,Ring),
                              bonded(A,C),
                              methyl(C).
```

The predicates `methyl`, `six_membered_carbon_ring`, and `meth_carbon_ring` will all succeed when provided the atom specifications for 3-chloro-toluene. An example of a molecular query predicate that will fail for this molecule is the hydroxide predicate. A hydroxide group is a hydrogen atom and an oxygen atom bonded to each other as in Figure 8.5. We identify a hydroxide group by looking for its oxygen atom since this is the part of the structure that can bond to other parts of the molecule.

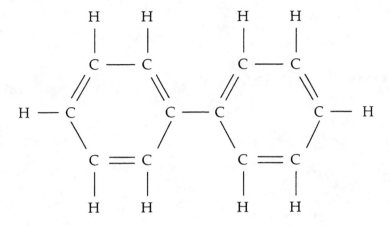

Figure 8.6 Structure of the diphenyl molecule.

```
hydroxide(O) :- element(O,oxygen),
                bonded(O,H),
                element(H,hydrogen).
```

Each substructure predicate we define can be used in definitions of other more complicated substructures. A library of molecular substructure predicates provides a powerful tool for reasoning about molecular structure and chemistry.

Exercise 8.6.1

The compound diphenyl has the structure shown in Figure 8.6. Number the atoms in the molecule and write a description of it in the **atom_specs** format. Do the following queries succeed for this molecule?

```
?- methyl(X).
?- six_membered_carbon_ring(X).
?- meth_carbon_ring(X).
?- hydroxide(X).
```

Exercise 8.6.2

A nitro group is an oxygen atom and a nitrogen atom in the arrangement shown in Figure 8.7. Notice that the bond between the oxygen atom and the nitrogen atom in a nitro group is a double bond. Write a procedure called **nitro** to find nitro groups in a molecule. Then write **atom_specs** for tri-nitro-toluene (TNT, Figure 8.8). Your **nitro** routine should find the three nitro groups in the tri-nitro-toluene molecule. Next, test your **nitro** routine on hydroxylamine (Figure 8.9). Since there is only a single bond between the oxygen atom and the nitrogen atom in this molecule, your nitro routine should fail.

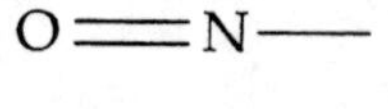

$$O = N—$$

Figure 8.7   Structure of the nitro group.

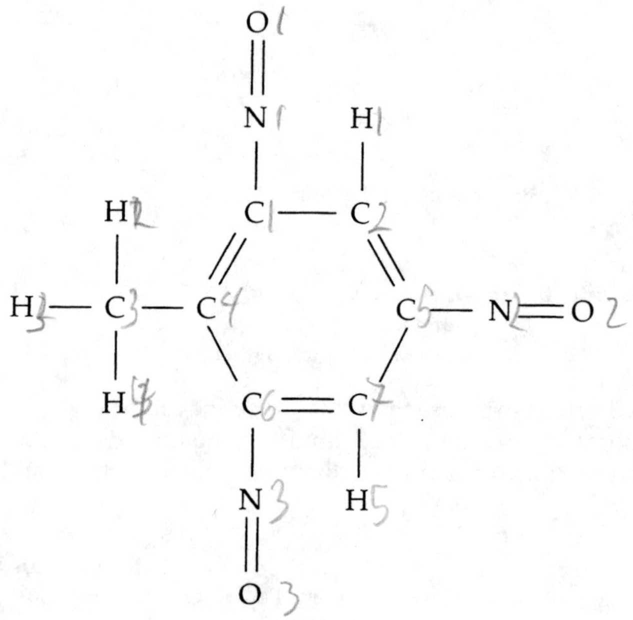

Figure 8.8   Structure of the tri-nitro-toluene molecule.

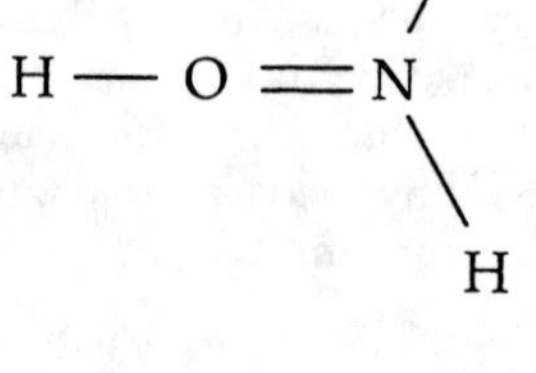

Figure 8.9   Structure of the hydroxylamine molecule.

8.6.1. Listing of CHEM.PL

```
% CHEM.PL
%   Molecular query predicates.

% Procedures to find bonds and identify elements.

bonded(A1,A2) :-
    atom_specs(A1,_,Neighbors),
    member(A2,Neighbors).

member(X,[X|_]).
member(X,[_|Y]) :- member(X,Y).

element(A1,Element) :- atom_specs(A1,Element,_).

% Procedures to identify molecular substructures.

methyl(C) :-
    element(C,carbon),
    bonded(C,H1), element(H1,hydrogen),
    bonded(C,H2), element(H2,hydrogen), H1 \== H2,
    bonded(C,H3), element(H3,hydrogen), H3 \== H1,
        H3 \== H2.

six_membered_carbon_ring([A1,A2,A3,A4,A5,A6]) :-
    element(A1,carbon), bonded(A1,A2),
    element(A2,carbon), bonded(A2,A3), A1 \== A3,
    element(A3,carbon), bonded(A3,A4),
        \+ member(A4,[A1,A2,A3]),
    element(A4,carbon), bonded(A4,A5),
        \+ member(A5,[A1,A2,A3,A4]),
    element(A5,carbon), bonded(A5,A6),
    element(A6,carbon), bonded(A6,A1),
        \+ member(A6,[A1,A2,A3,A4,A5]).

meth_carbon_ring([C|Ring]) :-
    six_membered_carbon_ring(Ring),
    member(A,Ring), bonded(A,C), methyl(C).

hydroxide(O) :- element(O,oxygen),
                    bonded(O,H),
                element(H,hydrogen).

%
% Demonstrations
%   A Prolog representation of a molecule such as the one in
%   3CTOLUEN.PL must be in memory before these demonstrations
%   are used.
%
```

```
demo1 :-      write('Searching for a methyl group...'), nl,
              methyl(X),
              write('Found one centered on atom: '),
              write(X), nl.
demo1 :-      write('No (more) methyl groups found.'), nl.

demo2 :-      write('Searching for a six-membered carbon ring...'),
              nl,
              six_membered_carbon_ring(List),
              write('Found one containing atoms: '),
              write(List), nl.
demo2 :-      write('No (more) six-membered carbon rings found.'),
              nl.
```

8.7. EXHAUSTIVE SEARCH, INTELLIGENT SEARCH, AND HEURISTICS

Exhaustive search can take longer than we would like to find a solution to a problem, especially when we place additional constraints on what counts as a solution. For example, consider a large, complex maze that has many different paths through it. Our goal is not simply to get through the maze, but to find a shortest, or at any rate a relatively short, path through the maze. This is a harder problem than just finding any path through the maze, and solving this problem is likely to take more computation and more time. With a very large maze, even finding a path may take more time than we would like.

Mazes are ordinarily thought of as amusements, but in fact we solve mazes every day. Anytime we try to move from one location to another through a piece of geography where our movement is constrained, we are solving a maze. This applies to driving to a restaurant for dinner, to planning a vacation trip, and to placing a long distance telephone call. Perhaps a friend will tell us how to get to the restaurant, the auto club will route our trip for us, and the telephone company directs our calls without any effort on our part. Somebody — or some computer — must solve these kinds of maze problems every day, and in every one of these cases, we are not willing to accept any path through the maze that gets us from point A to point B. We want the fastest, the most convenient, the most scenic, or the cheapest route we can find.

All this is leading up to a discussion of the difference between an *algorithm* and a *heuristic*. We will define these terms using a specific example. Suppose Acme Airlines serves ten cities in the United States: Atlanta, Boston, Chicago, Dallas, Denver, Los Angeles, Miami, New Orleans, Seattle, and Washington. Acme does not have direct flights between all the cities it serves. Figure 8.10 is a diagram showing the relative locations of the cities Acme serves. Where two cities are connected by a line in the diagram, Acme provides direct service between these two cities in both directions. The Acme diagram is a kind of maze, and the problem is to find flight plans, i.e., paths through the maze from any point to any other point. But we don't want just any flight plan. For example, the sequence Boston to Washington to Dallas to New Orleans to Miami to Atlanta to Denver to Los Angeles to Seattle to Chicago is not a reasonable route to take to get from Boston to Chicago (unless we are trying

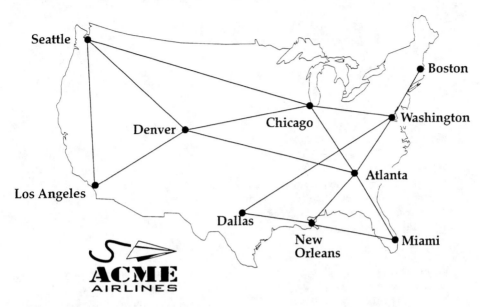

Figure 8.10   Acme Airlines flight map.

to maximize our frequent flyer miles!). If the best route is the shortest, then from the diagram it looks like the best route is Boston to Washington to Chicago.

Given our goal — finding the shortest flight plan between any two cities — there is a simple procedure that is guaranteed to give the right result. First, find *all* noncircuitous routes between the starting city and the destination. Second, compare the total distance traveled for each flight plan and pick a plan with a minimal total distance traveled. The problem with this procedure is that finding *one* path between two cities is relatively easy; finding *all* paths is daunting.

Suppose we had another procedure that searched our maze in some intelligent fashion. This procedure only finds one path, but it finds it fairly quickly and the path it finds is usually pretty short. Suppose the procedure usually takes about 10% as much time as the exhaustive search procedure we described in the last paragraph, and suppose the path it finds is usually no more than about 10% longer than the path found using exhaustive search. If we have to find new flight plans frequently, this second procedure sounds like a pretty good deal.

So we have two procedures, which we will call the exhaustive search procedure and the intelligent search procedure. Our original goal was to find a shortest flight path between any two cities that Acme Airlines serves. The exhaustive search procedure is guaranteed to satisfy this goal. Thus, it represents an *algorithmic* solution to the problem. The intelligent search procedure, on the other hand, is not *guaranteed* to find a shortest path although it usually finds a path of reasonable length. A procedure that usually produces an acceptable solution to a problem, although it is not guaranteed to find a maximal solution in every case, provides a *heuristic* solution to the problem. In fact, a heuristic procedure for solving a problem may sometimes fail to find any solution at all.

```
% ACME.PL
%
% Travel data for Acme Airlines.
%    The first two arguments in each clause list a pair of cities
%    served by Acme, the third argument gives the distance between
%    these cities, and the fourth tells whether Acme has direct
%    flights between these cities.
%
```

```
data(atlanta,boston,1108,n).          data(chicago,washington,696,y).
data(atlanta,chicago,715,y).          data(dallas,denver,797,n).
data(atlanta,dallas,808,n).           data(dallas,los_angeles,1431,n).
data(atlanta,denver,1519,y).          data(dallas,miami,1394,n).
data(atlanta,los_angeles,2091,n).     data(dallas,new_orleans,495,y).
data(atlanta,miami,862,y).            data(dallas,seattle,2222,n).
data(atlanta,new_orleans,480,y).      data(dallas,washington,1414,y).
data(atlanta,seattle,2954,n).         data(denver,los_angeles,1189,y).
data(atlanta,washington,618,y).       data(denver,miami,2126,n).
data(boston,chicago,976,n).           data(denver,new_orleans,1292,n).
data(boston,dallas,1868,n).           data(denver,seattle,1326,y).
data(boston,denver,2008,n).           data(denver,washington,1707,n).
data(boston,los_angeles,3017,n).      data(los_angeles,miami,2885,n).
data(boston,miami,1547,n).            data(los_angeles,new_orleans,1947,n).
data(boston,new_orleans,1507,n).      data(los_angeles,seattle,1193,y).
data(boston,seattle,3163,n).          data(los_angeles,washington,2754,n).
data(boston,washington,448,y).        data(miami,new_orleans,881,y).
data(chicago,dallas,936,n).           data(miami,seattle,3469,n).
data(chicago,denver,1017,y).          data(miami,washington,1096,n).
data(chicago,los_angeles,2189,n).     data(new_orleans,seattle,2731,n).
data(chicago,miami,1340,n).           data(new_orleans,washington,1099,n).
data(chicago,new_orleans,938,n).      data(seattle,washington,2880,n).
data(chicago,seattle,2184,y).
```

Figure 8.11 Listing of ACME.PL

There is some confusion in the way the term "algorithm" is used when talking about computer programs. In one sense, every syntactically correct program or procedure may be called an algorithm. Such a program should execute until it halts, reaches some error condition, or exhausts some computational resource. In fact, you may run across the phrase "heuristic algorithm" in the literature. This is not the sense in which we are using the term "algorithm," and we will always contrast the term "algorithm" with the term "heuristic." As we are using these terms, the same procedure may be called either an algorithm or a heuristic depending on the goal we are trying to reach when we use the procedure. If the procedure is guaranteed to solve the problem, then it is an algorithm relative to that problem. If the procedure is not guaranteed to solve the problem but usually produces an acceptable approximation of a solution, then it is a heuristic relative to that problem. A procedure could be an algorithm relative to one goal and a heuristic relative to another, but the way we are using these terms, the same procedure could not be both an algorithm and a heuristic relative to the same goal.

Getting back to our airline example, let's get some more information about the cities Acme serves. In the listing ACME.PL (Figure 8.11), we use the four-place predicate **data** to record this information. The first two arguments of a **data** clause represent two cities Acme serves, the third argument gives the distance between these two cities, and the fourth argument tells us whether Acme has direct flights between these two cities. Please note that the distances given are taken from road atlases and represent driving distances rather than distances by air. It is not important for our example that these distances be precise. This is all the information we will need to develop our exhaustive search and intelligent search procedures for finding flight plans for Acme Airlines.

We begin by defining a procedure that will find a path from our starting city to our destination without regard for total distance, but we will compute the total distance as part of the path. The predicate **plan** will take three arguments: the starting city, the destination, and the path.

```
plan(Start,Goal,Plan) :- planner(Goal,[0,Start],Path),
                         reverse(Path,[],Plan).
```

A path from one city to another will be a list whose first member is the total length of the path. The remaining members of the list will be a sequence of cities such that adjacent members of the list are connected by Acme flights. The initial list contains only 0 (since our initial path is a single city and has no length) and the name of the starting city. The auxiliary procedure **planner** looks for a city that can be reached from the starting city, adds it and the distance to it to the path, and recurses until it finally reaches the destination. **planner** constructs the path in reverse order and **plan** then reverses it to put it into the proper order.

```
planner(Goal,[Miles,Goal|Cities],[Miles,Goal|Cities]) :- !.
planner(Goal,[OldMiles,Current|Cities],Path) :-
        connected(Current,Next,MoreMiles),
        \+ member(Next,Cities),
        NewMiles is OldMiles + MoreMiles,
        planner(Goal,[NewMiles,Next,Current|Cities],Path).
```

```
connected(City1,City2,Miles)  :- data(City1,City2,Miles,y).
connected(City1,City2,Miles)  :- data(City2,City1,Miles,y).
```

We put a cut in the first clause for `planner` to prevent the procedure from trying to extend the path beyond the destination upon backtracking. This will be important later when we use `planner` in conjunction with `findall`. Notice that the only constraint on `planner` is that the same city can't be visited twice. But `planner`, and therefore `plan`, might come up with the kind of path we considered earlier: one where we visit every city Acme serves before arriving at our destination. The first path `plan` finds is a function only of the order in which we list our travel data.

We will use `planner` in defining an algorithm for finding a shortest path between any two cities.

```
best_plan(Start,Goal,[Min|Plan])  :-
      setof(Path,planner(Goal,[0,Start],Path),[[Min|Best]|_]),
      reverse(Best,[],Plan).
```

In the definition of `best_plan/3`, the call to `setof` uses `planner` to construct a list of all possible paths between the starting city and the destination. `setof` sorts these paths using their first element, which is their length. The first (shortest) member of the list of paths is pulled out and reversed to produce a shortest flight plan.

Our heuristic approach constructs a single path but uses information about the distances between cities to guide path construction. The top-level predicate, `good_plan`, looks very much like `plan` except that it calls the auxiliary predicate `smart_planner` instead of `planner`.

```
good_plan(Start,Goal,[Miles|Plan])  :-
      smart_planner(Goal,[0,Start],[Miles|Good]),
      reverse(Good,[],Plan).


smart_planner(Goal,[Miles,Goal|Cities],[Miles,Goal|Cities]).
smart_planner(Goal,[OldMiles,Current|Cities],Plan)  :-
      setof(option(Miles,City),
            X^(connected(Current,City,X),
               distance(City,Goal,Miles)),
            List),
      member(option(Min,Next),List),
      connected(Current,Next,MoreMiles),
      \+ member(Next,Cities),
      NewMiles is OldMiles + MoreMiles,
      smart_planner(Goal,[NewMiles,Next,Current|Cities],Plan).


distance(City,City,0).
distance(City1,City2,Miles)  :- data(City1,City2,Miles,_).
distance(City1,City2,Miles)  :- data(City2,City1,Miles,_).
```

The first clauses for `smart_planner` and `planner` are identical except that we don't need a cut for `smart_planner` because we never intend to backtrack into it. Both procedures stop when the goal city has been added to the path. But at each step in the construction, `smart_planner` is much pickier about the next city to be added to the path. The first thing `smart_planner` does at each step is to use `connected` in a call to `findall` to generate a list of cities that can be reached from the last city added to the path. Then `distance` is used in a call to `setof` to generate a sorted list of the distances from these cities to the *destination* `smart_planner` is trying to reach. The first member of this list is then used to pick the next city to place in the path. In this way, `smart_planner` always picks the next city that can be reached that is closest to the destination. If `smart_planner` goes down a blind alley and reaches a city from which no city can be reached that is not already in the path, it backtracks to a point where it can pick a city that is next-closest to the destination. Because `smart_planner` can backtrack, it will always find a path from any city in the network to any other, but because it isn't guaranteed to find a shortest path, `smart_planner` is a heuristic rather than an algorithm relative to the goal of finding a shortest path.

If we replaced the two clauses

```
setof(option(Miles,City),
        X^(connected(Current,City,X),
           distance(City,Goal,Miles)),
        List),
member(option(Min,Next),List),
```

in the second clause for the predicate `smart_planner` with the single clause

```
setof(option(Miles,City),
        X^(connected(Current,City,X),
           distance(City,Goal,Miles)),
        [option(Min,Next)|_]),
```

then `smart_planner` would be unable to backtrack from dead ends and in some cases it might not be able to find an existing path between two cities at all. This modification of `smart_planner` is an example of the *hill-climbing* heuristic. This heuristic gets its name from the search problem with which it is commonly associated: finding the highest point in a piece of terrain. The strategy is always to go uphill. The problem, of course, is that you could find yourself at the top of a hill that is not the highest hill in the region. Since you wouldn't be able to go directly to a higher point from that location, you would be stuck. This is sometimes called the problem of *local maxima* (or the *local minima* for tasks like minimizing the energy of a system). Seeking the global maximum, your search strategy has stranded you at a local maximum. In our example, higher points are cities closer to the destination, and the destination is the highest point (the global maximum). If you reach a city from which you cannot go to a city nearer your destination, you have reached a local maximum.

But `smart_planner` can retreat from local maxima and explore other paths. Still, it always moves to the *highest* untried location (the city next nearest the destination). This strategy is called *best-first* search. Each time `setof` is called, a stack of possible next cities is generated and ordered by a criterion of goodness (in this case, nearness to the destination). Then each option in the stack is tried *best first*.

From the ten cities served by Acme Airlines, we can choose 90 different combinations of starting cities and destination cities. `good_plan` finds the *shortest* path for 73 of these 90 pairs. In the worst case, `good_plan` finds a plan from Washington to Denver that is 2.28 times as long as the shortest plan. For all pairs of cities, the plan found by `good_plan` is on average 1.11 times as long as the shortest plan. For just the 17 pairs where `good_plan` does not produce the shortest path, the path it produces is on average 1.56 times as long as the shortest path.

For starting and destination cities connected by direct flights, `best_plan` invariably takes less time to compute a flight plan than `good_plan`. The reason for this is obvious: `smart_planner` always takes time to look at the distance from a candidate next city to the destination even when they are one and the same. As is typical of a heuristic, it is less efficient in the easiest cases. We could eliminate this advantage by making the following clause the first clause in the definition of `good_plan`:

```
good_plan(Start,Goal,[Miles,Start,Goal]) :-
        connected(Start,Goal,Miles).
```

Of course, we could add a similar clause to `best_plan`; then the two procedures would perform with equal speed on these cases. By adding these clauses, we increase the amount of time each procedure will require for other cases by a constant amount. Since either routine will find a flight plan quickly in these easiest cases, we shouldn't be too concerned about improving their performance here.

`good_plan` doesn't always give us a shortest plan, but it is supposed to find a good plan *faster* than `best_plan`. How efficient is `good_plan` relative to `best_plan`? We compared the time it took for `good_plan` to find paths between all 90 city pairs with the time `best_plan` took for the same task. `good_plan` took only 1.70 seconds while `best_plan` took 11.64 seconds. So `best_plan` took 6.8 times as long as `good_plan`. Of course, these timing figures will vary depending on your hardware and the Prolog implementation you use. But you should expect `good_plan` to be at least five times as fast as `best_plan` on average.

These figures give a clear example of the kind of trade-off we get when comparing algorithmic and heuristic approaches to the same problem. With an algorithm, we are guaranteed a best solution. The solutions we get with a heuristic may not always be maximal, but with a good heuristic we usually get quite good solutions much faster than we do with the algorithm. Of course, if no algorithm is known for a problem we have no choice but to rely on a heuristic.

Exercise 8.7.1

In the text, we describe a circuitous route from Boston to Chicago, one that stops at every city Acme serves. Arrange the Acme travel data so `plan` initially finds this route. Does the order of the clauses for `data` affect the flight plans that `best_plan` and `good_plan` find? Why or why not?

Exercise 8.7.2

Shortest total distance traveled is not the only consideration in making airline reservations. What other criteria might we use for comparing alternative flight paths? Pick one of these and modify `best_plan` and `good_plan` to search for best and good flight plans using this alternative criterion.

Exercise 8.7.3

> Define a predicate discrepancies of one argument that returns a list of all pairs of
> starting and destination cities such that best_plan and good_plan find different flight
> plans for these pairs. Of course, you may define whatever auxiliaries for discrepancies
> you require. Confirm our results that best_plan and good_plan produce the same flight
> plan in all but 17 of the 90 possible cases for Acme Airline.

Exercise 8.7.4

> Acme Airlines has just announced flights between Atlanta and San Francisco. Add the
> following clauses to ACME.PL:
>
> ```
> data(atlanta,san_francisco,2554,y).
> data(boston,san_francisco,3163,n).
> data(chicago,san_francisco,2233,n).
> data(dallas,san_francisco,1791,n).
> data(denver,san_francisco,1267,n).
> data(los_angeles,san_francisco,377,n).
> data(miami,san_francisco,3238,n).
> data(new_orleans,san_francisco,2300,n).
> data(san_francisco,seattle,786,n).
> data(san_francisco,washington,2897,n).
> ```
>
> Compare some flight plans between San Francisco and some other cities Acme serves
> generated by good_plan and best_plan. Describe and explain what you observe.

Exercise 8.7.5   (project)

> Here is an informal description of another algorithm for finding the shortest flight plan
> for any two cities. Generate an initial plan. Then begin generation of another plan. As
> you generate the second plan, check at each step to make sure that it is not longer than
> the plan you already have. If it is, backtrack and try again. If you generate a shorter
> plan, replace your original plan with the new, shorter plan and keep going. Stop when
> you have tried every plan. The plan you have at the end of this process will be a shortest
> plan. Define a predicate smartest_plan that implements this algorithm. Compare its
> efficiency with that of best_plan.

8.7.1. Listing of FLIGHT.PL

```
% FLIGHT.PL
% System for finding flight connections or flight plans.

%
% plan(+Start,+Goal,-Plan)
%    An algorithm for finding a flight plan linking the two cities
%    Start and Goal. The algorithm does not take total distance
%    traveled into account.
%


plan(Start,Goal,Plan) :- planner(Goal,[0,Start],Path),
                         reverse(Path,[],Plan).

%
```

```
% planner(+Goal,+PartialPlan,-CompletePlan)
%    Takes a partial flight plan and completes it all the way
%    to the destination city without regard to distances traveled.
%

planner(Goal,[Miles,Goal|Cities],[Miles,Goal|Cities]) :- !.
planner(Goal,[OldMiles,Current|Cities],Path) :-
        connected(Current,Next,MoreMiles),
        \+ member(Next,Cities),
        NewMiles is OldMiles + MoreMiles,
        planner(Goal,[NewMiles,Next,Current|Cities],Path).


%
% best_plan(+Start,+Goal,-Plan)
%    An algorithm for finding the shortest flight plan
%    linking two cities.
%

best_plan(Start,Goal,[Min|Plan]) :-
        findall(Path,planner(Goal,[0,Start],Path),PathList),
        setof(Miles,member([Miles|_],PathList),[Min|_]),
        member([Min|Best],PathList),
        reverse(Best,[],Plan).


%
% good_plan(+Start,+Goal,-Plan)
%    A heuristic for quickly finding a flight plan of
%    reasonable length linking two cities.
%

good_plan(Start,Goal,[Miles|Plan]) :-
        smart_planner(Goal,[0,Start],[Miles|Good]),
        reverse(Good,[],Plan).


%
% smart_planner(+Goal,+PartialPlan,-CompletePlan)
%    Takes a partial flight plan and completes it all the way
%    to the destination city, giving priority at each step to
%    those cities that can be reached from the current city
%    that are nearest the destination city.
%

smart_planner(Goal,[Miles,Goal|Cities],[Miles,Goal|Cities]).
smart_planner(Goal,[OldMiles,Current|Cities],Plan) :-
        findall(City,connected(City,Current,_),CityList),
        setof(Miles,distance(Goal,CityList,Miles),MilesList),
        member(Min,MilesList),
        distance(Next,[Goal],Min),
        connected(Current,Next,MoreMiles),
        \+ member(Next,Cities),
        NewMiles is OldMiles + MoreMiles,
```

```
            smart_planner(Goal,[NewMiles,Next,Current|Cities],Plan).

%
% Predicates for interpreting information about the travel data.
%

connected(City1,City2,Miles)  :- data(City1,City2,Miles,y).
connected(City1,City2,Miles)  :- data(City2,City1,Miles,y).

distance(City,[City|_],0).
distance(City1,[City2|_],Miles)  :- data(City1,City2,Miles,_).
distance(City1,[City2|_],Miles)  :- data(City2,City1,Miles,_).
distance(City1,[_|RestOfCities],Miles)  :- distance(City1,RestOfCities,Miles).

member(X,[X|_]).
member(X,[_|Y])  :- member(X,Y).

reverse([],List,List).
reverse([X|Tail],SoFar,List)  :-
        reverse(Tail,[X|SoFar],List).
```

8.8. SCHEDULING

In the last section, we ignored the rather crucial fact that Acme Airlines flights were scheduled for particular times. We acted as if the next flight we needed was available as soon as we stepped off the flight before it. This may not be the case. Suppose, for example, that there are flights every hour between Miami and Atlanta and between Atlanta and New Orleans, but there are only weekend flights from Miami to New Orleans. Then if today is Monday, we are in Miami, and we have to get to New Orleans today, we will go through Atlanta. It is no help at all that there is a direct flight available on Saturday.

Of course, we expect Acme Airlines to schedule its flights so we can make connections easily and fly whenever and wherever we need. Acme, on the other hand, wants to make sure that it is not flying empty airplanes around the country. The problem of developing flight schedules for airlines is overwhelming, requiring enormous computational resources. Even relatively simple scheduling problems can be demanding. In this section we will look at a simple scheduling problem and at how Prolog can be used to solve it.

The example we will use is fairly typical. Suppose we need to schedule workers for a small departmental library at a university. The library is only open from 8:00 A.M. until noon and from 1:00 P.M. until 5:00 P.M. Mondays through Fridays. We begin by dividing the work week into ten shifts, a morning shift and an afternoon shift each day. On each shift, we need two workers to shelve books and one worker to operate the checkout desk. We need an additional worker every morning shift to catalog items that arrive in the morning mail. So we have a total of 35 slots to fill where each kind of slot is represented by a shift and a job type. We will represent the seven Monday slots with the following clauses:

```
slots(mon,am,cataloger,1).
slots(mon,am,deskclerk,1).
slots(mon,pm,deskclerk,1).
slots(mon,am,shelver,2).
slots(mon,pm,shelver,2).
```

Besides this information, we also need to know what workers are available, when they can work, and what kinds of jobs they can do. We will record information about workers in clauses of a five-place predicate personnel where the first argument is the worker's name, the second is the minimum number of shifts the worker wants to work each week, the third is the maximum number of shifts the worker wants to work each week, the fourth is the maximum number of shifts the worker is willing to work in a single day, and the fifth is a list of days that the worker is available. (To simplify our task, we will assume that if a worker is willing to work at all on a particular day of the week, then he or she is willing to work either shift.) We will use a binary predicate job to record which workers are qualified for each job. Our three workers are Alice, Bob, Carol, Don, Ellen, and Fred. Here is the information for them:

```
personnel(alice,6,8,2,[mon,tue,thu,fri]).
personnel(bob,7,10,2,[mon,tue,wed,thu,fri]).
personnel(carol,3,5,1,[mon,tue,wed,thu,fri]).
personnel(don,6,8,2,[mon,tue,wed]).
personnel(ellen,0,2,1,[thu,fri]).
personnel(fred,7,10,2,[mon,tue,wed,thu,fri]).

job(cataloger,[alice,fred]).
job(deskclerk,[bob,carol,fred]).
job(shelver,[alice,bob,carol,don,ellen,fred]).
```

A weekly schedule will be a list of assignments of workers to all the slots for the week. The list will be constructed recursively in much the same way that solutions to puzzles and problems we have looked at earlier in this chapter have been constructed. At each step, we look for a worker who satisfies the requirements for some empty slot and assign him or her to that slot. If no one is available for a slot, we back up and try different combinations in our earlier assignments until someone becomes available. When the schedule is complete, we display it.

The top-level predicate in our program, schedule, is defined as follows:

```
schedule :-
        findall(slots(Day,Time,Job,Number),
                slots(Day,Time,Job,Number),Slots),
        schedule_aux(Slots,[],Schedule),
        write_report(Schedule).
```

schedule first calls findall to generate a list of the slots that need to be filled. These are then passed to the recursive procedure schedule_aux which actually generates the schedule.

The definition for schedule_aux is also relatively simple.

```
schedule_aux([],Schedule,Schedule).
schedule_aux([slots(_,_,_,0)|RestOfSlots],Partial,Schedule) :-
        schedule_aux(RestOfSlots,Partial,Schedule).
schedule_aux([slots(Day,Time,Job,Number)|RestOfSlots],Partial,Schedule) :-
        Number > 0,
        available(Day,Time,Job,Person,Partial),
        write('Trying: '),
        report(Day,Time,Job,Person),
        NewNumber is Number - 1,
        schedule_aux([slots(Day,Time,Job,NewNumber)|RestOfSlots],
                [sched(Day,Time,Job,Person)|Partial],Schedule).

report(Day,Time,Job,Person) :- write(Day),write(' '),
                               write(Time),write(' '),
                               write(Job),write(' '),
                               write(Person),nl.
```

As we would expect, the schedule is complete when the list of slots remaining to be filled is empty. This is what the first clause does. The second clause handles the case where we have filled all the slots of a particular kind. The third clause checks to be sure that there are slots of the kind under consideration to be filled, finds someone to assign to one of these slots, reduces the number of this kind of slot to be filled, and recurses. We have added two lines in the middle to give the user something to watch as the program runs. We will make further use of the procedure `report` in defining `write_report` later.

The predicate `available` defines when a worker fills the requirements for a particular assignment. First, the worker must be competent to perform the job. Second, the worker cannot already have an assignment for the time slot. Third, the worker must be available on the appropriate day. Fourth, the worker must not have already been assigned the maximum number of shifts that he or she is willing to work that day. Finally, we must take into account the number of shifts the worker has worked during the week. We begin with a clause that defines a worker as available if he or she has not yet been assigned to the minimum number of shifts desired for the week.

```
available(Day,Time,Job,Person,Partial) :-
        job(Job,JobList),
        member(Person,JobList),
        \+ member(sched(Day,Time,_,Person),Partial),
        personnel(Person,MinWeekly,_,Daily,Days),
        member(Day,Days),
        findall(T,member(sched(Day,T,J,Person),Partial),DList),
        length(DList,D),
        D < Daily,
        findall(T,member(sched(D,T,J,Person),Partial),WList),
        length(WList,W),
        W < MinWeekly.
```

If the first clause fails, meaning all workers who are otherwise suitable have already been assigned the minimum number of shifts they want, then we loosen the requirements in the second clause and consider all workers who have not yet been assigned the maximum number of shifts they can work in a week.

```
available(Day,Time,Job,Person,Partial) :-
        job(Job,JobList),
        member(Person,JobList),
        \+ member(sched(Day,Time,_,Person),Partial),
        personnel(Person,_,MaxWeekly,Daily,Days),
        member(Day,Days),
        findall(T,member(sched(Day,T,J,Person),Partial),DList),
        length(DList,D),
        D < Daily,
        findall(T,member(sched(D,T,J,Person),Partial),WList),
        length(WList,W),
        W < MaxWeekly.
```

The remainder of the program consists of routines for reporting the schedule once it is found. These display information about the schedule on the screen, but they could easily be modified to send the output to a file or to a printer. We put a cut at the end of **write_report** so the user can force backtracking to **schedule_aux** without backing into the middle of **write_report**.

The program is a *heuristic* for the assigned scheduling task since it is not guaranteed to satisfy all our intended constraints on a schedule. In fact, if you run the program you will find that it does not assign every worker the minimal number of shifts specified. Furthermore, if the list of clauses for the predicate **slots** is reordered, the program may take a very long time to find a schedule at all. We have taken advantage of another informal heuristic in ordering these clauses, putting the job types for which the fewest workers are qualified at the top of the list for each day. If this had not produced schedules fairly quickly, we could have gone a step further and placed all the clauses for these "bottleneck" jobs first without regard to the days of the week. Assigning workers their minimal numbers of shifts is a more difficult problem.

One way to handle a requirement like assigning each worker at least the minimal number of shifts indicated is by introducing a global constraint that a complete schedule must satisfy.

```
schedule :-
        findall(slots(Day,Time,Job,Number),
                slots(Day,Time,Job,Number),Slots),
        schedule_aux(Slots,[],Schedule),
        \+ violate_global_constraint(Schedule),
        write_report(Schedule).

violate_global_constraint(Schedule) :-
        personnel(Person,MinWeekly,_,_,_),
        findall(T,member(sched(D,T,J,Person),Schedule),List),
```

```
        length(List,L),
        L < MinWeekly.
```

The resulting program is an algorithm: If there exists a schedule that satisfies all our requirements, this program is guaranteed to find it. However, it is not a very efficient algorithm. The very first assignment made could render a schedule impossible. This algorithm will try all possible combinations of later assignments before it will backtrack far enough to revise that original assignment.

It is surprisingly difficult to find an algorithm, even for this relatively simple scheduling problem, that is significantly more efficient or to find a heuristic that routinely produces better schedules than the program we have looked at here. One thing that makes this so surprising is that we can look at the schedule produced by our program and see fairly quickly how to modify it to produce a schedule where every worker gets the minimum number of shifts. This suggests a third approach: use `schedule_aux` to generate an initial schedule and develop another program that corrects the faults in this schedule to produce a final schedule.

```
schedule :-
        findall(slots(Day,Time,Job,Number),
                slots(Day,Time,Job,Number),Slots),
        schedule_aux(Slots,[],IntermediateSchedule),
        improve_schedule(IntermediateSchedule,Schedule),
        write_report(Schedule).
```

Given a nearly-correct schedule, how can we define an improvement on it? This would be a schedule where a shift assigned in the original schedule to a worker who has more than the minimum number of shifts is reassigned to a worker who does not have the minimum number of shifts.

```
improve_schedule(Schedule,Schedule) :-
        \+ needs_shifts(_,Schedule).
improve_schedule(Current,Schedule) :-
        needs_shifts(Person1,Current),
        has_extra_shift(Person2,Current),
        personnel(Person1,_,_,Daily,Days),
        member(sched(Day,Time,Job,Person2),Current),
        member(Day,Days),
        \+ member(sched(Day,Time,_,Person1),Current),
        job(Job,JobList),
        member(Person1,Joblist),
        findall(T,member(sched(Day,T,J,Person1),Current),DList),
        length(DList,D),
        D < Daily,
        !,
        write('Rescheduling: '),
        report(Day,Time,Job,Person2),
        remove(sched(Day,Time,Job,Person2),Current,Partial),
        improve_schedule([sched(Day,Time,Job,Person1)|Partial],Schedule).
```

```
improve_schedule(Schedule,Schedule).

needs_shift(Person,Schedule) :-
        personnel(Person,MinWeekly,_,_,_),
        findall(T,member(sched(D,T,J,Person),Schedule),Shifts),
        length(Shifts,S),
        S < MinWeekly.

has_extra_shift(Person,Schedule) :-
        personnel(Person,MinWeekly,_,_,_),
        findall(T,member(sched(D,T,J,Person),Schedule),Shifts),
        length(Shifts,S),
        S > MinWeekly.

remove(X,[X|Y],Y) :- !.
remove(X,[Y|Z],[Y|W]) :- remove(X,Z,W).
```

The first clause for improve_schedule defines a schedule as improved if every worker already has at least his or her minimum number of shifts. The second clause defines a schedule as improved if a shift is reassigned from a worker with extra shifts to one who does not yet have his or her minimum number of shifts. This clause is recursive, and the program will continue to improve a schedule until it cannot find an acceptable reassignment. If this happens when there are still workers without their minimum numbers of shifts, then the first two clauses will fail and the third clause returns whatever schedule has been produced. After the report has been presented, the user can force failure and the program will backtrack and produce revisions of the original schedule.

Even with improve_schedule added, our scheduling program is a heuristic and not an algorithm for finding schedules. Suppose, for example, that we have three workers available for a particular job: George who can work any day, Henrietta who can only work on Monday, Wednesday, or Friday, and Inez who can only work on Tuesday or Thursday. schedule_aux might produce a schedule where George is scheduled for exactly his minimum number of shifts, Henrietta has extra shifts, and Inez has not been assigned her minimum number of shifts. Since George has no extra shifts, and since Henrietta and Inez don't work on the same days, there is no way for improve_schedule to make a change.

A scheduling problem involves assigning resources under a set of constraints. Since all kinds of constraints are possible, it is impossible to design a general scheduling program that fits every situation. We have seen that applying global constraints to completed schedules, thus forcing backtracking when these constraints are violated, will produce a scheduling algorithm. Such an algorithm is usually inefficient. A better strategy is to look for ways to design an intelligent search mechanism that takes constraints into account at each step of schedule construction. In our example, the predicate available and particularly the first clause of the predicate available does this. Even using this approach, we may be unable to produce perfect schedules in reasonable time, and we may be forced to accept a heuristic that generates schedules that usually come close to satisfying all of our constraints. We have seen how a second heuristic that takes a global view of a schedule produced by the first heuristic may produce improvements on a schedule faster than backtracking into the original heuristic. Arranging the data available to a scheduler so that it solves more difficult scheduling problems early while the schedule is still relatively fluid is another strategy that we used when we placed `slots` clauses for jobs that fewer workers can perform ahead of clauses for jobs that many workers can perform. This might be automated by writing programs that analyze the data before the scheduler is run and rearrange it to make the scheduler's job easier.

8.8.1. Listing of SCHEDULE.PL

```
% SCHEDULE.PL
% An example of a scheduling program.

schedule :-
        findall(slots(Day,Time,Job,Number),
                slots(Day,Time,Job,Number),Slots),
        schedule_aux(Slots,[],IntermediateSchedule),
        improve_schedule(IntermediateSchedule,Schedule),
        write_report(Schedule).

%
% Procedure to extend a partial schedule until it is complete.
%

schedule_aux([],Schedule,Schedule).
schedule_aux([slots(_,_,_,0)|RestOfSlots],Partial,Schedule) :-
        schedule_aux(RestOfSlots,Partial,Schedule).
schedule_aux([slots(Day,Time,Job,Number)|RestOfSlots],
                Partial,Schedule) :-
        Number > 0,
        available(Day,Time,Job,Person,Partial),
        write('Trying: '),
        report(Day,Time,Job,Person),
        NewNumber is Number - 1,
        schedule_aux([slots(Day,Time,Job,NewNumber)|RestOfSlots],
                [sched(Day,Time,Job,Person)|Partial],Schedule).

%
% available(+Day,+Time,+Job,-Person,+Partial)
%    finds a Person whom the Partial schedule leaves available
%    to perform Job at Time on Day.
%

available(Day,Time,Job,Person,Partial) :-
        job(Job,JobList),
        member(Person,JobList),
        \+ member(sched(Day,Time,_,Person),Partial),
        personnel(Person,MinWeekly,_,Daily,Days),
        member(Day,Days),
```

```
        findall(T,member(sched(Day,T,J,Person),Partial),DList),
        length(DList,D),
        D < Daily,
        findall(T,member(sched(D,T,J,Person),Partial),WList),
        length(WList,W),
        W < MinWeekly.

available(Day,Time,Job,Person,Partial) :-
        job(Job,JobList),
        member(Person,JobList),
        \+ member(sched(Day,Time,_,Person),Partial),
        personnel(Person,_,MaxWeekly,Daily,Days),
        member(Day,Days),
        findall(T,member(sched(Day,T,J,Person),Partial),DList),
        length(DList,D),
        D < Daily,
        findall(T,member(sched(D,T,J,Person),Partial),WList),
        length(WList,W),
        W < MaxWeekly.

%
% improve(+Current,-Better)
%    replaces the Current schedule with a Better schedule
%    by reassigning job slots occupied by persons with extra
%    shifts to persons who need additional shifts.
%

improve_schedule(Schedule,Schedule) :-
        \+ needs_shifts(_,Schedule).
improve_schedule(Current,Schedule) :-
        needs_shifts(Person1,Current),
        has_extra_shift(Person2,Current),
        personnel(Person1,_,_,Daily,Days),
        member(sched(Day,Time,Job,Person2),Current),
        member(Day,Days),
        \+ member(sched(Day,Time,_,Person1),Current),
        job(Job,JobList),
        member(Person1,JobList),
        findall(T,member(sched(Day,T,J,Person1),Current),DList),
        length(DList,D),
        D < Daily,
        !,
        write('Rescheduling: '),
        report(Day,Time,Job,Person2),
        remove(sched(Day,Time,Job,Person2),Current,Partial),
        improve_schedule([sched(Day,Time,Job,Person1)|Partial],Schedule).
improve_schedule(Schedule,Schedule).

%
% Procedures for finding persons who have fewer or more shifts
% than requested in a schedule.
```

```
%

needs_shift(Person,Schedule) :-
        personnel(Person,MinWeekly,_,_,_),
        findall(T,member(sched(D,T,J,Person),Schedule),Shifts),
        length(Shifts,S),
        S < MinWeekly.

has_extra_shift(Person,Schedule) :-
        personnel(Person,MinWeekly,_,_,_),
        findall(T,member(sched(D,T,J,Person),Schedule),Shifts),
        length(Shifts,S),
        S > MinWeekly.

remove(X,[X|Y],Y) :- !.
remove(X,[Y|Z],[Y|W]) :- remove(X,Z,W).

member(X,[X|_]).
member(X,[_|Y]) :- member(X,Y).

%
% Procedures for displaying schedules.
%

write_report(Schedule) :-
        nl, nl,
        write('Schedule for the Week: '), nl, nl,
        member(Day,[mon,tue,wed,thu,fri]),
        findall(sched(Day,Time,Job,Person),
                member(sched(Day,Time,Job,Person),Schedule),
                        DaySchedule),
        report_list1(DaySchedule), nl,
        write('Press key to continue. '), get0(_), nl, nl,
        Day = fri,
        findall(person(Person,Min,Max),
                personnel(Person,Min,Max,_,_),PersonList),
        report_list2(PersonList,Schedule),
        !.

report_list1([]).
report_list1([sched(Day,Time,Job,Person)|RestOfSchedule]) :-
        report(Day,Time,Job,Person),
        report_list1(RestOfSchedule).

report(Day,Time,Job,Person) :-
        write(Day), write(' '), write(Time),   write(' '),
        write(Job), write(' '), write(Person), nl.

report_list2([],_) :- write('Report finished.'), nl, nl.
report_list2([person(Person,Min,Max)|Rest],Schedule) :-
        write(Person), write('''s schedule ('),
```

```
                     write(Min),    write(' to '),
                     write(Max),    write(' shifts per week):'), nl, nl,
                     member(Day,[mon,tue,wed,thu,fri]),
                     findall(sched(Day,Time,Job,Person),
                             member(sched(Day,Time,Job,Person),Schedule),DaySchedule),
                     report_list2_aux(DaySchedule),
                     Day = fri, nl,
                     write('Press key to continue. '), get0(_), nl, nl,
                     report_list2(Rest,Schedule).

           report_list2_aux([]).
           report_list2_aux([sched(Day,Time,Job,_)|Rest]) :-
                     report(Day,Time,Job,''),
                     report_list2_aux(Rest).


           %
           % Sample scheduling data.
           %

           slots(mon,am,cataloger,1).
           slots(mon,am,deskclerk,1).
           slots(mon,pm,deskclerk,1).
           slots(mon,am,shelver,2).
           slots(mon,pm,shelver,2).
           slots(tue,am,cataloger,1).
           slots(tue,am,deskclerk,1).
           slots(tue,pm,deskclerk,1).
           slots(tue,am,shelver,2).
           slots(tue,pm,shelver,2).
           slots(wed,am,cataloger,1).
           slots(wed,am,deskclerk,1).
           slots(wed,pm,deskclerk,1).
           slots(wed,am,shelver,2).
           slots(wed,pm,shelver,2).
           slots(thu,am,cataloger,1).
           slots(thu,am,deskclerk,1).
           slots(thu,pm,deskclerk,1).
           slots(thu,am,shelver,2).
           slots(thu,pm,shelver,2).
           slots(fri,am,cataloger,1).
           slots(fri,am,deskclerk,1).
           slots(fri,pm,deskclerk,1).
           slots(fri,am,shelver,2).
           slots(fri,pm,shelver,2).

           personnel(alice,6,8,2,[mon,tue,thu,fri]).
           personnel(bob,7,10,2,[mon,tue,wed,thu,fri]).
           personnel(carol,3,5,1,[mon,tue,wed,thu,fri]).
           personnel(don,6,8,2,[mon,tue,wed]).
           personnel(ellen,0,2,1,[thu,fri]).
           personnel(fred,7,10,2,[mon,tue,wed,thu,fri]).
```

```
job(cataloger,[alice,fred]).
job(deskclerk,[bob,carol,fred]).
job(shelver,[alice,bob,carol,don,ellen,fred]).
```

8.9. FORWARD-CHAINING AND PRODUCTION-RULE SYSTEMS

A Prolog rule has a head and a body. Prolog tries to satisfy a current goal by matching it with a fact or with the head of a rule. If Prolog finds a rule whose head unifies with the goal, then the body of that rule becomes the current Prolog goal. An inference engine that starts with a goal and works toward facts that prove the goal in this way is called a *backward-chaining* inference engine.

There is another way we can use rules: We can work forward from available knowledge. Think of the head of a rule as describing some *action* to be performed and the body of the rule as describing the *condition* for performing this action. The inference engine is not given a goal in the form of a query. Instead, it looks at the facts stored in a temporary database. If these facts satisfy the condition of some rule, the inference engine *fires* that rule by performing the action that the rule specifies. An inference engine that begins with facts and works toward consequences like this is called a *forward-chaining* inference engine.

The action of a rule for a forward-chaining inference engine is usually more complex than the head of a Prolog rule. An action may add several new facts to the database. It may also delete some facts from the database, display some message for the user, or perform some other action. Since firing a rule typically *produces* a new situation, these rules are called *production rules*.

A forward-chaining inference engine has its goal built into it. It finds a rule to fire, fires it, then looks for another rule to fire. The goals of the user are different from the goal of the inference engine. The goals of the user are stored as special kinds of facts in the temporary database. Just as the actions of production rules can cause new information to be added to the temporary database, they can also cause new goals to be added to the database.

Let's consider an example of a very simple set of production rules to see how a forward-chaining production system works. We will write a production rule system for a robot to turn on a lamp. The goal will be `g(turn_on(lamp))`, and the situation will be described by either `f(status(lamp,on))` or `f(status(lamp,off))`. Initially, our database will contain the goal and one fact.

When the robot finds `g(turn_on(lamp))` in its database, what should it do? This will depend on the situation. If the lamp is already on, we will want it to do nothing except note that its goal is satisfied. The required production rule has three parts: an identifier, a condition, and an action. We could write our rule like this:

Rule 1: if   `g(turn_on(lamp))` *and*
           `f(status(lamp,on))`
           are in the database,
      then remove `g(turn_on(lamp))`
           from the database.

Now suppose the lamp is not on. Then the robot needs to flip the switch. Treating this as a new goal, we get a second rule:

Rule 2: if   `g(turn_on(lamp))` *and*
          `f(status(lamp,off))`
          are in the database,
     then add `g(flip(switch))`
          to the database.

Finally, we need two rules that actually cause the robot to perform some physical action.

Rule 3: if   `g(flip(switch))` *and*
          `f(status(lamp,on))`
          are in the database,
     then   flip the switch and
          remove `g(flip(switch))`
          from the database and
          remove `f(status(lamp,on))`
          from the database and
          add `f(status(lamp,off))`
          to the database.

Rule 4: if   `g(flip(switch))` *and*
          `fact(status(lamp,off))`
          are in the database,
     then   flip the switch and
          remove `g(flip(switch))`
          from the database and
          remove `f(status(lamp,off))`
          from the database and
          add `f(status(lamp,on))`
          to the database.

Let's see what happens when the robot is given these rules and a database containing `g(turn_on(lamp)` and `f(status(lamp,on))`. Only the condition for Rule 1 is satisfied, so Rule 1 is fired and `g(turn_on(lamp))` is removed from the database. Now the inference engine looks for another rule to fire. Every rule has a goal in its condition, but there are no goals in the database. So the inference engine stops.

Suppose the database contains `g(turn_on(lamp))` and `f(status(lamp,off))`. Only the condition for Rule 2 is satisfied; so it fires and `g(flip(switch))` is added to the database. Now there are two rules, Rule 2 and Rule 4, whose conditions are satisfied. Which shall the inference engine fire? Of course, we *want* the inference engine to fire Rule 4, but it may not.

We call the set of rules whose conditions are satisfied at any given time the current *conflict set*. When the conflict set is empty, the inference engine stops. When the conflict set has only one rule in it, that rule is fired. When the conflict set contains several rules, complex procedures may be necessary to decide which rule to fire. This decision can be very important. In our example, if we fire Rule 2 every time we can, we will be caught in a loop where we keep adding new instances of g(flip(switch)) to the database and never actually flip the switch.

When the forward-chaining inference engine selects some rule from the conflict set (using whatever principles it may), we say that it has *resolved* the conflict set. For our example, we will adopt the simple principle that the inference engine fires the first rule it finds whose condition is satisfied. This doesn't solve the looping problem we noticed. To do this, we must also specify that *every rule should change the database so its own condition is no longer satisfied*. This will stop loops of the kind we found in our example. In this case, we can eliminate the loop by adding a condition rather than an action to Rule 2:

Rule 2': if   g(turn_on(lamp))
             is in the database and
             f(status(lamp,off))
             is in the database and
             g(flip(switch))
             is not in the database,
      then add g(flip(switch))
             to the database.

Now after Rule 2' is fired, only the condition for Rule 4 is satisfied. After Rule 4 fires, the database contains only g(turn_on(lamp)) and f(status(lamp,on)). Rule 1 fires, and g(turn_on(lamp)) is removed from the database. Then there is no rule whose condition is satisfied and the robot (inference engine) stops. Three rules were fired: Rule 2', Rule 4, and Rule 1.

The problem with Rule 2 also points out a more general principle. All of the rules in a production system should operate independently of their order in the system. Exactly the same rules should fire in the same order no matter how the rules are arranged in the knowledge base. A forward-chaining inference engine that determines the entire conflict set and decides which of these rules to fire guarantees this. If the first rule that can be fired always fires, the user must guarantee that this is the only rule that can fire under the circumstances. This means that the rules should be written so a situation cannot arise where the conditions for two or more rules are satisfied. If such a situation did arise, then changing the order of the rules would cause different rules to fire. In effect, writing the rules so they are independent in this way ensures that the conflict set never has more than one member.

8.10. A SIMPLE FORWARD CHAINER

The listing FCHAIN.PL includes both a forward-chaining inference engine and a supervisory program for the inference engine. The basic form for the forward-chaining inference engine is very simple. All we want the inference engine to do is find the conflict set, resolve it, and perform the action of the selected rule. Then it should start again in the resulting situation. Here is a procedure that will do this.

```
forward_chainer :- findall(X,satisfied(X),ConflictSet),
                   resolve_set(ConflictSet,ID),
                   rule(ID),
                   write('Fired rule: '),
                   write(ID),
                   write('.'),
                   nl, !,
                   forward_chainer.
```

Of course, this is only the top level of the inference engine. We must still define `satisfied/1` and `resolve_set/2`. The first is rather easy. The second, of course, will depend on the particular conflict resolution principles we decide to use.

What makes the forward chainer so simple is the way we write our forward-chaining rules in Prolog. In backward-chaining, we look at the conclusion (the head) of the rule first and then look at the conditions (the body). As we saw in the last section, forward-chaining rules are usually written in the opposite order: conditions, then actions. We will be able to use a *translation* method that rewrites our production rules so the Prolog inference engine does most of the work for us. In a sense, the rules will satisfy and fire themselves.

Before we look at the way we will rewrite production rules in Prolog, let's define a few predicates that will make our rules easier to write. These predicates are part of the inference engine rather than part of any particular production rule set. Predicates `af/1` and `ag/1` add facts and goals to a database, and predicates `rf/1` and `rg/1` remove facts and goals. The predicate **then** does nothing and always succeeds. It serves only to separate the condition from the action in a production rule. The simple definitions for these predicates are found at the end of the listing for FCHAIN.PL.

8.11. PRODUCTION RULES IN PROLOG

A forward chaining production rule has the general form:

`Identifier: Condition, then Action.`

We want to write our rules so that Prolog does the least work possible. This means that the head, or conclusion, of the Prolog rule will be the identifier, not the action. Both the condition and the action will be subgoals.

Every Prolog production rule will have a head of the form `rule(ID)`, where ID is a number, phrase, or other identifier for the rule. This lets Prolog pick out the production rules stored in memory very quickly.

In the body of the rule, we will list the condition first and then the action. Because Prolog is trying subgoals in sequence one by one, the action will only be reached if the condition succeeds. The action should be a subgoal that always succeeds whenever the condition succeeds. We will separate the condition and the action with the special predicate **then** both to make the rule easier to read and to enable Prolog to distinguish conditions from goals in computing the conflict set. The general form of a Prolog production rule is:

```
rule(ID) :- Condition, then, Action.
```

To specify when the condition of a Prolog production rule is satisfied, we simply test the body of the rule until we reach the special predicate then:

```
satisfied(X) :- clause(rule(X),Body),
                satisfied_conditions(Body).
```

```
satisfied_conditions((then,_)) :- !.
satisfied_conditions((First,Rest)) :- First,
                                satisfied_conditions(Rest).
```

We could adopt any number of methods for resolving conflict sets. We could add an integer as a second argument to the head of the Prolog production rule and use this as an index to determine the priority of rules. We could look at the system clock to get a time stamp that we saved with each fact that we added to the temporary database, then prefer rules whose conditions were satisfied most recently. These and other methods have been used in production systems. We will use the very simple method of always firing the first rule whose condition is satisfied. Since we use findall to generate our conflict set, this will just be the first rule identified by findall:

```
resolve_set([ID|_],ID) :- !.
```

Using this resolution method, we will devise our production rules so the resolution set never has more than one member. If we can do this, then our resolution method will in practice give us the same results as every other resolution method.

Let's develop another set of production rules for our robot, this time in Prolog. Suppose we want our robot to stack cartons in a warehouse. Initially, the robot knows where each carton is and knows how the cartons are supposed to be stacked. Let's say there are four cartons marked a, b, c, and d. The two cartons a and b are on the warehouse floor, c is on top of b, and d is on top of c. The goal of the robot is to stack the cartons with a on the bottom, b on a, c on b, and d on d. We represent this initial situation in the robot's temporary database with five clauses:

```
f(supports(floor,a)).
f(supports(floor,b)).
f(supports,b,c)).
f(supports(c,d)).
g(stack([a,b,c,d])).
```

The robot can lift only one carton at a time. To stack the cartons, the robot will need to remove d from c and c from b. Thus it must set some intermediate goals for itself while remembering its original goal. That is, it must do some simple planning. We will not concern ourselves with the details of moving the robot hand, grasping and ungrasping cartons, and the like. We will tackle only the question of deciding which cartons to put where at each point in the process. Our rules will update the robot's temporary database as it moves the cartons. Thus the database reflects the changing positions fo the cartons and the robot's changing goals.

The first thing we want the robot to do is to stack **b** on **a**. In general, when the robot has a goal of stacking some cartons, it should try to stack the second carton on the first. If the second carton is already on the first, the robot moves on to stacking the third carton on the second.

```
rule(1) :- g(stack([X,Y|Rest])),
           f(supports(X,Y)),
               then,
           rg(stack([X,Y|Rest])),
           ag(stack([Y|Rest])).
```

Usually, the second carton to be stacked will not already be on the first carton. Then our robot must place the second carton on the first. It cannot do this if there is already a carton on either the first or the second carton. (We assume that only one carton can be stacked on another and that the robot can only lift one carton at a time.) The following rule picks up the second carton and puts it on top of the first, provided it is possible to do so:

```
rule(2) :- g(stack([X,Y|Rest])),
           \+ fact(supports(X,_)),
           \+ fact(supports(Y,_)),
           f(supports(Z,Y)),
               then,
           rf(supports(Z,Y)),
           af(supports(X,Y)),
           rg(stack([X,Y|Rest])),
           ag(stack([Y|Rest])).
```

If there is another carton on either the first or the second carton to be stacked, the robot must remove this obstacle before it can stack the two cartons. We need two rules to handle these possibilities:

```
rule(3) :- g(stack([X,Y|Rest]))),
           f(supports(X,Z)),
           Y \= Z,
           \+ g(remove(Z)),
               then,
           ag(remove(Z)).
```

```
rule(4) :- g(stack([_,X|Rest]))),
           f(supports(X,Y)),
           \+ g(remove(Y)),
               then,
           ag(remove(Y)).
```

Now we need to say how to remove an obstacle. Either the obstacle has another carton on it or it does not. Thus, two rules are needed:

```
rule(5) :- g(remove(X)),
           f(supports(X,Y)),
           \+ g(remove(Y)),
               then,
           ag(remove(Y)).

rule(6) :- g(remove(X)),
           \+ f(supports(X,_)),
           f(supports(Y,X)),
               then,
           rf(supports(Y,X)),
           af(supports(floor,X)),
           rg(remove(X)).
```

The terminating condition for the stacking operation is reached when there is only one carton left in the list of cartons to be stacked:

```
rule(7) :- g(stack([_])),
               .then,
           rg(stack([_])).
```

These rules and initial conditions are collected in the listing CARTONS.PL.

8.11.1. Listing of FCHAIN.PL

```
% FCHAIN.PL

% This file contains a simple forward chaining
% inference engine that accepts Prolog translations
% of production rules, plus a supervisory program
% for use with the inference engine.

:- dynamic f/1, g/1, rule/1.
:- multifile f/1, g/1, rule/1.

% forward-chainer
%    finds a production rule that can be fired,
%    fires it, and informs the user, then calls
%    itself to repeat the process.


forward_chainer :- findall(X,satisfied(X),ConflictSet),
                   resolve_set(ConflictSet,ID),
                   rule(ID),
                   write('Fired rule: '),
                   write(ID),
                   write('.'),
                   nl, !,
                   forward_chainer.
```

```
% satisfied(?Rule)
%    succeeds if every condition for rule(Rule) that comes
%    before the predicate then/0 succeeds.

satisfied(X) :- clause(rule(X),Body),
                satisfied_conditions(Body).

satisfied_conditions((then,_)) :- !.
satisfied_conditions((First,Rest)) :- First,
                                      satisfied_conditions(Rest).


% resolve(+ConflictSet,+RuleNumber)
% Returns the RuleNumber of the first member of the
%  ConflictSet (which is the first rule in the database
%  whose condition is satisfied).

resolve_set([ID|_],ID) :- !.

% The remaining predicates are provided to make
% writing and reading production rules easier.

af(X) :- asserta(f(X)).

rf(X) :- retract(f(X)).

ag(X) :- assert(g(X)).

rg(X) :- retract(g(X)).

then.

% Supervisory program

fc :-
    display_help_message,
    repeat,
    write('>'),
    read(X),
    ( X = stop,abolish(f/1),abolish(g/1)
      ;
      process(X), nl, fail
    ).

% display_help_message
%  provides a list of commands to use with the forward
%   chaining supervisor.

display_help_message :-
    nl, nl,
    write('FCHAIN - A Forward Chaining Inference Engine'),
```

```
        nl, nl,
        write('This is an interpreter for files containing production'),
        nl,
        write('rules written in the FCHAIN format.'),
        nl, nl,
        write('The > prompt accepts four commands:'), nl, nl,
        write('load. - prompts for names of rules files'), nl,
        write('         (enclose names in single quotes)'), nl,
        write('list. - lists facts and goals in working'), nl,
        write('         memory'),  nl,
        write('go.   - starts the forward chainer'), nl, nl,
        write('stop. - exits FCHAIN'), nl, nl,
        write('help. - display this message'), nl, nl.


% process(+Command)
%    provides procedures for processing each of the
%    four kinds of commands the user may give to the
%    supervisor.

process(go) :- nl, forward_chainer.

process(go) :- !.   /* if forward_chainer failed */

process(load) :- nl, write('File name? '),
                 read(Filename),
                 reconsult(Filename), !.

process(list) :- nl, write('Facts:'),
                 nl, f(X),
                 write('    '),
                 write(X), nl, fail.

process(list) :- nl, write('Goals:'),
                 nl, g(X),
                 write('    '),
                 write(X), nl, fail.

process(list) :- !.

process(list(X)) :- nl, f(X),
                    write('    '),
                    write(X), nl, fail.

process(list(_)) :- !.

% Starting query

:- fc.
```

8.11.2. Listing of CARTONS.PL

```
% CARTONS.PL

% This is a set of production rules for a robot that
% stacks cartons in a warehouse. The rules have been
% translated into Prolog rules that can be used with
% the forward-chaining inference engine in FCHAIN.PL.

:- dynamic f/1, g/1, rule/1.
:- multifile f/1, g/1, rule/1.

rule(1) :- g(stack([X,Y|Rest])),
           f(supports(X,Y)),
                then,
           rg(stack([X,Y|Rest])),
           ag(stack([Y|Rest])).

rule(2) :- g(stack([X,Y|Rest])),
           \+ f(supports(X,_)),
           \+ f(supports(Y,_)),
           f(supports(Z,Y)),
                then,
           rf(supports(Z,Y)),
           af(supports(X,Y)),
           rg(stack([X,Y|Rest])),
           ag(stack([Y|Rest])).

rule(3) :- g(stack([X,Y|Rest])),
           f(supports(X,Z)),
           Y \== Z,
           \+ g(remove(Z)),
                then,
           ag(remove(Z)).

rule(4) :- g(stack([_,X|Rest])),
           f(supports(X,Y)),
           \+ g(remove(Y)),
                then,
           ag(remove(Y)).

rule(5) :- g(remove(X)),
           f(supports(X,Y)),
           \+ g(remove(Y)),
                then,
           ag(remove(Y)).

rule(6) :- g(remove(X)),
           \+ f(supports(X,_)),
           f(supports(Y,X)),
```

```
                then,
            rf(supports(Y,X)),
            af(supports(floor,X)),
            rg(remove(X)).

rule(7) :- g(stack([_])),
                then,
            rg(stack([_])).

% initial facts and goals for the carton-stacking robot

f(supports(floor,a)).
f(supports(floor,b)).
f(supports(b,c)).
f(supports(c,d)).
g(stack([a,b,c,d])).

% End of CARTONS.PL
```

8.12. BIBLIOGRAPHICAL NOTES

For an entire book devoted to implementing AI techniques in Prolog, see Shoham (1994).

Chapter 9

A Simple Expert System Shell

9.1. EXPERT SYSTEMS

Expert systems are products of artificial intelligence research. They are computer programs designed to perform tasks that require special knowledge or problem-solving skills. Some expert systems must interact with a human user, while others operate without user interaction. Nearly all expert systems apply techniques developed in the artificial intelligence laboratories to practical problems.

Perhaps the most widely publicized expert systems are medical diagnostic systems. Among these are MYCIN (Shortliffe 1976), which diagnoses blood and meningitis infections; PUFF (Aikins, Kunz, and Shortliffe 1983), which diagnoses pulmonary diseases; and ABEL (Patil, Szolovitz, and Schwartz 1981), which diagnoses acid/base electrolyte disorders.

There are several expert systems for use in chemistry. DENDRAL (Lindsay et al. 1980) uses data produced by mass spectrometers to deduce the molecular structure of a chemical compound. SPARC (Karickhoff et al. 1991) works in the opposite direction and deduces the ultra-violet light absorption spectrum and other chemical and physical parameters of a compound from its molecular structure.

There are expert systems for many other domains besides medicine and chemistry. PROSPECTOR (Duda et al. 1978) evaluates sites for possible mineral deposits. XCON (O'Connor 1984) configures VAX computer systems for delivery to customers. Other systems, either experimental or operational, have been developed for use in education, engineering, law, management, manufacturing, and military applications.

Many expert systems are complex and require years to develop, but useful expert systems — on a smaller scale — can be built quickly by anyone who has access to some area of special expertise and an understanding of some basic principles of expert systems construction.

The domain of an expert system does not have to be anything as glamorous as medical diagnosis or as esoteric as mass spectroscopy. We can build an expert system to troubleshoot some electrical appliance like a stereo system, or to tell whether people qualify for social security benefits. The information needed to build many simple but useful expert systems can be found in user's manuals for appliances, government brochures, and other readily available sources. An expert system can be a more intelligent substitute for a reference book or handbook.

In this chapter, we will look at simple expert systems and how to build them. We will need to think about how an expert works and the different tasks an expert system needs to do. Then we will develop general tools and techniques for building small expert systems in Prolog.

9.2. EXPERT CONSULTANTS AND EXPERT CONSULTING SYSTEMS

Experts often serve as consultants. A client comes to the expert with some problem. Through consultation, the expert provides the client with one or both of two basic services: diagnosis and prescription. The client makes the final decision whether to accept the diagnosis and whether to act on the prescription.

The consulting expert does several things. He gathers information about the client's problem. Then he infers a diagnosis and perhaps a prescription. His diagnosis and prescription are based on the information the client gives him and the expert knowledge and special problem-solving skills that distinguish him from his client. Once he reaches his conclusions and reports them to the client, the consultant's job may still not be finished. The client may require an explanation of the expert's findings.

Let's consider a very simple case where you might consult an expert. You have discovered an ugly weed growing in your lawn and you want to get rid of it. You pull a few of the weeds and take them to your local lawn and garden shop.

The first thing the lawn expert will do is try to identify the weed for you. Perhaps he tells you the weed is crabgrass. This identification is a kind of diagnosis. Once you know that you have crabgrass in your lawn, you may need no further advice. You may already know, from books you have read or from some other source, how to get rid of crabgrass.

If you don't know how to get rid of crabgrass, the expert will suggest ways to do this. He might recommend sprays or other remedies. His recommendations may depend on the kind of grass and other plants you have in your lawn, the weather, the conditions of the lawn, and perhaps many other factors.

Suppose the lawn expert recommends that you use AJAX Weed Spray, but you have heard that AJAX Weed Spray isn't effective against crabgrass. So you ask the lawn expert why he recommends this product. If he is really an expert, he will be able to explain why he has made his recommendation.

We can divide what the expert has done into two parts. One of these parts is very obvious to the client while the other is hidden. The expert asks questions, listens, and talks. He communicates with the client. This is the obvious part of what he does. But the hidden part, the reason we consulted the expert in the first place, is his use of special knowledge and problem-solving skills.

9.3. PARTS OF AN EXPERT CONSULTING SYSTEM

How can we get a computer to do the things the consultant does? It will have to ask questions, report conclusions, and explain its conclusions. To reach its conclusions, it will have to contain some internal representation of expert knowledge, and it will have to be able to use this expert knowledge together with the knowledge supplied by the user to arrive at a diagnosis and possibly a solution to the user's problem.

To do this, every expert consulting system must have at least three basic subsystems. First, there is the part that holds the expert knowledge. We call this the knowledge base of the system.

Second, there is the part of the system that uses the knowledge base and information provided by the client to arrive at its conclusions. We call this the inference engine. It has special importance because the same knowledge base will really mean different things when teamed up with different inference engines. The knowledge base is just a set of electrical signals stored in the computer. For these signals to represent knowledge, they must be understood and used by the system in an appropriate way. It is the inference engine that determines how the signals stored in the computer are understood and used.

Third, there is the part of the system that we will call the user interface. This part of the system asks the user questions and converts the answers into a form the inference engine can understand. When the inference engine reaches a conclusion, the user interface must communicate it to the user. If the user questions a conclusion, the user interface must be able to explain to the user how the inference engine reached its conclusion.

Some expert systems are written in separate pieces with different modules for the knowledge base, the inference engine, and the user interface. Others mix them together. But we can always distinguish between these three functions even if the program does not have separate modules for each one. Expert systems that include different modules for these different functions are usually easier to understand, maintain, and expand.

9.4. EXPERT SYSTEM SHELLS

A number of products are being offered commercially as expert system "shells." Unlike a complete expert system, a shell is missing one of the three key ingredients of an expert system: it has no knowledge base. Instead, an expert system shell provides a subsystem called a knowledge base builder's interface that helps the user build a knowledge base. (Sometimes a knowledge base builder's interface is also provided with complete expert systems so that the user can modify or expand the knowledge base.)

The idea behind an expert system shell is that the user can produce a true expert system for whatever problem domain he wants by "filling" the shell with the expert knowledge needed for his application. These shells can simplify the task of building an expert system, but there is a price to be paid. Different problem domains may require different kinds of reasoning using different kinds of knowledge. Part of what makes an expert is his special problem-solving skills. These are often represented in expert systems by special features of their inference engines. We might also want different kinds of user interfaces for different domains. Thus, merely filling in the knowledge base may not be enough to build a satisfactory expert system.

The less expensive expert system shells usually support only one kind of inference. It is difficult or impossible to alter either the inference engine or the user interface provided by these shells. It is very important in choosing a shell to select a product that provides both the appropriate kind of inference engine and the appropriate kind of user interface for the application you have in mind.

Other expert system shells provide inference engines with a wide range of capabilities and provide user interfaces with great flexibility. These tend to be expensive, and the greater expense may not be justified for a particular application. You may need only a few of the features these systems provide, but you have paid for many more features that you may never use.

The alternative to using a shell for expert system development is to build the inference engine and user interface you need in some programming language. Prolog is a good choice for this because it comes with a built-in inference engine. Of course, you can build an inference engine in Lisp, Pascal, FORTRAN, or any other programming language. Indeed, you can build a Prolog interpreter in any of these languages. But Prolog has the advantage that a sophisticated inference engine is immediately available and ready to use.

Furthermore, Prolog provides a rudimentary user interface. We can enter a query, and Prolog will tell us whether it can satisfy the query from its knowledge base. If our query contains variables, Prolog will give us values for these variables that satisfy the query.

Prolog also offers a basic explanatory facility. To see how Prolog reaches a conclusion, all we need to do is invoke the trace function. Of course, this will slow down execution and it will usually give us much more information than we really want. But there is no doubt that tracing Prolog execution will provide us with a complete explanation of how Prolog reached its conclusions.

Notice that when you first enter the Prolog programming environment, the inference engine and the primitive user interface are already in place. Until you either consult a file containing some facts and rules or enter some facts and rules directly at the keyboard, the inference engine has no knowledge base to use in answering your queries. Prolog thus provides a very simple expert system shell.

Many expert system shells can perform the kind of inference Prolog performs and can use knowledge representations similar to Prolog facts and rules. Most shells offer user interfaces with more features than those available in Prolog. Why, then, would we ever use Prolog to develop expert systems? The reason is Prolog's flexibility combined with the relatively small price tag for a good Prolog interpreter or compiler. Not only does Prolog provide a useful inference engine, but it also provides the means to build far more powerful inference engines. Not only does Prolog provide a primitive user interface, but it is an excellent language to use to build more powerful user interfaces. In fact, some of the commercially available expert system shells are written in Prolog.

There is a trade-off here. Selecting the right expert system shell for a particular application takes time and effort. Sometimes we are forced to pay a high price to get the features we want. And it is usually impossible to modify the inference engine or user interface of a commercial expert system shell. Prolog, on the other hand, is relatively inexpensive and very flexible. But it takes time and effort to write your own user interface, and more time and effort if you need to modify the Prolog inference engine.

9.5. EXTENDING THE POWER OF PROLOG

In this and the next two chapters, we will look at different user interfaces and inference engines we can build in Prolog.

In the remainder of this chapter we will extend the Prolog user interface by adding simple routines that automatically ask appropriate questions when provided with suitable rules for a diagnosis, prescription, or other kind of identification. We will also develop a simple explanatory facility that will tell us the exact rule Prolog used to reach a conclusion. All of these features are collected in the file XSHELL.PL. We will also use XSHELL as the name for the system of utility predicates in the XSHELL.PL file.

We can easily distinguish the knowledge base, the inference engine, and the user interface in an XSHELL expert system. The user interface is the XSHELL program itself. The inference engine is standard Prolog. The knowledge base is a separate set of clauses for some special predicates the XSHELL routines use. We will give careful instructions for building XSHELL knowledge bases, and we will build some XSHELL knowledge bases as examples.

Chapter 10 presents a way to use confidence factors in our expert systems. We also build more tools for the user interface to fit the new features of the extended Prolog inference engine. The explanatory facilities in Chapter 10 are more sophisticated than those in XSHELL, and you may want to adapt them for other uses. All of this material is loosely based on recent developments in expert system technology.

In Chapter 11, we will build an additional inference engine for defeasible rules. Defeasible rules provide a way to represent uncertain or incomplete information without using confidence factors or other quantitative measures of uncertainty.

Exercise 9.5.1

What are the three major components of an expert system discussed in this chapter? Describe the function of each.

Exercise 9.5.2

What is the difference between an expert system and an expert system shell?

Exercise 9.5.3

Why do we claim that Prolog is a simple expert system shell?

9.5.1. Listing of XSHELL.PL

```
% XSHELL.PL

%
% An expert system consultation driver to be used
% with separately written knowledge bases.
%
% Procedures in the file include XSHELL, XSHELL_AUX,
% FINISH_XSHELL, PROP, PARM, PARMSET, PARMRANGE,
% EXPLAIN, MEMBER, and WAIT.
%
% Requires various procedures defined in the files
% READSTR.PL, READNUM.PL, and GETYESNO.PL from
% Chapter 5.
%


:- dynamic known/2.

:- ensure_loaded('readstr.pl').
:- ensure_loaded('readnum.pl').
:- ensure_loaded('writeln.pl').
:- ensure_loaded('getyesno.pl').


%
% xshell
%    The main program or procedure for the expert system
%    consultation driver. It always succeeds.
%

xshell :- xkb_intro(Statement),
          writeln(Statement), nl,
          wait,
          xkb_identify(RULE,TextList),
          asserta(known(identification,RULE)),
          append_list(TextList,Text),
          writeln(Text), nl,
          explain,
          xkb_unique(yes),
          !,
          xshell_aux.

xshell :- xshell_aux.
```

```
%
% xshell_aux
%    Prevents an abrupt end to a consultation that ends
% without an identification, or a consultation where
% multiple identifications are allowed.
%

xshell_aux :- \+ known(identification,_),
              writeln('I cannot reach a conclusion.'),
              !,
              finish_xshell.

xshell_aux :- xkb_unique(no),
              known(identification,_),
              writeln('I cannot reach any further conclusion.'),
              !,
              finish_xshell.

xshell_aux :- finish_xshell.

%
% finish_xshell
%    Erases the working database and asks if the user wants
%    to conduct another consultation.
%

finish_xshell :-
    retractall(known(_,_)),
    writeln('Do you want to conduct another consultation?'),
    yes, nl, nl,
    !,
    xshell.

finish_xshell.

%
% prop(+Property)
%    Succeeds if it is remembered from an earlier call that
%    the subject has the Property.  Otherwise the user is
%    asked if the subject has the Property and the user's
%    answer is remembered. In this case, the procedure call
%    succeeds only if the user answers 'yes'.
%

prop(Property) :- known(Property,Value),
```

```
                        !,
                        Value == y.

prop(Property) :- xkb_question(Property,Question,_,_),
                        writeln(Question),
                        yes, nl, nl,
                        !,
                        assert(known(Property,y)).

prop(Property) :- assert(known(Property,n)),
                        nl, nl,
                        !,
                        fail.


%
% parm(+Parameter,+Type,+Value)
%    Type determines whether Value is to be a menu choice, an
%    atom, or a number.  Value becomes the remembered value
%    for the parameter if there is one. Otherwise the user is
%    asked for a value and that value is remembered. Calls to
%    this procedure are used as test conditions for identification
%    rules. Value is instantiated before the procedure is called
%    and parm(Parameter,Type,Value) only succeeds if the remembered
%    value, or alternatively the value reported by the user,
%    matches Value.
%

parm(Parameter,_,Value) :- known(Parameter,StoredValue),
                              !,
                              Value = StoredValue.

parm(Parameter,m,Value) :- xkb_menu(Parameter,Header,Choices,_),
                              length(Choices,L),
                              writeln(Header),nl,
                              enumerate(Choices,1),
                              readnumber_in_range(1,L,N), nl, nl,
                              assert(known(Parameter,N)),
                              !,
                              Value = N.

parm(Parameter,a,Value) :- xkb_question(Parameter,Question,_,_),
                              writeln(Question),
                              readatom(Response), nl, nl,
                              assert(known(Parameter,Response)),
                              !,
                              Value = Response.
```

```
parm(Parameter,n,Value) :- xkb_question(Parameter,Question,_,_),
                           writeln(Question),
                           readnumber(Response), nl, nl,
                           assert(known(Parameter,Response)),
                           !,
                           Value = Response.

%
% parmset(+Parameter,+Type,+Set)
%   Type indicates whether the Parameter takes a character,
%   an atom, or a number as value, and Set is a list of
%   possible values for Parameter.  A call to the procedure
%   succeeds if a value for Parameter is established that is
%   a member of Set.
%

parmset(Parameter,Type,Set) :- parm(Parameter,Type,Value),
                               member(Value,Set).

%
% parmrange(+Parameter,+Minimum,+Maximum)
%   Parameter must take numbers as values, and Minimum and
%   Maximum must be numbers. A call to the procedure succeeds
%   if a value for Parameter is established that is in the
%   closed interval [Minimum,Maximum].
%

parmrange(Parameter,Minimum,Maximum) :-
    parm(Parameter,n,Value),
    Minimum =< Value,
    Maximum >= Value.

%
% explain and explain_aux
%   Upon request, provide an explanation of how an
%   identification was made.
%

explain :- xkb_explain(no), wait, !.

explain :- writeln(
           ['Do you want to see the rule that was used',
            'to reach the conclusion?']),
           \+ yes, nl, !.
```

```
explain :- known(identification,RULE),
           clause(xkb_identify(RULE,_),Condition),
           nl,nl,
           write('Rule '),
           write(RULE),
           write(': reach this conclusion IF'), nl,
           explain_aux(Condition), nl,
           wait, nl, !.

explain_aux((Condition,RestOfConditions)) :-
        !,
        interpret(Condition),
        explain_aux(RestOfConditions).
explain_aux(Condition) :-
        interpret(Condition).


%
% interpret(+Condition).
%    Uses questions and menus associated with a condition
%    and identification rule to display the condition in a
%    format that makes sense to the user.
%

interpret(prop(Property)) :-
        !,
        xkb_question(Property,_,Text,_),
            % Text is a message that says the subject to be
            % identified has the Property.
        write(Text), nl.
interpret(\+(prop(Property))) :-
        !,
        xkb_question(Property,_,_,Text),
            % Text is a message that says the subject to be
            % identified does not have the Property.
        write(Text), nl.
interpret(parm(Parameter,m,N)) :-
        !,
        xkb_menu(Parameter,_,Choices,Prefix),
            % Prefix is a phrase that informs the user which
            % Parameter is involved.
        nth_member(N,Text,Choices),
            % nth_member is used to retrieve the user's choice
            % from the menu associated with the Parameter.
        write(Prefix), write(Text), write('.'), nl.

interpret(\+(parm(Parameter,m,N))) :-
```

```
            !,
        xkb_menu(Parameter,_,Choices,Prefix),
            % Prefix is a phrase that informs the user which
            % Parameter is involved.
        nth_member(N,Text,Choices),
            % nth_member is used to retrieve the user's choice
            % from the menu associated with the Parameter.
        write(Prefix), write('NOT '), write(Text), write('.'), nl.
interpret(parm(Parameter,_,Value)) :-
        !,    % For any Parameter whose Value is not obtained
            % by using a menu.
        xkb_question(Parameter,_,Prefix,_),
        write(Prefix), write(Value), write('.'), nl.
interpret(\+(parm(Parameter,_,Value))) :-
        !,    % For any Parameter whose Value is not obtained
            % by using a menu.
        xkb_question(Parameter,_,Prefix,_),
        write(Prefix), write('NOT '), write(Value), write('.'), nl.
interpret(parmset(Parameter,m,Set)) :-
        !,
        xkb_menu(Parameter,_,Choices,Prefix),
        write(Prefix), write('one of the following -'), nl,
            % Since parmset is involved, any value for Parameter
            % included in Set would have satisfied the condition.
        list_choices_in_set(Set,Choices,1).
interpret(\+(parmset(Parameter,m,Set))) :-
        !,
        xkb_menu(Parameter,_,Choices,Prefix),
        write(Prefix), write('NOT one of the following -'), nl,
            % Since parmset is involved, any value for Parameter
            % not in Set would have satisfied the condition.
        list_choices_in_set(Set,Choices,1).
interpret(parmset(Parameter,_,Set)) :-
        !,    % For any Parameter whose Value is not obtained
            % by using a menu.
        xkb_question(Parameter,_,Prefix,_),
        write(Prefix), write('one of the following - '), nl,
        enumerate(Set,1).
interpret(\+(parmset(Parameter,_,Set))) :-
        !,    % For any Parameter whose Value is not obtained
            % by using a menu.
        xkb_question(Parameter,_,Prefix,_),
        write(Prefix), write('NOT one of the following - '), nl,
        enumerate(Set,1).

interpret(parmrange(Parameter,Min,Max)) :-
```

```
                !,
                xkb_question(Parameter,_,Prefix,_),
                write(Prefix), write('between '),
                write(Min), write(' and '), write(Max),
                write('.'), nl.
interpret(\+(parmrange(Parameter,Min,Max))) :-
                !,
                xkb_question(Parameter,_,Prefix,_),
                write(Prefix), write('NOT between '),
                write(Min), write(' and '), write(Max),
                write('.'), nl.
interpret(\+(Condition)) :-
                clause(Condition,Conditions),
                    % Any condition that does not have prop, parm,
                    % parmset, or parmrange as its functor must corres-
                    % pond to some Prolog rule with conditions of its
                    % own. Eventually, all conditions must terminate in
                    % conditions using prop, parm, parmset, or parmrange.
                write('A condition between here and "end" is NOT satisfied -'),
                nl,
                explain_aux(Conditions),
                write('    end'), nl.
interpret(Condition) :-
                clause(Condition,Conditions),
                    % Any condition that does not have prop, parm,
                    % parmset, or parmrange as its functor must corres-
                    % pond to some Prolog rule with conditions of its
                    % own. Eventually, all conditions must terminate in
                    % conditions using prop, parm, parmset, or parmrange.
                explain_aux(Conditions).


%
% enumerate(+N,+X)
%    Prints each atom in list X on a separate line, numbering
%    the atoms beginning with the number N. Used to enumerate
%    menu choices.
%

enumerate([],_).
enumerate([H|T],N) :- write(N),write('. '),write(H),nl,
                      M is N + 1,
                      enumerate(T,M).


%
% list_choices_in_set(+X,+Y,+N)
```

```
%   The members of the list of atoms Y corresponding to the
%   positions in the list indicated by the members of the list
%   of integers X are printed on separate lines and numbered
%   beginning with the number N.
%

list_choices_in_set([],_,_).
list_choices_in_set([N|Tail],Choices,M) :-
        nth_member(N,Choice,Choices),
        write(M), write('. '), write(Choice), nl,
        K is M + 1,
        list_choices_in_set(Tail,Choices,K).


%
% readnumber_in_range(+Min,+Max,-Response)
%   Evokes a numerical input from the user which must be
%   between Min and Max inclusively.
%

readnumber_in_range(Min,Max,Response) :-
        readnumber(Num),
        testnumber_in_range(Min,Max,Num,Response).


%
% testnumber_in_range(+Min,+Max,+Input,-Response)
%   Tests user Input to insure that it is a number between
%   Min and Max inclusively. If it is not, instructions for
%   the user are printed and readnum/1 is called to accept
%   another numerical input from the user.
%

testnumber_in_range(Min,Max,Num,Num) :-
        Min =< Num,
        Num =< Max,
        !.
testnumber_in_range(Min,Max,_,Num) :-
        write('Number between '),
        write(Min),
        write(' and '),
        write(Max),
        write(' expected. Try again. '),
        readnumber_in_range(Min,Max,Num).


%
% wait
%   Stops execution until the user presses a key. Used to
```

```
%   prevent information from scrolling off the screen before
%   the user can read it.
%

wait :- write('Press Return when ready to continue. '),
        get0(_), nl, nl.


%
% yes
%   Prompts the user for a response and succeeds if the
%   user enters 'y' or 'Y'.
%

yes :-  write('|: '),
        get_yes_or_no(Response),
        !,
        Response == yes.

member(X,[X|_]).
member(X,[_|Y]) :- member(X,Y).


%
% nth_member(+N,-X,+Y)
%   X is the nth element of list Y.
%

nth_member(1,X,[X|_]).
nth_member(N,X,[_|Y]) :- nth_member(M,X,Y),
                         N is M + 1.


append_list([],[]).
append_list([N|Tail],Text) :- append_list(Tail,Text1),
                              xkb_text(N,Text2),
                              append(Text2,Text1,Text).

%
% writeln(+Text)
%   Prints Text consisting of a string or a list of
%   strings, with each string followed by a new line.
%

writeln([]) :- !.

writeln([First|Rest]) :-
        !,
        write(First),
```

```
        nl,
        writeln(Rest).

writeln(String) :-
        write(String),
        nl.
```

9.6. XSHELL: THE MAIN PROGRAM

As we know, we can use either procedural or declarative approaches to programming in Prolog. We will think of XSHELL as a set of procedures for interaction between the user and the Prolog inference engine. Our basic approach in developing XSHELL, then, is procedural.

On the other hand, our approach in building knowledge bases to use with XSHELL should be declarative. The idea behind XSHELL is that it provides the auxiliary procedures we need to drive a consultation based on a declaratively developed knowledge base. Diagnosis and prescription are really just two different kinds of identification. Diagnosis is the identification of a problem, and prescription is the identification of a solution to a problem. XSHELL makes one or more identifications during a consultation by using information in its knowledge base and information provided by the user. While identification is the central task for XSHELL, it must also do several other jobs during a consultation. XSHELL should:

1. Tell the user what the expert system does and how it is used.

2. Make an identification, remember it, report it, and (if necessary) explain it.

3. If more than one identification is called for, keep making identifications until no more can be made. A system that both diagnoses a problem and offers a solution will usually make at least two identifications. Other systems may make even more.

4. End the consultation smoothly and ask the user if another consultation is wanted. If so, begin it. If not, stop.

Primary control of a consultation is handled by the three procedures `xshell`, `xshell_aux`, and `finish_xshell`. All other procedures used during a consultation are called by these three. We begin a consultation with the query

```
?- xshell.
```

(which, in many Prologs, can be embedded in the system as a starting query). The procedure `xshell` does the first three of the four jobs we have listed, then calls `xshell_aux`, which, together with `finish_xshell`, ends the consultation smoothly.

The `xshell` procedure has two clauses with the first doing most of the work. It first calls `xkb_intro/1`, which supplies an introductory message for the user. Note that a clause for `xkb_intro` must be included in our XSHELL knowledge base since it will be different for each expert system. The argument to `xkb_intro` is a list of atoms which are displayed using the `writeln/1` procedure from Chapter 5.

Next `xshell` attempts an identification. This is the meat of the system, and we will need several procedures to support the interaction needed to make an identification. All of these are called, indirectly, by the goal `xkb_identify(RULE,TextSet)`. The `xkb_` prefix is used to indicate that the identification rules will be part of the XSHELL knowledge base.

In order to remember every identification that has been made, `xshell` uses `asserta` to add a fact to the definition of a special predicate `known/2`. We will also use clauses for the predicate `known` to store other temporary information during a consultation. This is information supplied by the user or inferred from the user's information and the knowledge base. We will reserve the term KNOWLEDGE BASE for all the rules and facts the system has at the beginning of a consultation. We will call the temporary information or conclusions remembered during a consultation the WORKING DATABASE, and we will call predicates like `known` that are used to store this information DATABASE PREDICATES. The knowledge base is an integral part of the expert system, but the working database is a temporary phenomenon belonging only to a particular consultation.

Once it has made an identification, the system should inform the user of its findings. A system that identifies barnyard animals might say, "The animal is a cow." A medical diagnostic system might say, "A possible diagnosis is pneumonia." For any domain, there will probably be some standard phrases the system will use repeatedly to report conclusions. In these examples, the phrases are "The animal is a..." and "A possible diagnosis is...'. Rather than store the entire text for the conclusion in each rule, pieces of text are stored in the knowledge base in clauses for the predicate `xkb_text/2`. What is stored in the rules is a list of atoms corresponding to these pieces of text. The procedure `append_list/2` uses the list of text indices to assemble a list of atoms that are displayed by `writeln/1`.

Next XSHELL offers to explain how it reached its conclusion.

We mentioned a simple expert system that identifies animals commonly found in a barnyard. This identification system should only give one identification for each subject. But not all systems will work this way. A medical diagnostic system, for example, might give two or three possible diagnoses and a prescription for each. After an identification has been made, reported, and explained, the system should either end the consultation or backtrack to look for other identifications. If identification is unique for the domain of the knowledge base, the consultation should end. If identification is not unique, `xshell` should fail and backtrack.

We tell the system whether to try to find more than one identification by putting a special fact in the knowledge base — either `xkb_unique(yes)` or `xkb_unique(no)`. Then we include `xkb_unique(yes)` as a subgoal in `xshell`. If this subgoal succeeds, the cut in `xshell` is executed and `xshell_aux` is called. If `xshell` does not find `xkb_unique(yes)` in the knowledge base, it backtracks to look for another identification. Then `xshell` continues to bounce between `xkb_identify(RULE,TextList)` and `xkb_unique(yes)` until it can find no more identifications.

When `xkb_identify(RULE,TextList)` fails, execution moves to the second clause in the definition of `xshell`, and `xshell_aux` is called. It simply reports that no (further) conclusion can be reached, and calls `finish_xshell`, which erases the temporary database (retracts all clauses for the predicate `known`) and then offers to start another consultation.

Exercise 9.6.1

What is the difference between the Prolog inference engine and the XSHELL inference engine?

Exercise 9.6.2

In talking about XSHELL, we drew a distinction between a knowledge base and a working database. Explain this distinction. Why is it important?

9.7. ASKING ABOUT PROPERTIES IN XSHELL

Now we consider the most important task: how the system will make its diagnoses, prescriptions, or other identifications.

Let's think about our barnyard example again. Suppose the system must identify horses, cows, goats, pigs, chickens, ducks, cats, dogs, and rats. How would we identify a horse? It is an animal with hooves and a mane. None of the other animals we plan to include in our barnyard system has both hooves and a mane. So we could put a rule and some text to build a conclusion in our knowledge base like this:

```
xkb_identify(1,[isa,horse]) :- prop(hooves), prop(mane).

xkb_text(isa,['The animal is ']).
xkb_text(horse,['a horse.']).
```

Taken together, the rule and the associated text tell us "Identify the animal as a horse if it has the properties called hooves and mane." We will have other rules and text combinations in our knowledge base for the other animals we want to identify.

We need a routine `prop/1` that will automatically find out whether the animal to be identified has hooves or a mane. Our routine gets this information by asking the user, using the `yes` routine from Chapter 5. When it gets an answer, it remembers the answer in case it needs it later. It resembles the routines used in CAR.PL (Chapter 2) to collect information from the user.

```
prop(Property) :- known(Property,Value),
                  !,
                  Value == y.

prop(Property) :- xkb_question(Property,Question,_,_),
                  writeln(Question),
                  yes('>'), nl, nl,
                  assert(known(Property,y)),
                  !.
```

```
prop(Property) :- assert(known(Property,n)),
                  nl, nl,
                  !,
                  fail.
```

prop is called with the name of a property as its single argument. If it can be established that the subject has the property, the call to prop succeeds; otherwise it fails. In the process, one of three things happens.

1. First, prop looks in the working database to see if there is already information on the property. If there is, a cut is executed and the call to prop succeeds or fails conclusively (because of the cut) depending on whether the working database says the subject does or does not have the property.

2. Otherwise, prop asks the user about the property. To do this, it looks in the knowledge base for the appropriate form of the question, then uses the yes routine to get the user's answer. If the call to yes succeeds, prop records that the subject has the property and succeeds conclusively (ending with a cut).

3. If all attempts to establish that the subject has the property have failed, prop records that the subject does not have the property and fails conclusively.

We will store a separate question in the knowledge base for each property we include in an identification rule. For our horse example, we might use the following two questions.

```
xkb_question(hooves,'Does the animal have hooves?',
    'The animal has hooves.',
    'The animal does not have hooves.').
xkb_question(mane,
    'Does the animal have a mane of hair on its neck?',
    'The animal has a mane.',
    'The animal does not have a mane.')
```

The third and forth arguments to question/4 are used by the explanatory facility described later. Let's think about another animal in the barnyard for a moment. A cow is an animal with hooves, too. It also chews cud. We might put this identification rule and text in our knowledge base.

```
xkb_identify(3,[isa,cow]) :- prop(hooves), prop(chews_cud).
xkb_text(cow,['a cow.']).
```

Suppose the animal we are trying to identify is a cow. The first rule in the knowledge base is the rule for identifying horses. So prop will ask us if the animal has hooves, and we will answer yes. Then prop will ask us if the animal has a mane, and we will answer no. At this point, the rule for identifying horses will fail and Prolog will try the rule for cows. First, it will see if the animal has hooves. But we don't want it to ask us again if the animal has hooves — it should remember the answer we already gave.

This is exactly what `prop` does. It always looks in the database to see if the question has already been answered before asking the question again. The first time through, it does not find the answer in the database, so it asks the question. Later, it finds an answer recorded for the question that was asked previously.

The order for the clauses of `prop` may seem backward at first. The first thing `prop` does — asking the question — is described in the second clause, not the first clause. Remember, however, that the order of clauses specifies the order in which Prolog tries alternatives on each invocation of a predicate, not the order in which clauses will succeed in a series of invocations.

Notice that properties can also be used negatively in conditions for rules. Suppose, for example, that we were building a system for determining whether a student was eligible for certain kinds of financial aid at a particular university. To receive a graduate fellowship, the student must have received a baccalaureate degree; but to receive an undergraduate scholarship, the student must not have received a baccalaureate degree. But both graduate and undergraduate students are eligible for student loans. Then a rule for graduate fellowships would have

```
prop(baccalaureate)
```

as a condition, a rule for undergraduate scholarhips would have

```
\+ prop(baccalaureate)
```

as a condition, and a rule for student loans would have neither.

An `xkb_intro/1` clause and either `xkb_unique(yes)` or `xkb_unique(no)` will be in our knowledge base. It will also contain clauses for `xkb_identify/2`, `xkb_text/2/`, and `xkb_question/4`. If all the identification rules use only properties, we will have a question for each property used in any of the rules. Then our main program, together with the procedure `prop`, will be able to make our identifications for us.

9.8. ASKING ABOUT PARAMETERS IN XSHELL

It will be convenient if the identification rules in our knowledge bases can have other kinds of conditions. For example, an expert system that advises social security applicants about their eligibility for different benefits will want to know the applicant's age. We might have many "yes/no" properties like `age_less_than_18`, `age_between_18_and_60`, etc. But it will be tedious for the user to have to answer a series of questions like this. Instead, we will want to simply ask the subject's age and then use this information in different ways.

The first thing we do is define a routine called `parm/3` that asks the value of a given parameter, compares that value with the required value, and stores the reported value for later use. Of course, `parm` should look to see if it already knows the answer to its question before it asks, just as `prop` does.

The response to `parm` might be a selection from a menu, an atom (a name, for example), or a number. We will create an argument place for `parm` where we can tell it which kind of response to expect. This argument should always be an `m` for a menu choice, an `a` for an atom, or an `n` for a number. When we ask the user for the value of a parameter, we use different input routines depending on the type of answer we expect.

There are three arguments to `parm`: parameter name, parameter type, and parameter value. Usually all three of these arguments will already be instantiated, since the call to `parm` will be used as a condition in an identification rule. The call to `parm` succeeds if the parameter has the required value for the subject; otherwise, it fails. In the process, `parm` does one or the other of three things.

1. Looks in the working database to see if there is already information on the parameter. If there is, the call to `parm` succeeds or fails conclusively depending on whether the value given in the call to `parm` matches the one stored in the database.

2. If no value is stored and the expected type of response is a menu choice, `parm` finds the appropriate menu, prints the header for the menu, enumerates the choices, evokes a numerical response from the user corresponding to one of the choices, stores it, and tests it against the required value.

3. If no value is stored and the expected type of response is an atom or a number, `parm` retrieves and prints the appropriate question, evokes the appropriate type of response from the user, stores it, and tests it against the required value.

In the same way that properties can be used negatively in rules, so can parameters. For example, consider a system that determines the flight awards for which a frequent flyer is eligible. A frequent flyer with a certain number of miles might be eligible for a free round-trip ticket to anywhere in the United States except Alaska and Hawaii. We could use a `destination` parameter for this. The corresponding rule might say that the frequent flyer is entitled to a ticket provided he or she meets conditions including

```
\+ parm(destination,a,alaska),
\+ parm(destination,a,hawaii).
```

In this case, it is easier to indicate the destinations that are not allowed in negative conditions than to indicate the destinations that are allowed in positive conditions.

Another useful procedure is `parmset/3`, which uses the auxiliary predicate `member`.

```
parmset(+Parameter,+Type,+Set) :- parm(Parameter,Type,Value),
                                   member(Value,Set).
```

Suppose a condition for some identification rule is that the subject lives in New England. Rather than make this a property, we can make `lives_in_state` a parameter and make the condition succeed if the state is one of the New England states. Using two-letter postal codes for states, we can do this with the subgoal

```
parmset(lives_in_state,a,['CT','MA','ME','NH','RI','VT']).
```

For the accompanying question, we could use

```
question(lives_in_state,
        ['In which state do you live?',
         '(Enter two-letter postal code, all capitals.)'],
        'State of residence: ',
        '').
```

If we don't want to require that the postal code be given in capital letters, we could add Ct, ct, etc., to the set of values that satisfy the call to parmset.

We can represent the negative condition for frequent flyer eligibility in our earlier example more simply using parmset. It would be

```
\+ parmset(destination,a,[alaska,hawaii]).
```

Finally, we define a predicate parmrange/3 that checks to see if the numerical value of a parameter is in some specified range:

```
parmrange(Parameter,Minimum,Maximum)  :-
        parm(Parameter,n,Value),
        Minimum =< Value,
        Maximum >= Value.
```

This is the predicate we would use for our earlier examples age_less_than_18, age_between_18_and_60, etc. Instead of asking if the subject has each of these properties, we can use the subgoals parmrange(age,0,17) and parmrange(age,18,60). Notice that we don't need to tell parmrange the type of input to expect since it can only be numeric.

As with our earlier predicates, parmrange can of course be used in negative conditions. Suppose minors and senior citizens qualify for certain benefits under certain conditions. The rule for this might have either the condition

```
parmrange(age,0,20),
parmrange(age,65,1000)
```

or the simpler condition

```
\+ parmrange(age,21,64).
```

The advantage of using parmset and parmrange rather than a group of related properties is that the user only needs to answer a single question. This one answer is then used to satisfy or fail any number of conditions. Even if each condition specifies a unique value for a parameter rather than a set or range of acceptable values, it may be better to use parm instead of prop. Take the example of eye color. If the only eye color that ever shows up as a condition in any identification rule in the knowledge base is blue, then we might as well use the condition prop(blue_eyes). But some rules might require blue eyes, others brown eyes, and others green eyes. Then the conditions to use would have the form parm(eye_color,m,N) where the menu is

```
xkb_menu(eye_color,
        ['What color are your eyes?'],
        ['blue',
```

```
                    'green',
                    'brown',
                    'other.'],
                'Eye color: ').
```

With a single keystroke, the user gives information that can be used to satisfy or fail several different conditions.

These are all the tools we will need to make our identifications.

An XSHELL knowledge base will contain a set of identification rules, each of them a clause for the `xkb_identify` predicate. Each rule will use the predicates `prop`, `parm`, `parmset`, and `parmrange` in its conditions or subgoals. For every property or parameter named in a condition for an identification rule, we will also need to include an appropriate question or menu in the knowledge base. These will be stored in clauses for the predicates `xkb_question` and `xkb_menu`.

9.9. XSHELL'S EXPLANATORY FACILITY

The explanatory facility defined for XSHELL is quite simple. It displays the rule used to derive the last conclusion reported.

We will want to be able to turn our explanatory facility on and off. We do this with a clause in our knowledge base. If the clause `xkb_explain(no)` is in the knowledge base, XSHELL will not explain its conclusions. Otherwise, it will. If you want explanations, put the clause `xkb_explain(yes)` in your knowledge base. XSHELL will offer explanations even if this clause isn't in your knowledge base, but the clause will remind you that the explanatory facility is active.

When the procedure `explain/0` is called, it takes three successive courses of action until one succeeds.

1. It looks to see if `xkb_explain(no)` is in the knowledge base. If so, no explanation is required. So `explain` calls the auxiliary procedure `wait` and succeeds conclusively.

2. If (1) fails, then `xkb_explain(no)` is not in the knowledge base and an explanation should be offered. So `explain` asks the user if an explanation is wanted. If the answer is no, `explain` succeeds conclusively.

3. If (2) also fails, the user wants an explanation. So `explain` looks in the working database to find the last identification that was remembered and the rule that was used to derive it. This rule is displayed and explain succeeds.

Printing the rule that was used to make an identification in the form that the rule appears in the knowledge base will generally not be very helpful to the end user. It will be phrased using the predicates `prop`, `parm`, `parmset`, and `parmrange`, which the user may not understand. Also, it will use whatever short names the knowledge base builder gives to properties and parameters. The user may have difficulty associating these with the questions he has answered during the consultation. For this reason, a predicate `interpret/1` is provided that displays the conditions for rules in a format that the user is more likely to understand. This display is built out of information obtained from clauses for the predicates `xkb_question` and `xkb_menu`.

When xshell remembers an identification that has been made, it adds it to the working database using `asserta`. This puts the identification at the beginning of the clauses for the database predicate `known` where it will be found first by `explain`. We are using the predicate `known` in part as a stack for storing identifications with the most recent identification always on the top of the stack.

The procedure `explain` is invoked by `xshell` after a conclusion has been reached and reported. First `explain` checks whether `xkb_unique(no)` is in the knowledge base. If so, no explanation is required and the procedure `wait` is called. This procedure prints a message telling the user to press any key to continue and inputs a keystroke, allowing the user time to read the reported conclusion before the screen scrolls to print another question or menu.

If `xkb_explain(no)` is not in the knowledge base, `explain` asks the user if he would like to see the rule used to derive the last conclusion. If the user answers "no," `explain` succeeds without further action. If the user answers "yes," `explain` finds `known(identification,RULE)` to find the last identification rule that succeeded. It then prints the rule number and invokes `explain_aux/1`. This procedure does nothing more than pass individual conditions to the routine `interpret/1`, first separating complex conditions into their individual clauses. It is the procedure `interpret` that actually displays the conditions of the rule.

Corresponding to a property used in a rule is an `xkb_question/4` clause. The first argument for this clause is the internal property name and the second is the question itself. The third argument is a short piece of text saying that the subject has the property, and the fourth is a short piece of text saying that the subject does not have the property. The first clause in the definition of `interpret` prints the positive message as the interpretation of a `prop` condition, and the second clause prints the negative message as the interpretation of a `\+ prop` condition.

To interpret a condition involving a parameter where a menu is used to obtain the value of the parameter, the third clause for `interpret` uses the number in the condition indicating the menu choice to retrieve the text corresponding to that choice stored in the `xkb_menu/4` clause for that parameter. The auxiliary procedure `nth_member` is used for this. Also stored as the fourth argument for the `nth_member` clause is a short phrase identifying the parameter used in the condition. This phrase together with the text corresponding to the menu choice are printed to explain the condition.

For conditions involving parameters where the value of the parameter is entered as an atom or a number, `interpret` simply prints the short phrase identifying the parameter and the stored parameter value. For `parmset` and `parmrange` conditions, `interpret` prints, respectively, all allowable values or the maximum and minimum values. In interpreting negative conditions using `parm`, `parmset`, or `parmrange`, the only difference is that `NOT` is printed at an appropriate point in the display.

The last two clauses for `interpret` involve a kind of condition that we have not yet discussed. Consider once again a system for discovering the kinds of financial aid for which a student is eligible. There may be many scholarships available for juniors and seniors majoring in computer science who have a grade point average of

3.0 or higher. Each eligibility rule for these scholarships could contain the complex condition

```
parm(major,a,'computer science'),
parmset(year,a,[junior,senior]),
parmrange(gpa,3.0,4.0).
```

Alternatively, we could combine these conditions in defining a new condition that we might call good_upper_cs:

```
good_upper_cs :- parm(major,a,'computer science'),
                 parmset(year,a,[junior,senior]),
                 parmrange(gpa,3.0,4.0).
```

Then we can use good_upper_cs as a condition in the scholarship eligibility rules rather than the much longer complex condition. This makes the rules easier to write and easier to understand. But the user may not understand the condition good_upper_cs. So interpret must replace this condition with the parm, parmset, and parmrange conditions that define it. The next to last clause for interpret handles the case for negative defined conditions of this sort, and the last clause handles positive conditions. The clauses appear in this order because with the cuts in all earlier clauses, the final clause catches everything that drops through. These will be exactly the positive defined conditions.

For negative defined conditions, interpret reports that one of the defining conditions is not satisfied. The reports would become difficult to interpret if one negative condition were defined using another negative defined condition. However, this situation probably won't arise frequently.

Notice that all defined conditions must ultimately be grounded in conditions that use prop, parm, parmset, or parmrange, or interpret will fail. What other kinds of conditions might we include in XSHELL rules? An example might be a rule that required that the ratio of a person's body weight to height in inches should fall in a certain range. This complex condition could be represented as

```
parm(weight,n,W),
parm(height,n,H),
R is W/H,
Min <= R,
R <= Max.
```

If conditions like this occur in an XSHELL knowledge base, the explanatory facility should be turned off. Of course, it could be left on during system development since explain will at least print the rule number before encountering the uninterpretable condition and failing.[1]

As is clear from the code, interpret recurses until all the conditions upon which the rule depends have been interpreted.

---

[1]Notice also that variables occur in the two parm clauses in this example. This is not the usual case since this argument place is normally instantiated before parm is invoked.

9.10. CICHLID: A SAMPLE XSHELL KNOWLEDGE BASE

An XSHELL knowledge base will have eight things in it:

1. some initial clauses to load XSHELL if it is not already in memory and to erase any XSHELL knowledge base already in memory,

2. an introductory statement (a clause for `xkb_intro/1`),

3. `xkb_unique(yes)` or `xkb_unique(no)`,

4. `xkb_explain(yes)` or `xkb_explain(no)`,

5. a set of identification rules (clauses for `xkb_identify/2`),

6. text from which conclusions can be constructed (clauses for `xkb_text/2`),

7. a set of questions and menus for the properties and parameters used in the identification rules (clauses for `xkb_question/4` and `xkb_menu/4`), and

8. a starting query (`:- xshell.` or `?- xshell.`) to begin the consultation when the knowledge base is loaded, or instructions to tell the user how to type the starting query.

An example is the file CICHLID.PL, which contains an identification system that identifies tropical fish from the family *Cichlidae*. Rules for nine small or "dwarf" species are included. We will call the system itself CICHLID.

CICHLID has a lengthy introductory statement, given as a list of atoms to be printed by `writeln`. Also notice that we have included empty atoms where we want blank lines to appear in the message, and that quotation marks that are to be printed are written twice.

The identification of cichlids is not always easy. It is unlikely that anyone who knew much about these fish would confuse the species we have included in our knowledge base, but other species are difficult to distinguish. This is why we have allowed more than one identification (`xkb_explain(no)` is in the knowledge base) and use the phrase "Possible identification" in each of the conclusions we display. We include a line in the knowledge base to turn the explanatory facility on.

Some characteristics used to identify dwarf cichlids are the shape of the tail, the shape of the body, the shape of the other fins, and the presence or absence of a long stripe down the side of the body. We will use these features to make a first cut in identifying these fish.

The tail of a cichlid is either spear shaped with the tail coming to a point, lyre shaped with points at the top and bottom of the tail fin, or normal (rounded or triangular). These options are recorded in an `xkb_menu` clause for the parameter `caudal`. Two of our fish have spear-shaped tails, two have lyre-shaped tails, and the tails of the rest are normal. We use this parameter in the first condition of each identification rule.

The bodies of these fish are either long and narrow, short and deep, or what we might think of as a normal fish shape. Again, we have a parameter that can take one of three values. We use another short menu to ask the user for the fish's shape.

The dorsal (or top) fin of these fish may have some rays or spines near the front extended to form a crest or some rays at the back extended to form a streamer. The anal (or rear bottom) fin and the ventral (or front bottom) fins may also show a streamer. We represent each of these features as a distinct property the fish might have and provide an appropriate question for each.

The lateral stripe, or stripe down the side of the fish, is very distinct on some fish and irregular on others. On some fish, there is no lateral stripe at all. This gives us another parameter with three possible values.

Other features used to identify these fish visually include color and special markings. Color is represented in this knowledge base as a parameter. Other special markings are represented as properties. You can decipher these by comparing the names of the properties with their questions.

We have included far more information in our identification rules than we need to distinguish the nine species CICHLID can identify. However, all of this information would not be enough to make a positive identification if rules for other dwarf cichlids were added to the knowledge base. The knowledge base given here is actually an excerpt of a much larger knowledge base that includes dozens of species.

This raises an interesting dilemma for building knowledge bases. We could edit CICHLID.PL by eliminating many of the conditions in the identification rules. The resulting knowledge base would still allow us to identify all of the fish in the knowledge base, and the user would have to answer fewer questions. Shouldn't we do this?

If we are quite sure that we will never want to add any more species, then by all means we should simplify our rules. This will make the system easier to use. But if we anticipate adding more fish to the knowledge base, we should probably make each rule as complete as possible. We don't just want to give rules that will identify these nine species. We want rules that will help us distinguish these species from other species we might add to the knowledge base at a later time.

The knowledge base has another peculiarity. Only one fish is pale blue, only one fish has white-tipped fins, and other fish in the knowledge base have some property that distinguishes them from all the others. Why don't we put these distinguishing properties at the top of the rule in which they occur? Then we could identify each fish with a single, unique property.

Surprisingly, this approach will usually force the user to answer more questions rather than fewer.

Suppose each of our nine fish had some unique property. If these were the only properties listed, then a user would have to answer anywhere from one to nine questions to identify a particular fish. How many questions he had to answer would depend an how far down in the knowledge base the rule for his fish came. On average, he would have to answer five questions.

Suppose on the other hand that we could divide our nine fish into three groups of three with a single parameter. Then suppose we could divide each of these subgroups into individuals with another parameter. If we could do this, the user would always have to answer exactly two questions to identify any fish. Of course, this strategy is defeated because we have included more information than we really need just to tell these nine species apart. But the basic strategy is correct. Usually the best way to organize your rules will be to break the possible conclusions into large groups with a single question, then break each group into subgroups, and so on down to the level of the individual.

9.10.1. Listing of CICHLID.PL

```
% CICHLID.PL

% Contains an XSHELL knowledge base.
% Requires all procedures in XSHELL.PL.

:- ensure_loaded('xshell.pl').

%
% Any clauses for the predicates XKB_INTRO,
% XKB_REPORT, XKB_UNIQUE, XKB_EXPLAIN, XKB_IDENTIFY, and
% XKB_QUESTION should be removed from the knowledge base.
%

:- abolish(xkb_intro/1).
:- abolish(xkb_unique/1).
:- abolish(xkb_explain/1).
:- abolish(xkb_identify/2).
:- abolish(xkb_question/4).
:- abolish(xkb_menu/4).
:- abolish(xkb_text/2).

%
% XKB_IDENTIFY must be declared dynamic so the explanatory
% routine INTERPRET can access its clauses.
%

:- dynamic xkb_identify/2.

xkb_intro(
 ['',
  'CICHLID: An Expert System for Identifying Dwarf Cichlids',
  '',
  'The cichlids are a family of tropical fish.  Many of',
  'these fish are large and can only be kept in large',
  'aquariums. Others, called ''dwarf cichlids'', rarely',
  'exceed 3 inches and can be kept in smaller aquariums.',
  '',
  'This program will help you identify many of the more',
  'familiar species of dwarf cichlid.  Identification of',
  'these fish is not always easy, and the program may offer',
```

```
          'more than one possible identification.  Even then, you',
          'should consult photographs in an authoritative source',
          'such as Staek, AMERIKANISCHE CICHLIDEN I: KLEINE',
          'BUNTBARSCHE (Melle: Tetra Verlag, 1984), or Goldstein,',
          'CICHLIDS OF THE WORLD (Neptune City, New Jersey:',
          't.f.h. Publications, 1973) for positive identification.',
          '',
          'To use the program, simply describe the fish by',
          'answering the following questions.']).

xkb_unique(no).

xkb_explain(yes).

%
% xkb_identify(-Rule,-TextSet)
%    Each clause for this predicate provides a rule to be
%    used with the utility predicates in the XSHELL.PL file
%    to determine whether the fish to be identified is likely
%    to belong to the Species.
%

xkb_identify(1,[isa,agassizii]) :-
      parm(caudal,m,2),          % spear-shaped
      parm(body_shape,m,1),      % long and narrow
      parm(lateral_stripe,m,1),  % sharp, distinct
      prop(dorsal_streamer),
      prop(lateral_stripe_extends_into_tail).

xkb_identify(2,[isa,borelli]) :-
      parm(caudal,m,3),          % normal
      parm(body_shape,m,2),      % deep, heavy, short
      parm(lateral_stripe,m,2),  % irregular
      prop(dorsal_streamer),
      prop(ventral_streamer),
      prop(lateral_stripe_extends_into_tail),
      parm(color,m,5).    % yellow

xkb_identify(3,[isa,cockatoo]) :-
      parm(caudal,m,1),          % lyre-shaped
      parm(body_shape,m,2),      % deep, heavy, short
      parm(lateral_stripe,m,1),  % sharp, distinct
      prop(dorsal_crest),
      prop(dorsal_streamer),
      prop(anal_streamer),
      prop(stripes_in_lower_body),
```

```
      prop(lateral_stripe_extends_into_tail).

xkb_identify(4,[isa,trifasciata]) :-
      parm(caudal,m,3),              % normal
      parm(body_shape,m,3),          % normal
      parm(lateral_stripe,m,1),      % sharp, distinct
      prop(dorsal_crest),
      prop(dorsal_streamer),
      prop(anal_streamer),
      prop(ventral_streamer),
      prop(lateral_stripe_extends_into_tail),
      prop(angular_line_above_ventral).

xkb_identify(5,[isa,brichardi]) :-
      parm(caudal,m,1),              % lyre-shaped
      parm(body_shape,m,3),          % normal
      parm(lateral_stripe,m,3),      % not visible
      parm(color,m,2),               % pale gray
      prop(gill_spot),
      prop(fins_trimmed_white).

xkb_identify(6,[isa,krib]) :-
      parm(caudal,m,2),              % spear-shaped
      parm(body_shape,m,1),          % long and narrow
      prop(dorsal_streamer),
      prop(anal_streamer),
      prop(orange_spots_in_tail).

xkb_identify(7,[isa,ram]) :-
      parm(caudal,m,3),              % normal
      parm(body_shape,m,2),          % deep, heavy, short
      parm(lateral_stripe,m,3),      % not visible
      prop(dorsal_crest),
      parm(color,m,4).               % violet, yellow, claret

xkb_identify(8,[isa,nannacara]) :-
      parm(caudal,m,3),              % normal
      parm(body_shape,m,2),          % deep, heavy, short
      parm(lateral_stripe,m,3),      % not visible
      parm(color,m,3).               % metallic bronze, green

xkb_identify(9,[isa,nudiceps]) :-
      parm(caudal,m,3),              % normal
      parm(body_shape,m,1),          % long and narrow
      parm(lateral_stripe,m,3),      % not visible
      parm(color,m,1).               % pale blue
```

```
xkb_question(dorsal_crest,
     ['Are any fin rays at the front of the dorsal fin',
      'clearly extended above the rest of the fin?'],
     'Front rays of dorsal fin are extended.',
     'Front rays of dorsal fin are not extended.').

xkb_question(dorsal_streamer,
     ['Are any fin rays at the back of the dorsal fin',
      'clearly extended into a long streamer?'],
     'Rear rays of dorsal fin are extended.',
     'Rear rays of dorsal fin are not extended.').

xkb_question(anal_streamer,
     ['Are any fin rays at the back of the anal fin',
      'clearly extended into a long streamer?'],
     'Rear rays of anal fin are extended.',
     'Rear rays of anal fin are not extended.').

xkb_question(ventral_streamer,
     ['Are any fin rays at the bottom of the ventral',
      'fins clearly extended into streamers?'],
     'Rays of anal fin are extended.',
     'Rays of anal fin are not extended.').

xkb_question(lateral_stripe_extends_into_tail,
     ['Does the stripe down the side extend into the base',
      'of the tail?'],
     'The lateral stripe extends into the tail.',
     'The lateral stripe does not extend into the tail.').

xkb_question(stripes_in_lower_body,
     ['Are there horizontal stripes in the lower part',
      'of the body?'],
     'Horizontal stripes present in the lower body.',
     'There are no horizontal stripes in the lower body.').

xkb_question(angular_line_above_ventral,
     ['Is there an angular line above the ventral fin',
      'slanting from the pectoral downward toward the',
      'stomach region?'],
     'Slanting body line is present.',
     'Slanting body line is absent.').

xkb_question(orange_spots_in_tail,
     ['Are there black spots trimmed in orange in',
```

```
        'the tail fin?'],
        'Orange-trimmed black spots present in tail.',
        'There are no orange trimmed black spots in the tail.').

xkb_question(gill_spot,'Is there a dark spot on the gill?',
        'Dark spot present on gill.',
        'There is no dark spot on the gill.').

xkb_question(fins_trimmed_white,
        'Are the unpaired fins trimmed with a white edge?',
        'Unpaired fins are trimmed with white edge.',
        'The unpaired fins do not have a white edge.').

xkb_menu(caudal,
        ['What is the shape of the tail-fin?'],
        ['lyre-shaped',
         'spear-shaped',
         'normal, i.e, round or fan-shaped'],
        'Tail fin is ').

xkb_menu(body_shape,
        ['What is the shape of the body?'],
        ['long and narrow',
         'deep, heavy, and short',
         'normal fish shape'],
        'Body is ').

xkb_menu(lateral_stripe,
        ['Describe the line running the length of the body.'],
        ['sharp and distinct from eye to base of tail',
         'irregular, indistinct or incomplete',
         'not visible or barely visible'],
        'Lateral body stripe is ').

xkb_menu(color,
        ['What is the basic color of the body?'],
        ['pale blue',
         'pale gray',
         'metallic bronze or green',
         'violet, yellow and claret highlights',
         'yellow',
         'not listed'],
        'The basic body color is ').

xkb_text(isa,
['Possible identification: ']).
```

```
xkb_text(agassizii,
['Apistogramma agassizii ',
 '(Agassiz''s dwarf cichlid)']).

xkb_text(borelli,
['Apistogramma borelli ',
 '(Borell''s dwarf cichlid)']).

xkb_text(cockatoo,
['Apistogramma cacatuoides ',
 '(cockatoo dwarf cichlid)']).

xkb_text(trifasciata,
['Apistogramma trifasciata ',
 '(three-striped dwarf cichlid)']).

xkb_text(brichardi,
['Lamprologus brichardi']).

xkb_text(krib,
['Pelvicachromis pulcher ',
 '(krib or kribensis)']).

xkb_text(ram,
['Microgeophagus ramirezi ',
 '(Ram, or butterfly dwarf cichlid)']).

xkb_text(nannacara,
['Nannacara anomala']).

xkb_text(nudiceps,
['Nanochromis nudiceps']).

:- write('Type  xshell.  to start.').
```

9.11. A CONSULTATION WITH CICHLID

The following is a sample consultation session with the expert system composed of the XSHELL consultation driver and the CICHLID knowledge base.

```
?- consult('cichlid.pl').

CICHLID: An Expert System for Identifying Dwarf Cichlids
...
To use the program, simply describe the fish by
```

answering the following questions.

Press Return when ready to continue. <Return>

What is the shape of the tail-fin?

1. lyre-shaped
2. spear-shaped
3. normal, i.e, round or fan-shaped
>2

What is the shape of the body?

1. long and narrow
2. deep, heavy, and short
3. normal fish shape
>1

Describe the line running the length of the body.

1. sharp and distinct from eye to base of tail
2. irregular, indistinct or incomplete
3. not visible or barely visible
>1

Are any fin rays at the back of the dorsal fin
clearly extended into a long streamer?
>y

Does the stripe down the side extend into the base
of the tail?
>y

Possible identification:
Apistogramma agassizii (Agassiz's dwarf cichlid)

Do you want to see the rule that was used
to reach the conclusion?
>y

Rule 1: reach this conclusion IF
Tail fin is spear-shaped.
Body is long and narrow.

```
Lateral body stripe is sharp and distinct from eye to base of tail.
Rear rays of dorsal fin are extended.
The lateral stripe extends into the tail.

Press return when ready to continue. <Return>


Are any fin rays at the back of the anal fin
clearly extended into a long streamer?
>n

I cannot reach any further conclusion.
Do you want to conduct another consultation?
>n
yes
```

The program terminates by returning to the Prolog top level environment, which answers yes because the original query has succeeded.

Exercise 9.11.1

> *Lamprologus leleupi* is a small yellow cichlid with a long, narrow body and a rounded tail. It does not have streamers on any of its fins, and it does not have a line on the side of its body. Its iris is blue. Modify the CICHLID knowledge base so that it can identify *Lamprologus leleupi*.

9.12. PAINT: A SAMPLE XSHELL KNOWLEDGE BASE

An important area of expert system development is product recommendation. While selecting an appropriate product for a particular application is not so glamorous a domain as medical diagnosis or oil exploration, this is a common problem that all of us encounter regularly. In this section, we will describe the knowledge base for a relatively simple system for selecting an appropriate paint system for a typical interior application. PAINT.PL, like CICHLID.PL, represents a small piece of a large knowledge base. The larger system includes recommendations for both interior and exterior residential and industrial applications.

While CICHLID.PL is a typical classification system, PAINT.PL has more the flavor of a diagnostic system. The two knowledge bases were developed in different ways that correspond to the differences in how we conceive these two tasks. For CICHLID.PL, assuming that additional species will be added later, a reasonable approach is to include as complete a description as possible for each species included. In the case of PAINT.PL, a better approach is to examine the process that a paint store clerk might use to arrive at a recommendation. Typically, a customer would describe his or her application without much prompting in sufficient detail to allow the clerk to recommend an appropriate paint system. The clerk might ask a few questions to obtain additional information that the customer did not recognize as relevant. A flaw in the process is that the clerk might assume that the customer is more knowledgeable than he or she actually is and assume that certain considerations do not apply because the customer did not mention them. With our expert system, the user volunteers nothing and the system must elicit all information necessary to make a recommendation. An advantage of the expert system, of course, is that it cannot forget a relevant question or mistakenly draw conclusions from the silence of the user the way a human expert might. But this means that we must consider what the clerk would do in the case that the customer volunteers no more than the fact that he or she needs to paint something.

The first thing the clerk needs to know is what is to be painted: walls, floors, etc. Next the clerk needs to know the material that the surface to be painted is made of: wood, plaster, etc. Third, the clerk needs to know if the surface to be painted has been painted previously and, if so, the condition of this prior coating. Finally, the clerk needs to know something about the environment. We are assuming an interior environment; the only other question we will consider is whether the paint will be exposed to high moisture as it might be in a kitchen or bathroom. To keep our system simple, these are the only considerations we will include.

A reasonable way to proceed is with a flowchart. We put the first question to be asked at the top of the chart and draw arrows from it to other questions, one arrow for each possible answer to the first question. The completed chart represents the search space for our system. In the completed chart, each path from the top to the bottom of the chart represents a sequence of questions and answers that might take place between the clerk and the customer. Each of these paths also represents a rule in our knowledge base. Each question represents a property or parameter and each answer represents whether a property condition is positive or negative, or represents a value for a parameter. This is how PAINT.PL was developed.

In looking at the flow chart for PAINT.PL, we notice that certain combinations of questions and answers concerning prior coatings regularly occur together at mid-levels in paths. If the surface has been painted before, we need to know if the old paint is in sound condition. If it is, then we need to know whether the old paint is glossy. It was convenient to group the possibilities using one negative property condition and three defined conditions:

- `\+ prop(painted),`

- `bad_paint,`

- `glossy_paint,`

- `nonglossy_paint.`

A complete paint recommendation does not consist simply in recommending a product. Any professional painter will tell you that proper preparation of the surface to be painted is essential. Instructions for preparing the surface must be part of a complete recommendation. Once prepared, it may be necessary to apply more than one product in a certain sequence. For typical residential applications, it may be necessary to apply one product as a base coat or primer and a different product as the finish coat. In some industrial applications, a third product applied between the primer and the finish coat may be advisable. Thus, the computer should

recommend an appropriate paint *system*. This is where the advantage of representing
conclusions for rules as lists of boiler-plate text that can be assembled for the report
becomes obvious. Recommendations for preparation, primer, finish coat, and other
special instructions can be stored separately and assembled to fit a particular paint
application. This also simplifies maintenance of the system. If a new preparation
method were adopted for several paint applications, or if a new product became
available, it would only be necessary to revise the text in a few `xkb_text` clauses
rather than in affected `xkb_identify` clauses that might number in the hundreds in
a medium sized system.

9.12.1. Listing of PAINT.PL

```
% PAINT.PL

:- ensure_loaded('xshell.pl').

%
% Any clauses for the predicates XKB_INTRO,
% XKB_REPORT, XKB_UNIQUE, XKB_EXPLAIN, XKB_IDENTIFY, and
% XKB_QUESTION should be removed from the knowledge base.
%

:- abolish(xkb_intro/1).
:- abolish(xkb_unique/1).
:- abolish(xkb_explain/1).
:- abolish(xkb_identify/2).
:- abolish(xkb_question/4).
:- abolish(xkb_menu/4).
:- abolish(xkb_text/2).

%
% XKB_IDENTIFY and the following predicates defined in
% the knowledge base must be declared dynamic so the
% explanatory routine INTERPRET can access their clauses.
%

:- dynamic xkb_identify/2.
:- dynamic bad_paint/0.
:- dynamic glossy_paint/0.
:- dynamic nonglossy_paint/0.

xkb_intro(
['PAINT PRO:',
 '',
 'This system makes recommendations for common interior',
 'painting situations. The recommendations include advice',
```

```
    'on preparing the surface for painting and advice on the',
    'coating products to use for the job',
    '',
    'To use the system, just answer the following questions',
    'about your painting job.']).


xkb_unique(no).


xkb_explain(yes).


xkb_identify(1,[new_drywall_prep,enamel]) :-
        parm(surface,m,1),      % walls or ceilings
        parm(material1,m,1),    % drywall/sheetrock
        \+ prop(painted),
        prop(high_moisture).    % kitchen, bathroom, laundry


xkb_identify(2,[new_drywall_prep,latex]) :-
        parm(surface,m,1),      % walls or ceilings
        parm(material1,m,1),    % drywall/sheetrock
        \+ prop(painted),
        \+ prop(high_moisture).


xkb_identify(3,[standard_prep,stain_killer,enamel]) :-
        parm(surface,m,1),      % walls or ceilings
        parm(material1,m,2),    % wood or vinyl paneling
        \+ prop(painted),
        prop(high_moisture).    % kitchen, bathroom, laundry


xkb_identify(4,[standard_prep,stain_killer,latex]) :-
        parm(surface,m,1),      % walls or ceilings
        parm(material1,m,2),    % wood or vinyl paneling
        \+ prop(painted),
        \+ prop(high_moisture).


xkb_identify(5,[bare_plaster_prep,enamel]) :-
        parm(surface,m,1),      % walls or ceilings
        parm(material1,m,3),    % plaster
        \+ prop(painted),
        prop(high_moisture).    % kitchen, bathroom, laundry


xkb_identify(6,[bare_plaster_prep,latex]) :-
        parm(surface,m,1),      % walls or ceilings
        parm(material1,m,3),    % plaster
        \+ prop(painted),
        \+ prop(high_moisture).
```

```
xkb_identify(7,[bare_masonry_prep,latex_primer,enamel]) :-
        parm(surface,m,1),       % walls or ceilings
        parm(material1,m,4),     % masonry
        \+ prop(painted),
        prop(high_moisture).

xkb_identify(standard_prep,[bare_masonry_prep,latex_primer,latex]) :-
        parm(surface,m,1),       % walls or ceilings
        parm(material1,m,4),     % masonry
        \+ prop(painted),
        prop(high_moisture).

xkb_identify(9,[bad_paint_prep,enamel]) :-
        parm(surface,m,1),       % walls or ceilings
        parmset(material1,m,[1,2,3]),
                                 % sheetrock, paneling, or plaster
        bad_paint,
        prop(high_moisture).

xkb_identify(10,[bad_paint_prep,latex]) :-
        parm(surface,m,1),       % walls or ceilings
        parmset(material1,m,[1,2,3]),
                    % sheetrock, paneling, or plaster
        bad_paint,
        \+ prop(high_moisture).

xkb_identify(11,[glossy_prep,standard_prep,enamel,
              latex_over_oil_prep]) :-
        parm(surface,m,1),       % walls or ceilings
        parmset(material1,m,[1,2,3]),
                    % sheetrock, paneling, or plaster
        glossy_paint,
        prop(high_moisture).

xkb_identify(12,[glossy_prep,standard_prep,latex,
              latex_over_oil_prep]) :-
        parm(surface,m,1),       % walls or ceilings
        parmset(material1,m,[1,2,3]),
                    % sheetrock, paneling, or plaster
        glossy_paint,
        \+ prop(high_moisture).

xkb_identify(13,[standard_prep,enamel]) :-
        parm(surface,m,1),       % walls or ceilings
        parmset(material1,m,[1,2,3]),
                    % sheetrock, paneling, or plaster
```

```
        nonglossy_paint,
        prop(high_moisture).

xkb_identify(14,[standard_prep,latex]) :-
        parm(surface,m,1),      % walls or ceilings
        parmset(material1,m,[1,2,3]),
                    % sheetrock, paneling, or plaster
        nonglossy_paint,
        \+ prop(high_moisture).

xkb_identify(15,[painted_masonry_prep,enamel]) :-
        parm(surface,m,1),      % wall, ceilings, or floors
        parm(material1,m,4),    % masonry
        prop(painted),
        prop(high_moisture).

xkb_identify(16,[painted_masonry_prep,latex]) :-
        parm(surface,m,1),      % wall, ceilings, or floors
        parm(material1,m,4),    % masonry
        prop(painted),
        \+ prop(high_moisture).

xkb_identify(17,[bare_wood_prep,polyurethane]) :-
        parm(surface,m,2),       % wood doors, trim, cabinets
        \+ prop(painted).

xkb_identify(18,[bad_coating_on_wood_prep,polyurethane]) :-
        parm(surface,m,2),       % wood doors, trim, cabinets
        bad_paint.

xkb_identify(19,[glossy_prep,standard_prep,polyurethane,
                opaque_wood_finish,latex_over_oil_prep]) :-
        parm(surface,m,2),       % wood doors, trim, cabinets
        glossy_paint.

xkb_identify(20,[standard_prep,polyurethane,
                opaque_wood_finish]):-
        parm(surface,m,2),       % wood doors, trim, cabinets
        nonglossy_paint.

xkb_identify(21,[wood_floor_prep,polyurethane]) :-
        parm(surface,m,3),       % floors
        parm(material2,m,1).     % wood

xkb_identify(22,[painted_masonry_prep,masonry_sealer,
                trim_enamel]) :-
```

```
          parm(surface,m,3),       % floors
          parm(material2,m,2),     % masonry
          prop(painted).

xkb_identify(23,[bare_masonry_prep,masonry_sealer,
              trim_enamel]) :-
          parm(surface,m,3),       % floors
          parm(material2,m,2),     % masonry
          \+ prop(painted).

bad_paint :- prop(painted),
                  \+ prop(sound_paint).

glossy_paint :- prop(painted),
                  prop(sound_paint),
                  prop(glossy_paint).

nonglossy_paint :- prop(painted),
                  prop(sound_paint),
                  \+ prop(glossy_paint).

xkb_question(high_moisture,
['Are you painting in an area where you can expect',
 'high moisture or where frequent cleaning may be',
 'necessary (kitchen, bathroom, laundry)?'],
 'High moisture or frequent cleaning expected.',
 'Neither high moisture nor frequent cleaning expected.').

xkb_question(painted,
'Has the surface been painted or varnished before?',
'The surface has a previous coating.',
'The surface has no previous coating.').

xkb_question(sound_paint,
'Is the existing paint or varnish in sound condition?',
'Previous coating is in sound condition.',
'Previous coating is unsound.').

xkb_question(glossy_paint,
'Is the existing paint or varnish glossy?',
'Previous coating is glossy.',
'Previous coating is not glossy.').

xkb_menu(surface,
'What kind of surface do you plan to paint or varnish?',
['walls or ceiling',
```

```
'wood doors, trim, or cabinets',
 'floors'],
'Surface: ').

xkb_menu(material1,
'What kind of material is the surface made of?',
['drywall/sheetrock',
 'wood or vinyl paneling',
 'plaster',
 'masonry (concrete, concrete block, brick)'],
'Material: ').

xkb_menu(material2,
'What kind of material is the surface made of?',
['wood',
 'masonry (concrete, concrete block, brick)'],
'Material: ').

xkb_text(new_drywall_prep,
['Remove all dust from taping and finishing work using',
 'wet vac or damp (not wet) cloth.',
 'Prime with a latex enamel undercoater. Spot prime patches',
 'of drywall mud, then cover entire surface.']).

xkb_text(stain_killer,
['Prime vinyl paneling with a commercial stain killer.']).

xkb_text(bare_plaster_prep,
['Allow all new plaster to age at least 30 days before painting.',
 'Remove dust with damp (not wet) cloth.',
 'Prime with a latex enamel undercoater.']).

xkb_text(bare_masonry_prep,
['Efflorescence, a white powdery alkaline salt, is present in',
 'and on most masonry surfaces. This must be removed completely',
 'before painting. Wire brush all heavy deposits. Mix 1 part',
 'muriatic acid with three parts water and apply to surfaces.',
 'Rinse with clear water as soon as the foaming action stops.',
 'Never allow muriatic solution to dry on the surface before',
 'rinsing as this will damage the surface or cause premature',
 'coating failure. If acid etching is not practical, power wash',
 'the surface to remove all powdery deposits, chalk, dirt,',
 'grease, and oil.']).

xkb_text(bad_paint_prep,
['Scrape away all loose and peeling paint. Sand to a sound',
```

```
'surface. Sand adjoining area to feather into peeled area.',
'Prime any cracks, holes, or large repairs BEFORE patching',
'and then again AFTER patching. The primer provides a sound',
'bond for the patching material and then prepares the patch',
'for painting. Use an interior latex undercoater for spot',
'priming and to prime entire surface before painting.']).

xkb_text(glossy_prep,
['Sand glossy surfaces lightly.']).

xkb_text(latex_over_oil_prep,
['If existing paint is oil-based, prime with a commercial',
'stain killer before painting with latex paint.']).

xkb_text(standard_prep,
['Use a household detergent to clean away all dirt, dust,',
'grease, and oil from all surfaces to be painted. Rinse',
'and wipe all detergent residue from surfaces with clean',
'water before painting.']).

xkb_text(painted_masonry_prep,
['Scrape away peeling paint or use a power grinder to grind',
'away peeling paint.',
'Efflorescence, a white powdery alkaline salt, is present in',
'and on most masonry surfaces. This must be removed completely',
'before painting. Wire brush all heavy deposits. Mix 1 part',
'muriatic acid with three parts water and apply to worst areas.',
'Rinse with clear water as soon as the foaming action stops.',
'Never allow muriatic solution to dry on the surface before',
'rinsing as this will damage the surface or cause premature',
'coating failure. If acid etching is not practical, power wash',
'the surface to remove all powdery deposits, chalk, dirt,',
'grease, and oil.']).

xkb_text(bare_wood_prep,
['Sand lightly and remove dust with a wet vac or a damp cloth.']).

xkb_text(bad_coating_on_wood_prep,
['Scrape away all loose and peeling paint or varnish.',
'Sand to a sound surface. Sand adjoining area to feather',
'into peeled area. Lightly sand entire surface. Remove all',
'dust with a wet vac or a damp cloth.']).

xkb_text(wood_floor_prep,
['Sand smooth and remove all sanding dust. Remove or',
'neutralize residues from any wood lighteners (wood',
```

```
'bleach) or removers before finishing.']).

xkb_text(latex_primer,
['Prime with latex enamel undercoater.']).

xkb_text(masonry_sealer,
['Prime with an alkyd resin based masonry primer sealer.']).

xkb_text(enamel,
['Finish with interior latex semigloss enamel or interior alkyd',
 'enamel for resistance to moisture and easy cleaning.']).

xkb_text(latex,
['Finish with flat or semigloss interior latex paint.']).

xkb_text(polyurethane,
['Stain to desired shade and finish with a clear poly-',
 'urethane finish.']).

xkb_text(opaque_wood_finish,
['For opaque finishes, prime with an alkyd sealer primer',
 'and finish with a gloss or semigloss alkyd, acrylic latex,',
 'or polyurethane enamel.']).

xkb_text(trim_enamel,
['Paint with acrylic latex floor and trim enamel.']).

:- write('Type  xshell.  to start.').
```

9.13. DEVELOPING XSHELL KNOWLEDGE BASES

In this section we will suggest ways to go about building, verifying, debugging, and documenting an XSHELL knowledge base. The approach generally taken to expert system development is FAST PROTOTYPING. The idea is to get a prototype that represents part of the final system running quickly. Then the development goes through a cycle of acquiring more knowledge from experts or knowledge documents, analyzing the knowledge, converting the knowledge to the proper form to include in the developing knowledge base, and testing and evaluating the result. This process is repeated through as many iterations as are needed to bring the system to the level of performance required. Since this is the usual approach to expert system development, many of the methods included in this section are aimed at getting your prototype running as quickly as possible. The idea is to get the knowledge right before putting much time into carefully formulating your questions, menus, and conclusion reports.

An XSHELL consultation centers around making identifications. The first thing you should do in building an XSHELL knowledge base, then, is to decide on the kinds of identifications, diagnoses, prescriptions, or other conclusions you will want the finished expert system to make. These should be related in some way, belonging to a clearly defined domain. The same expert system wouldn't both identify tropical fish and make recommendations for paint applications.

As you build your rules, be sure to include comments in your code that indicate the situation a particular rule is intended to cover. Your choices of property and parameter names will help in this regard, but a brief comment combining several conditions into one clear statement can be invaluable to anyone trying to understand the knowledge base later. Also, notice how we have added comments to `parm` conditions that use menus to indicate the menu choice represented by the number in the condition.

At first, we suggest you use the name of a property or a parameter enclosed in asterisks (*) as its own question or menu heading. For example, you might have this question in your knowledge base:

```
xkb_question(age,'*age*',prefix,'').
```

As you add rules that use a particular property or parameter, you may refine your idea of what that property or parameter involves. This will affect the eventual form of the question. By putting in a placeholder initially, you avoid having to revise the question or menu repeatedly. Similarly, use short phrases for menu choices. When the rules are complete, you can then put your questions and menus into their final forms. By postponing exact formulation of questions and menus, you can also get your prototype system up and running faster.

Once you have your simplified rules and questions, you will need to add a few lines to your knowledge base to get it to run. First, put

```
xkb_intro('Introduction').
```

at the beginning. When you run XSHELL with your knowledge base, the word "Introduction" will appear when the consultation starts. Later you will replace this with a description of your expert system and instructions for using it.

You should already know whether your expert system will give only one identification or might give several. Put

```
xkb_unique(yes).
```

or

```
xkb_unique(no).
```

in your knowledge base to reflect this.

To turn on the explanatory facility, put

```
xkb_explain(yes).
```

in the knowledge base. You may want to change this later, but you will want to see explanations while you are verifying and debugging your knowledge base.

Notice in CICHLID.PL and PAINT.PL how we have used descriptive atoms to label the text stored in `xkb_text` clauses. Add the clause

```
xkb_text(X,[X]).
```

to your knowledge base. This will allow you to test and debug your system before you put in any actual text for conclusions. When a conclusion is reached, the system will report it by printing only the labels for the text blocks. If you use this strategy to get your prototype running quickly, be sure to remove this clause later when you enter your actual `xkb_text` clauses. Otherwise, you will get multiple reports for your conclusions containing combinations of text labels and actual text.

Eventually, you may want to put lines at the beginning of your knowledge base that erase any XSHELL knowledge base predicates already in memory when you load your knowledge base. You can copy these from the files CICHLID.PL or PAINT.PL. But for now just add the command line

```
:- ensure_loaded('xshell.pl').
```

at the very beginning of your knowledge base and, if your Prolog system accepts starting queries, the command line

```
:- xshell.
```

at the very end. (Some Prologs may not read the last line properly unless a blank line follows it.) These will automatically load XSHELL.PL if it is not already loaded, and then start the consultation after loading your knowledge base.

You are ready for your first run. Start your Prolog interpreter and load your knowledge base. If you get any error messages during loading, write them down and consult the user's manual for your Prolog interpreter. Common errors are omitted commas and misplaced periods. XSHELL.PL should load automatically when you load your knowledge base, and this file will in turn load various I/O files listed at the top of the XSHELL.PL listing. If your Prolog interpreter cannot find one of these files, this will cause an error.

Once you get your knowledge base to load properly (and to load XSHELL.PL and the other files properly), the consultation should begin automatically and the message 'Introduction' should appear on the screen. If the message doesn't appear and `xshell` fails immediately, you forgot to put an `xkb_intro` clause in your knowledge base.

Next you should be asked about the property or parameter in the first condition of the first identification rule of your knowledge base. If instead you get the message that no conclusion can be drawn, one of two things has probably happened: You have left out your identification rules, or you have left out your questions. Go back and correct this problem.

Once questions start appearing, give answers that will satisfy the conditions for your first identification rule. If XSHELL skips over any question for one of these conditions, it should be because you put the wrong parameter value in an earlier condition or you didn't provide a question for one of the conditions. Check for these common errors and make the corrections.

Eventually, you should be asked all the questions required by the first identification rule in your knowledge base. Give the required answers to each of these. Then a list of text labels corresponding to the conclusion of your first identification rule should appear on the screen. If instead XSHELL continues to ask you questions, you may have forgotten to put a list of text labels in your identification rule or you may have forgotten to put the clause

```
xkb_text(X,[X]).
```

in your knowledge base. To check to see if you gave the correct answers to satisfy the identification rule, break out of XSHELL and use the query

```
?- listing(known).
```

This will tell you what answers were recorded for the questions you were asked. You can compare these with your identification rules to try to pin down any problems. Be sure to retract all clauses for the predicate **known** to erase the working database before restarting your expert system.

Suppose XSHELL reports its identification but continues to ask questions even though only one identification was expected. Then you did not put `xkb_unique(no)` in your knowledge base.

You should be able to make any identification rule in your knowledge base succeed. Perhaps one rule is succeeding before you can get to the rule you are trying to make succeed. You may be able to solve the problem by reversing the order of these two rules. Or you may need to add another condition to the earlier rule. The second solution is preferred, since then the operation of the system will not depend on the order of the rules in the knowledge base. When rule order is an essential element of the knowledge base, the system becomes more difficult to maintain or to expand.

Another method you might try is to add one rule at a time to your knowledge base, verifying that each rule is working properly before you add the next. Put each new rule at the beginning of your knowledge base so you can make it succeed quickly. If you use this strategy, it is particularly important that you wait until all the rules have been added before you replace the short versions of your questions and menus with the final versions. A single parameter might be used by several identification rules, and you may find yourself continually rewriting the question or menu for a parameter if you don't leave this step for last.

Once you have verified your knowledge base in this simplified version, you can go back and replace your short introductory statement, properties, parameters, questions, menus, and conclusions text with the longer versions you want. You don't have to replace the names of properties and parameters with longer names, but longer, more descriptive names are helpful in documenting your knowledge base.

You will want to run your expert system again, trying to get each identification rule to succeed. This will let you see what each of your questions and conclusions looks like. If you use menus for any of your questions, trying to make each identification rule succeed will also point out choices that may have been omitted from menus.

These are some of the methods that you can use to get XSHELL running with your knowledge base. Of course, we are assuming that there are no bugs in your XSHELL.PL file itself. You can use the CICHLID.PL and PAINT.PL files to verify that XSHELL is operating properly. You can also use the trace facility in your Prolog interpreter to trace the actual execution during a consultation.

Developing a knowledge base for an expert system is difficult the first time you try it, but it is easier if you approach the job systematically. Don't try to do everything at once. By following the recommendations in this section, you should be able to get small to medium-sized systems running quickly. The difficult part is the acquisition and analysis of the knowledge to put into your system; but that problem goes well beyond the scope of this book.

Exercise 9.13.1

In this chapter, we described an expert system that can identify several barnyard animals: horses, cows, goats, pigs, chickens, ducks, crows, dogs, cats, and rats. Construct an XSHELL knowledge base for such a system; call it BARNYARD.PL.

Exercise 9.13.2

Add sheep to BARNYARD.PL. Did you have to change any of the rules that were already in BARNYARD.PL to get it to work properly? Why or why not?

Exercise 9.13.3

The file CAR.PL in Chapter 2 contains a simple expert system that diagnoses automobile starting problems. Compare CAR.PL with XSHELL.PL, explaining how similar jobs are done in each. Rewrite the CAR expert system using XSHELL.

9.14. BIBLIOGRAPHICAL NOTES

Expert system design is a broad subject; Jackson (1986) gives a good overview, with detailed information about MYCIN, DENDRAL, and other classic expert systems, as well as discussion of how various kinds of inference engines work. A popular text on expert systems is Luger (1989). Merritt (1989) and Bowen (1991) are devoted to expert system development in Prolog. Some leading journals are *Expert Systems* and *IEEE Expert*. Buchanan (1986) gives a 366-item bibliography dealing solely with expert systems that are now in practical (rather than experimental) use. Richer (1986) reviews the commercial expert system development tools ART, KEE, Knowledge Craft, and S.1, each of which comprises a shell and a powerful knowledge base building environment. Other references were given at the beginning of the chapter.

Chapter 10

An Expert System Shell
with Uncertainty

10.1. UNCERTAINTY, PROBABILITY, AND CONFIDENCE

About many things we can be certain. We are sure that the apple we are eating is red and sweet. We are sure that no bachelor is married. And we are sure that the sun rises in the east and sets in the west. About other things we are less than certain. We expect birds to fly. We expect matches to burn when they are struck. And we expect rain when we see dark clouds. But in none of these cases do we have the certainty that we have in the previous examples.

Despite our lack of certainty about many things, we must still make decisions based on what we believe or expect. We must arrive at conclusions based on incomplete or uncertain information, opinion or belief.

The use of expert systems cannot save us from the risk we take when we base our decisions on uncertain grounds. In fact, we run a greater risk if we rely on expert systems that take everything we tell them to be completely certain. People manage, and in many cases manage very well, even when there is some uncertainty in the evidence available to them. For expert systems to fulfill their promise, they must be able to distinguish between what is certain and what is not, and to arrive at conclusions based on uncertain information that compare well with the conclusions reached by a human expert.

When we do not know that something is so but the evidence leads us to believe that it is so, we often say that it is probably so. One way to deal with uncertainty would be to clarify what we mean when we say that something is probably so. There is a well developed mathematical theory of probability. We could extend the inference engine in Prolog, building a new inference engine that can reason about probabilities using this mathematical theory.

Attractive though this suggestion may sound, there are at least two good reasons why this approach usually is not taken. The first reason involves basic assumptions built into the mathematical theory of probabilities. The second is based on observation of human experts.

We will expect the probabilities of complex situations to be determined by the probabilities of their component situations. For example, the probability that interest will rise while unemployment falls will be a function of the probability that interest will rise and the probability that unemployment will fall. What is this function? Probability theory gives us an answer, provided interest rates and unemployment are causally independent. But there is reason to think that interest rates and unemployment are not independent. Where two situations are somehow dependent on each other, probability theory cannot tell us how to compute their joint probability from their individual probabilities.

Besides this, observation shows that human experts do not normally adjust their confidences in a way that fits probability theory. Actual practice suggests a different approach, one that has not yet been fully analyzed. Many different inference engines have been built around these observations, each an attempt to capture the way human experts reason with uncertain information.

Because the pattern of confidence human experts exhibit does not fit the mathematical theory of probability, we will not talk about the probabilities of different situations or outcomes at all. Instead, we will use the term confidence factor or certainty factor. The confidence factor of a hypothesis will be the measure of our inclination to accept or reject that hypothesis. Our confidence in some hypotheses does appear to determine our confidence in others, even if no final agreement has been reached about the correct method for computing this determination.

In this chapter, we will build another expert system shell. Unlike XSHELL, this new shell will extend the Prolog inference engine by providing one of many possible ways to reason with confidence factors. The user interface and explanatory facilities for this shell will also be different, providing the reader with additional techniques for handling these functions. We will call this expert system shell CONMAN, which is short for Confidence Manager. The complete program is in the accompanying listing titled CONMAN.PL.

10.2. REPRESENTING AND COMPUTING CONFIDENCE OR CERTAINTY

First we must decide on a way to represent confidence factors. The usual approach is to represent them as numbers. Some methods use a scale from 0 to 100, with 0 representing no confidence and 100 representing complete confidence. Others use a scale from −100 to 100, with negative numbers representing increasing confidence that the hypothesis is false. We will use a scale of 0 to 100, and we will follow the common practice of referring to these factors as percentages.

The confidence factor for a hypothesis can be determined in one of two ways. First, the user can tell CONMAN how confident he is that the hypothesis is true. Second, CONMAN can infer a confidence factor for the hypothesis from the confidence factors of other hypotheses.

To infer a confidence factor, CONMAN needs rules that say how much confidence one should have in the conclusion of the rule when the condition of the rule is satisfied. The knowledge base builder must supply the confidence factors for the rules. This is part of the expert knowledge built into the knowledge base.

Confidence factors come from two places. The rule itself has a confidence factor, and so do its premises or conditions. We may be 100% certain that the sun rises in the east, but if we are unsure whether it is dawn or dusk, we will not be certain whether the sun on the horizon indicates east or west. We will need a way to combine the confidence factor for the rule with the confidence factor for the condition to get the confidence factor for the conclusion.

To compute the confidence factor for the conclusion of a rule, we will multiply the confidence factor for the rule by the confidence factor for the condition, then divide by 100. If we are 80% certain that the stock market will go up if interest goes down, and we are 75% sure that interest will go down, then this method says we should be $(80 \times 75)/100\%$ or 60% sure that the stock market will go up.

Some rules will have complex conditions that involve the Boolean operators **not, and,** or **or.** We will therefore need methods for computing the confidence factor for the negation of a hypothesis, for the conjunction of two hypotheses, and for the disjunction of two hypotheses.

We will assume that the confidence factor for **not** H is 100 minus the confidence factor for H. If we are 83% confident that it will rain, then we are only 17% confident that it will not rain.

Confidence factors for conjunctions are trickier. Suppose our confidence that we turned off the lights this morning is 90% and our confidence that our teenage daughter turned of the radio is 30%. What should our confidence be that both the lights and the radio were turned off? If the two events are causally independent, probability theory says the combined confidence is $(30 \times 90)/100\%$ or 27%. If they are not independent, probability theory says the combined confidence can still never be higher than the lesser of the two confidences — in this case, 30%. It is this most optimistic figure that most expert systems using confidence or certainty factors accept. And so will we. If **H1** has a confidence factor of M and **H2** has a confidence of N, we will take the confidence factor for **H1 and H2** to be the lesser of M and N.

While optimism is the order of the day for **and,** most expert systems use the most pessimistic figure for **or.** Suppose we are 25% sure that it will rain today and 30% sure that our teenage son will remember to water the lawn today. What should be our confidence that one or the other will happen? The absolute lowest figure would be 25% since we would have this much confidence in the rain even if our son weren't involved. In fact, our confidence that one or the other will happen should be somewhat higher than our confidence that either alone will happen. But we will take the conservative approach and say that the confidence factor for **H1 or H2** is the greater of M and N where M and N are the confidence factors for **H1** and **H2** respectively.

Further, we may have more than one rule for a single hypothesis, and each rule may have a different confidence factor. What do we do in this case?

If a confidence factor of 0 means the hypothesis is certainly false and a confidence factor of 100 means it is certainly true, then a factor of 50 should mean that the evidence is evenly balanced. Furthermore, any factor below 50 shows a tendency to think the hypothesis is false. When we have more than one rule for a hypothesis giving us more than one confidence factor, we could combine the factors below 50 to get the evidence against the hypothesis, combine the factors above 50 to get the evidence for the hypothesis, then compare these to get the total evidence. Some expert systems do something like this.

We will adopt a simpler strategy for CONMAN. We will assume that a rule can only give evidence for a hypothesis, never evidence against. Furthermore, we will not take the evidence provided by the different rules as being cumulative. Instead we will think of each rule as making a case for the hypothesis, and we will base our opinion on the best case that can be made. So if three different rules recommend confidence factors of M, N, and K for our hypothesis, we will take the greatest of these three as the final confidence factor for the hypothesis.

These decisions about how we will represent and use confidence factors will guide our design of the inference engine for CONMAN. But before we start writing procedures for the inference engine, we must consider the form we will give to the special rules that will go into a CONMAN knowledge base.

10.3. CONFIDENCE RULES

Ordinary Prolog rules do not have confidence factors. We will represent our rules with confidence factors as Prolog facts using the predicate `c_rule`. Each `c_rule` clause will contain the conclusion, the confidence factor, and the conditions for the rule as the arguments for the predicate `c_rule`.

We will want to distinguish a condition of a confidence rule from something else we will call a PREREQUISITE. A prerequisite is some subordinate hypothesis that must be confirmed before we apply the rule. The confidence factor for the prerequisite is not used in computing the confidence factor for the conclusion of the rule, but it must be high enough to reach any threshold we set for counting a hypothesis as confirmed or the rule will provide no support for its conclusion at all.

Consider for example a rule we might find in an automotive repair system. Suppose fuel is reaching the carburetor but no fuel is coming through the carburetor jet. Then we might advise that we are 85% confident that cleaning the jet will restore the flow of fuel provided the jet is not damaged. In computing our confidence that cleaning the jet will solve the fuel problem, we only use our confidence that the jet is not damaged. But we do not use this rule at all unless we have already confirmed that fuel is reaching the carburetor but no fuel is coming through the carburetor jet. If no fuel is reaching the carburetor, we have no reason to think cleaning the jet will solve the problem regardless of the condition of the jet.

Our confidence rules will have the format:

```
c_rule(Hypothesis,
       ConfidenceFactor,
       Prerequisites,
       Conditions).
```

The `Hypothesis` of a confidence rule will be a quoted atom in English, showing what CONMAN should display when asking the user questions about the hypothesis or reporting its confidence in the hypothesis. The `ConfidenceFactor` of a confidence rule will be a number between 0 and 100, representing the confidence we would have in the conclusion if we were 100% confident in the condition. The `Prerequisites` of a confidence rule will be a list of hypotheses that must be confirmed (or disconfirmed) before the rule can be applied. If we want a hypothesis to be disconfirmed before a rule can be applied, we put the symbol "–" immediately before it in the list of prerequisites. The `Conditions` of a confidence rule will be a complex list of conditions and atoms representing the relationships between the conditions.

If the condition for a rule is a single hypothesis, `Conditions` will have two members: the hypothesis and the atom `yes`. If the condition for a rule is that a single hypothesis is false, then `Conditions` will have two members: the hypothesis and the atom `no`. For example, in our car repair example we had a rule with the condition that the carburetor jet was not damaged. This would be represented by the list:

```
['The carburetor jet is damaged.',no]
```

If the condition is a conjunction of two other conditions, then `Conditions` will have the form:

```
[and,Condition-1,Condition-2]
```

Of course, `Condition-1` and `Condition-2` can have any of the forms that `Conditions` itself can have. That is, conjunctions within conjunctions are permitted.

Finally, if the condition for a rule is a disjunction of two other conditions, then `Conditions` will have the form:

```
[or,Condition-1,Condition-2]
```

Again, `Condition-1` and `Condition-2` can have any of the forms that `Conditions` can have.

This gives us four basic ways to formulate a condition. Any condition with any of these four forms can be the second or third member of an **and** or an **or** condition.

Let's look at a complex example from a knowledge base for medical diagnosis that we will discuss in detail later. The object of the expert system is to diagnose the patient's illness and to prescribe for it. We are very confident (85%) that if the patient has nasal congestion without either a sore throat or chest congestion, then he is suffering from an allergy. There are no prerequisites for our rule, but it has a complex condition that requires one hypothesis to be confirmed and two others to be disconfirmed. Our rule has an empty list of prerequisites and looks like this:

```
c_rule('The patient has allergic rhinitis.',
       85,
       [],
       [and,['The patient has nasal congestion.',yes],
           [and,['The patient has a sore throat.',no],
               ['The patient has chest congestion.',no]
           ]
       ]).
```

Consider also the following rule for prescribing a medication. We have complete confidence that a decongestant should be given to a patient with nasal congestion provided the patient does not also suffer from high blood pressure. As our confidence that the patient has high blood pressure increases, our confidence that he should be given a decongestant decreases. We don't even consider giving the patient a decongestant unless he has nasal congestion, but our confidence in the prescription for a patient with nasal congestion depends only on our confidence in his having high blood pressure. So nasal congestion is a prerequisite, and not having high blood pressure is the only condition.

```
c_rule('Give the patient a decongestant.',
       100,
       ['The patient has nasal congestion.'],
       ['The patient has high blood pressure.',no]).
```

There are other examples of CONMAN confidence rules in the file MDC.PL. This file is a knowledge base for a toy medical diagnostic system. Of course, we are not physicians and the MDC expert system is not medically valid. It is only a demonstration of techniques.

10.4. THE CONMAN INFERENCE ENGINE

We can now build the CONMAN inference engine, which uses three main predicates: `confidence_in/2`, `evidence_that/2`, and `confirm/1`.

The first of these, `confidence_in`, takes as arguments a simple or compound condition and a confidence factor for this condition. Normally, the first argument is already instantiated and the second argument is computed from it. The first argument may have one of the following five forms:

1. `[]`, the empty condition,

2. `[Hypothesis,yes]`, the condition that some hypothesis is true,

3. `[Hypothesis,no]`, the condition that some hypothesis is false,

4. `[and,Conjunct1,Conjunct2]`, a conjunction of simpler conditions, or

5. `[or,Disjunct1,Disjunct2]`, a disjunction of simpler conditions.

Most of the work of `confidence_in` will involve option (2) above. There are four clauses to cover this case and one clause for each of the other cases. We will look at the other cases first, then return to the case of conditions of the form `[Hypothesis,yes]`.

The empty condition is always confirmed, and the first clause in the definition of `confidence_in` is

```
confidence_in([],100) :- !.
```

We assume that the confidence factor for a hypothesis being true and the confidence factor for a hypothesis being false will always add up to 100%. If we are 95% sure that it will rain, then we are 5% sure that it will not. Of course, we do not usually say things like, "I am 5% sure that it won't rain." Whenever our confidence falls below 50%, we don't say that we are sure but rather that we are unsure. Still, the lower our confidence that something is true, the higher our confidence that it is false. With this assumption, we build our inference engine to compute the confidence that something is false by first computing the confidence that it is true.

```
confidence_in([Hypothesis,no],CF) :-
        !,
        confidence_in([Hypothesis,yes],CF0),
        CF is 100 - CF0.
```

We decided earlier that our confidence in a conjunction would be equal to our confidence in the less likely of the two conjuncts, and that our confidence in a disjunction would be equal to our confidence in the more likely of the two disjuncts. These decisions are reflected in the following clauses.

```
confidence_in([and,Conjunct1,Conjunct2],CF) :-
        !,
        confidence_in(Conjunct1,CF1),
        confidence_in(Conjunct2,CF2),
        minimum([CF1,CF2],CF).
```

```
confidence_in([or,Disjunct1,Disjunct2],CF) :-
        !,
        confidence_in(Disjunct1,CF1),
        confidence_in(Disjunct2,CF2),
        maximum([CF1,CF2],CF).
```

The utility predicates `maximum/2` and `minimum/2` find, respectively, the largest and smallest numbers in a list, in the range 0 to 100.

When we call `confidence_in` with `[Hypothesis,yes]` as the first argument, the procedure will try to determine the confidence factor for the hypothesis using the following four methods.

1. Check to see if the confidence factor was determined and remembered earlier.

2. If appropriate, ask the user for the confidence factor.

3. Determine the confidence factor using the confidence rules in the knowledge base.

4. If none of the above produces a result, assign a confidence factor of 50, indicating that the weight of evidence for and against the hypothesis is evenly balanced.

We have a separate clause for each of these four methods. For the first, we have the clause:

```
confidence_in([Hypothesis,yes],CF) :-
        known(Hypothesis,CF,_), !.
```

The arguments for our database predicate known/3 represent the hypothesis, the confidence factor, and information about the way the confidence factor was determined. This last piece of information is used by the explanatory facilities we will examine later; we ignore it here.

The second clause asks the user for the confidence factor, if a method for doing so has been provided:

```
confidence_in([Hypothesis,yes],CF) :-
        ask_confidence(Hypothesis,CF),
        !,
        assert(known(Hypothesis,CF,user)).
```

We will describe the ask_confidence/2 procedure later; it is part of the CONMAN user interface.

If CONMAN cannot ask the user for the confidence factor, it must compute it using confidence rules and the confidence factors for other hypotheses that make up the prerequisites and conditions of these rules:

```
confidence_in([Hypothesis,yes],CF) :-
        asserta(current_hypothesis(Hypothesis)),      % Line 1
        findall(X,evidence_that(Hypothesis,X),List),  % Line 2
        retract(current_hypothesis(_)),
        findall(C,member([C,_],List),CFList),         % Line 3
        CFList \== [],
        !,
        maximum(CFList,CF),
        member([CF,Explanation],List),
        assert(known(Hypothesis,CF,Explanation)).
```

Line 1 leaves a message for the explanatory facility to tell it that confidence_in has begun to investigate a new hypothesis. At certain points, the user will have the opportunity to ask why any given question is being asked. The explanatory facility will use these clauses for current_hypothesis to construct an answer. Line 2 calls evidence_that, which instantiates its second argument to a list containing a confidence factor for the hypothesis, plus the prerequisites and conditions needed to infer it with that confidence factor. Since many rules can support the same hypothesis, evidence_that yields multiple solutions, and findall collects these into a list. Once evidence_that has done its work, the user will have no opportunity to ask about questions related to this hypothesis, so the clause added earlier to the working database predicate current_hypothesis is retracted. Line 3 gathers all the confidence factors in List and returns them as a list of confidence factors in the variable CFList. If there is no evidence for the hypothesis, CFList will be empty and the clause will fail. Otherwise, the confidence factor for the hypothesis becomes the maximum value in CFList. Information about the conditions that were used to compute the selected confidence factor is extracted from List. CONMAN remembers the confidence factor and the explanatory information by adding a clause to the working database predicate `known`.

The only way this method for finding a confidence factor for a hypothesis can fail is if there are no rules for the hypothesis whose prerequisites are satisfied. If this happens, the value of `CFList` will be the empty list. Then the following clause, which always succeeds, will be invoked:

```
confidence_in([Hypothesis,yes],50) :-
       assert(known(Hypothesis,50,no_evidence)), !.
```

The hypothesis gets a confidence factor of 50 because there was no evidence for it or against it.

This tells us how CONMAN determines the confidence factor for a hypothesis, except that we haven't said how `evidence_that` works. This crucial predicate is defined by a single clause:

```
evidence_that(Hypothesis,[CF,[CF1,Prerequisite,Condition]]) :-
       c_rule(Hypothesis,CF1,Prerequisite,Condition),
       confirm(Prerequisite),
       confidence_in(Condition,CF2),
       CF is (CF1 * CF2)//100.
```

That is, `evidence_that` finds a rule for the hypothesis. If the prerequisites for the rule have been confirmed, `evidence_that` calls `confidence_in` to get a confidence factor for the condition of the rule. This value is multiplied by the confidence factor for the rule itself, the result is divided by 100, and this figure is returned by `evidence_that` together with pertinent information about the content of the rule.

Notice that neither `confidence_in` nor `evidence_that` is directly recursive. However, each of them sometimes calls the other, and thus they are indirectly recursive.

In the knowledge base, we set a confidence factor threshold (call it `T`). We then consider a hypothesis confirmed if its confidence factor is higher than `T`, or disconfirmed if its confidence factor is lower than $100-T$. The prerequisite for each confidence rule is a list of hypotheses to be confirmed or disconfirmed. The hypotheses to be disconfirmed are preceded in the list by a hyphen. The predicate `confirm` then works through this list:

```
confirm([]).

confirm([-,Hypothesis|Rest]) :- !,
                         known(Hypothesis,CF,_),
                         kb_threshold(T),
                         M is 100 - CF,
                         M >= T,
                         confirm(Rest).

confirm([Hypothesis|Rest]) :- known(Hypothesis,CF,_),
                         kb_threshold(T),
```

```
CF >= T,
!,
confirm(Rest).
```

10.5. GETTING INFORMATION FROM THE USER

Every hypothesis that occurs in the confidence rules is automatically treated as a conjecture, and, if possible, CONMAN asks the user whether the conjecture is true. All hypotheses take the form of yes/no questions.

Unlike XSHELL, CONMAN cannot ask the user what value some parameter has. However, it can ask the user how sure he or she is that something is true or false. Thus, in a sense, the scale from "no" to "yes" is itself a parameter. The procedure that poses questions and gets the user's responses is `ask_confidence`, which gives the user a menu ranging from "no" through "unlikely" to "very likely" and "yes." The response is converted into a numerical confidence factor in every case except "don't know" and "why." If the response was "don't know," `ask_confidence` fails conclusively and `confidence_in` must find another way to compute a confidence factor. If the response was "why" `ask_confidence_aux` calls `explain_question` to display a brief explanation of why this hypothesis is being pursued. Then the question is asked again.

Not all hypotheses can be tested by questioning the user. For example in a medical diagnostic system, we will want CONMAN to ask about the patient's symptoms, but we will not want it to ask whether the patient has pneumonia. That is the kind of hypothesis CONMAN is supposed to evaluate by drawing inferences from other information. The predicate `kb_can_ask/1` identifies hypotheses that the user can be asked about. The first thing `ask_confidence` does when given a hypothesis is to check `kb_can_ask`. If `kb_can_ask` fails, so does `ask_confidence`; then the procedure that called it, namely `confidence_in`, must look for another way to investigate the hypothesis.

Menu responses are collected by the utility procedure `get0_only`, which works like `get0` except that the responses that will be accepted can be limited. A list of acceptable single character responses are passed to `get0_only` as its first parameter. When the user presses one of these characters, it is returned in the second argument for `get0_only`. If the user presses any key that is not in the list, `get0_only` prints an error message and asks for another response. You may find it useful to incorporate `get0_only` into other Prolog programs.

Exercise 10.5.1

The CONMAN procedure `ask_confidence` always displays the available responses. Rewrite `ask_confidence` so it only displays the available responses if the user asks to see them.

Exercise 10.5.2

Some expert systems that use confidence factors allow the user to enter either a word or a number to indicate his confidence in a hypothesis. Rewrite `ask_confidence` to allow the user to enter a confidence factor either as a word or as a number between 0 and 100.

10.6. THE CONMAN EXPLANATORY FACILITIES

The user can ask for an explanation at two different points in a CONMAN consultation. When CONMAN asks him whether a hypothesis is true, the user can ask why
the information is needed. And when CONMAN reports a conclusion, the user can
ask how the conclusion was obtained.

In exploring a hypothesis, the procedure `confidence_in` often calls the procedure `evidence_that`, which in turn accesses the confidence rules. Before it calls
`evidence_that`, the routine `confidence_in` adds a fact to the working database
predicate `current_hypothesis/1`. By looking at this predicate at any moment,
CONMAN can tell which hypotheses are being explored. There can be many facts
for `current_hypothesis` at one time because each confidence rule can have as a condition a new hypothesis that has to be explored. So clauses for `current_hypothesis`
function as a stack of working hypotheses with the most recent ones at the beginning
of the set. If the user responds to a question with "why?" the working hypotheses
are retrieved by `explain_question/0` and displayed, most recent first.

The second explanatory facility in CONMAN is organized under the predicate
`explain_conclusion/1`, which is called after any conclusion is reported to the user.
It asks the user if he or she wants an explanation. If the answer is yes, the explanation
is generated by `explain_conclusion_aux/1`.

Whereas `explain_question` builds its explanation from information stored under the predicate `current_hypothesis`, `explain_conclusion_aux` uses the working
database predicate `known/3`. Whenever `confidence_in` determines a confidence factor for any hypothesis, it remembers it by adding a fact to `known`. This fact includes
the hypothesis, the confidence factor, and information about how CONMAN arrived
at the confidence factor.

The confidence factor in turn may have come from any one of three places.
Either (1) the user gave it as a menu response, or (2) CONMAN computed it using a
confidence rule, or (3) CONMAN assigned a confidence factor of 50 because no other
evidence was available. Cases (1) and (3) are easily reported. In case (2) we want
CONMAN to display the rule in a reasonable format, then explain what confidence
factors it determined for the different hypotheses in the condition of the rule and
how it reached these conclusions. To do this, `explain_conclusion_aux` will have to
be recursive.

A condition for a rule must have one of these three forms:

1. `[Hypothesis,yes-or-no]`,

2. `[and,SubCondition1,SubCondition2]`,

3. `[or,SubCondition1,SubCondition2]`.

In cases (2) and (3), each of the subconditions can also have any of these three forms
— hence the recursion. To explain a condition, `explain_conclusion_aux` divides
the condition into two parts, explains the first part, and then explains the rest. Each
part may be divided up in the same way. Eventually, the part that remains to
be explained should be empty. When `explain_conclusion_aux` passes an empty
argument to itself, it should succeed with no further action. This gives us one
terminating condition for `explain_conclusion_aux`:

```
explain_conclusion_aux([]) :- !.
```

Besides this terminating condition, we need clauses for each of the three forms a condition can take:

```
explain_conclusion_aux([Hypothesis,_]) :-
        !,
        explain_conclusion_aux(Hypothesis).

explain_conclusion_aux([and,[Hypothesis,_],Rest]) :-
        explain_conclusion_aux(Hypothesis),
        explain_conclusion_aux(Rest), !.

explain_conclusion_aux([or,[Hypothesis,_],Rest]) :-
        explain_conclusion_aux(Hypothesis),
        explain_conclusion_aux(Rest),
        !.
```

The functions of these clauses are obvious.

Finally, we need procedures for explaining a simple hypothesis. First let's look at the case where the confidence factor was given to CONMAN by the user. This will be recorded in a fact for the predicate **known**. When CONMAN discovers this, it will next look to see if the confidence factor for the hypothesis confirms or disconfirms the hypothesis. Then it will report that it accepted or rejected the hypothesis because of the response the user gave when asked about the hypothesis.

```
explain_conclusion_aux(Hypothesis) :-
        known(Hypothesis,CF,user),
        kb_threshold(T),
        CF >= T,
        !,
        write(Hypothesis),
        writeln(' -'),
        write('From what you told me, I accepted this with '),
        write(CF),
        writeln('% confidence.'), nl.

explain_conclusion_aux(Hypothesis) :-
        known(Hypothesis,CF,user), !,
        DisCF is 100 - CF,
        write(Hypothesis),
        writeln(' -'),
        write('From what you told me, I rejected this with '),
        write(DisCF),
        writeln('% confidence.'), nl.
```

The case where the confidence factor was set at 50 because no evidence was available is easy:

```
explain_conclusion_aux(Hypothesis) :-
        known(Hypothesis,50,no_evidence),
        !,
        write(Hypothesis),
        writeln(' -'),
        writeln('Having no evidence, I assumed this was 50-50.'),
        nl.
```

The last and most complicated case is where a confidence rule was used to determine the confidence factor. The explanation is stored as a list with three members: the confidence factor for the rule that was used, the list of prerequisites for the rule, and the (possibly complex) condition for the rule. So CONMAN must display this information in a readable format. Each prerequisite is represented as something confirmed or disconfirmed, and each component hypothesis in the condition is represented as something to confirm or to disconfirm. Two auxiliary procedures, `list_prerequisites/1` and `list_conditions/1`, take care of this. Finally, `explain_conclusion_aux` passes the condition of the rule to itself recursively for further explanation:

```
explain_conclusion_aux(Hypothesis) :-
        !, known(Hypothesis,CF1,[CF,Prerequisites,Conditions]),
        writeln(Hypothesis),write('Accepted with '),
        write(CF1),
        writeln('% confidence on the basis of the following'),
        write('Rule: '),writeln(Hypothesis),
        write(' with confidence of '),
        write(CF),
        writeln('% if'),
        list_prerequisites(Prerequisites),
        list_conditions(Conditions), nl,
        explain_conclusion_aux(Conditions).
```

Eventually, every recursive call to `explain_conclusion_aux` will terminate with an empty condition or with a hypothesis that got its confidence factor from the user or got an arbitrary confidence factor of 50 because no other evidence was available. When this happens, `explain_conclusion_aux` succeeds.

10.7. THE MAIN PROGRAM

The two predicates `conman/0` and `finish_conman/0` control the entire CONMAN consultation system.

First `conman` gets the introductory statement from the CONMAN knowledge base and displays it. Then it finds the threshold confidence factor listed in the knowledge base. Now it will bounce between the goal `kb_hypothesis(Hypothesis)` and the `fail` at the end of the clause, making one pass for each hypothesis in the knowledge base.

We must tell CONMAN in the knowledge base which are the basic hypotheses it must investigate. We use clauses for the `kb_hypothesis/1` predicate to do this. We also determine the order CONMAN explores these hypotheses by the order of the clauses for `kb_hypothesis`. This order is very important since one hypothesis may be a prerequisite for a rule for another hypothesis. If the prerequisite hypothesis isn't investigated (and possibly confirmed) first, then the rule will never succeed.

Once a basic hypothesis is identified, its confidence factor is determined by `confidence_in` and compared with the threshold confidence factor. If it doesn't reach the threshold, `conman` backtracks and tries a different basic hypothesis. If it reaches the threshold, `conman` displays it and explains it. Then we hit the `fail` that causes `conman` to backtrack and get another basic hypothesis.

There may be many more subordinate hypotheses included in conditions for our confidence rules than there are basic hypotheses to be explored. When one of these subordinate hypotheses is confirmed, it is neither reported nor explained. The hypotheses that will be most important to the user, the ones that will be reported and explained when confirmed, must be identified in the knowledge base. However, CONMAN will explain how it confirmed or disconfirmed a subordinate hypothesis if this hypothesis is a condition in a rule used to confirm some basic hypothesis.

When `conman` can find no more basic hypotheses to investigate, execution moves to the second clause, which checks that at least one basic hypothesis was confirmed, then reports that no further conclusions can be reached, and finally calls `finish_conman` to clean up. If no hypotheses were confirmed, the third clause is executed. It prints a slightly different message and calls `finish_conman`, which eliminates the working database and asks the user whether to start another consultation.

10.7.1. Listing of CONMAN.PL

```
% CONMAN.PL
%    A simple expert system shell with uncertainty.


%
% Requires procedure defined in the file GETYESNO.PL
%


:- ensure_loaded('getyesno.pl').

:- dynamic known/3.


%
% CONMAN user interface
%    CONMAN modifies and extends the standard Prolog infer-
%    ence engine, providing the ability to use confidence
%    factors in reaching conclusions. As a result, we dis-
%    tinguish the procedures in CONMAN that handle communi-
%    cation with the user from the predicates that make up
```

```
%    the CONMAN inference engine.
%


%
% conman
%    Starts the consultation, calls the procedures making up
%    the inference engine, reports conclusions to the user, and
%    invokes the explanatory facility.
%

conman :- kb_intro(Statement),
          writeln(Statement),nl,
          kb_threshold(T),
          kb_hypothesis(Hypothesis),
          confidence_in([Hypothesis,yes],CF),
          CF >= T,
          write('Conclusion: '),
          writeln(Hypothesis),
          write('Confidence in hypothesis: '),
          write(CF),
          writeln('%.'),
          explain_conclusion(Hypothesis), fail.

conman :- kb_hypothesis(Hypothesis),
          confirm([Hypothesis]),!,
          writeln('No further conclusions.'),
          nl, finish_conman.

conman :- writeln('Can draw no conclusions.'),
          nl, finish_conman.


%
% finish_conman
%    Ends a consultation and begins another if requested.
%

finish_conman :-
    retractall(known(_,_,_)),
    write('Do you want to conduct another consultation?'),
    yes, nl, nl, !, conman.

finish_conman.


%
% ask_confidence(+Hypothesis,-CF)
%    Asks the user to express his/her confidence in the
```

```
%   Hypothesis under consideration. User chooses a descriptive
%   phrase in answer to the request. This phrase is converted
%   to a confidence factor CF between 0 and 100.
%

ask_confidence(Hypothesis,CF) :-
    kb_can_ask(Hypothesis),
    writeln('Is the following conjecture true? --'),
    write('  '), writeln(Hypothesis),
    writeln(['Possible responses: ',
            '  (y) yes          (n) no',
            '  (l) very likely  (v) very unlikely',
            '  (p) probably     (u) unlikely',
            '  (m) maybe        (d) don''t know.',
            '         (?) why?']),
    write('  Your response --> '),
    get_only([y,l,p,m,n,v,u,d,?],Reply), nl, nl,
    convert_reply_to_confidence(Reply,CF),
    !, Reply \== d,
    ask_confidence_aux(Reply,Hypothesis,CF).


%
% ask_confidence_aux(+Char,+Hypothesis,-CF)
%   If the user asks for a justification for a request
%   for information, this procedure invokes the explanatory
%   facility and then repeats the request for information.

ask_confidence_aux(Char,_,_) :- Char \== ?, !.

ask_confidence_aux(_,Hypothesis,CF) :-
    explain_question,
    !, ask_confidence(Hypothesis,CF).
%
% get_only(+List,-Reply)
%   An input routine that requires the user to press
%   one of the keys in the List, which the routine
%   returns as Reply.
%

get_only(List,Reply) :-
    get(Char),name(Value,[Char]),
    member(Value,List),Reply = Value, !.

get_only(List,Reply) :-
    write('  [Invalid response.  Try again.] '),
    !,
```

```
    get_only(List,Reply).

%
% convert_reply_to_confidence(+Char,-CF)
%   A table for converting characters to numerical
%   confidence factors.
%

convert_reply_to_confidence(?,_).
convert_reply_to_confidence(d,_).
convert_reply_to_confidence(n,0).
convert_reply_to_confidence(v,5).
convert_reply_to_confidence(u,25).
convert_reply_to_confidence(m,60).
convert_reply_to_confidence(p,80).
convert_reply_to_confidence(l,90).
convert_reply_to_confidence(y,100).


%
% explain_question
%   Justifies a request to the user for information by
%   reporting hypotheses the information will be used to
%   test.
%

explain_question :-
    current_hypothesis(Hypothesis),
    writeln(
'This information is needed to test the following hypothesis:'),
    writeln(Hypothesis), nl,
    writeln('Do you want further explanation?'),
    explain_question_aux,!.

explain_question :-
    writeln('This is a basic hypothesis.'),
    nl, wait.

%
% explain_question_aux
%   Inputs the user's indication whether further explanation
%   for a question is desired and, if so, forces explain_question
%   to backtrack and provide further explanation.
%

explain_question_aux :- \+ yes, nl, nl, !.
```

```
explain_question_aux :- nl, nl, fail.


%
% explain_conclusion(+Hypothesis)
%    Where Hypothesis is a conclusion just reported, this
%    routine asks the user whether he/she wants to see how
%    the conclusion was derived and, if so, invokes an
%    auxiliary routine that provides the explanation.
%

explain_conclusion(Hypothesis) :-
     writeln('Do you want an explanation?'),
     yes, nl, nl,
     explain_conclusion_aux(Hypothesis), wait, !.

explain_conclusion(_) :- nl, nl.


%
% explain_conclusion_aux(+Hypothesis)
%    Recursively reports all rules and facts used to
%    derive the Hypothesis.
%

explain_conclusion_aux([]) :- !.

explain_conclusion_aux([Hypothesis,_]) :-
     !, explain_conclusion_aux(Hypothesis).

explain_conclusion_aux([and,[Hypothesis,_],Rest]) :-
     !, explain_conclusion_aux(Hypothesis),
     explain_conclusion_aux(Rest).

explain_conclusion_aux([or,[Hypothesis,_],Rest]) :-
     !, explain_conclusion_aux(Hypothesis),
     explain_conclusion_aux(Rest).

explain_conclusion_aux(Hypothesis) :-
     known(Hypothesis,CF,user),
     kb_threshold(T),CF >= T,
     !, write(Hypothesis),writeln(' -'),
     write('From what you told me, I accepted this with '),
     write(CF),writeln('% confidence.'), nl.

explain_conclusion_aux(Hypothesis) :-
     known(Hypothesis,CF,user),
     !, DisCF is 100 - CF,
```

```
        write(Hypothesis),writeln(' -'),
        write('From what you told me, I rejected this with '),
        write(DisCF),writeln('% confidence.'), nl.

explain_conclusion_aux(Hypothesis) :-
        known(Hypothesis,50,no_evidence),
        !, write(Hypothesis),writeln(' -'),
        writeln(
            'Having no evidence, I assumed this was 50-50.'),
        nl.

explain_conclusion_aux(Hypothesis) :-
        !, known(Hypothesis,CF1,[CF,Prerequisites,Conditions]),
        writeln(Hypothesis),write('Accepted with '),
        write(CF1),
        writeln('% confidence on the basis of the following'),
        write('Rule: '),writeln(Hypothesis),
        write(' with confidence of '),
        write(CF),
        writeln('% if'),
        list_prerequisites(Prerequisites),
        list_conditions(Conditions), nl,
        explain_conclusion_aux(Conditions).

%
% list_prerequisites(+List)
%   Part of the explanatory facilty.
%   Reports whether the hypotheses in the List have
%   been confirmed or disconfirmed.
%

list_prerequisites([]) :- !.

list_prerequisites([-,Hypothesis|Rest]) :-
        !, write(' is disconfirmed: '),
        writeln(Hypothesis),
        list_prerequisites(Rest).

list_prerequisites([Hypothesis|Rest]) :-
        write(' is confirmed: '),
        writeln(Hypothesis),
        list_prerequisites(Rest).

%
% list_conditions(+Condition)
%   Part of the explanatory facilty.
```

```
%    Formats and displays a possibly complex Condition.
%

list_conditions([]) :- !.

list_conditions([and,Hypothesis,Rest]) :-
    list_conditions(Hypothesis),
    list_conditions(Rest).

list_conditions([or,Hypothesis,Rest]) :-
    writeln(' ['),
    list_conditions(Hypothesis),
    writeln('      or'),
    list_conditions(Rest), writeln(' ]').

list_conditions([Hypothesis,yes]) :-
    write('     to confirm: '),
    writeln(Hypothesis).

list_conditions([Hypothesis,no]) :-
    write('     to disconfirm: '),
    writeln(Hypothesis).

%
% wait
%    Prompts the user to press Return and then waits for
%    a keystroke.
%

wait :- write('Press Return when ready to continue. '),
        get0(_), nl, nl.

%
% CONMAN inference engine
%    The CONMAN inference engine computes the confidence in
%    compound goals and decides which of several rules best
%    support a conclusion. It remembers this information for
%    later use by itself, the main conman procedure, and the
%    explanatory facilities.
%

%
% confidence_in(+Hypothesis,-CF)
%    Computes the confidence factor CF for the possibly
%    complex Hypothesis from the confidence factors for
%    sub-hypotheses. Confidence factors for sub-hypotheses
```

```
%     come from the working database, are requested from the
%     user, or are determined by whatever evidence is provided
%     by rules that support each sub-hypothesis.
%

confidence_in([],100) :- !.

confidence_in([Hypothesis,yes],CF) :-
    known(Hypothesis,CF,_), !.

confidence_in([Hypothesis,yes],CF) :-
    ask_confidence(Hypothesis,CF), !,
    assert(known(Hypothesis,CF,user)).

confidence_in([Hypothesis,yes],CF) :-
    asserta(current_hypothesis(Hypothesis)),
    findall(X,evidence_that(Hypothesis,X),List),
    findall(C,member([C,_],List),CFList),
    retract(current_hypothesis(_)),
    CFList \== [],
    !, maximum(CFList,CF),
    member([CF,Explanation],List),
    assert(known(Hypothesis,CF,Explanation)).

confidence_in([Hypothesis,yes],50) :-
    assert(known(Hypothesis,50,no_evidence)), !.

confidence_in([Hypothesis,no],CF) :-
    !, confidence_in([Hypothesis,yes],CF0),
    CF is 100 - CF0.

confidence_in([and,Conjunct1,Conjunct2],CF) :-
    !, confidence_in(Conjunct1,CF1),
    confidence_in(Conjunct2,CF2),
    minimum([CF1,CF2],CF).

confidence_in([or,Disjunct1,Disjunct2],CF) :-
    !, confidence_in(Disjunct1,CF1),
    confidence_in(Disjunct2,CF2),
    maximum([CF1,CF2],CF).


%
% evidence_that(+Hypothesis,-Evidence)
%    Finds rules for Hypothesis whose prerequisites are
%    confirmed and determines the confidence factor for
%    the Hypothesis that can be derived from the rule.
```

```
%    The resulting Evidence consists in the confidence
%    factor together with information about the rule
%    used in determining the confidence factor.
%

evidence_that(Hypothesis,[CF,[CF1,Prerequisite,Condition]]):-
    c_rule(Hypothesis,CF1,Prerequisite,Condition),
    confirm(Prerequisite),
    confidence_in(Condition,CF2),
    CF is (CF1 * CF2)//100.


%
% confirm(+Hypothesis)
%    Checks to see if the confidence factor for the
%    Hypothesis reaches the threshold set in the
%    knowledge base.
%

confirm([]).

confirm([-,Hypothesis|Rest]) :-
    !, known(Hypothesis,CF,_),
    kb_threshold(T),
    M is 100 - CF, M >= T,
    confirm(Rest).

confirm([Hypothesis|Rest]) :-
    known(Hypothesis,CF,_),
    kb_threshold(T),CF >= T,
    !, confirm(Rest).

%
% minimum(+Values,-Minimum)
%    Returns the smaller value Minimum of the pair of
%    Values.
%

minimum([M,K],M) :- M < K, ! .
minimum([_,M],M).

%
% yes
%    Prompts the user for a response and succeeds if the
%    user enters 'y' or 'Y'.
%
```

```
yes :-  write('--> '),
        get_yes_or_no(Response),
        !,
        Response == yes.


%
% maximum(+Values,-Maximum)
%    Returns the largest value Maximum in a list of
%    Values.
%

maximum([],0) :- !.
maximum([M],M) :- !.
maximum([M,K],M) :- M >= K, !.
maximum([M|R],N) :- maximum(R,K), maximum([K,M],N).


%
% member(?X,?Y)
%    X is an element of list Y.
%

member(X,[X|_]).
member(X,[_|Z]) :- member(X,Z).


%
% writeln(+ListOfAtoms)
%    Prints text consisting of a string or a list of
%    atoms, with each atom followed by a new line.
%

writeln([]) :- !.

writeln([First|Rest]) :-
        !,
        write(First),
        nl,
        writeln(Rest).

writeln(Atom) :-
        write(Atom),
        nl.
```

10.8. CONMAN KNOWLEDGE BASES

A CONMAN knowledge base should contain clauses for the predicates `kb_intro`, `kb_threshold`, `kb_hypothesis`, `c_rule`, and `kb_can_ask`. We have provided two sample CONMAN knowledge bases in the files MDC.PL and PET.PL. The first of these contains the information needed for a "toy" medical diagnostic system. The second sample CONMAN knowledge base, PET.PL, drives a whimsical expert system that gives advice on what to feed a pet. Although written with tongue held firmly in cheek, PET.PL nevertheless provides a good demonstration of the CONMAN expert system shell. As we discuss the proper form for a CONMAN knowledge base, refer to these two files for examples.

We put goals at the beginning of a CONMAN knowledge base to make sure any clauses left from some previously consulted CONMAN knowledge base are eliminated from working memory:

```
:- abolish(kb_intro/1).
:- abolish(kb_threshold/1).
:- abolish(kb_hypothesis/1).
:- abolish(c_rule/4).
:- abolish(kb_can_ask/1).
```

In some implementations, the predicate `retractall` is used instead of `abolish`, and the syntax is slightly different.

The knowledge base should contain a single clause for each of the two predicates `kb_intro/1` and `kb_threshold/1`. The `kb_intro` clause contains a list of quoted atoms that CONMAN will print as the introductory message for the expert system. The `kb_threshold` clause contains the value between 50 and 100 that a confidence factor for a hypothesis must reach before the hypothesis is to be considered confirmed. In MDC.PL and PET.PL, the threshold is set at 65 and the introductory messages are simple.

Next the knowledge base must provide a set of hypotheses that CONMAN will try to confirm. Each of these will be stored in a clause for the predicate `kb_hypothesis`. The order of these clauses is very important since they will be investigated in exactly the order they appear in the knowledge base. Look at the hypotheses in the MDC knowledge base. You will notice that there are three diagnostic hypotheses followed by five prescriptive hypotheses. The MDC system will make all the diagnoses it can before it makes any prescriptions. If some prescription were only made in the case of a single diagnosis, for example if penicillin were only administered if pneumonia were diagnosed, we could put this prescription immediately after the diagnosis in the list of hypotheses.

Now come the all-important confidence rules. Each clause for `c_rule` has four arguments: a hypothesis, a confidence factor, a list of prerequisites, and a list of conditions. We have already discussed the form of these rules and the way they are used by the CONMAN inference engine. There are several examples in the files MDC.PL and PET.PL. We noticed that a confidence rule might have an empty set of prerequisites, but we now see that they may also have an empty list of conditions. The MDC rule for administering an antihistamine has a prerequisite but no conditions.

Finally, our knowledge base must specify which hypotheses the user can be asked about directly. These are enumerated in clauses for the predicate `kb_can_ask`. In the MDC knowledge base, these include hypotheses about the patient's symptoms and other items concerning the patient's condition and medical history.

Notice that no hypothesis shows up in clauses for both `kb_hypothesis` and `kb_can_ask`. This is normal. If a user can determine whether or not some hypothesis is true, then he or she does not need the help of the expert system to investigate the hypothesis. The expert system uses information about hypotheses the user is competent to investigate independently (and therefore competent to answer questions about) to arrive at conclusions the user is less competent to investigate independently.

Finally, we place the starting query

```
:- conman.
```

at the end of the CONMAN knowledge base if the Prolog implementation permits it. This goal will begin a consultation when the knowledge base is loaded. In some Prologs, this does not work as intended, so the distributed versions of the knowledge base simply print a message, "Type `conman.` to start."

Most of the advice in the last chapter for building and debugging an XSHELL knowledge base also applies to CONMAN knowledge bases. We will emphasize one particular point here. The hypotheses that show up in a CONMAN knowledge base are represented as complete English sentences. The sentence for a particular hypothesis must have exactly the same form in each of its occurrences. Typing errors will cause the system to perform erratically. Instead of typing each sentence repeatedly, we recommend using a short, distinctive word or syllable for each hypothesis as you build and debug your knowledge base. Later, use the global replace feature of a word processor to replace occurrences of these markers by the appropriate sentence. It is a good idea to keep the version of the knowledge base with the short markers to use if you ever expand or modify your knowledge base. Alternatively, you may wish to modify CONMAN to use the short names internally and maintain a lookup table that contains longer phrases to be used whenever a hypothesis is to be displayed on the screen.

Exercise 10.8.1

Suppose that red spots without nasal or chest congestion indicate measles with 85% confidence, but red spots with chest congestion and fever indicate rheumatic fever with 90% confidence. Write confidence rules for these two "facts" and add them to the MDC knowledge base. What else do you need to add to MDC to make the two rules work properly?

Exercise 10.8.2

Modify CONMAN so the text for hypotheses is stored in clauses for a predicate `kb_text/2`, allowing the CONMAN knowledge base builder to use short atoms in place of long text messages in CONMAN rules and elsewhere in the knowledge base. Refer to the way `kb_text/2` is used in XSHELL.

10.8.1. Listing of MDC.PL

```
% MDC.PL

%
% Contains a CONMAN knowledge base.
% Requires all utility procedures defined in file CONMAN.PL
%

:- (clause(conman,_) ; consult('conman.pl')).

% Any previously defined clauses for the predicates KB_INTRO,
% KB_THRESHOLD, KB_HYPOTHESIS, C_RULE, and KB_CAN_ASK should
% be removed from the knowledge base before loading the
% clauses below.

:- abolish(kb_intro/1).
:- abolish(kb_threshold/1).    % Should use retractall
:- abolish(kb_hypothesis/1).   % instead of abolish
:- abolish(c_rule/4).          % in some implementations
:- abolish(kb_can_ask/1).      % of Prolog

kb_intro(['',
          'MDC: A Demonstration Medical Diagnostic System',
          '          Using Confidence Rules',
          '']).

kb_threshold(65).

kb_hypothesis('The patient has allergic rhinitis.').
kb_hypothesis('The patient has strep throat.').
kb_hypothesis('The patient has pneumonia.').
kb_hypothesis('Give the patient an antihistamine.').
kb_hypothesis('Give the patient a decongestant.').
kb_hypothesis('Give the patient penicillin.').
kb_hypothesis('Give the patient tetracycline.').
kb_hypothesis('Give the patient erythromycin.').

c_rule('The patient has nasal congestion.',
       95,
       [],
       ['The patient is breathing through the mouth.',yes]).

c_rule('The patient has a sore throat.',
       95,
       [],
```

```
[and,['The patient is coughing.',yes],
       ['The inside of the patient''s throat is red.',
            yes]]]).

c_rule('The patient has a sore throat.',
       90,
       [],
       ['The inside of the patient''s throat is red.',yes]).

c_rule('The patient has a sore throat.',
       75,
       [],
       ['The patient is coughing.',yes]).

c_rule('The patient has chest congestion.',
       100,
       [],
       ['There are rumbling sounds in the chest.',yes]).

c_rule('The patient has allergic rhinitis.',
       85,
       [],
       [and,['The patient has nasal congestion.',yes],
            [and,['The patient has a sore throat.',no],
                 ['The patient has chest congestion.',no]]]).

c_rule('The patient has strep throat.',
       80,
       [],
       [and,['The patient has nasal congestion.',yes],
            ['The patient has a sore throat.',yes]]).

c_rule('The patient has pneumonia.',
       90,
       [],
       [and,['The patient has chest congestion.',yes],
            [and,['The patient has nasal congestion.',yes],
                 ['The patient has a sore throat.',no]]]).

c_rule('The patient has pneumonia.',
       75,
       [],
       [and,['The patient has chest congestion.',yes],
         ['The patient has nasal congestion.',yes]]).

c_rule('Give the patient an antihistamine.',
```

```
        100,
        ['The patient has allergic rhinitis.'],
        []).

   c_rule('Give the patient a decongestant.',
        100,
        ['The patient has nasal congestion.'],
        ['The patient has high blood pressure.',no]).

   c_rule('Give the patient penicillin.',
        100,
        ['The patient has pneumonia.'],
        ['The patient is allergic to penicillin.',no]).

   c_rule('Give the patient penicillin.',
        100,
        ['The patient has pneumonia.',
         'The patient is allergic to penicillin.'],
        [and,['The patient is in critical condition.',yes],
             ['The patient is allergic to tetracycline.',yes]]).

   c_rule('Give the patient tetracycline.',
        100,
        ['The patient has pneumonia.',
         -,'Give the patient penicillin.'],
        ['The patient is allergic to tetracycline.',no]).

   c_rule('Give the patient erythromycin.',
        100,
        ['The patient has strep throat.'],
        ['The patient is allergic to erythromycin.',no]).

kb_can_ask('The patient has nasal congestion.').
kb_can_ask('The patient has chest congestion.').
kb_can_ask('The patient has a sore throat.').
kb_can_ask('The patient has high blood pressure.').
kb_can_ask('The patient is allergic to penicillin.').
kb_can_ask('The patient is allergic to erythromycin.').
kb_can_ask('The patient is allergic to tetracycline.').
kb_can_ask('The patient is breathing through the mouth.').
kb_can_ask('The patient is coughing.').
kb_can_ask('The inside of the patient''s throat is red.').
kb_can_ask('There are rumbling sounds in the chest.').
kb_can_ask('The patient is in critical condition.').

:- write(' Type   conman.  to start.').
```

10.8.2. Listing of PET.PL

```
% PET.PL

%
% Contains a CONMAN knowledge base.
% Requires all utility procedures defined in file CONMAN.PL
%

:- ensure_loaded(conman).

%
% Any previously defined clauses for the predicates KB_INTRO,
% KB_THRESHOLD, KB_HYPOTHESIS, C_RULE, and KB_CAN_ASK should
% be removed from the knowledge base before loading the
% clauses below.
%

:- abolish(kb_intro/1).
:- abolish(kb_threshold/1).     % Should use retractall
:- abolish(kb_hypothesis/1).    % instead of abolish
:- abolish(c_rule/4).           % in some implementations
:- abolish(kb_can_ask/1).       % of Prolog

kb_intro(['',
          'Feeding Your Pet:',
          'A Whimsical Knowledge Base for CONMAN',
          '']).

kb_threshold(64).

kb_hypothesis('Your pet is a carnivore.').
kb_hypothesis('Your pet is a herbivore.').
kb_hypothesis('Feed your pet nerds.').
kb_hypothesis('Feed dog food to your pet.').
kb_hypothesis('Feed your aunt''s fern to your pet.').
kb_hypothesis('My pet is a carnivore.  Feed your pet to my pet.').

c_rule('Your pet is a carnivore.',
       100,
       [],
       [and,['Your pet has sharp claws.',yes],
            ['Your pet has sharp, pointed teeth.',yes]]).

c_rule('Your pet is a carnivore.',
       85,
```

```
                [],
                ['Your pet has sharp claws.',yes]).

        c_rule('Your pet is a herbivore.',
                100,
                [],
                [and,['Your pet has sharp claws.',no],
                    ['Your pet has sharp, pointed teeth.',no]]).

        c_rule('Your pet is a carnivore.',
                85,
                [],
                ['Your pet has sharp, pointed teeth.',yes]).

        c_rule('Feed your pet nerds.',
                100,
                ['Your pet is a carnivore.'],
                [or,['Nerds are available at a low price.',yes],
                    ['Dog food is available at a low price.',no]]).

        c_rule('Feed dog food to your pet.',
                100,
                ['Your pet is a carnivore.'],
                [and,['Dog food is available at a low price.',yes],
                    ['Nerds are available at a low price.',no]]).

        c_rule('Feed your aunt''s fern to your pet.',
                100,
                ['Your pet is a herbivore.'],
                ['Your aunt has a fern.',yes]).

        c_rule('My pet is a carnivore.  Feed your pet to my pet.',
                100,
                ['Your pet is a herbivore.'],
                ['Your aunt has a fern.',no]).

kb_can_ask('Nerds are available at a low price.').
kb_can_ask('Dog food is available at a low price.').
kb_can_ask('Your pet has sharp claws.').
kb_can_ask('Your pet has sharp, pointed teeth.').
kb_can_ask('Your aunt has a fern.').

:- write('Type   conman.   to start.').
```

10.9. NO CONFIDENCE IN "CONFIDENCE"

We must end this chapter on a negative note. While confidence factors are widely used in existing expert systems, we are suspicious of them for several reasons.

First, where do the confidence factors used in expert systems come from? Look at the rules in our MDC knowledge base. These are not intended to represent real medical expertise, of course, but what would a real rule for diagnosing pneumonia look like? We assume that there is some set of symptoms, test results, etc., which taken together indicate pneumonia. Do they indicate pneumonia conclusively, or is there room for error? If they indicate pneumonia conclusively, there is no need for confidence factors; we could use ordinary Prolog rules. Medical expert systems like MYCIN use confidence factors because their rules are to be applied in situations where the physician cannot reach a perfectly certain diagnosis. Somehow, confidence factors must be assigned to uncertain information and rules that deal with uncertain information.

One might assume that the confidence factors in expert systems are the result of statistical analysis of a large body of data. On this view, the confidence factor for a rule about pneumonia would come from analysis of the cases of lots of people who have had pneumonia. But in reality, confidence factors in expert systems do not come from statistical analysis, and as far as we know, nobody working on expert systems ever claimed that confidence factors were derived in this way.

Confidence factors come from experts' heads. They are numbers supplied by experts to represent their subjective confidence in some rule. This does not mean that the experts normally state their opinions as numbers or use numerical confidence factors in arriving at their conclusions. In fact, experts who become involved in expert system development projects typically say that they do not reach their conclusions in this way. They come up with the numbers only when someone asks them to place a numerical value on their confidence in a particular rule. For the most part, they find this unnatural and have difficulty assigning numbers to their rules in this way.

Moreover, knowledge bases with confidence factors have to be debugged after they are built. The numbers supplied by the experts are not directly useful and have to be adjusted extensively to make the answers come out right. The expert system may not work very much like the expert's mind, but we can always take the pragmatic approach that as long as it gives the same answers the expert gives, who cares?

This brings us to the second problem: Systems that use confidence factors are difficult to maintain and expand. The problem is that interactions between rules in a large system are hard to predict. A large system may require extensive refinement of its confidence factors before it regularly produces correct results. If even a few new rules are added to such a system after it has stabilized, the interactions of these rules can force another round of refinement. The number of rules that may require adjustment of their confidence factors can be very large. And there is still a chance of getting a grossly incorrect answer to a case that we happen not to have tried.

We have already alluded to our third problem with confidence factors: They do not give us a natural representation of how humans reason with incomplete or uncertain information. For example, we all know that birds fly. Of course, we also know that penguins don't fly. This means we have a rule about birds that we know has exceptions. If we are asked to build a cage for a large bird, we will plan to put a roof on it. If we learn that the bird is a penguin, we change our plans and omit the roof. We do not reason that we are 90% confident that birds fly, but we are 100% confident that penguins don't fly, and then use these two numbers in deciding whether to provide a roof. We don't even consider leaving off the roof until we learn that the bird is a penguin; then we don't even consider putting a roof on. The rules appear to be activated by the nature of the information in them, not by numbers on a scale.

Despite all our complaints, it cannot be denied that there is something attractive about confidence factors. Some impressive systems have been built that use them. Furthermore, we may have no choice but to use them to reason about uncertainty if no good alternative can be found. And of course most confidence-factor inference engines are more sophisticated than CONMAN. In the next chapter we will look at one system that can reason with uncertain or incomplete information without using confidence factors.

10.10. BIBLIOGRAPHICAL NOTES

Adams (1976) was one of the first to point out that MYCIN's confidence factors do not obey probability theory; his arguments are summarized by Jackson (1986:229–235). Several AI handbooks make much of Bayes' Theorem, a result in probability theory that allows inference about probabilities, while noting in passing that prominent expert systems do not actually use this formula. An example is Charniak and McDermott (1985). Others advocate systems that are frankly nonprobabilistic, such as the "fuzzy logic" of L. Zadeh, specifically intended to model subjective human confidence (see Mamdani and Gaines 1981).

Chapter 11

Defeasible Prolog

11.1. NONMONOTONIC REASONING AND PROLOG

If our reasoning is monotonic, the set of conclusions we draw from the information we have only gets larger as we get more and more information. Once we reach a conclusion, no additional information will cause us to reject it. When our reasoning is nonmonotonic, we may reject an earlier conclusion on the basis of new information.

Human reasoning is notoriously nonmonotonic. We make plans based on what we expect to happen, but we constantly revise our expectations, and our plans, as events unfold. For example, we make a date with a friend to meet for lunch on Friday. Then on Wednesday we learn that our friend had to leave town suddenly due to a family emergency. We revise our expectations and no longer believe our friend will keep his luncheon date.

The Prolog inference engine is nonmonotonic because of the way it handles negation. As we know, the query \+ Goal. succeeds in Prolog if and only if the query ?- Goal. fails. Consider this two-clause knowledge base:

```
flies(X) :- bird(X), \+ penguin(X).
bird(chilly).
```

The first clause says that something flies if it is a bird and we cannot prove that it is a penguin. The second says that Chilly is a bird. With this knowledge base, the query

```
?- flies(chilly).
```

succeeds. But if we add the fact `penguin(chilly)`, the same query will then fail because we are no longer unable to prove that Chilly is a penguin. With more information, Prolog rejects a goal it earlier accepted.

People often accept and use rules of thumb like "Birds fly," principles that they realize have exceptions. We use these rules, perhaps even unconsciously, unless we have reason to believe we are dealing with a case where the rule does not apply. We do not usually list all of the exceptions as part of the rule, and we realize that there may be many exceptions we don't know about. However, we can sometimes represent such rules in Prolog using negation-as-failure to list the exceptions. We shall see that this method will not work in all cases.

11.2. NEW SYNTAX FOR DEFEASIBLE REASONING

Generalizations like "Birds fly" and "Matches burn when they are struck" apply to usual, typical, or normal cases. Unusual, atypical, or abnormal cases are exceptions to the rule. We will say one of these generalizations is DEFEATED when we have information that tells us we are dealing with an exception to the rule. Because they can be defeated, we will call these generalizations DEFEASIBLE RULES.

Although Prolog can perform some kinds of nonmonotonic reasoning, Prolog rules are not defeasible. The rule about birds from the last section is not a defeasible rule because it is not affected by anything not stated in the rule itself. Prolog concludes that something flies if it satisfies the conditions of the rule no matter what else is in the knowledge base. A defeasible rule, on the other hand, is a rule that cannot be applied to some cases even though those cases satisfy its conditions, because some knowledge elsewhere in the knowledge base blocks it from applying.

This might lead one to think that a defeasible rule is simply an inexplicit Prolog rule. Not so. Some instances of defeasible reasoning cannot be reproduced in ordinary Prolog. As an example, suppose Wolf, Fox, and Hart are all running for the same elective office. Someone might say, "I presume Wolf will be elected, but if he isn't, then Fox will be." How could we represent this assertion in Prolog?

We might represent the presumption that Wolf will win by the fact

```
will_be_elected(wolf).
```

and we might represent the expectation that Fox will win if Wolf doesn't by the rule

```
will_be_elected(fox) :- \+ will_be_elected(wolf).
```

But this doesn't really capture the opinions expressed. First, the original statement was a presumption which might be defeated, but there is no way we can avoid the conclusion that Wolf will win the election once we have the fact about Wolf in our database. Second, there isn't much point in having the rule about Fox at all since its condition can never be satisfied so long as we have the fact about Wolf.

Perhaps our mistake is in the way we have represented the presumption. Instead of translating it into a Prolog fact, perhaps it should be a rule. But what rule? What is the condition for this rule? Maybe it should be

```
will_be_elected(wolf) :- \+ will_be_elected(fox).
```

Now the two rules about Wolf and Fox have exactly the same form and the same strength, but our presumption was that Wolf will be elected. Furthermore, the two rules taken together will cause Prolog to loop endlessly because each of them always calls the other when Prolog is given the query

```
?- will_be_elected(X).
```

Let's add some detail to our example. Suppose our political prognosticator goes on to say, "Of course, Wolf won't win the election if Bull withdraws and throws his support to Fox." How shall we represent this in Prolog? The obvious way to do it is

```
\+ will_be_elected(wolf) :- withdraws(bull),
                            supports(bull,fox).
```

But this is also obviously wrong since it is not a well-formed Prolog clause. The built-in predicate \+ cannot occur in the head of a Prolog clause. Typically, a Prolog interpreter will understand this rule as an attempt to redefine the predicate \+. Some interpreters will display an error message saying that this is not allowed.

What we need is a new way to represent defeasible rules and presumptions and an inference engine that knows how to use them. We also need a negation operator that is different from negation-as-failure so we can represent rules that tell us when something is positively not the case rather than just that we cannot *prove* that it is the case. These negative rules are needed to tell us when we have an exception to a defeasible rule, but they are desirable in their own right as well.

It's easy to represent defeasible rules. We arbitrarily pick a new operator to join the head and the body of the rule. We will use the operator :=/2. With this operator, we represent the defeasible rule that birds fly as

```
flies(X) := bird(X).
```

We will also introduce the negation operator **neg**/1. Unlike \+, **neg** can appear in a the head of a rule. Thus, we represent the claim that Wolf will not be elected if Bull withdraws from the election and throws his support to Fox as

```
neg will_be_elected(wolf) := withdraws(bull), supports(bull,fox).
```

Now comes the challenging part: building an inference engine that knows how to use these rules properly. Before we can do this, we must investigate further how reasoning with defeasible rules works.

Representing presumptions requires a bit more thought than representing ordinary defeasible rules. A presumption looks something like a defeasible fact. In Prolog the fact

```
yellow(sun).
```

is equivalent to the rule

```
yellow(sun) :- true.
```

The same relationship should hold between presumptions and defeasible rules. We will represent the presumption that Wolf will be elected by the defeasible rule

```
will_be_elected(wolf) := true.
```

This allows us to distinguish between presumptions and facts.

There is one other kind of statement that is important in understanding our use of defeasible rules. These are statements like "Wolf might not win if there is a poor voter turnout." How do these "might" rules work? If there is a poor voter turnout, does it follow that Wolf does not win? No. The rule is too weak to support this conclusion. But if there is a poor voter turnout, our presumption that Wolf will win gets defeated. Then the inference engine should conclude neither that Wolf will win nor that Wolf will not win. The sole purpose of these "might" rules is to interfere with conclusions that we might otherwise draw. They do not themselves allow us to draw any new conclusions.

This points out that there are two different ways that a defeasible rule can be defeated. First, we can have an ordinary Prolog rule or another defeasible rule that supports the opposite conclusion. When this happen, we say that the second rule *rebuts* the first rule. But that's not what is happening with these rules that use the word "might." They do not support the opposite conclusion or, for that matter, *any* conclusion. They simply point out a situation in which the rules they defeat might not apply. Rather than rebut, they *undercut* the rules they attack. So a defeasible rule might be either *rebutted* or *undercut*. Of course, two defeasible rules with opposite conclusions offer rebuttals for each other. It remains to be seen under what circumstances these rebuttals are successful. The other kind of defeater, the "might" defeater that does not itself support any conclusion, we will call an *undercutting* defeater or simply a *defeater*.

Of course, we will need some way to represent defeaters as well as defeasible rules and presumptions. We will use a new operator :^ to connect the head and the body of a defeater. We represent the defeater in our election example as

```
neg will_be_elected(wolf) :^ voter_turnout_is_poor.
```

We want an inference engine that recognizes defeasible rules, presumptions, defeaters and negations using **neg**, and knows how to use them. Our inference engine will be known as D-PROLOG ("defeasible Prolog"). To make the work of the defeasible inference engine easier, we will place some restrictions on the new kinds of rules we are introducing. We will not allow the use of disjunctions (;), cuts (!), or negation-as-failure (\+) in any of these rules. Then we don't have to tell our inference engine what to do when it finds these in a rule. By restricting the use of cuts and negation-as-failure, we restrict procedural control of the search for solutions and make it difficult to adopt a procedural style while using defeasible rules and defeaters. We assume that the procedural parts of our programs will still be written in ordinary Prolog. The use of disjunction in a defeasible reasoning system, on the other hand, raises special problems that we will not consider here.

11.3. STRICT RULES

Note that not all rules used in reasoning are defeasible. For example, the rule "Penguins are birds" can have no exceptions. This is because "bird" is part of the definition of "penguin." In general, rules which say that members of one NATURAL KIND are also members of another are nondefeasible or STRICT rules. Other examples include "Gold is a metal" and "Bats are mammals." We won't go into exactly what it means to say that something is a natural kind, and it isn't quite right to say that "bird" is part of the definition of the word "penguin," but the general idea should be clear enough.

Other examples of a strict rules are "Squares are rectangles" and "Marxists are communists." These rules are strict quite literally by definition. Of course, Marxists and communists aren't natural kinds (nor are squares and rectangles on most accounts), but that's why the relations between the terms are literally definitions. These are groups that man designed rather than groups found naturally.

Some other strict rules involve spatial and temporal regularities, such as, "Every living person born in Atlanta was born in Georgia" and "Every living person born before 1950 is more than forty years old today."

Besides the kinds of rules listed here, most other rules are defeasible. Even strong causal claims like "Litmus paper turns red when it is dipped in acid" should be treated as defeasible, as should strong regularities like "Members of the John Birch Society are conservative." No causal generality can ever be completely confirmed, and of course a group like the John Birch Society might be infiltrated by the A.C.L.U. or some other liberal group.

We will represent strict rules as ordinary Prolog rules. Whenever the antecedent condition of a strict rule is derivable, so is its consequent. But suppose the condition of a strict rule is only *defeasibly* derivable? Suppose, for example, that we have evidence that some animal is a bat and we also have evidence that it is a bird, but our evidence for neither claim is conclusive. Then the conditions for the two strict rules

```
mammal(X)  :- bat(X).
neg mammal(X) :- bird(X).
```

are both defeasibly derivable in the case of our mystery animal. What should we conclude? If our strict rules are correct, then some of our evidence must be incorrect. But we can't tell whether it is our evidence that the animal is a bat or our evidence that it is a bat that is flawed. We do know, though, that the animal can't both *be* a mammal and *not be* a mammal. In this situation, we should refrain from drawing any conclusion about whether the animal is a mammal. We may still be in the peculiar situation of concluding at least tentatively that it is both a bat and a bird, but we do a certain amount of damage control by stopping short of the blatant contradiction that it both is and is not a mammal.

There are two lessons to be learned from this example. First, we have to distinguish between what is strictly derivable and what is only defeasibly derivable. A conclusion is strictly derivable if it is derivable from facts and strict rules alone. We will say that any conclusion that is strictly derivable is also (at least) defeasibly derivable, but other conclusions that depend on presumptions and defeasible rules are also defeasibly derivable. Second, to limit the damage when we have conflicting evidence for competing strict rules, we will allow strict rules to be rebutted by other strict rules in at least those cases where the condition for the rebutted strict rule is only defeasibly derivable.

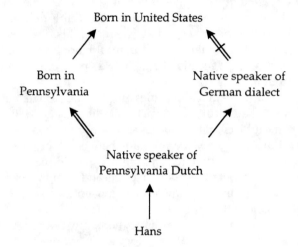

Figure 11.1   The Pennsylvania Dutch Example.

What about cases where strict rules compete with defeasible rules? Let's consider another example. Pennsylvania Dutch is a dialect of German. Ordinarily, native speakers of Pennsylvania Dutch are born in Pennsylvania. Of course, anyone born in Pennsylvania was born in the United States. But typically, native speakers of a German dialect are not born in the United States. Hans speaks Pennsylvania Dutch. We represent all this information as follows;

```
native_speaker(X,german_dialect) :- native_speaker(X,pa_dutch).
born(X,pennsylvania) := native_speaker(X,pa_dutch).
born(X,usa) :- born(X,pennsylvania).
neg born(X,usa) := native_speaker(X,german_dialect).
native_speaker(hans,pa_dutch).
```

We can also represent this information in a graph, as we have done in Figure 11.1 using → for strict rules and ⇒ for defeasible rules. We use bars through the arrows to show when the negation of the term at the head of the arrow is indicated by the rule.

First, we notice that Hans must definitely be a native speaker of a German dialect. Second, we have evidence that Hans was born in Pennsylvania and no evidence to the contrary. So we conclude defeasibly that Hans was in fact born in Pennsylvania. But now we have conflicting evidence in the strict rule saying Hans was born in the United States and the defeasible rule saying that he was not. Even though the condition of the strict rule is only defeasibly derivable while the condition of the defeasible rule is strictly derivable, the strict rule is superior. So we conclude defeasibly that Hans was born in the United States. Another way to put this is to strengthen our previous observation: *A strict rule can only be defeated if its condition is only defeasibly derivable, and then only by a fact or by another strict rule that rebuts it.*

11.4. INCOMPATIBLE CONCLUSIONS

We call simple Prolog clauses that do not contain the functor :- ATOMIC clauses or simply ATOMS (logical atoms, not Prolog atoms, of course!). We call atoms and negations of atoms formed using the predicate **neg** LITERALS. Where **Atom** is a logical atom, we say that **Atom** and **neg Atom** are COMPLEMENTS of each other. As we remarked earlier, both positive and negative literals may occur as the heads of rules in d-Prolog. And rules whose heads are complements of each other may rebut each other.

This is not the only way that two rules might conflict. It is impossible for one and the same animal to be both a bird and a mammal, and it is impossible for one and the same man to be both a Marxist and a capitalist. (We are not talking about *membership* in some Marxist group, now, but actually *being* a Marxist.) But of course **bird(animal)** and **mammal(animal)** are not complements of each other, nor are **marxist(man)** and **capitalist(man)** Yet we would surely want to say that evidence that an animal is a bird conflicts with any evidence that it is a mammal, and evidence that a man is a Marxist conflicts with any evidence that he is a capitalist. How can we indicate this?

Consider the example of Ping, who was born in the People's Republic of China but who emigrated to this country, where she now owns a restaurant. Is Ping a capitalist? We might represent the situation as follows:

```
capitalist(X) := owns(X,restaurant).
neg capitalist(X) :- marxist(X).
marxist(X) := born(X,prc).
neg marxist(X) :- capitalist(X).
owns(ping,restaurant).
born(ping,prc).
```

This set of d-Prolog rules and facts certainly captures the incompatibility of being both a Marxist and a capitalist. But consider what would happen if we asked whether we could defeasibly derive that Ping is a capitalist. Since she owns a restaurant, we have evidence that she is a capitalist. But the rule we would use is defeasible; so we must make sure that it is not defeated. We find the competing rule that says she is not a capitalist if she is a Marxist. This will defeat our rule unless we can show that there is no way to derive that Ping is a Marxist, i.e., that the rule is not SATISFIED. But since Ping was born in the People's Republic of China, we have evidence that she is a Marxist. Of course, this also depends on a defeasible rule; so we will still be okay if we can show that this rule is defeated. We have a competitor in the strict rule that says that capitalists are not Marxists. So now we need to show that Ping is a capitalist in order to show that Ping is a capitalist! We are in a loop and have no way to get out.

Our solution to this problem is similar to the solution to the problem of using biconditionals discussed in Chapter 6. We will introduce a predicate **incompatible/2** which will tell d-Prolog when two clauses that are not complements of each other are nevertheless incompatible. So in our examples, we would use the clauses

```
incompatible(bird(X),mammal(X)).
```

and

```
incompatible(marxist(X),capitalist(X)).
```

When we implement our defeasible logic, we must tell the d-Prolog inference engine how to use this information without looping.

We say two clauses `Clause1` and `Clause2` are CONTRARIES in a d-Prolog database if one is the complement of the other or if either of the two clauses

```
incompatible(Clause1,Clause2).
```

or

```
incompatible(Clause2,Clause1).
```

is in the database. We say that two rules COMPETE or CONFLICT with each other and that they are COMPETITORS if their heads are contraries. These definitions are implemented in Prolog as follows:

```
contrary(Clause1,Clause2) :- incompatible(Clause1,Clause2).

contrary(Clause1,Clause2) :- incompatible(Clause2,Clause1).

contrary(Clause1,Clause2) :- comp(Clause1,Clause2).

comp(neg Atom,Atom) :- !.

comp(Atom,neg Atom).
```

11.5. SUPERIORITY OF RULES

Let's consider the Chinese restaurant example again. We can represent this information by the graph in Figure 11.2. Here we have two defeasible rules, each rebutting the other. But, intuitively, what would we conclude about someone who emigrated from the People's Republic of China to the United States and opened a restaurant? We would conclude that this person is probably a capitalist. We would consider the evidence of running a business for profit superior to the evidence of place of birth. So our capitalist rule is superior to our Marxist rule.

We need a way to tell d-Prolog that one rule is superior to another. For this, we introduce the predicate sup/2. In our example, we add the clause

```
sup((capitalist(X) := owns(X,restaurant)),
    (marxist(X) := born(X,prc))).
```

We say Rule 1 is INFERIOR to Rule 2 if Rule 2 is superior to Rule1. The importance of this notion to our defeasible logic is that a defeasible rule cannot be rebutted by an inferior defeasible rule. In our example, the Marxist rule is rebutted by the capitalist rule, but the capitalist rule is not rebutted by the Marxist rule. So we conclude that `capitalist(ping)` is defeasibly derivable.

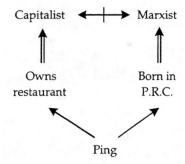

Figure 11.2   The Chinese Restaurant Example.

Similarly, a defeasible rule cannot be undercut by an inferior defeater. For example, people normally can walk. But if someone is very young, he or she might not yet walk.

```
walks(X) := human(X).
neg walks(X) :^ infant(X).
```

But suppose we incorporate into this same database information about animals other than humans. Antelope, for example, can walk within hours of birth. We would not want our defeater for young creatures to undercut the rule for deer.

```
walks(X) := deer(X).
sup((walks(X) := deer(X)),(neg walks(X) :^ infant(X))).
```

So the rule about normal deer locomotion is superior to the defeater about infant locomotion and is not undercut by it. But the rule about human locomotion is not superior to the defeater and is therefore undercut by it.

11.6. SPECIFICITY

Sometimes we can tell that one rule is superior to another without being told. Consider the following example.

```
flies(X) := bird(X).
neg flies(X) := penguin(X).
bird(X) :- penguin(X).
penguin(opus).
```

Is Opus a bird? Definitely. Does Opus fly? Apparently, not. An example like this has been around for some time involving a bird named Tweety. The corresponding graph is shown in Figure 11.3. Because of the shape of the graph, this kind of example is often called a "Tweety Triangle."

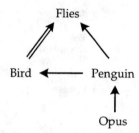

Figure 11.3   A "Tweety Triangle."

Remember that defeasible rules tell us about the normal or typical cases. Typical birds fly. But a penguin is a special kind of bird. Because of our strict rule, we immediately know that something is a bird as soon as we know that it is a penguin. The converse, of course, is not true: many birds are not penguins. So any rule for penguins is more specific than any rule for birds. Penguin rules take into account more information than do bird rules. When one rule is more specific than another, the first rule is superior to the second.

How can we tell that penguin rules are more specific than bird rules? By noticing that the strict rule

```
bird(X) :- penguin(X).
```

is in our database. But the connection between birds and penguins might have been less direct and it might have involved defeasible rules as well as strict rules. Here is another example.

```
conservative(X) := affiliate(X,chamber_of_commerce).
neg conservative(X) := theatrical_agent(X).
busnessperson(X) := theatrical_agent(X).
affiliate(X,chamber_of_commerce) := businessperson(X).
theatrical_agent(Taylor).
```

In this case, the rule for nonconservativism is more specific than and therefore superior to the rule for conservativism. That's because we have a chain of rules linking the condition for nonconservativism (being a theatrical agent) to the condition for conservativism (being a businessperson). Put another way, we can DEFEASIBLY DERIVE that Taylor is an affiliate of the Chamber of Commerce from her activities as a theatrical agent, but we cannot defeasibly derive how she makes her living from her membership in the Chamber of Commerce.

It is not enough to establish specificity that we have rules linking the condition of one competing rule to the condition of another. If those links are defeasible, then they must be undefeated or specificity cannot be inferred. As an example of what can go wrong, assume that college students are normally adults and that normally adults are employed, but that college students normally are not employed.

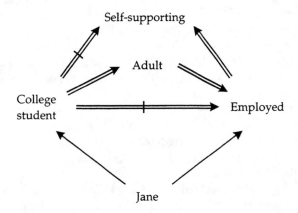

Figure 11.4 The College Student Example.

Furthermore, employed persons typically are self-supporting while college students typically are not self-supporting. Finally, we stipulate that Jane is a college student who is employed. Does Jane support herself? The rules and facts relevant to this example are:

```
adult(X) := college_student(X).
neg employed(X) := college_student(X).
neg self_supporting(X) := college_student(X).
employed(X) := adult(X).
self_supporting(X) := employed(X).
college_student(jane).
employed(jane).
```

The corresponding graphic representation is shown in Figure 11.4. We have two conflicting rules, one for college students and another for employed persons. Is either more specific than the other? Since college students are normally adults and adults are normally employed, it might appear at first glance that the rule for college students is more specific than the rule for employed persons. However, rules about college students are not really more specific than rules about employed persons because the link from college students to employed persons is itself defeated. Or to put it differently, we cannot defeasibly derive that Jane is employed from her status as a college student because we have a rule that says college students normally are not employed. This rule is more specific than the rule for adults that occurs in the path from college students to employed persons. So neither rule about self-support is more specific, and each rule is rebutted by the other.

    This points out a crucial fact about our defeasible reasoning. Most of the time, we are using everything we know as the basis for our conclusions. But sometimes, when we are trying to figure out which rules are more specific, we use only the information in the conditions of the rules together with other rules that may link these. When we do this, we ignore any facts or presumptions we may have available and rely only on the conditions of the two rules being compared and the other rules available to us. For example, part of the information we have in the college student example is the fact that Jane is employed. If we are allowed to use this, then we can infer that Jane is employed from any other information at all. But that certainly doesn't mean that it follows even defeasibly from Jane's being a college student that she is employed.

In summary, then, at any given time we may be reasoning from part of our information. We will call these different sets of information KNOWLEDGE BASES. Normally we will be reasoning from the entire d-Prolog database. We will call this the ROOT knowledge base. When we test to see whether one rule is more specific than another, we limit ourselves to the clauses in the condition of one of the two rules being compared together with all the strict rules, defeasible rules, and defeaters in the root knowledge base. We leave out any facts or presumptions in the root knowledge base during this part of our reasoning. Remembering that the strict rules, defeasible rules, and defeaters from the root knowledge base get added in, we can think of each condition of a rule as itself determining a knowledge base. It will be important in designing our inference engine to remember that we must always keep track of the knowledge base in use at each stage of reasoning.

11.6.1. Listing of DPROLOG.PL

```
% DPROLOG.PL
%
% A defeasible inference engine for Prolog.
%


init :- nl, nl,
        write('d-Prolog - A Defeasible Extension of Prolog'),
        nl, nl,
        write('"preempt" toggles preemption of defeaters.'),
        nl, nl, nl,
        op(1100,fx,@),
        op(900,fx,neg ),
        op(1100,xfy,:=),
        op(1100,xfy,:^).


:- init.

:- dynamic (neg)/1, (:=)/2, (:^)/2.
:- multifile (neg)/1, (:=)/2, (:^)/2.
:- prolog_flag(unknown,_,fail).


%
% @(+Goal)
%     Succeeds if Goal is defeasibly derivable from
%     the d-Prolog knowledge base.
%
```

```
@ Goal :- def_der(root,Goal).

%
% strict_der(+KB,+Goal)
%    Succeeds if Goal is derivable from the ordinary Prolog
%    facts and rules in the d-Prolog knowledge base.
%

strict_der(root,Goal) :-
        % A goal is derivable from the complete d-Prolog
        % knowledge base if and only if it succeeds.
          !,
          call(Goal).

strict_der(KB,(First,Rest)) :-
        % A conjunction is strictly derivable if and only if
        % both of its conjuncts are strictly derivable.
          !,
          strict_der(KB,First),
          strict_der(KB,Rest).

strict_der(KB,Goal) :-
        % A goal is strictly derivable from a knowledge base
        % other than the complete knowledge base if it is
        % contained in that knowledge base.
          conjunct(Goal,KB).

strict_der(KB,Goal) :-
        % A goal is strictly derivable from a knowledge base
        % other than the complete knowledge base if it is
        % the head of an ordinary Prolog rule in the complete
        % knowledge base whose nonempty condition is strictly
        % derivable from that knowledge base.
          clause(Goal,Condition),
          Condition \== true,
          strict_der(KB,Condition).

%
% def_der(+KB,+Goal)
%    Succeeds if Goal is defeasibly derivable from the
%    knowledge base KB.
%

def_der(_,true) :- !.
        % 'true' is defeasibly derivable from any
        % knowledge base.

def_der(KB,(First,Rest)) :-
        % A conjunction is defeasibly derivable if
        % and only if both conjuncts are defeasibly
        % derivable.
```

```
        !,
        def_der(KB,First),
        def_der(KB,Rest).

def_der(_,Goal) :-
        predicate_property(Goal,built_in),
        \+ functor(Goal,',',_),
        % A goal with a built-in functor is defeasibly
        % derivable if and only if it succeeds. The test
        % used here is for Quintus Prolog. This test may
        % be different for another version of Prolog.
        !,
        Goal.

def_der(KB,Goal) :-
        % A goal is defeasibly derivable if it is
        % strictly derivable.
        strict_der(KB,Goal).

def_der(KB,Goal) :-
        % A goal is defeasibly derivable if it is
        % the head of an ordinary Prolog rule whose
        % condition is defeasibly derivable and which
        % is not rebutted.
        clause(Goal,Condition),
        Condition \== true,
        def_der(KB,Condition),
        not_rebutted(KB,(Goal :- Condition)).

def_der(KB,Goal) :-
        % A goal is defeasibly derivable if it is
        % the head of a defeasible rule whose
        % condition is defeasibly derivable and which
        % is neither rebutted nor undercut.
        def_rule(KB,(Goal := Condition)),
        def_der(KB,Condition),
        not_rebutted(KB,(Goal := Condition)),
        not_undercut(KB,(Goal := Condition)).

def_der(KB,Goal) :-
        preemption,
        % If defeater preemption is enabled, then
        % a goal is defeasibly derivable if it is
        % the head of a defeasible rule whose condition
        % is defeasibly derivable, provided every
        % rebutting or undercutting defeater for that
        % rule is itself rebutted by a strict rule or
        % a superior defeasible rule.
        def_rule(KB,(Goal := Condition)),
        \+ (contrary(Goal,Contrary1),
            strict_der(KB,Contrary1)),
```

```
            def_der(KB,Condition),
            \+ (contrary(Goal,Contrary2),
                clause(Contrary2,Condition2),
                Condition2 \== true,
                def_der(KB,Condition2)),
            \+ (contrary(Goal,Contrary3),
                def_rule(KB,(Contrary3 := Condition3)),
                def_der(KB,Condition3),
                \+ (preempted(KB,(Contrary3 := Condition3)))),
            \+ (contrary(Goal,Contrary4),
                (Contrary4 :^ Condition4),
                def_der(KB,Condition4),
                \+ (preempted(KB,(Contrary4 :^ Condition4)))).


%
% contrary(+Clause1,-Clause2)
%    Discovers Clause2 which either is the complement of
%    Clause1 or is incompatible with Clause1.
%

contrary(Clause1,Clause2) :-
        incompatible(Clause1,Clause2).

contrary(Clause1,Clause2) :-
        incompatible(Clause2,Clause1).

contrary(Clause1,Clause2) :-
        comp(Clause1,Clause2).


%
% comp(+Clause1,-Clause2)
%    Succeeds if Clause1 is neg Clause2 or if Clause2 is
%    is neg Clause1.
%

comp(neg Atom,Atom) :-
        !.

comp(Atom,neg Atom).


%
% not_rebutted(+KB,+Rule)
%    Succeeds if \+ rebutted(+KB,Rule) succeeds. This
%    predicate is added to introduce a cut in a way that
%    reduces the number of duplicate solutions.
%

not_rebutted(KB,Rule) :-
        \+ rebutted(KB,Rule),
        !.
```

```
%
% rebutted(+KB,+Rule)
%    Succeeds if the Rule is defeated in the knowledge
%    base KB by a rebutting defeater (an ordinary
%    Prolog rule or a defeasible rule to which the Rule
%    is not superior).
%

rebutted(KB,Rule) :-
        % Any rule is rebutted if a contrary of
        % its head is strictly derivable.
          Rule =.. [_,Head,_],
          contrary(Head,Contrary),
          strict_der(KB,Contrary).

rebutted(KB,Rule) :-
        % Any rule may be rebutted by an ordinary
        % Prolog rule with a contrary head.
          Rule =.. [_,Head,_],
          contrary(Head,Contrary),
          clause(Contrary,Body),
          Body \== true,
          def_der(KB,Body).

rebutted(KB,(Head := Body)) :-
        % Defeasible rules may be rebutted by other
        % defeasible rules with contrary heads.
          contrary(Head,Contrary),
          def_rule(KB,(Contrary := Condition)),
          def_der(KB,Condition),
          \+ sup_rule((Head := Body),(Contrary := Condition)).

%
% not_undercut(+KB,+Rule)
%    Succeeds if \+ undercut(+KB,Rule) succeeds. This
%    predicate is added to introduce a cut in a way that
%    reduces the number of duplicate solutions.
%

not_undercut(KB,Rule) :-
          \+ undercut(KB,Rule),
          !.

%
% undercut(+KB,+Rule)
%    Succeeds if the Rule is defeated in the knowledge
%    base KB by an undercutting defeater.
%

undercut(KB,(Head := Body)) :-
        % Only defeasible rules may be undercut by pure
```

```
            % defeaters.
              contrary(Head,Contrary),
              (Contrary :^ Condition),
              def_der(KB,Condition),
              \+ sup_rule((Head := Body),(Contrary :^ Body)),
              !.


%
% sup_rule(+Rule1,+Rule2)
%    Succeeds if the body of Rule2 is defeasibly derivable
%    from the body of Rule1, but the body of Rule1 is not
%    defeasibly derivable from the body of Rule2. The user
%    can also force superiority by adding clauses for the
%    predicate 'sup'.
%

sup_rule(Rule1,Rule2) :-
        sup(Rule1,Rule2).

sup_rule((_ := Body1),(_ := Body2)) :-
        def_der(Body1,Body2),
        \+ def_der(Body2,Body1).

sup_rule((_ := Body1),(_ :^ Body2)) :-
        def_der(Body1,Body2),
        \+ def_der(Body2,Body1).


%
% conjunct(+Clause1,+Clause2)
%

conjunct(Clause,Clause) :- !.

conjunct(Clause,(Clause,_)) :- !.

conjunct(Clause,(_,Rest)) :-
        conjunct(Clause,Rest).


%
% def_rule(+KB,+Rule)
%    Succeeds if KB is the entire d-Prolog knowledge base
%    and Rule is any defeasible rule in KB, or if Rule is a
%    defeasible rule in the d-Prolog knowledge base and the
%    body of Rule is not the atom 'true'.
%

def_rule(root,(Head := Body)) :-
        !,
        (Head := Body).

def_rule(_,(Head := Body)) :-
```

```
                    (Head := Body),
                    Body \== true.


%
% preempted(+KB,+Rule)
%    Succeeds if the Rule is defeated in the knowledge
%    base KB by a superior rebutting defeater (an ordinary
%    Prolog rule or a defeasible rule which is superior
%    to the Rule).
%

preempted(KB,Rule) :-
        % Any rule is preempted if a contrary of
        % its head is strictly derivable.
          Rule =.. [_,Head,_],
          contrary(Head,Contrary),
          strict_der(KB,Contrary),
          !.


preempted(KB,Rule) :-
        % Any rule may be preempted by an ordinary
        % Prolog rule with a contrary head.
          Rule =.. [_,Head,_],
          contrary(Head,Contrary),
          clause(Contrary,Body),
          Body \== true,
          def_der(KB,Body).

preempted(KB,(Head := Body)) :-
        % Defeasible rules may be preempted by superior
        % defeasible rules with contrary heads.
          contrary(Head,Contrary),
          def_rule(KB,(Contrary := Condition)),
          def_der(KB,Condition),
          sup_rule((Contrary := Condition),(Head := Body)),
          !.


%
% preempt
%    Toggles the preemption of defeaters feature between
%    enabled and disabled.
%

preempt :-
        retract(preemption),
        !,
        write('Preemption is disabled.'), nl.


preempt :-
        assert(preemption),
        write('Preemption is enabled.'), nl.
```

```
:- abolish(preemption/0).

:- consult('dputils.pl').
```

11.7. DEFINING STRICT DERIVABILITY IN PROLOG

The defeasible inference engine will be built around a special predicate @/1 just as
the inference engine for biconditionals in Chapter 6 was built around the special
predicate prove/1. For any Goal, we will want the query

```
?- @(Goal).
```

to succeed if the defeasible inference engine can derive Goal from the database,
including defeasible rules, presumptions, defeaters, and negations with neg. If the
inference engine cannot prove Goal using these resources, we will want the query to
fail. Basically, then, the inference engine must define the predicate @.

   We will make @ a prefix operator so we can express the above query without
parentheses as

```
?- @ Goal.
```

   In fact, we define four new operators :=/2, :^/2, neg/1, and @/1 using the
built-in predicate op/3 discussed in Chapter 6. File DPROLOG.PL thus begins with
a procedure init/0 containing the op declarations, followed immediately by a query
invoking it. If the op declarations were not executed at this time, Prolog would be
unable to understand the rest of the clauses in the file. (Some implementations may
require moving the op declarations outside of init to get them recognized at the
proper time.)

   Remember that a literal may be either strictly or defeasibly derivable either
from the complete d-Prolog database (the root knowledge base) or from the literals
in the condition of some rule (together with the strict rules, defeasible rules, and
defeaters in the root knowledge base). The query

```
?- @ Goal.
```

succeeds if Goal is at least defeasibly derivable from the root knowledge base. We
need another binary predicate that takes both the knowledge base and the goal as
arguments. Thus, we define @ by

```
@ Goal :- def_der(root,Goal).
```

   Before defining def_der/2, we will attack the easier task of defining the predicate for strict derivability, strict_der/2. For the root knowledge base, strict derivability is just ordinary derivability in Prolog.

```
strict_der(root,Goal) :- !, call(Goal).
```

We include the cut because we do not want the inference engine to apply any later clauses upon backtracking since these are intended only for knowledge bases other than the root knowledge base.

A literal is strictly derivable from a knowledge base KB if it is in KB or if it is the head of a strict rule in the root knowledge base whose condition is strictly derivable from KB. Since conditions may be conjunctions of literals, we will handle this case first. A conjunction of literals is strictly derivable from KB if each conjunct is strictly derivable from KB.

```
strict_der(KB,(First,Rest)) :-
        !,
        strict_der(KB,First),
        strict_der(KB,Rest).
```

We put this clause first and include a cut so the inference engine will not try to apply any of the clauses intended for literals to a complex condition before it has broken the condition into individual literals.

For any knowledge base KB other than the root knowledge base, we have two cases left to consider. One is where the literal we are trying to derive is in KB and the other is where it is the head of a strict rule whose condition is strictly derivable from KB. We have a separate clause for each of these situations. Remember that any knowledge base other than the root knowledge base will be identified with the condition of some other rule. So it will be a conjunction of literals. A literal is in a conjunction of literals if it is one of the conjuncts.

```
strict_der(KB,Goal) :-
        conjunct(Goal,KB).
```

```
strict_der(KB,Goal) :-
        clause(Goal,Condition),
        Condition \== true,
        strict_der(KB,Condition).
```

We eliminate rules in the second clause above whose conditions are the built-in predicate true because these rules are the facts in the root knowledge base. Remember that if we don't do this, then any fact in the root knowledge base will be strictly derivable from any rule condition whatsoever. So, for example, if we know that Opus is both a bird and a penguin, we would be able to show that being a penguin follows from being a bird. Since we certainly don't want to be able to do that, we have the restriction.

The auxilliary predicate conjunct/2 is easily defined.

```
conjunct(Clause,Clause) :- !.
```

```
conjunct(Clause,(Clause,_)) :- !.
```

```
conjunct(Clause,(_,Rest)) :- conjunct(Clause,Rest).
```

What we have done in defining strict derivability is to call the Prolog interpreter for the root knowledge base and to define a Prolog interpreter in Prolog for other knowledge bases.

11.8. D-PROLOG: PRELIMINARIES

Before looking at how we apply defeasible rules, we must attend to some other details. Remember that a presumption is a defeasible rule of the form

```
Goal := true.
```

In using presumptions, an inference engine will eventually contend with the query `?- def_der(KB,true)`. Of course, this query should succeed. So the first clause in the definition of `def_der/2` is simply

```
def_der(KB,true) :- !.
```

As with strict derivability, the inference engine will sometimes need to show that the condition of a rule is defeasibly derivable. To do this, it must break the condition down into its individual literals.

```
def_der(KB,(First,Rest)) :-
        !,
        def_der(KB,First),
        def_der(KB,Rest).
```

When the inference engine encounters a built-in Prolog predicate, it must evaluate the goal containing that predicate using the built-in definition of the predicate regardless of the knowledge base upon which the derivation is based. The test for a built-in predicate used in the clause below is the correct test in Quintus Prolog. This test may have to be modified for other versions of Prolog.

```
def_der(_,Goal) :-
        predicate_property(Goal,built_in),
        \+ functor(Goal,',',_),
        !,
        Goal.
```

Of course, a literal is *at least* defeasibly derivable from a knowledge base if it is *strictly* derivable from that knowledge base.

```
def_der(KB,Goal) :- strict_der(KB,Goal).
```

The last clause before looking at defeasible rules defines how strict rules may be involved in defeasible derivations. Since strict rules can't be undercut, they apply if their conditions are at least defeasibly satisfied and they are not rebutted.

```
def_der(KB,Goal) :-
        clause(Goal,Condition),
        Condition \== true,
        def_der(KB,Condition),
        not_rebutted(KB,(Goal :- Conditional)).
```

We eliminate strict rules with `true` as their condition since these are facts and cannot be used in deriving a literal from the condition of another rule in testing for specificity.

Notice that in the last paragraph, we used a predicate `not_rebutted` rather than `\+ rebutted`. We define this new predicate simply as

```
not_rebutted(KB,Rule) :- \+ rebutted(KB,Rule),  !.
```

We do this because in some Prologs, `\+` will succeed more than once, producing identical solutions to a defeasible query. In similar fashion, we use `not_undercut` below.

How can a strict rule be rebutted? It is rebutted if a contrary of its head is strictly derivable (when we know conclusively that the head of the rule is false). Otherwise, it can only be rebutted by another strict rule.

```
rebutted(KB,Rule) :-
        Rule =.. [_,Head,_],
        contrary(Head,Contrary),
        strict_der(KB,Contrary),
        !.


rebutted(KB,Rule) :-
        Rule =.. [_,Head,_],
        contrary(Head,Contrary),
        clause(Contrary,Body),
        Body \== true,
        def_der(KB,Body).
```

Notice that these two clauses apply to all rules, including defeasible rules. Naturally, any set of circumstances that will rebut a strict rule will also rebut a defeasible rule.

11.9. USING DEFEASIBLE RULES

Under what circumstances can we apply a defeasible rule? As an example, let's take the simple rule

```
flies(X) := bird(X).
```

To use this rule to conclude tentatively that Opus flies, we need to establish three things:

1. We conclude at least tentatively that Opus is a bird.

2. Our rule is not rebutted.

3. Our rule is not undercut.

An initial attempt at representing this as a general principle in Prolog is simple. First we find a defeasible rule whose head unifies with our goal. Then we apply the three tests listed above.

```
def_der(KB,Goal) :-
        def_rule(KB,(Goal := Condition)),
        def_der(KB,Condition),
        not_rebutted(KB,(Goal := Condition)),
        not_undercut(KB,(Goal := Condition)).
```

We must define which rules belong in a knowledge base because we only use presumptions when we are reasoning from the root knowledge base. This gives us a simple definition of `def_rule/2`:

```
def_rule(root,(Head := Body)) :-
        !,
        (Head := Body).

def_rule(KB,(Head := Body)) :-
        (Head := Body),
        Body \== true.
```

Of course, we need to specify the conditions in which a defeasible rule is rebutted or defeated. Recall from the last section that any rule, strict or defeasible, is rebutted if a contrary of its head is either strictly derivable or is the head of some strict rule that is at least defeasibly satisfied. But defeasible rules can also be rebutted by other competing, noninferior defeasible rules with contrary heads.

```
rebutted(KB,(Head := Body)) :-
        contrary(Head,Contrary),
        def_rule(KB,(Contrary := Condition)),
        def_der(KB,Condition),
        \+ sup_rule((Head := Body),(Contrary := Condition)).
```

We use a cut because we are never interested in knowing that there are different ways to rebut a rule. If it is rebutted at all, then it cannot be applied.

One rule is superior to another if we have a clause for the predicate sup/2 that indicates this, or if the first rule is more specific than the second. The later situation holds when the body of the second rule is defeasibly derivable from the body of the first, but at least one literal in the body of the first rule is not defeasibly derivable from the body of the second.

```
sup_rule(Rule1,Rule2) :-
        sup(Rule1,Rule2).

sup_rule((Head1 := Body1),(Head2 := Body2)) :-
        def_der(Body1,Body2),
        \+ def_der(Body2,Body1).
```

Defeasible rules are undercut by defeaters in much the same way they are rebutted by other defeasible rules. The only difference is that a defeater does not support an argument for a contrary conclusion.

```
undercut(KB,(Head := Body)) :-
        contrary(Head,Contrary),
        (Contrary :^ Condition),
        def_der(KB,Condition),
        \+ sup_rule((Head := Body),(Contrary :^ Body)).
```

Once again, the cut is used because we only need to know that there is at least one way that the rule is undercut. Since superiority also applies to defeaters, we need another clause for sup_rule/2:

```
sup_rule((Head1 := Body1),(Head2 :^ Body2)) :-
        def_der(Body1,Body2),
        \+ def_der(Body2,Body1).
```

11.10. PREEMPTION OF DEFEATERS

Arguably, our requirement that we cannot apply a defeasible rule unless it is superior to every competing defeasible rule or defeater that is satisfiable is too strong. We will look at an example that illustrates the problem with this requirement. To begin, we know that southerners are typically conservatives and conservatives are typically Republicans, even though southerners typically are not Republicans. Furthermore, movie stars are typically rich and rich folks are typically Republicans, even though movie stars typically are not Republicans. Kim Basinger is a southern movie star. The d-Prolog representation of all this information is as follows:

```
[1]   republican(X) := conservative(X).
[2]   republican(X) := rich(X).
[3]   neg republican(X) := southerner(X).
[4]   neg republican(X) := movie_star(X).
[5]   conservative(X) := southern(X).
[6]   rich(X) := movie_star(X).
      southerner(kim).
      movie_star(kim).
```

The question, of course, is whether we should conclude that Kim Basinger is a Republican. The intuitively correct answer is that she is not.

The structure of the rules is perhaps easier to see in the graph in Figure 11.5. You will probably recognize this as an example of twin Tweety Triangles. When we look at these rules, we see that [3] is superior to [1] (since it is more specific) but not to [2], while [4] is superior to [2] (since it is more specific) but not to [1]. So neither of the two rules supporting the intuitively correct rule that Kim is not a Republican is superior to all competitors. How can we save the situation?

Based on examples like this, we can insist that any defeasible rule that is itself rebutted by a superior defeasible rule loses its capacity to rebut any other rule. Then since [1] is rebutted by the superior rule [3] and [2] is rebutted by the superior rule [4], neither [1] nor [2] has the capacity to rebut either [3] or [4]. In this case, we say that the rules [1] and [2] have been PREEMPTED as defeaters.

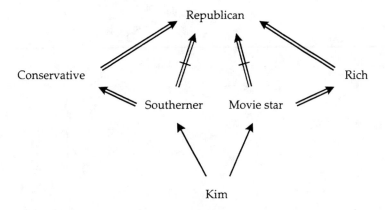

Figure 11.5   Twin Tweety Triangles.

Perhaps a defeasible rule should be preempted as a potential defeater if it is either rebutted or undercut by a superior rule. This, however, appears to be too strong as the following modification of our original Tweety Triangle shows. Remember that birds normally fly, that penguins normally don't fly, and that penguins are birds. Now suppose we develop a genetically altered penguin with large wings and correspondingly large "flight" muscles. Can these genetically altered penguins fly? We should probably take the information that a particular penguin has this genetic alteration as a reason to suspend our usual judgment that it can not fly. We are assuming, of course, that the genetic alteration envisioned is not so great that the creatures cease to be penguins. They are still penguins albeit strange ones. Suppose Folio is one of these genetically altered penguins. (A folio is a kind of opus, isn't it?) In the graphic representation of this example (Figure 11.6), we use a wavy arrow for the defeater. The following is the d-Prolog representation of the same example:

```
flies(X) := bird(X)
neg flies(X) := penguin(X).
flies(X) :^ ga_penguin(X).
bird(X) :- penguin(X).
penguin(X) :- ga_penguin(X).
ga_penguin(folio).
```

The important point to note about this example is that we are inclined to withhold judgment about whether Folio can fly; we are not inclined to infer even tentatively that he *can* fly. But if the penguin rule were preempted by the undercutting defeater for genetically altered penguins, then it could no longer rebut the bird rule and we could then use the bird rule to infer that apparently Folio flies. Since this runs contrary to our intuitions about this kind of example, we conclude that potential defeaters are not preempted when they are only undercut by superior defeaters. They must actually be rebutted by a superior rule to be preempted.

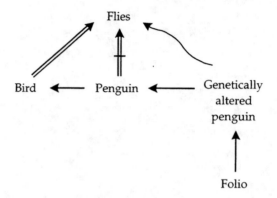

Figure 11.6 An Example of an Undercut Defeater.

Putting all of this together we get another, rather complicated, clause for the predicate `def_der/2`:

```
def_der(KB,Goal) :-
[1]     preemption,
[2]     def_rule(Goal := Condition),
[3]     \+ (contrary(Goal,Contrary1),
             strict_der(KB,Contrary1)),
[4]     def_der(KB,Condition),
[5]     \+ (contrary(Goal,Contrary2),
             clause(Contrary2,Condition2),
             Condition2 \== true,
             def_der(KB,Condition2)),
[6]     \+ (contrary(Goal,Contrary3),
             def_rule(KB,(Contrary3 := Condition3)),
             def_der(KB,Condition3),
             \+ (rebutted(KB,(Contrary3 := Condition3)))),
[7]     \+ (contrary(Goal,Contrary4),
             (Contrary4 :^ Condition4),
             def_der(KB,Condition4),
             \+ (rebutted(KB,(Contrary4 :^ Condition4)))).
```

We will examine these conditions one at a time.

This clause is considerably more complex than our earlier clauses for applying defeasible rules. If we add it to our inference engine, Prolog will have much more work to do to check to see whether a literal is defeasibly derivable. At the same time, twin Tweety Triangles are relatively unusual. So we give the d-Prolog developer the option of enabling or disabling preemption of defeaters. If it is enabled, the clause **preemption** will be found in the database and condition [1] of our rule will be satisfied. Otherwise, condition [1] will fail and Prolog will ignore the rest of the clause. We define a predicate `preempt/0` which toggles between enabling and disabling preemption of defeaters, and by default preemption is disabled when d-Prolog is loaded.

```
preempt :-
        retractall(preemption),
        !,
        write('Preemption is disabled.'), nl.

preempt :-
        assert(preemption),
        write('Preemption is enabled.'), nl.


:- retractall(preemption).
```

Condition [2] finds any available defeasible rule that we might try to apply, condition [3] makes sure that no contrary of the head of the rule (after unifying with the goal) is strictly derivable, and condition [4] checks to see if the rule is satisfiable. The rest of our conditions check to make sure that the rule is not defeated in one of several ways. Condition [5] checks to see that the rule is not rebutted by any strict rule (which can never be preempted). Conditions [6] and [7] check to see that every defeasible rule or defeater that might otherwise rebut or undercut the rule is preempted. The definition for the auxiliary predicate `preempted/2` is just like the definition for `rebutted/2` except that in the last clause, the rebutting defeasible rule must be superior to the rule it preempts rather than just not inferior.

```
preempted(KB,Rule) :-
        Rule =.. [_,Head,_],
        contrary(Head,Contrary),
        strict_der(KB,Contrary),
        !.

preempted(KB,Rule) :-
        Rule =.. [_,Head,_],
        contrary(Head,Contrary),
        clause(Contrary,Body),
        Body \== true,
        def_der(KB,Body).

preempted(KB,(Head := Body)) :-
        contrary(Head,Contrary),
        def_rule(KB,(Contrary := Condition)),
        def_der(KB,Condition),
        sup_rule((Contrary := Condition),(Head := Body)),
        !.
```

This completes the definition of our defeasible inference engine.

11.10.1. Listing of DPUTILS.PL

```
% DPUTILS.PL
%
% Utilities for d-Prolog.
%

:- op(1100,fx,@@).

:- dynamic have_seen_predicate_before/2.
:- dynamic dPrologDictionary/2.


%
% @@(+Goal)
%    Tests to see if Goal is strictly or defeasibly
%    derivable from the d-Prolog knowledge base. Goal
%    may not contain an uninstantiated variable.
%

@@ Goal :-
        Goal =.. [_|ArgumentList],
        member(Argument,ArgumentList),
        var(Argument),
        write('Improper argument for @@.'), nl,
        write('Argument contains an uninstantiated variable.'),
        nl,
        !,
        fail.

@@ Goal :-
        strict_der(root,Goal),
        contrary(Goal,Contrary),
        Contrary,
        !,
        write('definitely, yes -'), nl,
        write('and definitely, no - contradictory.'), nl.

@@ Goal :-
        strict_der(root,Goal),
        !,
        write('definitely, yes.'), nl.

@@ Goal :-
        contrary(Goal,Contrary),
        Contrary,
        !,
        write('definitely, no.'), nl.

@@ Goal :-
        def_der(root,Goal),
```

```
          !,
          write('presumably, yes.'), nl.

@@ Goal :-
          contrary(Goal,Contrary),
          def_der(root,Contrary),
          !,
          write('presumably, no.'), nl.

@@ _ :-
          write('can draw no conclusion.'), nl.

%
% member(?X,?Y)
%    Succeeds if X is a member of the list Y.
%

member(X,[X|_]).

member(X,[_|Y]) :- member(X,Y).

%
% dlisting(+Predicate)
%    Lists all ordinary Prolog clauses, defeasible rules, and
%    defeaters in memory which have heads of the form
%    Predicate(...Arguments...) or of the form
%    neg Predicate(...Arguments...).
%

dlisting(Predicate) :-
          listing(Predicate),
          fail.

dlisting(Predicate) :-
          clause(neg Head,Body),
          functor(Head,Predicate,_),
          pprint(neg Head,' :-',Body),
          fail.

dlisting(Predicate) :-
          (Head := Body),
          dfunctor(Head,Predicate,_),
          pprint(Head,' :=',Body),
          fail.

dlisting(Predicate) :-
          (Head :^ Body),
          dfunctor(Head,Predicate,_),
          pprint(Head,' :^',Body),
          fail.
```

```
dlisting(Predicate) :-
        clause(incompatible(Clause1,Clause2),Body),
        dfunctor(Clause1,Predicate,_),
        pprint(incompatible(Clause1,Clause2),' :-',Body),
        fail.

dlisting(Predicate) :-
        clause(incompatible(Clause1,Clause2),Body),
        dfunctor(Clause2,Predicate,_),
        pprint(incompatible(Clause1,Clause2),' :-',Body),
        fail.

dlisting(Predicate) :-
        clause(sup(Clause1,Clause2),Body),
        rule_functor(Clause1,Predicate,_),
        pprint(sup(Clause1,Clause2),' :-',Body),
        fail.

dlisting(Predicate) :-
        clause(sup(Clause1,Clause2),Body),
        rule_functor(Clause2,Predicate,_),
        pprint(sup(Clause1,Clause2),' :-',Body),
        fail.

dlisting(_).

%
% dlist
%   dlists all predicates in the d-Prolog dictionary.
%

dlist :-
        dPrologDictionary(Predicate,_),
        dlisting(Predicate),
        fail.

dlist.

%
% dfunctor(+Clause,-Predicate,-Arity)
%   Returns the d-Prolog Predicate of Clause
%   together with its Arity.
%

dfunctor(neg Clause,Predicate,Arity) :-
        functor(Clause,Predicate,Arity),
        !.

dfunctor(Clause,Predicate,Arity):-
        functor(Clause,Predicate,Arity).
```

```
%
% rule_functor(+Rule,-Predicate,-Arity)
%   Returns the d-Prolog Predicate of the head of
%   the Rule together with its Arity.
%

rule_functor((Head :- _),Predicate,Arity) :-
        dfunctor(Head,Predicate,Arity),
        !.

rule_functor((Head := _),Predicate,Arity) :-
        dfunctor(Head,Predicate,Arity),
        !.

rule_functor((Head :^ _),Predicate,Arity) :-
        dfunctor(Head,Predicate,Arity),
        !.


%
% pprint(+Head,+Operator,+Body)
%   A formatting routine for printing ordinary Prolog clauses,
%   defeasible rules, and defeaters.
%

pprint(Head,' :-',true) :-
        !,
        write(Head), write('.'), nl.

pprint(Head,Operator,Clause) :-
        write(Head), write(Operator), nl,
        pprint(Clause).

pprint((First,Rest)) :-
        !,
        write('     '), write(First), write(','), nl,
        pprint(Rest).

pprint(Clause) :-
        write('     '), write(Clause), write('.'), nl.


%
% rescind(+Predicate/+Arity)
%   Removes all ordinary Prolog clauses, defeasible rules,
%   or defeaters whose heads are of the form
%   Predicate(...Arguments...) or of the form
%   neg Predicates(...Argument...).
%

rescind(Predicate/Arity) :-
        abolish(Predicate/Arity),
        functor(Clause,Predicate,Arity),
```

```
        retractall(Clause),
        retractall(neg Clause),
        retractall((Clause := _)),
        retractall((neg Clause := _)),
        retractall((Clause :^ _)),
        retractall((neg Clause :^ _)),
        retractall(incompatible(Clause,_)),
        retractall(incompatible(_,Clause)),
        retractall(incompatible(neg Clause,_)),
        retractall(incompatible(_,neg Clause)),
        retractall(sup((Clause := _),_)),
        retractall(sup(_,(Clause := _))),
        retractall(sup((neg Clause := _),_)),
        retractall(sup(_,(neg Clause := _))),
        retractall(sup((Clause :^ _),_)),
        retractall(sup(_,(Clause :^ _))),
        retractall(sup((neg Clause :^ _),_)),
        retractall(sup(_,(neg Clause :^ _))),
        retractall(dPrologDictionary(Predicate,Arity)).

%
% rescindall
%    Removes from memory the entire d-Prolog knowledge base,
%    provided it was loaded into memory using reload.
%

rescindall :-
        dPrologDictionary(Predicate,Arity),
        rescind(Predicate/Arity),
        fail.

rescindall.

%
% dload(+Filename)
%    Consults a file containing a d-Prolog knowledge base.
%

dload(Filename) :-
        concat([Filename,'.dpl'],NewFilename),
        see(NewFilename),
        repeat,
        read(Term),
        execute_term(Term),
        remember_predicate(Term),
        add_to_memory(Term),
        Term == end_of_file,
        seen,
        !.

%
```

```
% reload(+Filename)
%    Reconsults a file containing a d-Prolog knowledge base.
%

reload(Filename) :-
        concat([Filename,'.dpl'],NewFilename),
        see(NewFilename),
        repeat,
        read(Term),
        execute_term(Term),
        rescind_previous_clauses(Term),
        add_to_memory(Term),
        Term == end_of_file,
        retractall(have_seen_predicate_before(_,_)),
        seen,
        !.


%
% execute_term(+Term)
%    During a dload or a reload, executes any queries
%    read from a d-Prolog knowledge base.
%

execute_term((:- Goal)) :-
        Goal,
        !,
        fail.

execute_term(_).

%
% add_to_memory(+Clause)
%    Adds clauses to memory during a reload.
%

add_to_memory((:- _)) :- !.

add_to_memory(end_of_file) :- !.

add_to_memory(Term) :-
        assertz(Term).


%
% remember_predicate(+Term)
%    Adds new predicates to the dPrologDictionary
%    during a dload.
%

remember_predicate((:- _)) :- !.

remember_predicate(end_of_term) :- !.
```

```
remember_predicate(Rule) :-
        rule_functor(Rule,Predicate,Arity),
        add_to_dictionary(Predicate,Arity),
        !.

remember_predicate(sup(Rule1,Rule2)) :-
        rule_functor(Rule1,Predicate1,Arity1),
        add_to_dictionary(Predicate1,Arity1),
        rule_functor(Rule2,Predicate2,Arity2),
        add_to_dictionary(Predicate2,Arity2),
        !.

remember_predicate(incompatible(Goal1,Goal2)) :-
        dfunctor(Goal1,Predicate1,Arity1),
        add_to_dictionary(Predicate1,Arity1),
        dfunctor(Goal2,Predicate2,Arity2),
        add_to_dictionary(Predicate2,Arity2),
        !.

remember_predicate(Goal) :-
        dfunctor(Goal,Predicate,Arity),
        add_to_dictionary(Predicate,Arity).

%
% add_to_dictionary(+Predicate,+Arity)
%    Adds a clause to dPrologDictionary/2 for
%    Predicate and Arity if one is not already
%    present.
%

add_to_dictionary(Predicate,Arity) :-
        \+ dPrologDictionary(Predicate,Arity),
        functor(DummyGoal,Predicate,Arity),
        assert(DummyGoal),
        retract(DummyGoal),
        assert(dPrologDictionary(Predicate,Arity)).

add_to_dictionary(_,_).

%
% rescind_previous_clauses(+Term)
%    Removes from memory all ordinary Prolog clauses,
%    defeasible rules, or defeaters that were not loaded
%    during the current invocation of reload and that,
%    from the perspective of the d-Prolog inference engine,
%    are clauses for the same predicate as Term.
%

rescind_previous_clauses((:- _)) :- !. % Query to execute.
```

```
rescind_previous_clauses(end_of_file) :- !.

rescind_previous_clauses((Head :- _)) :-
        rescind_previous_clauses(Head),
        !.

rescind_previous_clauses((Head := _)) :-
        rescind_previous_clauses(Head),
        !.

rescind_previous_clauses((Head :^ _)) :-
        rescind_previous_clauses(Head),
        !.

rescind_previous_clauses(incompatible(X,Y)) :-
        rescind_previous_clauses(X),
        rescind_previous_clauses(Y),
        !.

rescind_previous_clauses(sup(Rule1,Rule2)) :-
        rescind_previous_clauses(Rule1),
        rescind_previous_clauses(Rule2),
        !.

rescind_previous_clauses(Clause) :-
        dfunctor(Clause,Predicate,Arity),
        \+ have_seen_predicate_before(Predicate,Arity),
        asserta(have_seen_predicate_before(Predicate,Arity)),
        rescind(Predicate/Arity),
        remember_predicate(Clause),
        !.

rescind_previous_clauses(_).

%
% dictionary
%   Prints a list of all predicates and their arities that
%   occur in a d-Prolog knowledge base loaded into memory
%   using dload or reload.
%

dictionary :-
        dPrologDictionary(Predicate,Arity),
        write(Predicate),
        write('/'),
        write(Arity),
        nl,
        fail.

dictionary.
```

```
%
% contradictions
%    Finds all contradictory goals for the d-Prolog knowledge
%    base that succeed, displays them, and stores them as
%    clauses for the predicate contradictory_pair/2.
%

contradictions :-
        abolish(contradictory_pair/2),
        fail.

contradictions :-
        dPrologDictionary(Predicate,Arity),
        functor(Clause1,Predicate,Arity),
        clause(Clause1,_),
        contrary(Clause1,Clause2),
        contradictions_aux(Clause1,Clause2),
        assert(contradictory_pair(Clause1,Clause2)),
        write(Clause1), write(' - '), write(Clause2), nl,
        fail.

contradictions.

contradictions_aux(X,Y) :-
        \+ contradictory_pair(X,Y),
        \+ contradictory_pair(Y,X),
        X,
        Y,
        !.

%
% whynot(+Goal)
%    Explains why Goal is not defeasibly derivable.
%

whynot(Goal) :-
        Goal, nl,
        write('Why not indeed!'), nl,
        write(Goal),
        write(' is strictly derivable!'), nl.

whynot(Goal) :-
        (@ Goal), nl,
        write('Why not indeed!'), nl,
        write(Goal),
        write(' is defeasibly derivable!'), nl.

whynot(Goal) :-
        \+ initial_evidence(Goal), nl,
        write('There are no rules in the database for '), nl,
        write(Goal), nl,
```

```
        write('whose antecedent is defeasibly derivable.'), nl,
        fail.

whynot(Goal) :-
        setof(pair(Rule,Defeater),
              obstruct(Goal,Rule,Defeater),
              List),
        say_why_not(List).

obstruct(Goal,(Goal :- Body),Opposite) :-
        clause(Goal,Body),
        (@ Body),
        contrary(Goal,Opposite),
        Opposite.

obstruct(Goal,(Goal :- Body),Opposite) :-
        clause(Goal,Body),
        (@ Body),
        contrary(Goal,Opposite),
        \+ Opposite,
        clause(Opposite,Tail),
        (@ Tail).

obstruct(Goal,(Goal := Body),Opposite) :-
        def_rule(root,(Goal := Body)),
        (@ Body),
        contrary(Goal,Opposite),
        Opposite.

obstruct(Goal,(Goal := Body),(Opposite :- Tail)) :-
        def_rule(root,(Goal := Body)),
        (@ Body),
        contrary(Goal,Opposite),
        clause(Opposite,Tail),
        \+ Opposite,
        (@ Tail).

obstruct(Goal,(Goal := Body),(Opposite := Tail)) :-
        def_rule(root,(Goal := Body)),
        (@ Body),
        contrary(Goal,Opposite),
        def_rule(root,(Opposite := Tail)),
        (@ Tail),
        \+ sup_rule((Goal := Body),(Opposite := Tail)).

obstruct(Goal,(Goal := Body),(Opposite :^ Tail)) :-
        def_rule(root,(Goal := Body)),
        (@ Body),
        contrary(Goal,Opposite),
        defeater((Opposite :^ Tail)),
        (@ Tail),
```

```
                \+ sup_rule((Goal := Body),(Opposite :^ Tail)).

%
% say_why_not(+List)
%    displays a list of rules and defeaters for a failed
%    goal.
%

say_why_not([]).

say_why_not([pair((Goal :- Body),(Opposite :- Tail))|Rest]) :-
        !,
        write('The antecedent of the strict rule'), nl, nl,
        pprint(Goal,' :- ',Body), nl,
        write('is defeasibly derivable;'), nl,
        write('but the condition of the strict rule'), nl, nl,
        pprint(Opposite,' :- ',Tail), nl,
        write('is also defeasibly derivable.'), nl, nl,
        pause,
        say_why_not(Rest).

say_why_not([pair((Goal :- Body),Opposite)|Rest]) :-
        !,
        write('The antecedent of the strict rule'), nl, nl,
        pprint(Goal,' :- ',Body), nl,
        write('is defeasibly derivable;'), nl,
        write('but the condition of the strict rule'), nl, nl,
        pprint(Opposite), nl,
        write('is also strictly derivable.'), nl, nl,
        pause,
        say_why_not(Rest).

say_why_not([pair((Goal := Body),(Opposite :- Tail))|Rest]) :-
        !,
        write('The antecedent of the defeasible rule'), nl, nl,
        pprint(Goal,' := ',Body), nl,
        write('is defeasibly derivable;'), nl,
        write('but the condition of the strict rule'), nl, nl,
        pprint(Opposite,' :- ',Tail), nl,
        write('is also defeasibly derivable.'), nl, nl,
        pause,
        say_why_not(Rest).

say_why_not([pair((Goal := Body),(Opposite := Tail))|Rest]) :-
        !,
        write('The antecedent of the defeasible rule'), nl, nl,
        pprint(Goal,' := ',Body), nl,
        write('is defeasibly derivable;'), nl,
        write('but the condition of the defeasible rule'), nl, nl,
        pprint(Opposite,' := ',Tail), nl,
        write('is also defeasibly derivable.'), nl, nl,
```

```
              pause,
              say_why_not(Rest).

say_why_not([pair((Goal := Body),(Opposite :^ Tail))|Rest]) :-
          !,
          write('The antecedent of the defeasible rule'), nl, nl,
          pprint(Goal,' := ',Body), nl,
          write('is defeasibly derivable;'), nl,
          write('but the condition of the defeater'), nl, nl,
          pprint(Opposite,' :^ ',Tail), nl,
          write('is also defeasibly derivable.'), nl, nl,
          pause,
          say_why_not(Rest).

say_why_not([pair((Goal := Body),Opposite)|Rest]) :-
          !,
          write('The antecedent of the defeasible rule'), nl, nl,
          pprint(Goal,' := ',Body), nl,
          write('is defeasibly derivable;'), nl,
          write('but'), nl, nl,
          pprint(Opposite), nl,
          write('is strictly derivable.'), nl, nl,
          pause,
          say_why_not(Rest).

pause :-
          nl,nl,
          write('Press any key to continue. '),
          get0(_),
          nl,nl.


%
% initial_evidence(+Goal)
%    Succeeds if there is a rule supporting Goal that
%    is satisfied, i.e., whose body is at least
%    defeasibly derivable.
%

initial_evidence(Goal) :-
          clause(Goal,Body),
          (@ Body).

initial_evidence(Goal) :-
          def_rule(root,(Goal := Body)),
          (@ Body).


%
% concat(+List,-String)
%    Concatenates a List of strings into a single
%    String.
%
```

```
concat(List,String) :-
      concat_aux(List,[],String).

concat_aux([],Chars,String) :-
      name(String,Chars).

concat_aux([First|Rest],Chars,String) :-
      name(First,List),
      append(Chars,List,NewChars),
      !,
      concat_aux(Rest,NewChars,String).
```

11.11. DEFEASIBLE QUERIES AND EXHAUSTIVE RESPONSES

The query ?- @ Goal, where Goal contains no variables, evokes a response of yes or no from d-Prolog. If the answer is yes, we do not know whether defeasible rules were used in the derivation of Goal; if the answer is no, we do not know if d-Prolog is able to show that Goal is positively false (i.e., that ?- @ neg Goal succeeds) or merely that d-Prolog is unable to defeasibly derive Goal. To get all this information, we need to try some combination of the following four queries:

1. ?- Goal.

2. ?- neg Goal.

3. ?- @ Goal.

4. ?- @ neg Goal.

A utility predicate is provided to make this process simpler.

The first line in DPUTILS.PL is a query that declares a new operator, @@/1. This operator is used to ask d-Prolog to provide an exhaustive response to a defeasible query without variables. It would be very difficult to give an exhaustive response to a query containing variables since different responses would be appropriate for different instantiations of the variables. So the first clause in the definition of @@ checks to see if an uninstantiated variable occurs in the goal. If it does, the user is informed of the problem and the query succeeds. We should remember here that disjunctions, cuts, and negations-as-failure also may not appear in the argument for @@ just as they may not appear in the argument for @. If this restriction is violated, then the user will not be warned but the behavior of the inference engine is unpredictable.

Having determined that the goal contains no uninstantiated variables, the next clause tests to see if both the goal and some contrary of the goal are strictly derivable. If so, then there is a contradiction in the knowledge base and the user is so informed. If the system does not find a contradiction, it tests again to see if the goal is strictly derivable. If so, the response to the user is

```
definitely, yes.
```

If not, the system tests to see if any contrary of the goal is strictly derivable. If so, the response to the user is

```
definitely, no.
```

If neither the goal nor any contrary is strictly derivable, the system checks to see if the goal or any contrary is defeasibly derivable. If so, the response is, respectively,

```
presumably, yes.
```

or

```
presumably, no.
```

We do not have to worry about getting both answers here since the only way that a goal and a contrary of that goal can be both defeasibly derivable is if both are strictly derivable. That case is handled by an earlier clause.

Finally, the system may be unable to strictly or defeasibly derive either the goal or any contrary of the goal. Then the response to the user is

```
can draw no conclusion.
```

11.12. LISTING DEFEASIBLE PREDICATES

In response to the query

```
?- dlisting(pred).
```

d-Prolog lists all clauses which d-Prolog recognizes as belonging to the predicate `pred`. So `dlisting/1` is the d-Prolog equivalent of the built-in Prolog predicate `listing`. We need a special utility to list the d-Prolog clauses for a predicate because Prolog will recognize the clauses

```
neg p.
p := q.
neg p :^ r.
sup((p := q),(neg p :^ r)).
incompatible(p,(neg s)).
```

as belonging to the predicates `neg/1`, `:=/2`, `:^/2`, `sup/2`, and `incompatible/2`, respectively. Prolog will list none of these clauses in response to the query

```
?- listing(p).
```

However, the query

```
?- dlisting(p).
```

will list these clauses and any others in memory that belong to the predicate p from the perspective of d-Prolog.

The definition of dlisting includes many clauses to cover all the possible cases, but there is nothing very difficult to understand about any of these clauses and we will not discuss them in detail. The predicate dlisting also uses the auxiliary predicate pprint/1 to format rules.

Another utility predicate, dlist/0, will perform a listing for all predicates in the d-Prolog dictionary. This dictionary is created by the two utilities dload/1 and reload/1 described in the next section.

11.13. CONSULTING AND RECONSULTING D-PROLOG FILES

As we saw in the previous section, Prolog does not recognize the same clauses for a predicate that the d-Prolog inference engine recognizes. We also have to take this difference between Prolog and d-Prolog into account when we reconsult a d-Prolog file. Normally all the clauses for a given predicate are contiguous in a file; that is, clauses for one predicate are not interrupted by clauses for any other predicate. Many Prologs expect this during a reconsult and discard all clauses currently in memory for a predicate whenever a new block of clauses for that predicate is encountered. For example, if a file containing only the three clauses odd(1), even(2), and odd(3) were reconsulted by a Prolog that behaves in this way, clause odd(1) would not be in memory after the reconsult. Because the clauses for the predicate odd are interrupted by a clause for even, Prolog treats the clause odd(3) as though it were a clause for a new predicate and deletes all clauses for odd currently in memory. So Prolog adds odd(1) to memory, then deletes it before adding odd(3) to memory during the reconsult.

The problem, of course, is that Prolog sees all defeasible rules as clauses for the predicates :=, all undercutting defeaters as clauses for the predicate :^, and so on. If we reconsult a file containing the clauses

```
red(X)    := apple(X).
yellow(X) := banana(X).
grape(this_fruit).
purple(X) := grape(X).
```

only the last defeasible rule in the file will be in memory after the reconsult. (Not all Prolog implementations behave this way, of course, but some do.)

We solve this problem by developing our own reconsult utility reload/1 defined in DPUTILS.PL. The proper query to reconsult a d-Prolog file is

```
?- reload(filename).
```

Here filename should not include an extension; reload expects the file to have the extension .DPL for d-Prolog. The utility reads terms from the specified file one by one. First it tries to execute them. This allows the user to include queries in a file which are executed whenever the file is consulted or reconsulted. Next, if the term is a clause and not a query, reload determines the d-Prolog predicate for the term. If it has not seen a term for the predicate before, it stores the predicate and its arity in a clause for the predicate `have_seen_predicate_before/2`, and it uses the utility predicate `rescind/1` (see next section) to remove all d-Prolog clauses for the predicate from memory. It also stores the predicate and its arity in a clause for the predicate `dPrologDictionary`. Finally, the utility adds the clause to memory. It processes each term in the file in this manner until it encounters an `end_of_file` marker. Then it removes all clauses for `have_seen_predicate_before` from memory but leaves the d-Prolog dictionary in memory for later use by other utilities explained below.

Consulting a file is a much simpler operation since nothing has to be removed from memory during a consult. But we nevertheless provide a d-Prolog utility `dload/1` to consult d-Prolog files. The proper query to consult a d-Prolog file is

```
?- dload(filename).
```

Once again, no extension should be included in `filename`; `dload` expects the file to have the extension `.DPL`. The only difference between using `dload` and `consult` for d-Prolog files is that `dload` builds the d-Prolog dictionary used by other d-Prolog utilities.

The two utilities `dload` and `reload` take longer to consult or to reconsult a file than do the built-in utilities `consult` and `reconsult`. This is to be expected since they are doing more work.

11.14. THE D-PROLOG DICTIONARY

In the last section, we described how the d-Prolog utility predicates `dload` and `reload` build a d-Prolog dictionary as they consult or reconsult d-Prolog files. The dictionary consists of the clauses for the predicate `dPrologDictionary/2`. Each clause has the form

```
dPrologDictionary(Pred,Arity).
```

where `Pred` is the name of some d-Prolog predicate loaded into memory using `dload` or `reload`, and `Arity` is the arity of that predicate.

The first utility to use the d-Prolog dictionary is the predicate `dictionary/0`. d-Prolog lists all predicates and their arities stored in the d-Prolog dictionary in response to the query ?- `dictionary`.

11.15. RESCINDING PREDICATES AND KNOWLEDGE BASES

On occasion a user may want to remove all clauses for a particular predicate from memory. For many Prolog implementations there is a built-in predicate `abolish/1` that will remove all clauses from memory for a Prolog predicate. The appropriate query for a predicate `Pred` with arity `Arity` is

```
?- abolish(Pred/Arity).
```

Of course, we will run into the same complication here that we do with the built-in predicate `listing`: many clauses that belong to the predicate `Pred` from the perspective of d-Prolog will belong to the predicates `neg`, `:=`, `:^`, `sup`, and `incompatible` from the perspective of Prolog.

A predicate `rescind/1` is defined in the file DPUTILS.PL which fills this gap. The query

```
?- rescind(Pred/Arity).
```

will remove from memory all d-Prolog clauses that belong to the predicate `Pred` with arity `Arity`.

A user may also want to eliminate all d-Prolog predicates from memory without removing the d-Prolog inference engine itself. The predicate `rescindall/0`, defined in DPUTILS.PL, removes all `dPrologDictionary` clauses and all clauses for predicates recorded in the d-Prolog dictionary. So all d-Prolog clauses loaded into memory using the d-Prolog utility predicates `dload` and `reload` can be removed from memory with a single, simple command.

11.16. FINDING CONTRADICTIONS

An important difference between a Prolog and a d-Prolog program is that a Prolog program can never contain a contradiction while contradictions are possible in d-Prolog programs. The only kind of negation available in Prolog is negation-as-failure, represented by the built-in predicate `\+`. The only way a query

```
?- \+ Goal.
```

can succeed is if the query

```
?- Goal.
```

fails. This is, after all, exactly what negation-as-failure means. The clause `\+ Goal` says that `Goal` cannot be proved, not that it is false.

In d-Prolog we have implemented a positive negation operator `neg`. The only way the query

```
?- neg Goal.
```

can succeed is if there is a fact or rule in memory whose head unifies with `neg Goal`. But nothing is simpler than to construct a contradictory program in d-Prolog. A simple example is:

```
p.
neg p.
```

A more interesting example is:

```
p.
q.
incompatible(p,q).
```

The first example is contradictory since it says that the same atom is both true and false. The second is contradictory since it says both that two atoms are true and that they cannot both be true.

A d-Prolog program containing a contradiction must contain some false statements. In general, a d-Prolog developer will not intend to incorporate contradictions into his or her program. They are more likely to occur as a result of the interactions of several rules. While d-Prolog is expressively more powerful because contradictions can be expressed in it, contradictions are in principle a bad thing. So when we have them, we want to be able to find them. Once we find them, we can begin the task of figuring out which of our facts or rules is incorrect. This can be a difficult task, but it is a problem in knowledge acquisition rather than a problem in logic programming. Our job is only to provide a tool to find the contradictions.

The d-Prolog utility `contradictions/0`, defined in DPUTILS.PL, does this for us. In response to the query

```
?- contradictions.
```

d-Prolog constructs dummy queries from the predicates found in the d-Prolog dictionary. Then it tries to derive strictly both the query and any contrary of the query. If it succeeds, it informs the user. The d-Prolog dictionary is essential to this process since otherwise there would be no way to generate the test queries.

As it finds contradictions, d-Prolog displays them to the user and stores them in clauses for the predicate `contradictory_pair/2`. These clauses are not removed from memory after the contradictions have been identified; they are left in memory for the convenience of the user. It can take a long time to check a large program for contradictions, and it is faster to check the clauses for `contradictory_pairs` than to run the utility again. However, whenever the utility is invoked, it removes all clauses for `contradictory_pairs` from memory before testing for contradictions. Thus any contradictions corrected by the user will not show up again.

Notice that besides the contradictory pairs, a great deal more may be displayed when the `contradictions` utility is invoked. d-Prolog will call every query it can construct from the predicates in the d-Prolog dictionary. Any queries that use `write` will produce text on the screen when `contradictions` is used. More importantly, any other input or output operations included in your code will be performed, including writes to files using `tell/1` or changes in the contents of memory using `assert/1` or `retract/1`. So great care should be used with the `contradictions` utility. Still, with care, it can be a valuable tool for testing d-Prolog knowledge bases for consistency.

11.17. A SPECIAL EXPLANATORY FACILITY

A simple Prolog query either contains \+ or it doesn't. In either case, there is only one possible explanation for why a query failed. If it does not contain \+, then it failed because it did not unify with any fact or with the head of any rule whose body succeeded. If it contains \+, then it failed because the clause following the \+ succeeded. Although simple in principle, it is often difficult to work through a complex Prolog program carefully to see how the clauses interact and why a query fails.

With d-Prolog, however, defeasible queries can fail in new and interesting ways. They can fail because no rule supporting them is satisfied, but they can also fail even though some rule supporting them is satisfied because that rule is rebutted or undercut. This is why the rules are called defeasible.

The last of the utilities defined in DPUTILS.PL is the predicate whynot/1. Given a query of the form

```
?- whynot(Goal).
```

the utility will respond in one of the following ways.

1. If the query ?- @ Goal succeeds, whynot reports this and stops.

2. If there is no fact that will unify with Goal and no rule supporting Goal that is satisfiable, whynot reports this and stops. The auxiliary predicate initial_evidence/1 is used here.

3. If there is a strict or defeasible rule supporting Goal that is satisfiable, whynot displays this rule, finds the competing rule or fact that defeats it, and displays it as well.

It takes several clauses to cover all the cases, but the clauses are not difficult to understand once one understands the d-Prolog inference engine.

11.18. A SUITE OF EXAMPLES

The file KBASES.DPL contains a representative selection of d-Prolog examples that illustrate many of the features discussed in this chapter. You must load DPROLOG.PL before loading this file. Otherwise, Prolog will not understand the operators :=, :^, neg, and @, and you will see various error messages. We suggest that you always use dload or reload to load KBASES.DPL or any other d-Prolog files.

The first predicate defined in KBASES.DPL is examples/0, which simply prints a list of the examples that have been loaded. This predicate is invoked in a query at the end of the file so the user will immediately see the list of examples as soon as the file is loaded.

The Tweety Triangle, the Chinese Restaurant, the Pennsylvania Dutch, and the Twin Tweety Triangle examples discussed earlier in this chapter are included in KBASES.DPL. Also included are an example of inheritance with exceptions (Naked Nautilus), an example of multiple inheritance (modified Nixon Diamond), an example of defeasible temporal reasoning (Yale Shooting Problem), and a complex example involving several features of defeasible reasoning (Election). We will look at some of these examples in detail.

11.18.1. Listing of KBASES.DPL

```
% KBASES.DPL - a sampler of d-Prolog knowledge bases

examples:-
```

```
nl,
write('Tweety Triangle is loaded.'), nl,
        write('Chinese Restaurant example is loaded.'), nl,
write('Pennsylvania Dutch example is loaded.'), nl,
        write('Twin Tweety Triangle is loaded.'), nl,
write('Naked nautilus example is loaded.'), nl,
write('Modified Nixon Diamond is loaded.'), nl,
write('Yale Shooting Problem is loaded.'), nl,
write('Election example is loaded.'), nl, nl.


%
% Tweety Triangle, plus some refinements involving
% undercutting defeaters.
%

flies(X):=  bird(X).
neg flies(X):= penguin(X).
neg flies(X):^ sick(X),bird(X).

flies(X) :^ ga_penguin(X).
flies(superman) := true.

bird(tweety).
bird(X):- penguin(X).

penguin(opus).
penguin(X) :- ga_penguin(X).

ga_penguin(folio).

%
% Chinese Restaurant Example - illustrating use of
% the predicate incompatible/2.
%

incompatible(marxist(X),capitalist(X)).

capitalist(X) := owns(X,restaurant).

marxist(X) := born(X,prc).

owns(ping,restaurant).

born(ping,prc).

%
% Pennsylvania Dutch Example - showing superiority
% of strict rules over defeasible rules.
%

native_speaker(X,german_dialect) :- native_speaker(X,pa_dutch).
```

```
native_speaker(hans,pa_dutch).

born(X,pennsylvania) := native_speaker(X,pa_dutch).
born(X,usa) :- born(X,pennsylvania).
neg born(X,usa) := native_speaker(X,german_dialect).


%
% Twin Tweety Triangles - an example of preemption
% of defeaters.
%

republican(X) := conservative(X).
neg republican(X) := southerner(X).
conservative(X) := southerner(X).

republican(X) := rich(X).
neg republican(X) := movie_star(X).
rich(X) := movie_star(X).

southerner(kim).
movie_star(kim).

%
% The Naked Nautilus - an example of inheritance with
% exception.
%

has_shell(X) := mollusc(X).
neg has_shell(X) := cephalopod(X).
has_shell(X) := nautilus(X).
neg has_shell(X) := naked_nautilus(X).

mollusc(X) :- cephalopod(X).
mollusc(fred).

cephalopod(X) :- nautilus(X).

nautilus(X) :- naked_nautilus(X).

%
% Nixon Diamond - an example of multiple inheritance
% with resolution of the conflict forced by specifying
% superiority of the rule for Republicans.
%

pacifist(X) := quaker(X).
neg pacifist(X) := republican(X).

quaker(nixon).

republican(nixon).
```

```
sup((neg pacifist(X) := republican(X)),
         (pacifist(X) := quaker(X))).


%
% The Yale Shooting Problem - an example involving
% temporal persistence.
%

holds(alive,s).
holds(loaded,s).

holds(F,result(E,S)) := holds(F,S).

incompatible(holds(alive,S),holds(dead,S)).

holds(dead,result(shoot,S)) :=
        holds(loaded,S),
        holds(alive,S).


%
% The Election Example - an extended example of
% some complexity.
%

neg runs(dove) := true.

backs(hawk,crow).
neg backs(X,Y) :- backs(X,Z),
                        Y \== Z.

nominate(animals,wolf) := true.
neg nominate(animals,wolf):=
        neg backs(bull,wolf).
nominate(animals,fox):=
        neg nominate(animals,wolf).
neg nominate(animals,fox) :=
        involved_in_scandal(fox),
        neg nominate(animals,wolf).
nominate(animals,hart):=
        neg nominate(animals,wolf),
        neg nominate(animals,fox).

nominate(birds,dove):= true.
neg nominate(birds,dove) :-
        neg runs(dove).
nominate(birds,crow):=
        neg nominate(animals,wolf),
        neg runs(dove).
neg nominate(birds,crow):=
        nominate(animals,wolf),
```

```
        neg runs(dove).
nominate(birds,crane):=
        neg nominate(birds,dove),
        neg nominate(birds,crow).

elected(Animal):=
        nominate(animals,Animal),
        nominate(birds,Bird),
        backs(hawk,Bird).
elected(dove):=
        nominate(birds,dove),
        nominate(animals,Animal),
        neg backs(bull,Animal).

p.
neg p.

:- examples.
```

11.19. SOME FEATHERED AND NONFEATHERED FRIENDS

This example contains a number of claims about what normally flies and what normally does not fly. In English, these claims are:

- Normally, birds fly.

- Normally, penguins don't fly.

- A sick bird might not fly.

- A genetically altered penguin might fly.

- Presumably, Superman flies.

We also have the following information about what are penguins and what are birds:

- Tweety is a bird.

- All penguins are birds.

- Opus is a penguin.

- All genetically altered penguins are penguins.

- Folio is a genetically altered penguin.

With this example in memory, we conduct the following dialog with d-Prolog:

```
?- @ flies(X).

X = tweety ->;
```

```
X = superman ->;

no
?- @ neg flies(X).

X = opus ->;

no
?- assert(sick(tweety)).

yes
?- assert(sick(superman)).

yes
?- @ flies(X).

X = superman ->;

no
?- @@ flies(opus).
presumably, no.

yes
?- @@ flies(folio).
can draw no conclusion.

yes
?-
```

Notice that when we tell d-Prolog that Tweety and Superman are sick, it no longer concludes that Tweety can fly, although it continues to conclude that Superman can fly. This is because the undercutting defeater only applies to sick birds. Since the system cannot infer that Superman is a bird, it does not use the defeater in Superman's case. Notice also that the system can draw no conclusion about Folio. The rule for genetically altered penguins undercuts the rule for penguins, but the undercut rule can still rebut the rule for birds.

11.20. INHERITANCE REASONING

A kind of reasoning often found in expert systems is INHERITANCE reasoning. Our genetically altered penguin is an example of inheritance reasoning. Since genetically altered penguins are penguins and penguins are birds, genetically altered penguins INHERIT characteristics from both penguins and birds. Two common problems with inheritance reasoning are exceptions and multiple inheritance. Additional examples of inheritance reasoning illustrating these two problems and how they might be resolved in d-Prolog are included in KBASES.DPL.

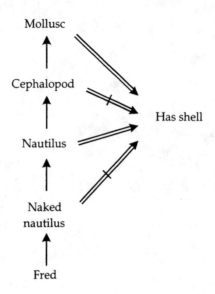

Figure 11.7   The Naked Nautilus

Molluscs are a large group of sea creatures including oysters and clams. Squid and octopuses make up a subcategory of molluscs called cephalopods. A nautilus is a kind of cephalopod. It looks like a squid with a shell. The shell might be long and spiraling or coiled like a typical snail shell. For the example, we invent a special kind of nautilus that has lost its shell. We call this creature a *naked nautilus*. An interesting feature of this sequence of groups and subgroups is that molluscs and nautili normally have shells while cephalopods and naked nautili normally do not. The situation is represented graphically in Figure 11.7 and in d-Prolog by the clauses in the Naked Nautilus example in KBASES.DPL.

We start with the information that Fred is a mollusc. We subsequently learn that he is a cephalopod, then that he is a nautilus, and finally that he is a naked nautilus. The following dialog with d-Prolog shows how these disclosures should affect our beliefs about whether Fred has a shell.

```
?- @@ has_shell(fred).
presumably, yes.

yes
?- assert(cephalopod(fred)).

yes
?- @@ has_shell(fred).
presumably, no.
```

```
yes.
?- assert(nautilus(fred)).

yes
?- @@ has_shell(fred).
presumably, yes.

yes
?- assert(naked_nautilus(fred)).

yes
?- @@ has_shell(fred).
presumably, no.

yes
```

The Naked Nautilus is an example where we have a linear hierarchy of groups with each group directly inheriting from its immediate supergroup. We can think of properties flowing from each group to its subgroups. Multiple inheritance, on the other hand, involves cases where the inheritance relations between the groups and individuals form a nonlinear structure. An example is the Nixon Diamond illustrated graphically in Figure 11.8. Here the individual Nixon inherits from two groups, Republicans and Quakers, and neither group is more specific than the other. Furthermore, members of one group normally have a characteristic that members of the other group normally do not. So Nixon inherits from multiple groups with incompatible characteristics. In general, we can draw no conclusions in a Nixon Diamond since the two inheritance rules rebut each other. But in d-Prolog we can force resolution of the conflict by specifying with a clause for the predicate **sup** which of the two rules should dominate. Notice that resolving the conflict in this way does not involve a claim that Republicans are normally Quakers or that Quakers are normally Republicans. Neither rule becomes more specific than the other. Instead, stipulating superiority of the Republican rule simply declares that for purposes of determining whether a person is a pacifist, being a Republican counts for more than being a Quaker. For another case where Republicans and Quakers tend to differ in their characteristics, we might specify that being a Quaker is more important or we might leave the issue unresolved.

11.21. TEMPORAL PERSISTENCE

Things tend to remain the same and yet eventually everything changes. We expect to find our car where we parked it, to find our home where we left it, to find our friend's hair the same color as the last time we saw it. Yet we also believe that if we abandoned our car it would eventually be moved, that our house will someday be demolished, and that our friend's hair will turn gray or even disappear over the course of the years. The tendency things have to stay the same we will call TEMPORAL PERSISTENCE. This is a kind of inertia that sooner or later will be overcome by the

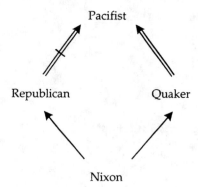

Figure 11.8   The Nixon Diamond

forces of change.

Temporal persistence is a very important feature of the world, one that we rely upon routinely. Suppose you want a green chair in your bedroom and you have a green chair in your living room. You might try to achieve your goal by moving the chair from the living room to the bedroom. But how can you infer that this action will accomplish your goal? How do you know that after you move the chair it will still be green? Why do you even believe that it will still be a chair? More to the point from the perspective of artificial intelligence, how can a machine infer this? It may have a rule that says that after something is moved from location A to location B, it is in location B in the resulting situation. But it seems the system must also have a rule that says that green things remain green and chairs remain chairs when they are moved. And other rules that say chairs remain chairs and things maintain their locations when they are painted. And so on. It would appear that we will need more rules telling us what does *not* change as the result of some event than we do to tell us what changes.

This problem, which is a problem of knowledge representation, was dubbed the FRAME PROBLEM by McCarthy and Hayes (1969). Specifically, the problem is to represent the information a system needs to make all the necessary inferences about what remains unchanged when some event occurs. The kinds of rules we have mentioned which state that some feature of a situation remains unchanged after some event are called FRAME AXIOMS. The point that McCarthy and Hayes make is that it looks like we will need lots and lots of frame axioms, probably more than all our other rules combined.

A proposal to solve the Frame Problem is to formulate one very general temporal persistence principle that says, essentially, that everything tends to stay the same. Then, unless we can show that something would change as a consequence of some event having occurred, we are justified in inferring that it has not changed. We can formulate such a principle using McDermott's (1982) Situation Calculus together with d-Prolog.

In the Situation Calculus situations are indicated by constants or as the situations that result from the occurrence of certain events in other situations. For example, we could indicate an initial situation by the constant s. If some event e1 occurs at s, we would represent the resulting situation by `result(e1,s)`. If in this situation another event e2 were to occur, the resulting situation would be represented by `result(e2,result(e1,s))`.

Besides representing situations and the events that produce them, we also want to represent what holds in different situations. In the initial situation s of the last paragraph, for example, it may be the case that a particular chair is green and that it is in the living room. We could represent this information by the following clauses:

```
holds(chair(c),s).
holds(green(c),s).
holds(in(c,living_room),s).
```

Now suppose the event e1 is the event of the chair being moved from the living room to the bedroom. Then we believe that in the resulting situation, the chair is still a chair and is still green, but it is no longer in the living room.

```
holds(chair(c),result(e1,s)).
holds(green(c),result(e1,s)).
holds(neg in(c,living_room),result(e1,s)).
```

We now have enough machinery to formulate our temporal persistence principle. It will be a defeasible rule containing variables indicating that it applies to all situations, events, and fluents (possible states that may or may not hold in a situation):

```
holds(F,result(E,S)) := holds(F,S).
```

Basically, this rule says that if some fact F holds in situation S, then presumably it also holds after event E occurs. This single principle should be the only frame axiom we need since it applies to all fluents, all events, and all situations.

This solution to the Frame Problem, or something very much like it, was proposed by McDermott (1987). But he later decided it didn't work because of some very simple examples that did not easily submit to this treatment using the nonmonotonic formalisms with which McDermott was familiar. One famous example constructed by Hanks and McDermott (1987) has come to be called the Yale Shooting Problem. We include a version of the YSP in KBASES.DPL which is simplified but which nevertheless captures the problematic features of the original.

Our version of the YSP concerns Frankie and Johnnie, lovers of ballad fame. Frankie shot Johnnie for his infidelity. We come in late in the story. Frankie enters Johnnie's empty room with a loaded gun. She waits until he returns, then points the gun at his head and pulls the trigger. Intuitively, we do not expect Johnnie to survive this story. How do we represent the story in d-Prolog so the system can infer the expected outcome? Like this:

```
holds(alive,s).
holds(loaded,s).
```

```
holds(F,result(E,S)) := holds(F,S).

incompatible(holds(alive,S),holds(dead,S)).

holds(dead,result(shoot,S)) :=
        holds(loaded,S),
        holds(alive,S).
```

The first two clauses say that in the initial situation, s, Johnnie is alive and Frankie's gun is loaded. The next is our temporal persistence principle. The fourth says that Johnnie can't be both alive and dead in the same situation. The final clause is a causal rule that says that normally Johnnie's status would be changed from alive to dead if a loaded gun were fired at his head. In the brief act of the story that we witness only two events occur: Frankie waits until Johnnie arrives and then she fires the gun at him. The crucial query, then, is

```
?- @@ holds(alive,result(shoot,result(wait,s))).
```

d-Prolog gives the correct answer: presumably, Johnnie is not alive at the end of the story.

Notice that it is important in the last clause of the example that holds(alive,S) is a condition. Otherwise, this defeasible rule would not be more specific than the temporal persistence principle in the appropriate instance and the two rules would rebut each other. It is reasonable to include this condition since we are trying to represent a causal rule. Causal rules tell us how events tend to change things. So the condition of the rule naturally includes the feature of the situation which will be changed. This is all that is needed for the solution to work.

Why did McDermott's nonmonotonic logic and the other nonmonotonic formalisms with which he was familiar fail to resolve the example so simply? Because these systems allow MULTIPLE EXTENSIONS of a knowledge base. Basically, an extension is any completion of the knowledge base that violates a minimum number of the defeasible rules in the knowledge base. In the YSP, there are at least three ways we can complete the story that only violate one defeasible rule.

1. Violate the persistence principle going from the first situation to the second so the gun is no longer loaded when Johnnie arrives.

2. Violate the causal principle going from the second situation to the last so Johnnie is still alive at the end of the story.

3. Violate the persistence principle going from the second situation to the last so Johnnie is dead at the end of the story.

Thus, the story has multiple extensions. In the first two extensions, Johnnie survives. Why do we prefer the third extension, the only one that d-Prolog supports? Because we have a *reason* to reject the persistence principle in this case: It conflicts with the more specific causal principle.

11.22. THE ELECTION EXAMPLE

The object of the Election Example is to deduce who will represent two political parties in a campaign and who will in fact be elected. Wolf, Fox, and Hart seek the nomination of the Animals; Crow and Crane seek the nomination of the Birds. Dove is a Bird who has been discussed as a potential candidate, but it is presumed that she will not run. Hawk, a highly visible but discredited Bird, backs Crow. We stipulate that no one supports two different candidates. We represent this information with the following clauses:

```
neg runs(dove):=true.

backs(hawk,crow).
neg backs(X,Y) :- backs(X,Z),
                  Y \== Z.
```

It is presumed that Wolf will represent the Animals in the election, although he cannot get the nomination without Bull's support. If Wolf should for some reason not get the nomination, Fox is expected to get it. But Fox will not be nominated if he is involved in a scandal, even if Wolf is not nominated. And if both Wolf and Fox fail, the nomination is expected to go to Hart.

```
nominate(animals,wolf) := true.
neg nominate(animals,wolf):=
        neg backs(bull,wolf).
nominate(animals,fox):=
        neg nominate(animals,wolf).
neg nominate(animals,fox) :=
        involved_in_scandal(fox),
        neg nominate(animals,wolf).
nominate(animals,hart):=
        neg nominate(animals,wolf),
        neg nominate(animals,fox).
```

The situation is murkier for the Birds. Presumably, Dove would get the nomination if she ran. But Crow will apparently get the nomination if, as expected, Dove does not run, and if the Animals do not nominate Wolf. Of course, Dove will not be nominated if she does not run. Furthermore, Crow will not be nominated if Wolf is nominated by the Animals, even if Dove does not run. If for some reason neither Crow nor Dove is nominated by the Birds, then the nomination will apparently go to Crane.

```
nominate(birds,dove):= true.
neg nominate(birds,dove) :- neg runs(dove).
nominate(birds,crow):= neg nominate(animals,wolf), neg runs(dove).
neg nominate(birds,crow):= nominate(animals,wolf), neg runs(dove).
nominate(birds,crane):= neg nominate(birds,dove), neg nominate(birds,crow).
```

We expect that the Animal candidate will win the election if Hawk, a well-known but discredited Bird, backs the Bird candidate. We might call this the "kiss

of death" rule. Second, we expect Dove to win if she is nominated and if the Animal
candidate does not have Bull's support. This is as much as we can predict regarding
the actual outcome of the election.

```
elected(Animal):=
        nominate(animals,Animal),
        nominate(birds,Bird),
        backs(hawk,Bird).
elected(dove):=
        nominate(birds,dove),
        nominate(animals,Animal),
        neg backs(bull,Animal).
```

With this information, d-Prolog can deduce that apparently Wolf will receive
the Animal nomination and Crow will receive the Bird nomination. It cannot predict
the eventual winner in the election. If we add the information that Bull backs
Hart, d-Prolog concludes that apparently Fox will receive the Animal nomination,
Crow will receive the Bird nomination, and Fox will be elected. If we add the
further information that Fox is involved in a scandal, then d-Prolog concludes that
apparently the Animals will nominate Hart, the Birds will still nominate Dove,
and the election will go to Hart. Here is the corresponding dialog with d-Prolog,
including some additional scenarios.

```
?- @ nominate
| ?- @ (nominate(animals,A),nominate(birds,B)).

A = wolf,
B = crane

| ?- @ elected(X).

no
| ?- retract(backs(hawk,crow)),assert(backs(hawk,crane)).

yes
| ?- @ elected(X).

X = wolf

| ?- assert(backs(bull,hart)).

yes
| ?- @ (nominate(animals,A),nominate(birds,B)).

A = fox,
B = crow

| ?- @ elected(X).
```

```
X = fox

| ?- assert(involved_in_scandal(fox)).

yes
| ?- @ (nominate(animals,A),nominate(birds,B)).

A = hart,
B = crow

| ?- @ elected(X).

X = hart

| ?- assert(runs(dove)).

yes
| ?- @ (nominate(animals,A),nominate(birds,B)).

A = hart,
B = dove

| ?- @ elected(X).

no
| ?- retract(backs(bull,hart)),assert(backs(bull,fox)).

yes
| ?- @ (nominate(animals,A),nominate(birds,B)).

A = hart,
B = dove

| ?- @ elected(X).

X = dove
```

Careful examination of the information represented in the example should convince you that these are the correct conclusions. However, it is not a simple task to sort through the information and reach the correct conclusions. This example shows d-Prolog's ability to handle complex combinations of interacting rules.

Exercise 11.22.1

Notice that d-Prolog sometimes offers the same solution several times to the query

```
?- @ nominate(Party,Candidate).
```

Explain this. If one clause is deleted from the definition of the predicate `def_der/2`, this solution is not repeated. Which clause can we eliminate to accomplish this? Despite the fact that it sometimes produces duplicate queries, we do not want to delete this clause. Why not?

Exercise 11.22.2

When we assert clauses indicating that Bull supports Hart, Hawk supports Dove, and Dove is running, d-Prolog deduces that both Fox and Dove are elected President. We can avoid this by using the perdicate `runs` to list all the candidates that are running and then adding a clause for the predicate `incompatible/2` which has a condition using the predicate `runs/1`. When done properly, d-Prolog will no longer be able to deduce that two different candidates who are running can both be elected. How do we do this? Why do we need to use the `runs` predicate to make this work?

11.23. D-PROLOG AND THE CLOSED WORLD ASSUMPTION

In working with databases, we often make the Closed World Assumption. The CWA is the assumption that if some piece of data were correct, it would be included in the database. For example, consider a database in Prolog containing information about employees of some company. The database will include such information as employees' names, social security numbers, position, salary, birth date, etc. Suppose we want to know whether Jones is a secretary. When we query the database

```
?- position(jones,secretary).
```

we get the response `no`. We conclude that Jones is not a secretary since, if he were, that fact would have been in the database and the query would have succeeded.

Consider another example. We want to know all employees who are not secretaries and who make less than $25,000 per year. The appropriate query is

```
?- salary(X,Y), Y < 25000, \+ position(X,secretary).
```

If the subgoal `\+ position(X,secretary).` succeeds, then X must not be a secretary. But this is only so if the CWA is correct for the predicate `position/2`. Notice that the variable X is bound by the time the subgoal containing `\+` is called. This is important since otherwise the subgoal will only succeed if no one in the company is a secretary.

Negation-as-failure is only appropriate where the CWA is justified. But when the CWA is justified, we can use `\+` in Prolog to invoke it. This would seem to present a problem for d-Prolog. The CWA is often very useful, but the d-Prolog inference engine will not interpret `\+` correctly. The solution to this problem is simple, and in fact, d-Prolog gives us additional control over when we do and when we do not make the Closed World Assumption. In our example, we invoke the CWA for the predicate `position/2` by including in our database the presumption

```
neg position(X,Y) := true.
```

The presumption, then, is that nobody has *any* position in the company. Of course, presumptions are always overridden by facts. They are also overridden by any competing defeasible rule whose body is something other than `true`. So the presumption that nobody has any position in the company is overridden by any positive evidence whatsoever that some individual holds some position in the company. We can then rephrase our earlier query about employees making less than $25,000 who are not secretaries as

```
?- @ salary(X,Y), Y < 25000, neg position(X,secretary).
```

In some cases, we may not be justified in making the CWA. Then we will not add the corresponding presumption. Suppose, for example, the senior partner in our fictional company has entered data in the database concerning whether the other employees like chocolates. Her reason for doing this is to help her keep track of what to give the other employees for Christmas. If they like chocolates, that's what she gives them. If they don't like chocolates, she gives them something else. If she doesn't know, she tries to work chocolates into the conversation and find out. But she would not *assume* that someone does not like chocolates just because the database doesn't include the information that they *do* like chocolates. That's just not the kind of information one can assume would be included. The partner will have to enter an explicit fact to show that a particular employee does not like chocolate.

The Closed World Assumption example in KBASES.DPL includes information about positions, salaries, and attitudes toward chocolates for all the people working in the small dental clinic Dewey, Pullem, and Howe. The CWA is made only for the predicate `position`.

Exercise 11.23.1   (project)

> Write a set of Prolog rules, defeasible rules, and defeaters for a predicate `prescribe/2` that captures the following principles for prescribing medication.
>
> 1. Normally, prescribe a medication for a diagnosed illness if the medication is effective in treating that illness.
> 2. Normally, don't prescribe a medication for a diagnosed illness if there are counter-indications (allergies, etc.).
> 3. Normally, prescribe a medication for a diagnosed illness even if the medication is counter-indicated, if the medication is effective in treating the illness and the patient's condition is critical (the patient will die if not treated).
> 4. Never prescribe a counter-indicated medication for an illness if there is another medication that is effective in treating the illness and is not counter-indicated.

Exercise 11.23.2   (project)

> Rewrite the CONMAN knowledge base in the file MDC.PL as a set of Prolog rules, defeasible rules, and defeaters for the predicate `diagnosis/1`. Use the prescription rules from the preceding exercise as part of your knowledge base.

11.24. BIBLIOGRAPHICAL NOTES

There is a growing literature on nonmonotonic and defeasible reasoning. For a collection of early papers see Ginsberg (1987); for more recent papers, see Gabbay, Hogger, and Robinson (1994). The inference engine d-Prolog is based on the theoretical work reported by Nute (1992, 1994).

Chapter 12

Natural Language Processing

12.1. PROLOG AND HUMAN LANGUAGES

Natural language processing (NLP) is the study of how to make computers understand human languages such as English and French. By "understand" we do not mean that the computer must approach language with humanlike consciousness and respond to every poetic nuance. We mean only that human beings should be able to use their native languages to put information into computers, rather than resorting to artificial languages such as BASIC, Pascal, or Prolog.

NLP is an important area of artificial intelligence for two reasons. First, language understanding is a task for which complete algorithms are not presently known, yet the human brain obviously accomplishes the task in some way. Hence the problem is one of emulating, on a computer, a human cognitive capacity. Second, in order to process the information conveyed by human language, we need more powerful ways to represent and use knowledge.

Prolog is an ideal programming language for natural language processing. It has a simple knowledge representation system already built in; this can be extended to represent other kinds of information as needed. More importantly, the Prolog unification mechanism provides a convenient way to build and compare representations of the structures of natural-language utterances.

Natural language processing is not, at present, a solved problem. Systems have been built that perform impressively in limited contexts. For instance, Canadian weather reports are routinely translated from English to French by a computer (Slocum 1985), and software packages such as Lotus's HAL and Symantec's Q&A

use a subset of English as a command language. But present-day researchers are a long way from a complete understanding of how language works.

In what follows we will explore the linguistic theory that underlies NLP and show how it can be applied in practical Prolog programs. First we present a template system that can be implemented even by programmers who have studied no linguistics. Then we present more advanced techniques that illustrate current research issues. You should be aware that, in this chapter, many shortcuts have been taken because there is not room to explain the topic fully. For a more comprehensive treatment of natural language processing in Prolog, see Covington (1994).

12.2. LEVELS OF LINGUISTIC ANALYSIS

The goal of NLP is to translate spoken or typed utterances into information that the computer can use. To do this, the computer must analyze language on several levels, corresponding to the traditional subfields of linguistics:

- PHONOLOGY is the analysis and recognition of speech sounds. The phonological component of an NLP system translates a continuum of sound waves into a string of discrete symbols chosen from the set of sounds (called PHONEMES) used by a particular language.

- MORPHOLOGY is the analysis of word forms. For example, it is a fact of morphology that most English nouns form their plurals by adding s. English morphology is much simpler than that of most other languages, and NLP systems built by English speakers tend to neglect morphology.

- SYNTAX is the analysis of sentence structure. The syntactic part of an NLP system is called a PARSER. The input to a parser is called the INPUT STRING, even though it is usually a list of words rather than a string of characters.

- SEMANTICS is the analysis of meaning. The semantic part of an NLP system identifies the information conveyed by utterances.

- PRAGMATICS deals with the relation of language to context. The pragmatic part of an NLP system determines how to respond appropriately to each utterance, distinguishing statements from questions and taking into account information from prior utterances.

Although the five levels are qualitatively different, we do not claim that they can be processed separately. Often an ambiguity on one level can only be resolved by referring to another level. Most NLP systems interleave the levels to some extent.

Nor do researchers understand all five levels equally well. Phonology is full of difficult problems in waveform analysis that require special computer hardware; fortunately, we can bypass phonology by using typewritten input. Morphology is usually thought to be relatively simple, but few linguists have built explicit theoretical models of it. Syntax is complex but a lot is known about it, and there are several rival theories of how it should be analyzed. Semantics is a much newer field; there was little substantial work in it until around 1970. Pragmatics is even less developed.

Exercise 12.2.1

Classify each of the following facts about English as phonological, morphological, syntactic, semantic, or pragmatic:

1. The sentence *Can you close the door?* is normally understood as a polite request even though it is literally a question.

2. The sound /h/ never occurs at the end of a syllable.

3. The plural noun *trousers* has no singular form.

4. The verb *run* has a large number of different meanings.

5. The verb *denounce* is normally followed by a noun phrase.

Exercise 12.2.2

Compare the morphology of a foreign language that you are acquainted with to the morphology of English. Does the morphology of the other language convey kinds of information that English morphology does not?

12.3. TOKENIZATION

The first step in designing any NLP system is to write down some examples of sentences it should process. Our goal in this chapter will be to build a system that can carry on conversations like that shown in Figure 12.1. The computer will accept information from the user and use it to answer questions. For simplicity, we have chosen trivial subject matter, but our techniques will work equally well with almost any Prolog knowledge base.

The first problem that we face is TOKENIZATION. We want to represent an utterance as a list of words, but the user types it as a string of characters. The string must therefore be broken up into words. Additionally, we will discard punctuation marks, convert all uppercase letters to lowercase, and then convert the words into Prolog atoms. Thus, "How are you today?" will become [how,are,you,today].

This is done by the recursive procedure shown in TOKENIZE.PL (Figure 12.2). To understand how it works, first consider the following procedure, which copies a list one element at a time:

```
copy_list([],[]).
copy_list([X|Y],[X|Z]) :- copy_list(Y,Z).
```

This is an inefficient way to copy a list; unification could duplicate the whole list in a single step. But `copy_list` can be modified so that it looks at the list and stops copying at a particular point. This is how `grab_word` (in TOKENIZE.PL) works: It stops copying when it reaches a blank. Then it returns two results: the word that it found, and the list of characters remaining in the input string. Thus, successive calls to `grab_word` extract successive words in a string.

This tokenizer makes no attempt to recognize or classify words. It is a "generic" tokenizer designed for NLP systems that deal with word recognition and morphology elsewhere. In practice, most systems can be made more efficient by combining part of the morphological component with the tokenizer, to avoid the waste of effort

```
> Cathy is a child.
> Fido is a big brown dog.
> Cathy likes animals.
> Does Cathy like a dog?
Not as far as I know.
> Dogs are animals.
> Does Cathy like Fido?
Yes.
> Does Fido like Cathy?
Not as far as I know.
> Big dogs chase cats.
> Felix is a cat.
> Is Fido big?
Yes.
> Does Fido chase cats?
Yes.
> Does Felix chase Fido?
Not as far as I know.
```

Figure 12.1   Design goal: a possible "conversation" with our system. The computer will reason solely from the information given to it in human language.

that comes from collapsing lists of characters into atoms, then taking them apart again later for morphological analysis. We have chosen not to do this so that we will not have to modify the tokenizer as we refine the syntactic and semantic parts of the system.

Exercise 12.3.1

Get TOKENIZE.PL working on your computer. Demonstrate that it correctly handles queries such as this:
```
?- tokenize("This is a test.",What).
What = [this,is,a,test]
```

Exercise 12.3.2

What does TOKENIZE.PL presently do if words are separated by multiple blanks ("like   this")? Modify it to handle multiple blanks correctly. Call your version TOKENIZ1.PL.

Exercise 12.3.3

Further modify TOKENIZ1.PL so that punctuation marks are not discarded, but instead are treated as one-character tokens. Call this version TOKENIZ2.PL.

12.4. TEMPLATE SYSTEMS

Our system will translate English sentences into Prolog. Translations of statements will then be added to the knowledge base; translations of questions will be executed

```
% File TOKENIZE.PL

% tokenize(+String,-Result)
% Breaks String (a list of ASCII code) into a list of atoms,
% discarding punctuation and converting all letters to lowercase.

tokenize([],[]) :- !.

tokenize(String,[Word|Rest]) :-
  grab_word(String,Chars,NewString),
  name(Word,Chars),                    % use atom_codes if available
  tokenize(NewString,Rest).


% grab_word(+String,-Chars,-Rest)
% Splits String into first token (Chars) and remainder (Rest).

grab_word([32|Tail],[],Tail) :- !.      % stop upon hitting a blank

grab_word([],[],[]).                    % stop at end of list

grab_word([Char|Tail],Chars,Rest) :-    % skip punctuation marks
  punctuation_mark(Char), !,
  grab_word(Tail,Chars,Rest).

grab_word([Char|Tail1],[NewChar|Tail2],Rest) :-
  grab_word(Tail1,Tail2,Rest),
  lowercase(Char,NewChar).              % if within a word, keep going


% punctuation_mark(+Char)
% Succeeds if Char is a punctuation mark.

punctuation_mark(Char) :- Char =< 47.
punctuation_mark(Char) :- Char >= 58, Char =< 64.
punctuation_mark(Char) :- Char >= 91, Char =< 96.
punctuation_mark(Char) :- Char >= 123.


% lowercase(+Char,-NewChar)
% Translates any ASCII code to lower case.

lowercase(Char,NewChar) :-      % Add 32 to code of uppercase letter
  Char >= 65, Char =< 90, !,
  NewChar is Char+32.

lowercase(Char,Char).           % Leave all others unchanged
```

Figure 12.2 A tokenizer for natural language input.

as queries. Thus, "Dogs are animals" will translate to

```
animal(X) :- dog(X).
```

and "Is Fido a dog?" will become:

```
?- dog(fido).
```

One way to perform these translations is to match tokenized sentences to TEMPLATES, or stored sentence patterns, each of which is accompanied by a translation schema. Thus, [X,is,a,Y] will translate into the fact Y(X) regardless of what X and Y may be. In practice, Prologs does not allow variable functors, so we must use =.. to build the translation. The rules will look like this:

```
process([X,is,a,Y]) :- Fact =.. [Y,X], assert(Fact).
process([is,X,a,Y]) :- Query =.. [Y,X], call(Query).
```

Some analysis of words is unavoidable. We want to distinguish "Dogs sleep" from "Fido sleeps," since their translations have different structures: the first is sleep(X) :- dog(X) and the second is sleep(fido). To do this we must distinguish singulars from plurals, and perhaps distinguish names from common nouns.

Program TEMPLATE.PL (Figure 12.3) contains a template-matching system that can carry on simple conversations; Figure 12.4 shows an example of what it can do. By adding more templates, we could make it accept a greater variety of sentence types, and it could obviously benefit from a more thorough treatment of morphology. The present version naively assumes that all nouns ending in *s* are plural and all verbs ending in *s* are singular.

Template systems are powerful enough for a wide range of NLP applications. They are especially appropriate for creating English-based command languages in which the vocabulary may be large but the repertoire of sentence structures is small. Moreover, template systems can be implemented without performing extensive analysis of the human language that they are to accept. Thus, they are especially suitable for implementation by programmers who have no training in linguistics.

A template system can be made more versatile by discarding unnecessary words in advance. "Give me the names of people in accounting with salaries above $30,000" can be turned into "names in accounting, salaries above $30,000" by the tokenizer. A more sophisticated approach, called KEYWORD ANALYSIS, scans the sentence for important words and uses them as clues to determine which other words are important. Keyword analysis is widely used in commercial NLP systems. Another approach is to combine template matching with limited parsing capability, as is done in the program PARRY (Parkinson et al. 1977), which has over 2,000 templates. But no template system, even with keyword analysis, is powerful enough to cover all the sentence structures of a human language.

Exercise 12.4.1

Get TEMPLATE.PL working and modify it so that it knows that *children* is the plural of *child* (so that you can say *girls are children* and *Cathy is a girl* and have it infer that Cathy is a child).

```
% File TEMPLATE.PL
% Simple natural language understander using templates

% Uses READSTR.PL (Chapter 5) and TOKENIZE.PL (Chapter 12).

:- ensure_loaded('readstr.pl').   % Use reconsult if necessary
:- ensure_loaded('tokenize.pl').


% process(+Wordlist)
%   translates Wordlist into Prolog and asserts it if it
%   is a statement or queries it if it is a question.

% Note that this procedure assumes that whenever a word ends in S,
%   the S is an affix (either noun plural or verb singular).

process([X,is,a,Y]) :-          % [fido,is,a,dog] => dog(fido).
    !,
    Fact =.. [Y,X],
    note(Fact).

process([X,is,an,Y]) :-         % same, with "an"
    !,
    process([X,is,a,Y]).

process([is,X,a,Y]) :-          % [is,fido,a,dog] => ?-dog(fido).
    !,
    Query =.. [Y,X],
    check(Query).

process([is,X,an,Y]) :-         % same, but with "an"
    !,
    process([is,X,a,Y]).

process([X,are,Y]) :-           % [dogs,are,animals] =>
    !,                          %     animal(X) :- dog(X).
    remove_s(X,X1),
    remove_s(Y,Y1),
    Head =.. [Y1,Z],
    Tail =.. [X1,Z],
    note((Head :- Tail)).
```

Figure 12.3 A program that implements a simple template system. (Continued on following pages.)

```
process([does,X,Y]) :-         % [does,fido,sleep] => ?-sleep(fido).
    !,
    Query =.. [Y,X],
    check(Query).

process([X,Y]) :-              % [fido,sleeps] => sleep(fido).
    \+ remove_s(X,_),
    remove_s(Y,Y1),
    !,
    Fact =.. [Y1,X],
    note(Fact).

process([X,Y]) :-              % [dogs,sleep] => sleep(X) :- dog(X).
    remove_s(X,X1),
    \+ remove_s(Y,_),
    !,
    Head =.. [Y,Z],
    Tail =.. [X1,Z],
    note((Head :- Tail)).

process(_) :-
    write('I do not understand.'),
    nl.


% remove_s(+Word,-NewWord)
%   removes final S from Word, or fails if Word does not end in S.

remove_s(X,X1) :-
    name(X,XList),
    remove_s_list(XList,X1List),
    name(X1,X1List).

remove_s_list("s",[]).

remove_s_list([Head|Tail],[Head|NewTail]) :-
    remove_s_list(Tail,NewTail).
```

Figure 12.3 (Continued).

```
% check(+Query)
%    Try Query. Report whether it succeeded.

check(Query) :- % write('Trying query: ?- '),
                % write(Query),       % Un-comment these lines
                % nl,                 % to see the translations
                call(Query),
                !,
                write('Yes.'),
                nl.

check(_) :-     write('Not as far as I know.'),
                nl.


% note(+Fact)
%    Asserts Fact and prints acknowledgment.

note(Fact) :-   % write('Adding to knowledge base: '),
                % write(Fact),        % Un-comment these lines
                % nl,                 % to see the translations
                asserta(Fact),
                write('OK'),
                nl.


% do_one_sentence
%  Accept and process one sentence.

do_one_sentence :- write('>'), read_str(S), tokenize(S,T), process(T).


% start
%  Main procedure.

start :- write('TEMPLATE.PL at your service.'),nl,
         write('Terminate by pressing Break.'),nl,
         repeat,
           do_one_sentence,
         fail.
```

Figure 12.3 (Continued).

```
TEMPLATE.PL at your service.
Terminate by pressing Break.
>Fido is a dog.
OK
>Dogs are animals.
OK
>Animals eat.
OK
>Does Fido eat?
Yes.
>Does Fido sleep?
Not as far as I know.
```

Figure 12.4   A conversation with TEMPLATE.PL.

Exercise 12.4.2   (project)

Use template technology to make your computer process operating system commands in English. Instead of constructing a Prolog query from the input, construct a command and pass it to the operating system. For example, *What files do I have?* would translate as `dir` in DOS or `ls` in UNIX. Most Prologs have a built-in predicate that passes strings or atoms to the operating system as commands.

12.5. GENERATIVE GRAMMARS

Templates are inadequate to describe human language because every human language has an infinite number of sentence structures. To see that this is so, consider the sentences:

John arrived.
Max said John arrived.
Bill claimed Max said John arrived.
Mary thought Bill claimed Max said John arrived.

What we have is a recursive structure that can contain another structure like itself. There is no limit, in principle, to the number of structures that can be formed this way, and each one requires a different template. Moreover, this is only one of many recursive structures that occur in English, and there are analogues in all known languages.

The linguist Noam Chomsky first pointed this out in 1957. He suggested that, instead of trying to list the sentence types of each language, linguists should treat syntax as a problem in set theory — how to give a finite description of an infinite set.

One way to describe an infinite set is to give a generative procedure that "generates," or points out, all the members of the set. For example, here is a generative procedure for the set of even numbers:

- 0 is an even number.

- From any even number you can get another even number by adding or subtracting 2.

With just two rules, this procedure describes an infinite number of numbers, because the second rule can apply recursively to its own output. You can show that 1,988 is even by applying the first rule once and then applying the second rule 994 times.

A procedure that generates the sentences of a human language is called a GENERATIVE GRAMMAR. What kinds of rules should a generative grammar contain? Chomsky's initial conclusion was that two kinds of rules are sufficient. Most sentence structures can be generated satisfactorily by CONTEXT-FREE PHRASE STRUCTURE RULES (PS-rules for short), which we will discuss next; rules of another type, called TRANSFORMATIONS, are needed to generate structures that we will discuss later.

The following is a small grammar consisting of context-free phrase structure rules. Here we are using the notation commonly used in linguistics; the notation used in Prolog programs is slightly different.

(1) $S \rightarrow NP\ VP$
(2) $NP \rightarrow D\ N$
(3) $VP \rightarrow V\ NP$
(4) $VP \rightarrow V\ S$
(5) $D \rightarrow$ the
(6) $D \rightarrow$ a
(7) $N \rightarrow$ dog
(8) $N \rightarrow$ cat
(9) $N \rightarrow$ boy
(10) $N \rightarrow$ girl
(11) $V \rightarrow$ chased
(12) $V \rightarrow$ saw
(13) $V \rightarrow$ said
(14) $V \rightarrow$ believed   (etc.)

The first rule says, "A sentence (S) can consist of a noun phrase (NP) followed by a verb phrase (VP)." That is, it EXPANDS S into NP and VP. The other rules work the same way; D stands for "determiner," N for "noun," and V for "verb." In many cases there are alternative expansions of the same symbol; rules 3 and 4, for example, both specify expansions of VP. The words introduced by rules 6 to 14 are called TERMINAL SYMBOLS because they have no further expansions.

Figure 12.5 shows one of the sentences generated by this grammar, together with a tree diagram that shows how the rules generate it. The diagram divides the sentence into phrases called CONSTITUENTS, each comprising the expansion of one symbol.

This grammar generates an infinite number of structures. Rule 1 expands S into NP VP, and rule 4 expands VP into V S. Each of these rules can apply to the output of the other, and the resulting loop can generate arbitrarily long sentences (Figure 12.6). Thus the grammar is a finite description of an infinite set.

Our grammar does generate some nonsensical sentences, such as "The boy chased the cat saw the girl." We could block generation of these sentences by using more sophisticated rules. Alternatively, we could say that they are syntactically

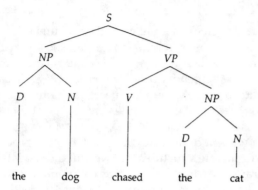

Figure 12.5 A sentence generated by our phrase structure grammar, with a tree diagram showing the rules used to generate it.

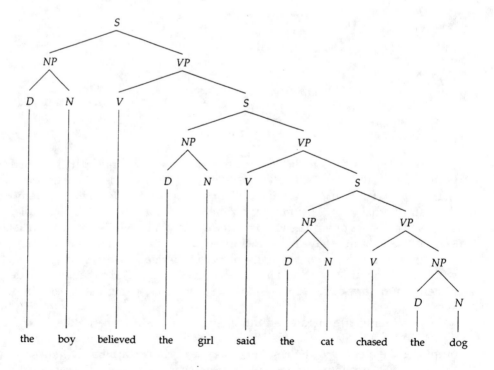

Figure 12.6 Recursion enables our grammar to generate arbitrarily long sentences.

acceptable but semantically ill-formed; that is, their structures are legitimate but no coherent meanings can be assigned to them because of the particular words used.

Exercise 12.5.1

Using the generative grammar given in the text of this section, draw tree diagrams of the following sentences:

A dog chased the boy.

The cat believed the dog saw the girl.

Exercise 12.5.2

Which of these sentences are generated by the grammar given in the text of this section?

The boy saw the boy.

A boy chased.

The dog slept.

The cat said the cat said the cat said the cat.

The the cat said the dog chased the boy.

Exercise 12.5.3

Give an example of a recursive syntactic structure in English other than those mentioned in the text.

Exercise 12.5.4

Write a generative procedure (in English or any appropriate notation) that generates the following infinite set of strings:

ab

aabb

aaabbb

aaaabbbb

aaaaabbbbb

⋮

Exercise 12.5.5

Does the human brain generate sentences by the same process as the grammar described in this section? Or does it use some other process? What, in your opinion, is the relation between the generative grammar (or a more comprehensive one like it) and the brain of a person who speaks English?

12.6. A SIMPLE PARSER

We know how to use the grammar to generate sentences. How do we do the opposite — take a sentence and see whether the grammar generates it? One way of doing this is called RECURSIVE DESCENT PARSING; it relies on the fact that PS-rules can be paraphrased as ordinary Prolog rules. For example:

(1)   **X** is an S if **X** consists of an NP followed by a VP.
(2)   **X** is an NP if **X** consists of a D followed by an N.
(3)   **X** is a VP if **X** consists of a V followed by an NP.
    ⋮
(5)   **X** is a D if **X** is *the*.
    ⋮

Rule 1 calls rules 2 and 3; rule 2 calls rule 5 and another rule much like it; and so on. The process continues until all the words in the sentence have been recognized.

This kind of parser can handle multiple expansions of the same symbol, because if one alternative fails, it backtracks and tries another. It can handle recursion because the rules can call themselves recursively. The only thing that it cannot handle is LEFT RECURSION, as in the PS-rule

$$A \rightarrow A\ B$$

because the procedure for parsing A would call itself before doing anything else, and an endless loop would result. Fortunately, any PS-grammar that uses left recursion can be transformed into an equivalent grammar that does not.

To perform recursive descent parsing, we need to keep track of two things: the list of words that we are starting with, and the list of words that will be left over after a particular constituent has been removed. Call these **X** and **Z** respectively. We will render $S \rightarrow NP\ VP$ into Prolog as:

```
sentence(X,Z) :- noun_phrase(X,Y), verb_phrase(Y,Z).
```

In English: "To remove a sentence from **X** leaving **Z**, first remove a noun phrase from **X** leaving **Y**, then remove a verb phrase from **Y** leaving **Z**."

The rules for terminal symbols refer directly to the elements of the list:

```
noun([dog|Z],Z).
```

To ask whether *The cat saw the dog* is a sentence, we execute the query:

```
?- sentence([the,cat,saw,the,dog],[]).
```

The second argument is [] so that no words will be left over at the end. This is important; we want to distinguish *The cat saw the dog*, which is grammatical, from *The cat saw the dog the the*, which is not, and if we try to parse *The mouse ate the cheese*, we do not want to stop with *The mouse ate*.

File PARSER1.PL (Figure 12.7) shows a complete parser constructed in this way. As shown, it merely tests whether a list is generated by the grammar, without constructing a representation of the structure found. However, note that it is reversible — it can generate as well as parse. The query

```
?- sentence(X,[]).
```

means "generate a sentence," and you can backtrack to get as many different sentences as you wish. In fact, you can even issue a query such as

```
% File PARSER1.PL
% Simple parser using Prolog rules

sentence(X,Z) :- noun_phrase(X,Y),
                 verb_phrase(Y,Z).

noun_phrase(X,Z) :- determiner(X,Y),
                    noun(Y,Z).

verb_phrase(X,Z) :- verb(X,Y),
                    noun_phrase(Y,Z).

verb_phrase(X,Z) :- verb(X,Y),
                    sentence(Y,Z).

determiner([the|Z],Z).
determiner([a|Z],Z).

noun([dog|Z],Z).
noun([cat|Z],Z).
noun([boy|Z],Z).
noun([girl|Z],Z).

verb([chased|Z],Z).
verb([saw|Z],Z).
verb([said|Z],Z).
verb([believed|Z],Z).
```

Figure 12.7   A parser that uses Prolog rules to determine whether a list of atoms is generated by the grammar.

```
?- sentence([W,X,Y,Z,cat|T],[]).
```

to get a sentence whose fifth word is "cat" — a feature that can be useful for solving puzzles and breaking codes.

Exercise 12.6.1

> Get PARSER1.PL working on your computer, and use it to generate all possible sentences whose third word is *believed*. What do you get?

Exercise 12.6.2

> Using your solution to Exercise 12.5.4, implement a parser that will test whether a list consists of a number of a's followed by the same number of b's (such as [a,a,a,b,b,b]).

Exercise 12.6.3

> Consider the work done by a recursive descent parser using the rules
>
> $a \rightarrow b\,c$
>
> $a \rightarrow b\,d$
>
> $a \rightarrow b\,e$
>
> $a \rightarrow f\,g$
>
> when the input string is [f,g,e]. What operations are needlessly repeated during the parsing? Suggest a way to reduce the duplication of effort.

12.7. GRAMMAR RULE (DCG) NOTATION

Rules like those in PARSER1.PL are tedious to write because each functor has two arguments whose arrangement is entirely predictable. Prolog provides an alternative notation in which these arguments are supplied automatically. Clauses written in the alternative notation have the infix operator --> in place of :-, thus:

```
sentence --> noun_phrase, verb_phrase.
```

This is functionally equivalent to the rule

```
sentence(X,Z) :- noun_phrase(X,Y), verb_phrase(Y,Z).
```

although its internal implementation may be different (see Appendix B).

In grammar rule notation, nonterminal symbols are written in lists:

```
noun --> [dog].
```

The list can contain more than one element, representing words that occur in immediate succession:

```
verb --> [gives,up].
```

This rule treats *gives up* as a single verb. The list can even be empty, indicating an element that can be left out:

```
determiner --> [].
```

This rule says that the grammar can act as if a determiner is present even if it doesn't actually find one.

What about queries? A query to the rule such as

```
sentence --> noun_phrase, verb_phrase.
```

will rely on the fact that the rule is equivalent to

```
sentence(X,Z) :- noun_phrase(X,Y), verb_phrase(Y,Z).
```

and will therefore use `sentence/2` as the predicate:

```
?- sentence([the,dog,chased,the,cat],[]).
yes
```

In fact, if you use `listing`, you will find that grammar rules are actually translated into ordinary Prolog clauses when they are loaded into memory. Remember that grammar rule notation is merely a notational device. It adds no computing power to Prolog; every program written with grammar rules has an exact equivalent written without them.

PARSER2.PL (Figure 12.8) is a parser written in grammar rule notation. Here are some examples of its operation:

```
?- sentence([the,dog,chased,the,cat],[]).
yes
?- sentence([the,dog,the,cat],[]).
no
?- sentence([the,dog,believed,the,boy,saw,the,cat],[]).
yes
?- sentence([A,B,C,D,cat|E],[]).
A=the,B=dog,C=chased,D=the,E=[]
A=the,B=dog,C=chased,D=a,E=[]
A=the,B=dog,C=saw,D=the,E=[]      % etc.
```

Like Prolog goals, grammar rules can use semicolons to mean "or":

```
noun --> [dog];[cat];[boy];[girl].
```

Grammar rules can even include Prolog goals, in curly brackets, interspersed among the constituents to be parsed:

```
sentence --> noun_phrase, verb_phrase,
                    { write('Sentence found'), nl }.
```

Grammar rules are executed in the same way as ordinary clauses; in fact, they are clauses in which some of the arguments are supplied automatically. Thus it may even make sense to embed a cut in a grammar rule:

```
sentence --> [does], {!}, noun_phrase, verb_phrase.
```

This rule parses a question that begins with *does*. The cut says that if *does* has been found, no other rule for `sentence` should be tried.

Most importantly, nonterminal symbols in grammar rules can take arguments. Thus

```
% File PARSER2.PL
% A parser using grammar rule notation

sentence --> noun_phrase, verb_phrase.

noun_phrase --> determiner, noun.

verb_phrase --> verb, noun_phrase.
verb_phrase --> verb, sentence.

determiner --> [the].
determiner --> [a].

noun --> [dog].
noun --> [cat].
noun --> [boy].
noun --> [girl].

verb --> [chased].
verb --> [saw].
verb --> [said].
verb --> [believed].
```

Figure 12.8   A parser written in grammar rule notation.

```
sentence(N) --> noun_phrase(N), verb_phrase(N).
```

is equivalent to

```
sentence(N,X,Z) :- noun_phrase(N,X,Y), verb_phrase(N,Y,Z).
```

although some Prologs may put N after the automatically supplied arguments instead of before them.

A grammar in which nonterminal symbols take arguments is called a *definite-clause grammar* (DCG); it is more powerful than a context-free phrase-structure grammar. The arguments undergo instantiation just as in ordinary clauses; they can even appear in embedded Prolog goals. Grammar rule notation is often called DCG notation.

Exercise 12.7.1

Get PARSER2.PL running on your computer. Show how to use it to:

- Parse the sentence *The girl saw the cat.*
- Test whether *The girl saw the elephant* is generated by the grammar rules.
- Generate a sentence with 8 words (if possible).

Exercise 12.7.2

Reimplement your parser for *ab, aabb, aaabbb...* using grammar rule notation.

12.8. GRAMMATICAL FEATURES

Arguments in grammar rules can be used to handle grammatical agreement phenomena. In English, the present tense verb and the subject agree in number; if one is plural, so is the other. Thus we cannot say *The dogs chases the cat* or *The dog chase the cat.* Determiners also reflect number: *a* and *an* can only be used with singulars, and the null (omitted) determiner is normally used with plurals. Thus we can say *A dog barks* and *Dogs bark* but not *A dogs bark.*

One way to handle agreement would be to distinguish two kinds of noun phrases and two kinds of verb phrases:

```
sentence --> singular_noun_phrase, singular_verb_phrase.
sentence --> plural_noun_phrase, plural_verb_phrase.

singular_noun_phrase --> singular_determiner, singular_noun.
plural_noun_phrase    --> plural_determiner, plural_noun.

singular_verb_phrase --> singular_verb, singular_noun_phrase.
singular_verb_phrase --> singular_verb, plural_noun_phrase.
plural_verb_phrase    --> plural_verb, singular_noun_phrase.
plural_verb_phrase    --> plural_verb, plural_noun_phrase.

singular_determiner  --> [a];[the].
```

```
plural_determiner      --> [];[the].

singular_noun          --> [dog];[cat];[boy];[girl].
plural_noun            --> [dogs];[cats];[boys];[girls].

singular_verb          --> [chases];[sees];[says];[believes].
plural_verb            --> [chase];[see];[say];[believe].
```

This grammar works correctly but is obviously very redundant. Most rules are duplicated, and one of them — the rule for verb phrases — has actually split into four parts because the verb need not agree with its object. Imagine how the rules would proliferate a language whose constituents agree not only in number but also in gender and case.

AGREEMNT.PL (Figure 12.9) shows a much better approach. Number is treated as an argument (or, as linguists call it, a FEATURE) of certain non-terminal symbols (Figure 12.10). The first rule says that a sentence consists of a noun phrase with some number feature, followed by a verb phrase with the same number:

```
sentence --> noun_phrase(N), verb_phrase(N).
```

N is instantiated to `singular` or `plural` when a word that can be identified as singular or plural is parsed. Thus, when looking for `noun(N)`, we could use the rule

```
noun(plural) --> [dogs].
```

which, if successful, will instantiate N to plural.

The rule for verb phrases uses an anonymous variable to show that the number of the object does not matter:

```
verb_phrase(N) --> verb(N), noun_phrase(_).
```

Anonymous variables are an ideal computational mechanism to handle features that are NEUTRALIZED (disregarded) at particular points in the grammar. Notice that we can't leave out the argument altogether, because `noun_phrase` (without arguments) will not unify with `noun_phrase(singular)` or `noun_phrase(plural)`. Here are some examples of queries answered by AGREEMNT.PL:

```
?- sentence([the,dog,chases,cats],[]).
yes
?- sentence([the,dog,chase,cats],[]).
no
?- noun_phrase(X,[the,dogs],[]).
X=plural
?- noun_phrase(X,[a,dog],[]).
X=singular
?- noun_phrase(X,[a,dogs],[]).
no
```

Note in particular that you need not parse an entire sentence; you can tell the computer to parse a noun phrase or something else.

```
% File AGREEMNT.PL
% Illustration of grammatical agreement features

% The argument N is the number of
% the subject and main verb.
% It is instantiated to 'singular'
% or 'plural' as the parse progresses.

sentence --> noun_phrase(N), verb_phrase(N).

noun_phrase(N) --> determiner(N), noun(N).

verb_phrase(N) --> verb(N), noun_phrase(_).
verb_phrase(N) --> verb(N), sentence.

determiner(singular) --> [a].
determiner(_)        --> [the].
determiner(plural)   --> [].

noun(singular) --> [dog];[cat];[boy];[girl].
noun(plural)   --> [dogs];[cats];[boys];[girls].

verb(singular) --> [chases];[sees];[says];[believes].
verb(plural)   --> [chase];[see];[say];[believe].
```

Figure 12.9   A parser that implements subject-verb number agreement.

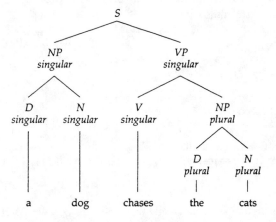

Figure 12.10   Number features on nonterminal symbols. Some constituents, such as adverbs and prepositional phrases, are not marked for number.

Exercise 12.8.1

> Get AGREEMNT.PL working and add the determiners *one, several, three, every, all,* and *some.*

12.9. MORPHOLOGY

AGREEMNT.PL is still redundant in one respect: it lists both singular and plural forms of every word. Most English noun plurals can be generated by adding an *s* to the singular. Likewise, almost all third person singular verbs are formed by adding an *s* to the plural (unmarked) form. In MORPH.PL (Figure 12.11), we implement these morphological rules and at the same time allow them to have exceptions.

The trick is to use Prolog goals embedded in grammar rules. A rule such as

```
noun(N) --> [X], { morph(verb(N),X) }.
```

means: "Parse a noun with number feature N by instantiating X to the next word in the input list, then checking that `morph(verb(N),X)` succeeds." Here `morph` is an ordinary Prolog predicate that handles morphology.

The clauses for `morph` comprise both rules and facts. The facts include all the singular nouns as well as irregular plurals:

```
morph(noun(singular),dog).
morph(noun(singular),cat).
    :
    :
morph(noun(plural),children).
```

The rules compute additional word forms from the ones listed in the facts. They use `remove_s`, a predicate defined originally in TEMPLATE.PL; `remove_s(X,Y)` succeeds if X is an atom ending in *s* and Y is the same atom without the *s*. This provides a way to form regular plural nouns from singulars:

```
morph(noun(plural),X) :-
    remove_s(X,Y),
    morph(noun(singular),Y).
```

A similar rule forms third person singular verbs from plurals.

Exercise 12.9.1

> As shown, MORPH.PL accepts *childs* as well as *children.* Modify it so that only the correct form of each irregular plural is accepted. Call your version MORPH1.PL.

Exercise 12.9.2

> Can you use MORPH.PL to generate, as well as analyze, the forms of a word? If not, why not? Explain.

```
% File MORPH.PL
% Parser with morphological analysis

sentence --> noun_phrase(N), verb_phrase(N).

noun_phrase(N) --> determiner(N), noun(N).

verb_phrase(N) --> verb(N), noun_phrase(_).
verb_phrase(N) --> verb(N), sentence.

determiner(singular) --> [a].
determiner(_)        --> [the].
determiner(plural)   --> [].

noun(N) --> [X], { morph(noun(N),X) }.
verb(N) --> [X], { morph(verb(N),X) }.


% morph(-Type,+Word)
%   succeeds if Word is a word form
%   of the specified type.

morph(noun(singular),dog).        % Singular nouns
morph(noun(singular),cat).
morph(noun(singular),boy).
morph(noun(singular),girl).
morph(noun(singular),child).
```

Figure 12.11   A parser that recognizes *s* suffixes. (Continued on next page.)

```
        morph(noun(plural),children).      % Irregular plural nouns

        morph(noun(plural),X) :-           % Rule for regular plural nouns
            remove_s(X,Y),
            morph(noun(singular),Y).

        morph(verb(plural),chase).         % Plural verbs
        morph(verb(plural),see).
        morph(verb(plural),say).
        morph(verb(plural),believe).

        morph(verb(singular),X) :-         % Rule for singular verbs
            remove_s(X,Y),
            morph(verb(plural),Y).


    % remove_s(+X,-X1) [lifted from TEMPLATE.PL]
    %  removes final S from X giving X1,
    %  or fails if X does not end in S.

    remove_s(X,X1) :-
        name(X,XList),
        remove_s_list(XList,X1List),
        name(X1,X1List).

    remove_s_list("s",[]).

    remove_s_list([Head|Tail],[Head|NewTail]) :-
        remove_s_list(Tail,NewTail).
```

Figure 12.11 (Continued).

12.10. CONSTRUCTING THE PARSE TREE

All of these parsers merely tell us whether a sentence is generated by the grammar; they do not give its structure. Hence they do not get us any closer to a mechanism for "understanding" the sentences.

 We can remedy this by using arguments to keep records of the structure found. The idea is that whenever a rule succeeds, it will instantiate an argument to show the structure that it has parsed. Within the arguments will be variables that have been instantiated by the lower-level rules that this rule has called.

 For simplicity, we will abandon number agreement and go back to the grammar in PARSER2.PL. However, we want to emphasize that it would be perfectly all right to use two arguments on each nonterminal symbol, one for the structure and one for the number.

 We can represent a parse tree as a Prolog structure in which each functor represents a nonterminal symbol and its arguments represent its expansion. For example, the structure

```
sentence(
    noun_phrase(
        determiner(the),
        noun(dog)
            ),
    verb_phrase(
        verb(chased),
        noun_phrase(
            determiner(the),
            noun(cat)
                )
            )
        )
```

can represent the parse tree in Figure 12.5 above. (It is indented purely for readability; a few Prologs have a "pretty-print" utility that can print any structure this way.)

 To build these structures, we rewrite the grammar rules as in this example:

```
sentence(sentence(X,Y)) --> noun_phrase(X), verb_phrase(Y).
```

That is: Instantiate the argument of sentence to `sentence(X,Y)` if you can parse a noun phrase, instantiating its argument to `X`, and then parse a verb phrase, instantiating its argument to `Y`.

 The complete parser is shown in STRUCTUR.PL (Figure 12.12). A query to it looks like this:

```
?- sentence(X,[the,dog,chased,the,cat],[]).
```

and `X` becomes instantiated to a structure representing the parse tree.

 Grammars of this kind, with clause heads such as `sentence(sentence(X,Y))`, are obviously somewhat redundant; there are more concise ways to build parsers that simply output the parse tree. Behind the redundancy, however, lies some hidden

```
% File STRUCTUR.PL
% Parser like PARSER2.PL, but building a
% parse tree while parsing

sentence(sentence(X,Y)) -->
    noun_phrase(X), verb_phrase(Y).

noun_phrase(noun_phrase(X,Y)) -->
    determiner(X), noun(Y).

verb_phrase(verb_phrase(X,Y)) -->
    verb(X), noun_phrase(Y).
verb_phrase(verb_phrase(X,Y)) -->
    verb(X), sentence(Y).

determiner(determiner(the)) --> [the].
determiner(determiner(a)) --> [a].

noun(noun(dog)) --> [dog].
noun(noun(cat)) --> [cat].
noun(noun(boy)) --> [boy].
noun(noun(girl)) --> [girl].

verb(verb(chased)) --> [chased].
verb(verb(saw)) --> [saw].
verb(verb(said)) --> [said].
verb(verb(believed)) --> [believed].
```

Figure 12.12 A parser that builds a representation of the parse tree.

power; the grammar can build a structure that is *not* the parse tree but is computed in some way while the parsing is going on. Instead of building up a phrase-structure representation of each constituent, we can build a semantic representation. But before we begin doing so, we have one more syntactic issue to tackle.

Exercise 12.10.1

Get STRUCTUR.PL working and show how to use it to obtain the parse tree of the sentence *The girl believed the dog chased the cat.*

Exercise 12.10.2

What is the effect of the following query to STRUCTUR.PL? Explain.

```
?- sentence(sentence(noun_phrase(_),verb_phrase(verb(_),sentence(_))),What,[]
```

12.11. UNBOUNDED MOVEMENTS

Questions that begin with the "WH-words" *who* or *what* cannot be generated straight-
forwardly by context-free PS-rules. To see why, consider these sentences:

Max thought Bill believed Sharon saw Cathy.
Who ␣ *thought Bill believed Sharon saw Cathy?*
Who did Max think ␣ *believed Sharon saw Cathy?*
Who did Max think Bill believed ␣ *saw Cathy?*
Who did Max think Bill believed Sharon saw ␣ *?*

The first sentence contains four noun phrases, and a question can be formed to
inquire about any of them. When this is done, the questioned NP disappears, and
who or *who did* is added at the beginning of the sentence.

Crucially, each WH-question is missing exactly one noun phrase, marked by ␣
in the examples above. Yet the sentences have a recursive structure that provides, in
principle, an infinite number of different positions from which the missing NP may
come, so we can't just enumerate the positions. Nor can the PS-rules say that these
NPs are optional, for we would then get sentences with more than one NP missing.

In Chomsky's generative grammars, the PS-rules generate *who* or *what* in the position of the missing NP, and another rule, called a TRANSFORMATION, then moves the
WH-word to the beginning of the sentence (Figure 12.13). A grammar of this type is
called a TRANSFORMATIONAL GRAMMAR; this transformation is called WH-MOVEMENT
and is an example of an UNBOUNDED MOVEMENT because it can lift a constituent out
of an unlimited amount of recursive structure. Chomsky uses transformations for
many other purposes — for example, relating actives to passives — but unbounded
movement phenomena provide the strongest evidence that transformations are necessary.

Transformational parsing is difficult. In order to undo the transformation, we
must know the structure that it produced — but we must do the parsing in order to
discover the structure. The strategy we'll use here is different. When a WH-word is
encountered, we'll save it, and whenever we fail to find an expected NP, we'll use
the saved WH-word instead, thereby pairing up the WH-word with the missing NP
position.

For this to work, most of the nonterminal symbols will need two more arguments. One will be a list of WH-words that were saved prior to parsing that
constituent, and the other will be a list of WH-words remaining after that constituent
has been parsed. One of the rules for VP, for instance, will be:

```
verb_phrase(X,Z,verb_phrase(V,NP)) --> verb(V), noun_phrase(X,Z,NP).
```

This rule passes the saved WH-word list **X** unchanged to **noun_phrase**, which may or
may not use it; then **noun_phrase** instantiates **Z** to the new WH-word list and passes
it back to this rule.

Crucially, one of the rules can pull a noun phrase out of the WH-word list rather
than the input string:

```
noun_phrase([X|Tail],Tail,noun_phrase(X)) --> [].
```

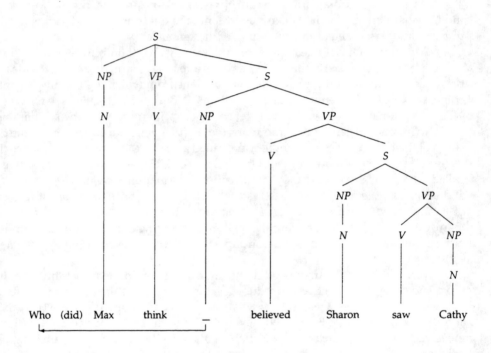

Figure 12.13 A transformational grammar generates a WH-word in place and then moves it to the beginning of the sentence. Another transformation inserts *did*.

The other noun phrase rules accept a noun phrase from the input string without altering the WH-word list.

WHPARSER.PL (Figure 12.14) is a parser that uses this technique. For the sentence [who,did,the,boy,believe,saw,the,girl] it produces the parse tree

```
sentence(
    noun_phrase(
        determiner(the),
        noun(boy)
            ),
    verb_phrase(
        verb(believed),
        sentence(
            noun_phrase(who),
            verb_phrase(
                verb(saw),
                noun_phrase(
                    determiner(the),
                    noun(girl)
                        )
                )
            )
        )
    )
```

with the WH-word *who* in the position of the missing NP, where it would have appeared if the movement transformation had not taken place.

Each WH-question contains only one preposed WH-word, so we don't really need a list in which to store it. The usefulness of lists shows up with relative clauses, which can have WH-words introducing multiply nested constructions: *The man whom the dog which you saw belonged to claimed it.* In parsing such sentences, the WH-word list might acquire two or even three members. However, sentences that require more than two items on the list are invariably confusing to human hearers. The human brain apparently cannot maintain a deep pushdown stack while parsing sentences.

Exercise 12.11.1

Why does WHPARSER.PL accept *Who did the boy believe the girl saw?* but reject *Who did the boy believe the girl saw the cat?* That is, how does WHPARSER.PL guarantee that if the sentence begins with *who,* an NP must be missing somewhere within it?

12.12. SEMANTIC INTERPRETATION

Now let's build the complete natural language understanding system that we envisioned at the beginning of the chapter. Figure 12.1 showed the kind of dialogue that it should be able to engage in. The completed program is shown in file NLU.PL (Figure 12.17).

The program parses a subset of English somewhat different from what we have been handling so far. Figure 12.15 summarizes the syntax of this subset, in Prolog

```
% File WHPARSER.PL
% Parser that handles WH-questions as well as statements.
% For simplicity, morphology is neglected.

% Each phrase that can contain a WH-word has 3 arguments:
%       (1) List of WH-words found before starting to
%              parse this constituent;
%       (2) List of WH-words still available after
%              parsing this constituent;
%       (3) Structure built while parsing this
%              constituent (as in STRUCTUR.PL).


sentence(X,Z,sentence(NP,VP)) -->   % Sentence that does not
     noun_phrase(X,Y,NP),           % begin with a WH-word,
     verb_phrase(Y,Z,VP).           % but may be embedded in
                                    % a sentence that does.


sentence(X,Z,sentence(NP,VP)) -->
     wh_word(W),                    % Sentence begins with WH-word.
     [did],                         % Put the WH-word on the list,
     noun_phrase([W|X],Y,NP),       % absorb "did," and continue.
     verb_phrase(Y,Z,VP).


noun_phrase(X,X,noun_phrase(D,N)) -->
     determiner(D),                 % Ordinary NP that does
     noun(N).                       % not use saved WH-word

noun_phrase([X|Tail],Tail,noun_phrase(X)) --> [].
     % Missing NP supplied by picking a
     % stored WH-word off the list

verb_phrase(X,Z,verb_phrase(V,NP)) -->
     verb(V),
     noun_phrase(X,Z,NP).
```

Figure 12.14   A parser that can undo unbounded movements. (Continued on next page.)

```
verb_phrase(X,Z,verb_phrase(V,S)) -->
     verb(V),
     sentence(X,Z,S).

determiner(determiner(a))   --> [a].
determiner(determiner(the)) --> [the].

noun(noun(dog))  --> [dog].
noun(noun(cat))  --> [cat].
noun(noun(boy))  --> [boy].
noun(noun(girl)) --> [girl].

% Two forms of every verb:
%   "The boy saw the cat" vs. "Did the boy see the cat?"

verb(verb(chased))   --> [chased];[chase].
verb(verb(saw))      --> [saw];[see].
verb(verb(said))     --> [said];[say].
verb(verb(believed)) --> [believed];[believe].

wh_word(who)  --> [who].
wh_word(what) --> [what].


% Sample queries

test1 :- sentence([],[],Structure,
          [who,did,the,boy,believe,the,girl,saw],[]),
         write(Structure),
         nl.

test2 :- sentence([],[],Structure,
          [who,did,the,boy,believe,saw,the,girl],[]),
         write(Structure),
         nl.
```

Figure 12.14 (Continued).

Rule:	Example:
sentence → *noun_phrase verb_phrase*	Dogs chase cats.
sentence → *noun_phrase copula verb_phrase*	Dogs are animals.
sentence → *noun_phrase copula adj_phrase*	Dogs are big.
sentence → *aux_verb noun_phrase verb_phrase*	Do dogs chase cats?
sentence → *copula noun_phrase noun_phrase*	Are dogs animals?
sentence → *copula noun_phrase adj_phrase*	Are dogs big?
verb_phrase → *verb noun_phrase*	chase cats
adj_phrase → *adjective*	big
noun_phrase → *determiner noun_group*	a big brown dog
noun_group → *adjective noun_group*	big brown dog
noun_group → *common_noun*	dog
noun_group → *proper_noun*	Fido

Figure 12.15   Phrase-structure rules used in the language understander.

grammar rule notation, and Figure 12.16 shows some of the structures that these rules generate. For simplicity, we completely neglect morphology. However, we introduce several new types of sentences, including yes–no questions and sentences that have the copula *is* or *are* rather than a main verb.

We compute the meaning of each sentence in two stages. First, the parser constructs a representation of the meaning of the sentence; then other procedures convert this representation into one or more Prolog rules, facts, or queries. The representations constructed by the parser have the form

`statement(EntityList,Predicate)`

or

`question(EntityList,Predicate)`

where `EntityList` is a list of the people, places, or things that the sentence is about, and `Predicate` is the central assertion made by the sentence. The principal functor, `statement` or `question`, of course identifies the type of sentence.

The items in `EntityList` represent meanings of noun phrases. We assume that every noun phrase refers to a subset of the things that exist in the world — specifically, to the thing or things that meet particular conditions. We therefore represent entities as structures of the form:

`entity(Variable,Determiner,Conditions)`

Here `Variable` is a unique variable that identifies the entity; if the entity has a name, the variable is instantiated to that name. `Determiner` is the determiner that introduces the noun phrase; in this subset of English, the only determiners are a and null. Finally, `Conditions` is a Prolog goal specifying conditions that the entity must meet. Here are a few examples:

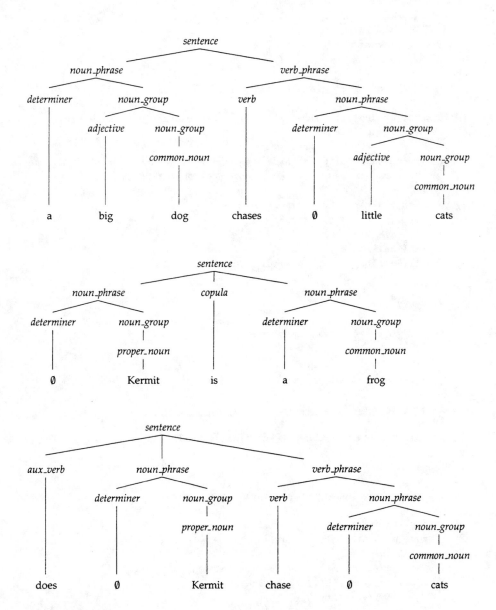

Figure 12.16   Some structures that the language understander will parse.

```
% File NLU.PL
% A working natural language understander

%%%%%%%%%%%%%%%%%
% Preliminaries %
%%%%%%%%%%%%%%%%%

:- write('Loading program. Please wait...'),nl,nl.

:- ensure_loaded('tokenize.pl').      % Use reconsult if necessary.
:- ensure_loaded('readstr.pl').

% Define the ampersand (&) as a compound goal constructor
%    with narrower scope (lower precedence) than the comma.

:- op(950,xfy,&).       % syntax of &

GoalA & GoalB  :-
    call(GoalA),
    call(GoalB).        % semantics of &


%%%%%%%%%%
% Parser %
%%%%%%%%%%


%    sentence --> noun_phrase, verb_phrase.

sentence(statement([Subj|Tail],Pred)) -->
    noun_phrase(Subj),
    verb_phrase(verb_phrase([Subj|Tail],Pred)).


%    sentence --> noun_phrase, copula, noun_phrase.
%    sentence --> noun_phrase, copula, adj_phrase.

sentence(statement([NewSubj],Pred)) -->
    noun_phrase(Subj),
    copula(Cop),
    (noun_phrase(Comp) ; adj_phrase(Comp)),
    { change_a_to_null(Subj,NewSubj) },
    { NewSubj = entity(S,_,_) },
    { Comp = entity(S,_,Pred) }.
```

Figure 12.17 A Prolog program that understands a small subset of English. (Continued on following pages.)

```
%    sentence --> aux_verb, noun_phrase, verb_phrase.

sentence(question([Subj|Tail],Pred)) -->
    aux_verb(_),
    noun_phrase(Subj),
    verb_phrase(verb_phrase([Subj|Tail],Pred)).


%    sentence --> copula, noun_phrase, noun_phrase.
%    sentence --> copula, noun_phrase, adj_phrase.

sentence(question([NewSubj],Pred)) -->
    copula(Cop),
    noun_phrase(Subj),
    (noun_phrase(Comp) ; adj_phrase(Comp)),
    { change_a_to_null(Subj,NewSubj) },
    { NewSubj = entity(S,_,_) },
    { Comp = entity(S,_,Pred) }.


% change_a_to_null(+Entity,-NewEntity)
%    Special rule to change determiner 'a' to 'null'.
%    Invoked when parsing sentences with copulas so that
%    "A dog is an animal" will mean "Dogs are animals."

change_a_to_null(entity(V,a,C),entity(V,null,C)) :- !.

change_a_to_null(X,X). % if it didn't match the above


%    verb_phrase --> verb, noun_phrase.

verb_phrase(verb_phrase([Subj,Obj],Pred)) -->
    verb(V),
    noun_phrase(Obj),
    { Subj = entity(Su,_,_) },
    { Obj  = entity(Ob,_,_) },
    { Pred =.. [V,Su,Ob] }.


%    adj_phrase --> adjective.

adj_phrase(entity(X,_,Cond)) -->
    adjective(A),
    { Cond =.. [A,X] }.
```

Figure 12.17 (Continued).

```
%    noun_phrase --> determiner, noun_group.

noun_phrase(entity(X,D,Conds)) -->
    determiner(D),
    noun_group(entity(X,_,Conds)).


%    noun_group --> adjective, noun_group.

noun_group(entity(X,_,(Cond & Rest))) -->
    adjective(A),
    { Cond =.. [A,X] },
    noun_group(entity(X,_,Rest)).


%    noun_group --> common_noun.

noun_group(entity(X,_,Cond)) -->
    common_noun(N),
    { Cond =.. [N,X] }.


%    noun_group --> proper_noun.

noun_group(entity(N,_,true)) -->
    proper_noun(N).


%%%%%%%%%%%%%%%
% Vocabulary %
%%%%%%%%%%%%%%%

copula(be)           --> [is];[are].
aux_verb(do)         --> [do];[does].
determiner(a)        --> [a];[an].
determiner(null)     --> [].

verb(chase)          --> [chase];[chases].
verb(see)            --> [see];[sees].
verb(like)           --> [like];[likes].

adjective(green)     --> [green].
adjective(brown)     --> [brown].
adjective(big)       --> [big].
adjective(little)    --> [little].
```

Figure 12.17 (Continued).

```
common_noun(dog)     --> [dog];[dogs].
common_noun(cat)     --> [cat];[cats].
common_noun(frog)    --> [frog];[frogs].
common_noun(boy)     --> [boy];[boys].
common_noun(girl)    --> [girl];[girls].
common_noun(person)  --> [person];[people].
common_noun(child)   --> [child];[children].
common_noun(animal)  --> [animal];[animals].

proper_noun(cathy)   --> [cathy].
proper_noun(fido)    --> [fido].
proper_noun(felix)   --> [felix].
proper_noun(kermit)  --> [kermit].


%%%%%%%%%%%%%%%%%%%%%%%%%%%%%%%%%%%%
% Procedure to drive the parser %
%%%%%%%%%%%%%%%%%%%%%%%%%%%%%%%%%%%%

% parse(+List,-Structure)
%    parses List as a sentence, creating Structure.

parse(List,Structure) :-
    sentence(Structure,List,[]),
    !.
    % Commit to this structure, even if there
    % are untried alternatives, because we are
    % going to modify the knowledge base.

parse(List,'PARSE FAILED').
    % if the above rule failed


%%%%%%%%%%%%%%%%%%%%%%%%%%%%%%%%%%%%%
% Translation into Prolog rules %
%%%%%%%%%%%%%%%%%%%%%%%%%%%%%%%%%%%%%

% make_rule(+EntityList,+Pred,-Rule)
%    rearranges EntityList and Pred to make a Prolog-like rule,
%    which may be ill-formed (with a compound left side).

make_rule(EntityList,Pred,(Pred :- Conds)) :-
    combine_conditions(EntityList,Conds).
```

Figure 12.17 (Continued).

```
% combine_conditions(EntityList,Result)
%    combines the conditions of all the entities
%    in EntityList to make a single compound goal.

combine_conditions([entity(_,_,Cond),Rest1|Rest], Cond & RestConds) :-
    combine_conditions([Rest1|Rest],RestConds).


combine_conditions([entity(_,_,Cond)],Cond).


%%%%%%%%%%%%%%%%%%%%%%%%%%%%%%%%
% Processing of statements %
%%%%%%%%%%%%%%%%%%%%%%%%%%%%%%%%

% dummy_item(-X)
%    Creates a unique dummy individual (a structure of
%    the form dummy(N) where N is a unique number).

dummy_item(dummy(N)) :-
    retract(dummy_count(N)),
    NewN is N+1,
    asserta(dummy_count(NewN)),
    !.


dummy_count(0).


% substitute_dummies(+Det,+Elist,-NewElist)
%    Substitutes dummies for all the entities in Elist
%    whose determiners match Det and whose identifying
%    variables are not already instantiated.
%    If Det is uninstantiated, it is taken as matching
%    all determiners, not just the first one found.

substitute_dummies(Det,[Head|Tail],[NewHead|NewTail]) :-
    !,
    substitute_one(Det,Head,NewHead),
    substitute_dummies(Det,Tail,NewTail).

substitute_dummies(_,[],[]).

substitute_one(Det,entity(V,D,Conds),entity(V,D,true)) :-
    var(V),
    (var(Det) ; Det == D),
    !,
    dummy_item(V),
    assert_rule((Conds :- true)).
```

Figure 12.17 (Continued).

```
substitute_one(_,E,E).
  % for those that didn't match the above

% assert_rule(Rule)
%   Adds Rule to the knowledge base.
%   If the left side is compound, multiple rules
%   with simple left sides are created.

assert_rule(((C1 & C2) :- Premises)) :-
    !,
    Rule = (C1 :- Premises),
    message('Adding to knowledge base:'),
    message(Rule),
    assert(Rule),
    assert_rule((C2 :- Premises)).

assert_rule(Rule) :-
    % Did not match the above
    message('Adding to knowledge base:'),
    message(Rule),
    assert(Rule).


%%%%%%%%%%%%%%%%%%%%%%%%%%%%%%%
% Processing of questions %
%%%%%%%%%%%%%%%%%%%%%%%%%%%%%%%

% move_conditions_into_predicate(+Det,+E,+P,-NewE,-NewP)
%   E and P are original entity-list and predicate, respectively.
%   The procedure searches E for entities whose determiner
%   matches Det, and transfers their conditions into P.
%   Results are NewE and NewP.

move_conditions_into_predicate(Det,[E1|E2],P,[E1|NewE2],NewP) :-
    E1 \= entity(_,Det,_),
    !,
    % No change needed in this one
    move_conditions_into_predicate(Det,E2,P,NewE2,NewP).
move_conditions_into_predicate(Det,[E1|E2],P,
                                    [NewE1|NewE2],Conds & NewP) :-
    E1 = entity(V,Det,Conds),
    !,
    NewE1 = entity(V,Det,true),
    move_conditions_into_predicate(Det,E2,P,NewE2,NewP).

move_conditions_into_predicate(_,[],P,[],P).
```

Figure 12.17 (Continued).

```
% query_rule(+Rule)
%    Tests whether Rule expresses a valid generalization.
%    This procedure always succeeds.

query_rule((Conclusion :- Premises)) :-
    message('Testing generalization:'),
    message(for_all(Premises,Conclusion)),
    for_all(Premises,Conclusion),
    !,
    write('Yes.'),nl.

query_rule(_) :-
    % Above clause did not succeed
    write('No.'),nl.


% for_all(+GoalA,+GoalB)
%    Succeeds if:
%    (1) All instantiations that satisfy GoalA also satisfy GoalB,
%    (2) There is at least one such instantiation.

for_all(GoalA,GoalB) :-
    \+ (call(GoalA), \+ call(GoalB)),
    call(GoalA),
    !.


%%%%%%%%%%%%%%%%%%
% User interface %
%%%%%%%%%%%%%%%%%%

% message(+Msg)
%    Prints Msg only if message_flag(true).

message(X) :-
    message_flag(true),
    !,
    write(X),nl.

message(_).

message_flag(true).
    % Change to false to suppress messages
```

Figure 12.17 (Continued).

```
% process(+Structure)
%     Interprets and acts upon a sentence.
%     Structure is the output of the parser.

process('PARSE FAILED') :-
                write('I do not understand.'),
                nl.

process(statement(E,P)) :-
                substitute_dummies(a,E,NewE),
                make_rule(NewE,P,Rule),
                assert_rule(Rule),
                substitute_dummies(_,NewE,_).

process(question(E,P)) :-
                move_conditions_into_predicate(a,E,P,NewE,NewP),
                make_rule(NewE,NewP,Rule),
                query_rule(Rule).

% main_loop
%     Top-level loop to interact with user.

main_loop :-  repeat,
                  message(' '),
                  message('Enter a sentence:'),
                  read_str(String),nl,
                  tokenize(String,Words),
                  message('Parsing:'),
                  parse(Words,Structure),
                  message(Structure),
                  process(Structure),
                fail.


% start
%     Procedure to start the program.

start :-  write('NATURAL LANGUAGE UNDERSTANDER'),nl,
          write('Copyright 1987, 1994 Michael A. Covington'),nl,
          nl,
          write('Type sentences. Terminate by hitting Break.'),nl,
          main_loop.
```

Figure 12.17 (Continued).

a frog	=	`entity(X,a,frog(X))`
dogs	=	`entity(Y,null,dog(Y))`
Fido	=	`entity(fido,null,true)`

Here **true** serves as an "empty"condition — a goal that always succeeds and thus can be inserted where no other goal is needed. **X** and **Y** stand for unique uninstantiated variables.

The sentence *Do dogs chase a cat?* is thus represented as:

`question([entity(X,null,dog(X)),entity(Y,a,cat(X))],chase(X,Y))`

Predicates and conditions can be compound. To form compound goals, we use the ampersand, defined as an operator synonymous with the comma but with lower precedence, exactly as in Chapter 6. Some examples of compounding follow:

a big green frog	=	`entity(X,a,big(X) & green(X) & frog(X))`
little Cathy	=	`entity(cathy,null,little(cathy) & true)`

Big dogs chase little cats	=	`statement([entity(X,null,big(X) & dog(X)),`
		`            entity(Y,null,little(X) & cat(X))],`
		`    chase(X,Y))`

Notice that **true** occurs redundantly in the translation of *little Cathy*. This is because the translation of *Cathy* is `entity(cathy,null,true)`, and when *little* is added, none of the existing structure is removed. We could write more complex rules to remove redundancies such as this, but there is little point in doing so, since the extra occurrence of **true** does not affect the conditions under which the compound goal succeeds.

Exercise 12.12.1

What representation would NLU.PL use for each of the following phrases or sentences?

1. *Cathy chases a green frog.*
2. *Kermit is an animal.*
3. *Is Cathy a cat?*

12.13. CONSTRUCTING REPRESENTATIONS

Recall that if we want a parser to build a parse tree, we have to use rules such as

```
sentence(sentence(X,Y)) -->
        noun_phrase(X), verb_phrase(Y).
```

The arguments contain the same information as the rule itself; that's why the end result is a structure showing how the rules generate the sentences.

But in NLU.PL, we don't want to build a parse tree. Instead, we want to build a semantic representation. And the first rule in the grammar is therefore this:

```
sentence(statement([Subj|Tail],Pred)) -->
        noun_phrase(Subj),
        verb_phrase(verb_phrase([Subj|Tail],Pred).
```

Paraphrasing this in English: "To parse a sentence, parse a noun phrase and unify its representation with `Subj`, and then parse a verb phrase and unify its representation with `verb_phrase([Subj|Tail],Pred)`."

  To see how this works, note that the representation of a verb phrase is like that of a sentence except that most of the information about the subject is uninstantiated. For instance:

a dog   =
`entity(X,a,dog(X))`

chases a cat   =
`verb_phrase([entity(Y,Y1,Y2),entity(Z,a,cat(Z))],chase(Y,Z))`

To combine these into a sentence, we unify `Subj` first with `entity(X,a,dog(X))` and then with `entity(Y,YDet,YConds)`. This sets up the following instantiations:

```
Y = X
Y1 = a
Y2 = dog(X)
Subj = entity(X,a,dog(X))
Tail = [entity(Z,a,cat(Z))]
Pred = chase(Y,Z) = chase(X,Z)
```

And when we combine all of these, the argument of `sentence` becomes:

`statement([entity(X,a,dog(X)),entity(Z,a,cat(Z))],chase(X,Z))`

That is: "This is a statement about two entities, `X`, which is a dog, and `Z`, which is a cat. The fact being stated is `chase(X,Z)`." The parser works this way throughout; it builds representations of small units and combines them to represent larger units.

  If the sentence has a copula (*is* or *are*) rather than a verb, then its predicate comes from the noun phrase or adjective phrase that follows the copula. To parse *Fido is a dog* we first represent the constituents as follows:

 Fido   =   `entity(fido,null,true)`

 a dog   =   `entity(X,a,dog(X))`

Upon finding the copula, the parser unifies `X` with `fido` and moves the conditions of *a dog* into the predicate, creating the structure:

`statement([entity(fido,null,true)],dog(fido))`

This accounts for the fact that *a dog* is understood, in this context, as a description of Fido, not as another entity to which Fido is related in some way.

  The semantic representations must next be converted into Prolog facts, rules, or queries. This is done by the procedure **process** and various other procedures that it calls. Consider first the simple statement:

Children like animals.

```
statement([entity(X,null,child(X)),entity(Y,null,animal(Y))],
          like(X,Y))
```

From this we want to build a Prolog rule something like this:

```
like(X,Y) :- child(X) & animal(Y).
```

This is easily done: Put the predicate of the sentence on the left and the conditions of all the entities on the right. That is done by the procedures `combine_conditions` and `make_rule`.

The same procedure works for sentences with names in them. The sentence

Cathy likes Fido.

```
statement([entity(cathy,null,true),entity(fido,null,true)],
          like(cathy,fido))
```

becomes

```
like(cathy,fido) :- true & true.
```

which is correct, if slightly wordy.

Exercise 12.13.1

> What is the semantic representation for *Green frogs are animals*? What is the Prolog rule into which this statement should be translated? (Disregard dummy entities, which will be discussed in the next section.)

12.14. DUMMY ENTITIES

A problem arises when we want to translate questions. If the question refers only to individuals, it poses no problem: "Does Cathy like Fido?" can become

```
?- like(cathy,fido).
```

which is an ordinary Prolog query.

Consider, however, what happens if the question is "Does Cathy like dogs?" or a similar generalization. This could mean either "Does Cathy like all of the dogs in the knowledge base?" or "Is there a rule from which we can deduce that Cathy likes all dogs?"

To handle such questions we must make an ad hoc extension to the Prolog inference engine. Recall that in Chapter 6 we defined a predicate `for_all(Goal1,Goal2)`, which succeeds if all instantiations that satisfy `Goal1` also satisfy `Goal2` (and there is at least one such instantiation). Thus, the query

```
?- for_all(dog(X),like(cathy,X)).
```

enables us to ask whether Cathy likes all of the dogs in the knowledge base. But if, without naming any dogs, we have simply asserted, "Cathy likes dogs," the query will fail.

We can get more natural behavior by postulating dummy entities, whose names will be `dummy(0)`, `dummy(1)`, `dummy(2)`, and so on. Whenever we assert a generalization, we will also assert that there is a dummy entity to which the generalization applies. Thus, if the user types "Children like big animals," we will assert not only

```
like(X,Y) :- child(X) & big(Y) & animal(Y).
```

but also

```
child(dummy(0)).
animal(dummy(1)).
big(dummy(1)).
```

That is, if we say that children like big animals, we will assert that there exists at least one child and at least one big animal. As a result, if we later ask "Do children like big animals?" or even "Do children like animals?" we will get an affirmative answer.

Dummy entities also provide a way to deal with the determiner *a*. When we say "Cathy likes a dog," we are asserting that there is a dog and that Cathy likes it:

```
dog(dummy(2)).
like(cathy,dummy(2)).
```

Similarly, when we translate "A dog chases a cat," we will assert that there is a dummy dog and a dummy cat and that the dog chases the cat:

```
dog(dummy(3)).
cat(dummy(4)).
chase(dummy(3),dummy(4)).
```

Dummy entities are inserted into statements by the procedure `substitute_dummies`, which creates dummies for all the entities with a particular determiner. As an example, consider how we process the statement:

Dogs chase a little cat.

```
statement([entity(X,null,dog(X)),entity(Y,a,little(Y) & cat(Y))],
          chase(X,Y))
```

First, `substitute_dummies` searches for entities whose determiner is *a*. It instantiates their identifying variables to unique values and asserts their conditions. Thus, in this step, we instantiate Y to `dummy(5)`, make the assertions

```
little(dummy(5)).
cat(dummy(5)).
```

and change the representation of the sentence to:

```
statement([entity(X,null,dog(X)),entity(dummy(5),a,true)],
          chase(X,dummy(5)))
```

In effect, we have changed the sentence to "Dogs chase `dummy(5)`" and asserted that `dummy(5)` is a little cat.[1]

Next we turn the representation into a Prolog rule in the normal manner, and assert it:

```
chase(X,dummy(5)) :- dog(X) & true.
```

Finally, we need to ensure that there is some individual to which this generalization applies, so we make another pass through the representation, this time picking up all the entities that remain. `X` is still uninstantiated, so we can instantiate it to `dummy(6)` and assert:

```
dog(dummy(6)).
```

This gives the expected behavior with queries that use `for_all`. In fact, we use `for_all` to process all questions, not just those that involve generalizations. If we ask, "Is Fido a dog?" the query that we generate is

```
?- for_all(true,dog(fido)).
```

which is trivially equivalent to `?- dog(fido)`.

The actual process of translating a question into Prolog is simple. Given a question such as

Does a dog chase Felix?

```
question([entity(X,a,dog(X)),entity(felix,null,true)],
         chase(X,felix))
```

the first step is to move into the predicate the conditions of all the entities whose determiner is *a*. (These are the ones that we want to have implicit existential rather than universal quantifiers in Prolog.) The result is:

```
question([entity(X,a,true),entity(felix,null,true)],
         chase(X,felix) & dog(X))
```

Next we transform the representation into a Prolog rule using the same procedure as if it were a statement:

```
chase(X,felix) & dog(X) :- true.
```

But instead of adding the rule to the knowledge base, we pass it to the procedure `query_rule`, which transforms it into a query that uses `for_all`:

```
?- for_all(true,chase(X,felix) & dog(X)).
```

This query succeeds if the answer to the question is yes.

---

[1]Logicians will recognize that this use of dummy entities is a crude form of SKOLEMIZATION, the elimination of the quantifier ∃ by replacing each ∃-bound variable with a function. In our examples this function has no arguments and can be viewed as a constant; in more complex cases, the Skolem function would have all unbound variables as arguments.

Exercise 12.14.1   (small project)

Get NLU.PL running and modify it to handle sentences with the determiner *every,* such as *Every dog chases every cat* and *Does every dog chase a cat?*

Exercise 12.14.2   (small project)

Modify NLU.PL so that it can answer WH-questions such as *Who saw the cat?*

Exercise 12.14.3   (project)

Using techniques from NLU.PL, construct a practical natural language interface for a database that is available to you.

12.15. BIBLIOGRAPHICAL NOTES

See Covington (1994) for much more extensive coverage of natural language processing in Prolog. NLP is a large field, comprising many rival theories and methodologies. Allen (1987) surveys NLP comprehensively; Grishman (1986) gives a good brief overview; and Grosz et al. (1986) reprint many classic papers. Readers who are not familiar with linguistics may want to read Fromkin and Rodman (1993) to learn the terminology and basic concepts.

Chomsky (1957) is still, in many ways, the best introduction to generative grammar, though the specific theory presented there is obsolete; Newmeyer (1983, 1986) chronicles the development of later theories and surveys their conclusions. Sells (1985) gives lucid expositions of three current generative formalisms.

Pereira and Shieber (1987) specifically address the use of Prolog in natural language processing; they presume more knowledge of linguistics than of logic programming. Dahl and Saint-Dizier (1985, 1988) present collections of articles on NLP applications of Prolog. Other important articles on this topic include Pereira and Warren (1980), Pereira (1981), Warren and Pereira (1982), Dahl and McCord (1983), and Matsumoto, Tanaka, and Kiyono (1986). In addition, Shieber (1986) describes several kinds of generative grammar in which unification plays a crucial role.

Appendix A

Summary of ISO Prolog

This appendix is a summary of the 1995 ISO standard for the Prolog language, ISO/IEC 13211-1:1995 ("Prolog: Part 1, General core"). As this is written (September 1995), standard-conforming Prolog implementations are just beginning to appear.[1] Section A.9 summarizes the August 1995 proposal for implementing modules ("Prolog: Part 2, Modules — Working Draft 8.1," ISO/IEC JTC1 SC22 WG17 N142); this is not yet an official standard and is subject to change.

The information given here is only a sketch; anyone needing definitive details is urged to consult the ISO documents themselves.

The ISO standard does not include definite-clause grammars (DCGs), nor the Edinburgh file-handling predicates (`see, seen, tell, told`, etc.). Implementors are, however, free to keep these for compatibility, and nothing that conflicts with them has been introduced.

The standard does not presume that you are using the ASCII character set. The numeric codes for characters can be whatever your computer uses.

---

[1]A draft of this appendix was circulated by Internet; I want to thank Jan Burse, Jo Calder, Klaus Daessler, Markus Fromherz, Fergus Henderson, Andreas Kagedal, Koen de Bosschere, Paul Holmes-Higgin, and especially Roger Scowen for pointing out errors and making helpful suggestions.

A.1. SYNTAX OF TERMS

A.1.1. Comments and Whitespace

Whitespace ("layout text") consists of blanks, end-of-line marks, and comments. Implementations commonly treat tabs and formfeeds as equivalent to blanks.

You can put whitespace before or after any term, operator, bracket, or argument separator, as long as you do not break up an atom or number and do not separate a functor from the opening parenthesis that introduces its argument list. Thus f(a,b,c) can be written f(a , b , c), but there cannot be whitespace between f and (.

Whitespace is sometimes required, for example between two graphic tokens. For example, * * is two occurrences of the atom *, but ** is one atom. Also, whitespace is required after the period that marks the end of a term.

There are two types of comments. One type begins with /* and ends with */; the other type begins with % and ends at the end of the line. Comments can be of zero length (e.g., /**/).

It is not possible to nest comments of the same type (for example, /* /* */ is a complete, valid comment). But a comment of one type can occur in a comment of the other type (/* % thus */).

STYLE NOTE: Because nesting is not permitted, we recommend using % for ordinary comments and using /* */ only to comment out sections of code.

A.1.2. Variables

A variable name begins with a capital letter or the underscore mark (_) and consists of letters, digits, and/or underscores. A single underscore mark denotes an anonymous variable.

A.1.3. Atoms (Constants)

There are four types of atoms:

- A series of letters, digits, and/or underscores, beginning with a lowercase letter.

- A series of 1 or more characters from the set

$$ \# \ \$ \ \& \ * \ + \ - \ . \ / \ : \ < \ = \ > \ ? \ @ \ \char`\^ \ \char`\~ \ \backslash $$

  provided it does not begin with '/*' and is not a period followed by whitespace. Such atoms are called GRAPHIC TOKENS.

- The special atoms [] and {} (see Section A.1.6 below).

- A series of arbitrary characters in single quotes.

Within single quotes, a single quote is written double (e.g., 'don''t panic'). A backslash at the very end of the line denotes continuation to the next line, so that

```
'this is \
 an atom'
```

is equivalent to `'this is an atom'` (that is, the line break is ignored). Note however that when used this way, the backslash must be at the physical end of the line, not followed by blanks or comments. (In practice, some implementations are going to have to permit blanks because it is hard or impossible to get rid of them.)[2]

Another use of the backslash within a quoted atom is to denote special characters, as follows:

`\a`	alert character (usually the beep code, ASCII 7)
`\b`	backspace character
`\f`	formfeed character
`\n`	newline character or code (implementation dependent)
`\r`	return without newline
`\t`	(horizontal) tab character
`\v`	vertical tab character (if any)
`\x23\`	character whose code is hexadecimal 23 (using any number of hex digits)
`\23\`	character whose code is octal 23 (using any number of octal digits)
`\\`	backslash
`\'`	single quote
`\"`	double quote
`` \` ``	backquote

The last two of these will never be needed in a quoted atom. They are used in other types of strings that take these same escape sequences, but are delimited by double quotes or backquotes.

A.1.4. Numbers

Integers are written in any of the following ways:

- As a series of decimal digits, for example `012345`;

- As a series of octal digits preceded by `0o`, such as `0o567`;

- As a series of hexadecimal digits preceded by `0x`, such as `0x89ABC`;

- As a series of binary digits preceded by `0b`, such as `0b10110101`;

- As a character preceded by `0'`, such as `0'a`, which denotes the numeric code for the character a. (The character is written exactly as if it were in single quotes; that is, if it is a single quote it must be written twice, and an escape sequence such as `\n` is treated as a single character.)

---

[2]A line break written as such cannot be part of the atom; for example,
```
'this and
that'
```
is not a valid atom. Instead, use the escape sequence `\n`.

Floating-point numbers are written only in decimal. They consist of at least one digit, then (optionally) a decimal point and more digits, then (optionally) E, an optional plus or minus, and still more digits. For example:

234   2.34   2.34E5   2.34E+5   2.34E-10

Note that .234 and 2. are not valid numbers.

A minus sign can be written before any number to make it negative (e.g., -3.4). Notice that this minus sign is part of the number itself; hence -3.4 is a number, not an expression.

A.1.5. Character Strings

The ISO standard provides four ways of representing character-string data:

- As atoms ('like this'). Unfortunately, atoms take up space in the symbol table, and some implementations limit the size of each atom, or the total number of atoms, or both. The standard itself does not recognize any such limits.

- As lists of one-character atoms ([l,i,k,e,' ',t,h,i,s]).

- As lists of numeric codes (e.g., "abc" = [97,98,99]).

- As strings delimited by backquotes ('like this') *if* the implementor wants to implement them. No operations are defined on this type of string, and they are not required to be implemented at all.

As you might guess, these four options reflect considerable disagreement among the standardizers.

Strings written in double quotes ("like this") can be interpreted in any of three ways: as atoms, as lists of characters, or as lists of codes. The choice depends on the value of the Prolog flag double_quotes, which can be set by the user (see A.5 below). The standard does not specify a default, but we expect that most implementors will adopt lists of codes as the default, for compatibility with Edinburgh Prolog.

The quotes that delimit a string or atom, whichever kind they may be, are written double if they occur within the string ('it''s', "it""s", 'it''s'). Double quoted strings and backquoted strings recognize the same backslash escape sequences as are used in quoted atoms (Section A.1.3).

Table A.1 shows all the built-in predicates that relate to character string operations. Most perform operations on atoms or lists of characters rather than lists of numeric codes.

A.1.6. Structures

The ordinary way to write a structure is to write the functor, an opening parenthesis, a series of terms separated by commas, and a closing parenthesis: f(a,b,c). We call this FUNCTOR NOTATION, and it can be used even with functors that are normally written as operators (e.g., 2+2 = +(2,2)).

TABLE A.1 BUILT-IN PREDICATES FOR CHARACTER-STRING OPERATIONS.

`atom_length(Atom,Integer)`
> Length (in characters) of `Atom` is `Integer`.

`atom_concat(Atom1,Atom2,Atom3)`
> Concatenating `Atom1` and `Atom2` gives `Atom3`. (Either `Atom3`, or both `Atom1` and `Atom2`, must be instantiated.)

`sub_atom(Atom,NB,L,NA,Sub)`
> Succeeds if `Atom` can be broken into three pieces consisting of `NB`, `L`, and `NA` characters respectively, where `L` is the length of substring `Sub`. Here `Atom` must be instantiated; the other arguments enjoy full interchangeability of unknowns and give multiple solutions upon backtracking.

`char_code(Char,Code)`
> Relates a character (i.e., a one-character atom) to its numeric code (ASCII, or whatever the computer uses). (Either `Char` or `Code`, or both, must be instantiated.)

`atom_chars(Atom,Chars)`
> Interconverts atoms with lists of the characters that represent them, as in `atom_chars(abc,[a,b,c])`. (Either `Atom` or `Chars`, or both, must be instantiated.)

`atom_codes(Atom,String)`
> Like `atom_chars`, but uses a list of numeric codes, i.e., a string.

`number_chars(Num,Chars)`
> Interconverts numbers with lists of the characters that represent them, as in `number_chars(23.4,['2','3','.','4'])`. (Either `Num` or `Chars`, or both, must be instantiated.)

`number_codes(Num,String)`
> Like `number_chars`, but uses a list of numeric codes, i.e., a string.

These predicates raise error conditions if an argument is the wrong type. Note that `name/2` is not included in the standard.

TABLE A.2   PREDEFINED OPERATORS OF ISO PROLOG.

Priority	Specifier	Operators
1200	xfx	:- -->
1200	fx	:- ?-
1100	xfy	;
1050	xfy	->
1000	xfy	,
900	fy	\+
700	xfx	= \= == \== @< @=< @> @>= is =:= =\= < =< > >= =..
600	xfy	: (not yet official; for module system)
500	yfx	+ - /\ \/
400	yfx	* / // rem mod << >>
200	xfx	**
200	xfy	^
200	fy	\ -

Lists are defined as rightward-nested structures using the functor '.' (which is not an infix operator). For example,

```
[a]         =  .(a, [])
[a, b]      =  .(a, .(b, []))
[a, b | c]  =  .(a, .(b, c))
```

There can be only one | in a list, and no commas after it.

    Curly brackets have a special syntax that is used in implementing definite clause grammars, but can also be used for other purposes. Any term enclosed in { } is treated as the argument of the special functor '{}':

```
{one}  =  {}(one)
```

Recall that commas can act as infix operators; thus,

```
{one,two,three} = {}(','(one,','(two,three)))
```

and likewise for any number of terms.

    The standard does not include definite clause grammars, but does include this syntactic "hook" for implementing them. You are, of course, free to use curly brackets for any other purpose.

A.1.7. Operators

The predefined operators of ISO Prolog are shown in Table A.2. The meanings of the operators will be explained elsewhere in this appendix as they come up; : is to be used in the module system (Part 2 of the standard, not yet official). Some operators, such as ?- and -->, are not given a meaning in the standard, but are preserved for compatibility reasons.

The SPECIFIER of an operator, such as **xfy**, gives both its CLASS (infix, prefix, or postfix) and its ASSOCIATIVITY. Associativity determines what happens if there are two infix operators of equal priority on either side of an argument. For example, in 2+3+4, 3 could be an argument of either the first or the second +, and the associativity **yfx** specifies that the grouping on the left should be formed first, treating 2+3+4 as equivalent to (2+3)+4. The Prolog system parses an expression by attaching operators to their arguments, starting with the operators of the lowest priority, thus:

```
2 + 3 * 4 =:= X          (original expression)
2 + *(3,4) =:= X         (after attaching *, priority 400)
+(2,*(3,4)) =:= X        (after attaching +, priority 500)
=:=(+(2,*(3,4)),X)       (after attaching =:=, priority 700)
```

Terms that are not operators are considered to have priority 0.

The same atom can be an operator in more than one class (such as the infix and prefix minus signs). To avoid the need for unlimited lookahead when parsing, the same atom cannot be both an infix operator and a postfix operator.

A.1.8. Commas

The comma has three functions: it separates arguments of functors, it separates elements of lists, and it is an infix operator of priority 1000. Thus (a,b) (without a functor in front) is a structure, equivalent to ','(a,b).

A.1.9. Parentheses

Parentheses are allowed around any term. The effect of parentheses is to override any grouping that may otherwise be imposed by operator priorities. Operators enclosed in parentheses do not function as operators; thus 2(+)2 is a syntax error.

A.2. PROGRAM STRUCTURE

A.2.1. Programs

The standard does not define "programs" per se, because Prolog is not a (wholly) procedural language. Rather, the standard defines PROLOG TEXT, which consists of a series of clauses and/or directives, each followed by '.' and then whitespace.

The standard does not define **consult** or **reconsult**; instead, the mechanism for loading and querying a Prolog text is left up to the implementor.

A.2.2. Directives

The standard defines the following set of directives (declarations):

```
:- dynamic(Pred/Arity).
```
    The specified predicate is to be dynamic (modifiable at run time). (See also Section A.9.) This directive can also be written

```
:- dynamic([Pred/Arity,Pred/Arity...]). or
:- dynamic((Pred/Arity,Pred/Arity...)).
```
to declare more than one predicate at once.

```
:- multifile(Pred/Arity).
```
The specified predicate can contain clauses loaded from more than one file. (The `multifile` declaration must appear in each of the files, and if the predicate is declared dynamic in any of the files, it must be declared dynamic in all of them.) This directive can also be written
```
:- multifile([Pred/Arity,Pred/Arity...]). or
:- multifile((Pred/Arity,Pred/Arity...)).
```
to declare more than one predicate at once.

```
:- discontiguous(Pred/Arity).
```
The clauses of the specified predicate are not necessarily together in the file. (If this declaration is not given, the clauses of each predicate are required to be contiguous.) This directive can also be written
```
:- discontiguous([Pred/Arity,Pred/Arity...]). or
:- discontiguous((Pred/Arity,Pred/Arity...)).
```
to declare more than one predicate at once.

```
:- op(Priority,Associativity,Atom).
```
The atom is to be treated syntactically as an operator with the specified priority and associativity (e.g., `xfy`).

CAUTION: An **op** directive in the program file affects the syntax while the program is being loaded; the standard does not require that its effect persist after the loading is complete. Traditionally, an **op** declaration permanently changes the syntax used by the Prolog system (until the end of the session), thus affecting all further **reads**, **writes**, and **consults**; the standard permits but does not require this behavior. See also Section A.9.

However, **op** can also be called as a built-in predicate while the program is running, thereby determining how **read** and **write** will behave at run time.

Any operator except the comma can be deprived of its operator status by declaring it to have priority 0 (in which case its class and associativity have no effect, but must still be declared as valid values).

```
:- char_conversion(Char1,Char2).
```
This specifies that if character conversion is enabled (see "Flags," Section A.5), all occurrences of `Char1` that are not in quotes should be read as `Char2`. Note that, to avoid painting yourself into a corner, you should normally put the arguments of `char_conversion` in quotes so that they won't be subject to conversion.

The situation with `char_conversion` is analogous to **op** — the standard does not require its effect to persist after the program finishes loading. However, you can also call `char_conversion` as a built-in predicate at execution time, to determine how characters will be converted at run time.

```
:- set_prolog_flag(Flag,Value).
```
Sets the value of a Prolog flag (see Section A.5). As with `char_conversion`,

it is up to the implementor whether the effect persists after the program finishes loading, but you can also call `set_prolog_flag` as a built-in predicate at execution time.

`:- initialization(Goal).`

This specifies that as soon as the program is loaded, the goal `Goal` is to be executed. There can be more than one `initialization` directive, in which case all of the goals in all of them are to be executed, in an order that is up to the implementor.

`:- include(File).`

Specifies that another file is to be read at this point exactly as if its contents were in the main file. (Apparently, a predicate split across two files using `include` does not require a `multifile` declaration, since the loading is all done at once.)

`:- ensure_loaded(File).`

Specifies that in addition to the main file, the specified file is to be loaded. If there are multiple `ensure_loaded` directives referring to the same file, it is only loaded once.

Note that *directives are not queries* — the standard does not say you can embed arbitrary queries in your program, nor that you can execute directives as queries at run time (except for `op`, `char_conversion`, and `set_prolog_flag`, which are, explicitly, also built-in predicates). Traditionally, directives have been treated as a kind of query, but the standard, with advancing compiler technology in mind, does not require them to be.

A.3. CONTROL STRUCTURES

A.3.1. Conjunction, Disjunction, `fail`, and `true`

As in virtually all Prologs, the comma (`,`) means "and," the semicolon (`;`) means "or," `fail` always fails, and `true` always succeeds with no other action.

A.3.2. Cuts

The cut (`!`) works in the traditional way. When executed, it succeeds and throws away all backtrack points between itself and its CUTPARENT. Normally, the cutparent is the query that caused execution to enter the current clause. However, if the cut is in an environment that is OPAQUE TO CUTS, the cutparent is the beginning of that environment. Examples of environments that are opaque to cuts are:

- The argument of the negation operator (`\+`).

- The argument of `call`, which can of course be a compound goal, such as `call((this,!,that))`.

- The left-hand argument of '`->`' (see below).

- The goals that are arguments of once, catch, findall, bagof, and setof (and, in general, any other goals that are arguments of predicates).

A.3.3. If-Then-Else

The "if-then-else" construct (Goal1 -> Goal2 ; Goal3) tries to execute Goal1, and, if successful, proceeds to Goal2; otherwise, it proceeds to Goal3. The semicolon and Goal3 can be omitted. Note that:

- Only the first solution to Goal1 is found; any backtrack points generated while executing Goal1 are thrown away.

- If Goal1 succeeds, execution proceeds to Goal2, and then:
  - If Goal2 fails, the whole construct fails.
  - If Goal2 succeeds, the whole construct succeeds.
  - If Goal2 has multiple solutions, the whole construct has multiple solutions.

- If Goal1 fails, execution proceeds to Goal3, and then:
  - If Goal3 fails, the whole construct fails.
  - If Goal3 succeeds, the whole construct succeeds.
  - If Goal3 has multiple solutions, the whole construct has multiple solutions.

- If Goal1 fails and there is no Goal3, the whole construct fails.

- Either Goal2 or Goal3 will be executed, but not both (not even upon backtracking).

- If Goal1 contains a cut, that cut only has scope over Goal1, not the whole clause. That is, Goal1 is opaque to cuts.

- The whole if-then-else structure has multiple solutions if Goal1 succeeds and Goal2 has multiple solutions, or if Goal1 fails and Goal3 has multiple solutions. That is, backtrack points in Goal2 and Goal3 behave normally.

- Cuts in Goal2 and Goal3 have scope over the entire clause (i.e., behave normally).

Note that the semicolon in Goal1 -> Goal2 ; Goal3 is not the ordinary disjunction operator; if it were, you would be able to get solutions to Goal1 -> Goal2 and then, upon backtracking, also get solutions to Goal3. But this never happens. Rather, -> and ; have to be interpreted as a unit.

STYLE NOTE: We do not recommend mixing cuts with if-then or if-then-else structures.

A.3.4. Variable Goals, call

Variables can be used as goals. A term G which is a variable occurring in place of a goal is converted to the goal call(G). Note that call is opaque to cuts.

A.3.5. `repeat`

The predicate `repeat` works in the traditional way, that is, whenever backtracking reaches it, execution proceeds forward again through the same clauses as if another alternative had been found.

A.3.6. `once`

The query `once(Goal)` finds exactly one solution to `Goal`. It is equivalent to `call((Goal,!))` and is opaque to cuts.

A.3.7. Negation

The negation predicate is written `\+` and is opaque to cuts. That is, `\+ Goal` is like `call(Goal)` except that its success or failure is the opposite. Note that extra parentheses are required around compound goals (e.g., `\+ (this, that)`).

A.4. ERROR HANDLING

A.4.1. `catch` and `throw`

The control structures `catch` and `throw` are provided for handling errors and other explicitly programmed exceptions. They make it possible to jump out of multiple levels of procedure calls in a single step.

The query `catch(Goal1,Arg,Goal2)` is like `call(Goal1)` except that if, at any stage during the execution of `Goal1`, there is a call to `throw(Arg)`, then execution will immediately jump back to the `catch` and proceed to `Goal2`. Here `Arg` can be a variable or only partly instantiated; the only requirement is that the `Arg` in the `catch` must match the one in the `throw`. Thus, `Arg` can include information to tell `catch` what happened.

In `catch`, `Goal1` and `Goal2` are opaque to cuts.

A.4.2. Errors Detected by the System

When the system detects a runtime error, it executes `throw(error(ErrorType,Info))`, where `ErrorType` is the type of error and `Info` contains other information that is up to the implementor.

If the user's program has executed a matching `catch`, execution jumps back to there; otherwise, the system prints out an error message and stops. Thus, you can use `catch` to catch system-detected errors, not just your own calls to `throw`.

The possible values of `ErrorType` are:

`instantiation_error`
An argument was uninstantiated in a place where uninstantiated arguments are not permitted.

type_error(Type,Term)
>   An argument should have been of type Type (atom, body (of clause), callable (goal), character, compound (= structure), evaluable (arithmetic expression), integer, list, number, etc., as the case may be), but Term is what was actually found.

domain_error(Domain,Term)
>   Like type_error, except that a DOMAIN is a set of possible values, rather than a basic data type. Examples are character_code_list and stream_or_alias. Again, Term is the argument that caused the error.

existence_error(ObjType,Term)
>   Something does not exist that is necessary for what the program is trying to do, such as reading from a nonexistent file. Here, again, Term is the argument that caused the error.

permission_error(Operation,ObjType,Term)
>   The program attempted something that is not permissible (such as repositioning a nonrepositionable file). Term and ObjType are as in the previous example, and Operation is access_clause, create, input, modify, or the like. Reading past end of file gets a permission_error(input,past_end_of_stream,Term).

representation_error(Error)
>   An implementation-defined limit has been violated, for example by trying to handle 'ab' as a single character. The possible values of Error are character, character_code, in_character_code, max_arity, max_integer, or min_integer.

evaluation_error(Error)
>   An arithmetic error has occurred. Types are float_overflow, int_overflow, underflow, zero_divisor, and undefined.

resource_error(Resource)
>   The system has run out of some resource (such as memory or disk space).

syntax_error(Message)
>   The system has attempted to read a term that violates Prolog syntax. This can occur during program loading, or at run time (executing read or read_term).

system_error
>   This is the catchall category for other implementation-dependent errors.

For further details see the latest ISO documents.

A.5. FLAGS

A FLAG is a parameter of the implementation that the program may need to know about. Programs can obtain and, where applicable, change flags by using the built-in predicates current_prolog_flag(Flag,Value) and set_prolog_flag(Flag,Value).

Table A.3 lists the flags defined in the standard. Any specific implementation is likely to have many more.

TABLE A.3   FLAGS DEFINED IN THE ISO PROLOG STANDARD.

`bounded` (`true` or `false`)

> True if integer arithmetic gives erroneous results outside a particular range (as when you add $32767 + 1$ on a 16-bit computer and get -32768). False if the range of available integers is unlimited (as with Lisp "bignums").

`max_integer` (an integer)

> The greatest integer on which arithmetic works correctly. Defined only if `bounded` is true.

`min_integer` (an integer)

> The least integer on which arithmetic works correctly. Defined only if `bounded` is true.

`integer_rounding_function` (`down` or `toward_zero`)

> The direction in which negative numbers are rounded by `//` and `rem`.

`char_conversion` (`on` or `off`)

> Controls whether character conversion is enabled. Can be set by the program.

`debug` (`on` or `off`)

> Controls whether the debugger is in use (if so, various predicates may behave nonstandardly). Can be set by the program.

`max_arity` (an integer or `unbounded`)

> The maximum permissible arity for functors.

`unknown` (`error`, `fail`, or `warning`)

> Controls what happens if an undefined predicate is called. Can be set by the program.

`double_quotes` (`chars`, `codes`, or `atom`)

> Determines how strings delimited by double quotes (`"like this"`) are interpreted upon input: as lists of characters, lists of codes, or atoms. The standard specifies no default, but most implementors are expected to choose `codes` for Edinburgh compatibility.

TABLE A.4   FUNCTORS THAT CAN BE USED IN ARITHMETIC EXPRESSIONS.

`N + N`	Addition
`N - N`	Subtraction
`N * N`	Multiplication
`N / N`	Floating-point division
`I // I`	Integer division
`I rem I`	Remainder
`I mod I`	Modulo
`N ** N`	Exponentiation (result is floating-point)
`-N`	Sign reversal
`abs(N)`	Absolute value
`atan(N)`	Arctangent (in radians)
`ceiling(N)`	Smallest integer not smaller than `N`
`cos(N)`	Cosine (argument in radians)
`exp(N)`	Natural antilogarithm, e^N
`sqrt(N)`	Square root
`sign(N)`	Sign (-1, 0, or 1 for negative, zero, or positive `N`)
`float(N)`	Convert to floating-point
`float_fractional_part(X)`	Fractional part of `X` (negative if `X` is negative)
`float_integer_part(X)`	Integer part of `X` (negative if `X` is negative)
`floor(X)`	Largest integer not greater than `X`
`log(N)`	Natural logarithm, $\log_e N$
`sin(N)`	Sine (argument in radians)
`truncate(X)`	Integer equal to the integer part of `X`
`round(X)`	Integer nearest to `X`
`I >> J`	Bit-shift `I` rightward `J` bits
`I << J`	Bit-shift `I` leftward `J` bits
`I /\ J`	Bitwise **and** function
`I \/ J`	Bitwise **or** function
`\ I`	Bitwise complement (reverse all bits of `I`)

Here `I` and `J` denote integers, `X` denotes floating-point numbers, and `N` denotes numbers of either type.

A.6. ARITHMETIC

A.6.1. Where Expressions are Evaluated

Arithmetic expressions are evaluated in the following contexts:

- The right-hand argument of is (e.g., **X** is 2+3).

- Both arguments of the comparison predicates =:= =\= < > =< >=.

A.6.2. Functors Allowed in Expressions

The EVALUABLE FUNCTORS that are permitted in expressions are listed in Table A.4.

The arithmetic system of the ISO standard is based on other ISO standards for computer arithmetic; see the standard itself for full details. The Prolog standard requires all arithmetical operations to give computationally reasonable results or raise error conditions.

A.7. INPUT AND OUTPUT

A.7.1. Overview

Except for `read`, `write`, `writeq`, and `nl`, the traditional Edinburgh input-output predicates are not included in the standard. Instead, a new, very versatile i-o system is presented. Here is a simple example of file output:

```
test :- open('/usr/mcovingt/myfile.txt',write,MyStream,[type(text)]),
        write_term(MyStream,'Hello, world',[quoted(true)]),
        close(MyStream,[force(false)]).
```

Notice that each input-output operation can name a STREAM (an open file) and can give an OPTION LIST. To take the defaults, the option lists can be empty, and in some cases even omitted:

```
test :- open('/usr/mcovingt/myfile.txt',write,MyStream,[]),
        write_term(MyStream,'Hello, world',[]),
        close(MyStream).
```

A.7.2. Opening a Stream

A STREAM is an open file (or other file-like object) that can be read or written sequentially. You can refer to a stream either by its HANDLE (an implementation-dependent term that gets instantiated when you open the stream) or its ALIAS (a name that you give to the stream).

By default, the streams `user_input` and `user_output` are already open, referring to the keyboard and the screen respectively, and are the current input and output streams. But current input and output can be redirected.

To open a stream, use the predicate `open(Filename,Mode,Stream,Options)`, where:

- `Filename` is an implementation-dependent file designator (normally a Prolog atom);

- `Mode` is `read`, `write`, or `append`;

- `Stream` is a variable that will be instantiated to an implementation-dependent "handle";

- `Options` is an option list, possibly empty.

The contents of the option list can include:

- `type(text)` (the default) or `type(binary)`. A text file consists of printable characters arranged into lines; a binary file contains any data whatsoever, and is read byte by byte.

- `reposition(true)` or `reposition(false)` (the default). A repositionable stream (e.g., a disk file) is one in which it is possible to skip forward or backward to specific positions.

- `alias(Atom)` to give the stream a name. For example, if you specify the option `alias(accounts_receivable)`, you can write `accounts_receivable` as the `Stream` argument of subsequent operations on this stream.

- A specification of what to do upon repeated attempts to read past end of file:

  - `eof_action(error)` to raise an error condition;
  - `eof_action(eof_code)` to make each attempt return the same code that the first one did (e.g., −1 or `end_of_file`); or
  - `eof_action(reset)`, to examine the file again and see if it is now possible to read past what used to be the end (e.g., because of data written by another concurrent process).

Somewhat surprisingly, the standard specifies no default for this option.

Implementors are free to add other options.

A.7.3. Closing a Stream

The predicate `close(Stream,Options)` closes a stream; `close(Stream)` is equivalent if the option list is empty.

The option list can include `force(false)` (the default) or `force(true)`; the latter of these says that if there is an error upon closing the stream (e.g., a diskette not in the drive), the system shall assume that the stream was successfully closed anyway, without raising an error condition.

A.7.4. Stream Properties

The predicate `stream_property(Stream,Property)` lets you determine the properties of any currently open stream, like this:

```
?- stream_property(user_input,mode(What)).
What = read
```

Properties include the following:

- `file_name(...)`, the file name;

- `mode(M)`, where `M` is `input` or `output`;

- `alias(A)`, where `A` is the stream's alias, if any;

- `position(P)`, where P is an implementation-dependent term giving the current position of the stream;

- `end_of_stream(E)`, where E is at, past, or no, to indicate whether reading has just reached end of file, has gone past it, or has not reached it.

- `eof_action(A)`, where A is as in the options for open.

- `reposition(B)`, where B is true or false to indicate repositionability.

- `type(T)`, where T is text or binary.

Implementations are free to define other properties.

A.7.5. Reading and Writing Characters

Tables A.5 and A.6 summarize the input-output predicates that deal with single characters. The char and code predicates are for text files and the byte predicates are for binary files.

The standard *does not specify whether keyboard input is buffered or unbuffered*; that is considered to be an implementation-dependent matter.

A.7.6. Reading Terms

Table A.7 shows the predicates for reading terms. Each of them reads a term from a text stream; the term must be followed by a period and then by whitespace, and must conform to Prolog syntax.

A new feature in the standard gives you some access to the variables in the input. Traditionally, if you read a term with variables in it, such as f(X,Y,X), then you get a term in which the relative positions of the variables are preserved, but the names are not, such as f(_0001,_0002,_0001).

Now, however, by specifying the option `variable_names(List)`, you can also get a list that pairs up the variables with their names, like this:

```
?- read_term(Term, [variable_names(Vars)]).
f(X,Y,X).  (typed by user)
Term = f(_0001,_0002,_0001)
Vars = [_0001='X',_0002='Y']
```

The import of this is that it lets you write your own user interface for the Prolog system (or any Prolog-like query processor). You can accept a query, store a list that gives the names of its variables, and then eventually print out the names alongside the values.

There are also two less elaborate options. The option `singletons(List)` gives you a list, in the same format, of just the variables that occurred only once in the term — useful if you're reading Prolog clauses and want to detect misspelled variable names. And `variables(List)` gives you a list of just the variables, without their names (such as [_0001,_0002]).

TABLE A.5 SINGLE-CHARACTER INPUT AND OUTPUT PREDICATES.

`get_char(Stream,Char)`
> Reads a character (as a one-character atom). Returns `end_of_file` at end of file.

`get_char(Char)`
> Same, using the current input stream.

`peek_char(Stream,Code)`
> Returns the next character waiting to be read, without removing it from the input stream. Returns `end_of_file` at end of file.

`peek_char(Code)`
> Same, using current input stream.

`put_char(Stream,Char)`
> Writes `Char`, which must be a one-character atom. (Equivalent to `write(Char)`, but presumably faster.)

`put_char(Char)`
> Same, using the current output stream.

`get_code(Stream,Code)`
> Reads a character as a numeric code. Returns −1 at end of file.

`get_code(Code)`
> Same, using the current input stream.

`peek_code(Stream,Code)`
> Returns the code of the next character waiting to be read, without removing it from the input stream. Returns −1 at end of file.

`peek_code(Code)`
> Same, using current input stream.

`put_code(Stream,Code)`
> Writes a character given its numeric code.

`put_code(Code)`
> Same, using the current output stream.

TABLE A.6   BINARY SINGLE-BYTE INPUT AND OUTPUT PREDICATES.

`get_byte(Stream,Code)`
>   Reads a byte as a numeric value. Returns −1 at end of file.

`get_byte(Code)`
>   Same, using current input stream.

`peek_byte(Stream,Code)`
>   Returns the numeric value of the next byte waiting to be read, without removing it from the input stream. Returns −1 at end of file.

`peek_byte(Code)`
>   Same, using current input stream.

`put_byte(Stream,Code)`
>   Writes a byte given its numeric value.

`put_byte(Code)`
>   Same, using the current output stream.

TABLE A.7   PREDICATES FOR READING TERMS.

`read_term(Stream,Term,Options)`
>   Reads a term from `Stream` using options in list.

`read_term(Term,Options)`
>   Same, using current input stream.

`read(Stream,Term)`
>   Like `read_term(Stream,Term,[])`.

`read(Term)`
>   Like `read_term(Term,[])`.

All of these return the atom `end_of_file` at end of file.

TABLE A.8 PREDICATES FOR WRITING TERMS.

`write_term(Stream,Term,Options)`
    Outputs a term onto a text stream using the option list.
`write_term(Term,Options)`
    Same, using the current output stream.
`write(Stream,Term)`
    Like `write_term(Stream,Term,[numbervars(true)])`.
`write(Term)`
    Same, using the current output stream.
`write_canonical(Stream,Term)`
    Like `write_term` with the options `[quoted(true), ignore_ops(true)]`.
`write_canonical(Term)`
    Same, using current output stream.
`writeq(Stream,Term)`
    Like `write_term` with the options `[quoted(true), numbervars(true)]`.
`writeq(Term)`
    Same, using current output stream.

A.7.7. Writing Terms

Table A.8 lists the predicates for writing terms. The following options are available:

- `quoted(true)` puts quotes around all atoms and functors that would require them in order to be read by `read/1`.

- `ignore_ops(true)` writes all functors in functor notation, not as operators (e.g., `+(2,2)` in place of 2+2).

- `numbervars(true)` looks for terms of the form `'$VAR'(1)`, `'$VAR'(2)`, etc., and outputs them as A, B, etc.

  The significance of this is that `'$VAR'`–terms are often used to replace variables when there is a need to instantiate all the variables in a term. By printing the term out with this option, its variables can be made to look like variables again.

A.7.8. Other Input-Output Predicates

Table A.9 lists some additional input-output predicates.

A.8. OTHER BUILT-IN PREDICATES

This section briefly describes all the other built-in predicates described in the ISO standard.

TABLE A.9 MISCELLANEOUS INPUT-OUTPUT PREDICATES.

`current_input(Stream)`
  Unifies `Stream` with the handle of the current input stream.

`current_output(Stream)`
  Unifies `Stream` with the handle of the current output stream.

`set_input(Stream)`
  Redirects current input to `Stream`.

`set_output(Stream)`
  Redirects current output to `Stream`.

`flush_output(Stream)`
  Causes all output that is buffered for `Stream` to actually be written.

`flush_output`
  Same, but uses current output stream.

`at_end_of_stream(Stream)`
  True if the stream is at or past end of file (i.e., the last character or byte has been read).
  (A `read` or `read_term` does not consume any of the whitespace following the term that
  it has read, so after reading the last term on a file, the file will not necessarily be at end
  of stream.)

`at_end_of_stream`
  Same, using current input stream.

`set_stream_position(Stream,Pos)`
  Repositions a stream (use `stream_property` to obtain a term that represents a
  position).

`nl(Stream)`
  Starts a new line on `Stream` (which should be text).

`nl`
  Same, using current output stream.

`op(Priority,Specifier,Term)`
  Alters the set of operators during execution. See Sections A.1.7, A.2.2.

`current_op(Priority,Specifier,Term)`
  Determines the operator definitions that are currently in effect. Any of the arguments,
  or none, can be instantiated. Gives multiple solutions upon backtracking as
  appropriate.

`char_conversion(Char1,Char2)`
  Alters the set of character conversions during execution. See Sections A.2.2, A.5.

`current_char_conversion(Char1,Char2)`
  True if `char_conversion(Char1,Char2)` is in effect (see Sections A.2.2, A.5). Either
  argument, or none, may be instantiated. Gives multiple solutions upon backtracking.

A.8.1. Unification

`Arg1 = Arg2`
> Succeeds by unifying `Arg1` with `Arg2` in the normal manner (i.e., the same way as when arguments are matched in procedure calls). Results are undefined if you try to unify a term with another term that contains it (e.g., `X = f(X)`, or `f(X,g(X)) = f(Y,Y)`). (Commonly, such a situation produces cyclic pointers that cause endless loops when another procedure later tries to follow them.)

`unify_with_occurs_check(Arg1,Arg2)`
> Succeeds by unifying `Arg1` with `Arg2`, but explicitly checks whether this will attempt to unify any term with a term that contains it, and if so, fails:

> ```
> ?- unify_with_occurs_check(X,f(X)).
> no
> ```

> This version of unification is often assumed in work on the theory of logic programming.

`Arg1 \= Arg2`
> Succeeds if the two arguments cannot be unified (using the normal unification process).

A.8.2. Comparison

(See also the arithmetic comparison predicates < =< > >= =:= in Section A.6.)

`Arg1 == Arg2`
> Succeeds if `Arg1` and `Arg2` are the same term. Does not unify them and does not attempt to instantiate variables in them.

`Arg1 \== Arg2`
> Succeeds if `Arg1` and `Arg2` are not the same term. Does not unify them and does not attempt to instantiate variables in them.

`Arg1 @< Arg2`
> Succeeds if `Arg1` precedes `Arg2` in alphabetical order. All variables precede all floating-point numbers, which precede all integers, which precede all atoms, which precede all structures. Within terms of the same type, the alphabetical order is the collating sequence used by the computer, and shorter terms precede longer ones.

`Arg1 @=< Arg2`
> Succeeds if `Arg1 @< Arg2` or `Arg1 == Arg2`. Does not perform unification or instantiate variables.

`Arg1 @> Arg2`
> Like `@<` with the order of arguments reversed.

`Arg1 @>= Arg2`
> Like `@=<` with the order of arguments reversed.

A.8.3. Type Tests

`var(Arg)`
>   Succeeds if `Arg` is uninstantiated.

`nonvar(Arg)`
>   Succeeds if `Arg` is at least partly instantiated.

`atomic(Arg)`
>   Succeeds if `Arg` is an atom or a number.

`compound(Arg)`
>   Succeeds if `Arg` is a compound term (a structure, including lists but not []).

`atom(Arg)`
>   Succeeds if `Arg` is an atom.

`number(Arg)`
>   Succeeds if `Arg` is a number (integer or floating-point).

`integer(Arg)`
>   Succeeds if `Arg` is an integer. Note that this tests its data type, not its value. Thus `integer(3)` succeeds but `integer(3.0)` fails.

`float(Arg)`
>   Succeeds if `Arg` is a floating-point number. Like `integer`, `float` tests the data type, not the value. Thus `float(3.3)` and `float(30).` succeed but `float(3)` fails.

A.8.4. Creating and Decomposing Terms

`functor(Term,F,A)`
>   Succeeds if `Term` is a compound term, `F` is its functor, and `A` (an integer) is its arity; or if `Term` is an atom or number equal to `F` and `A` is zero. (Either `Term`, or both `F` and `A`, must be instantiated.) Some examples:

```
?- functor(f(a,b),F,A).
F = f
A = 2

?- functor(What,f,2).
What = f(_0001,_0002)

?- functor(What,f,0).
What = f

?- functor(What,3.1416,0).
What = 3.1416
```

`arg(N,Term,Arg)`
>   Succeeds if `Arg` is the Nth argument of `Term` (counting from 1):

```
?- arg(1,f(a,b,c),What).
What = a
```

Both N and Term must be instantiated.

Term =.. List

Succeeds if List is a list consisting of the functor and all arguments of Term, in order. Term or List, or both, must be at least partly instantiated.

```
?- f(a,b) =.. What.
What = [f,a,b]
```

```
?- What =.. [f,a,b]
What = f(a,b)
```

copy_term(Term1,Term2)

Makes a copy of Term1 replacing all occurrences of each variable with a fresh variable (like changing f(A,B,A) to f(W,Z,W)). Then unifies that copy with Term2.

```
?- copy_term(f(A,B,A),What).
A = _0001
B = _0002
What = f(_0003,_0004,_0003)
```

A.8.5. Manipulating the Knowledge Base

Note that *only dynamic predicates can be manipulated.* Static predicates are compiled into a form that is inaccessible to some or all of the built-in predicates described here. Nonetheless, some implementations may treat static predicates as dynamic.

clause(Head,Body)

Succeeds if Head matches the head of a dynamic predicate, and Body matches its body. The body of a fact is considered to be true. Head must be at least partly instantiated. Thus, given

```
green(X) :- moldy(X).
green(kermit).
```

we get:

```
?- clause(green(What),Body).
What = _0001, Body = moldy(_0001)  ;
What = kermit, Body = true
```

current_predicate(Functor/Arity)

Succeeds if Functor/Arity gives the functor and arity of a currently defined non-built-in predicate, whether static or dynamic:

```
?- current_predicate(What).
What = green/1
```

Gives multiple solutions upon backtracking.

Note that `current_predicate(Functor/Arity)` succeeds even if all the clauses of the predicate have been retracted (or if the predicate was declared dynamic but no clauses were ever asserted), but not if the predicate has been abolished.

`asserta(Clause)`

Adds `Clause` at the beginning of the clauses for its predicate. If there are no clauses for that predicate, the predicate is created and declared to be dynamic. If the predicate already has some clauses and is static, an error condition is raised.

`assertz(Clause)`

Like `asserta`, but adds the clause at the end of the other clauses for its predicate. *Note:* `assert` (without a or z) is not included in the standard.

`retract(Clause)`

Removes from the knowledge base a dynamic clause that matches `Clause` (which must be at least partly instantiated). Gives multiple solutions upon backtracking.

Note that the fact `green(kermit)` could be retracted by any of the following queries:

```
?- retract(green(kermit)).
?- retract((green(kermit) :- true)).
?- retract((green(_) :- _)).
```

Note: `retractall` is not included in the standard.

`abolish(Functor/Arity)`

Completely wipes out the dynamic predicate designated by `Functor/Arity`, as if it had never existed. Its dynamic declaration is forgotten, too, and `current_predicate` no longer recognizes it.

This is a more powerful move than simply retracting all the clauses, which would leave the dynamic declaration in place and leave `current_predicate` still aware of the predicate.

A.8.6. Finding All Solutions to a Query

`findall(Term,Goal,List)`

Finds each solution to `Goal`; instantiates variables to `Term` to the values that they have in that solution; and adds that instantiation of `Term` to `List`. Thus, given

```
green(kermit).
green(crabgrass).
```

we get the following results:

```
?- findall(X,green(X),L).
L = [kermit,crabgrass]
```

```
?- findall(f(X),green(X),L).
L = [f(kermit),f(crabgrass)]
```

This is the simplest way to get a list of the solutions to a query. The solutions found by findall are given in the order in which the normal searching-and-backtracking process finds them.

bagof(Term,Goal,List)

Like findall(Term,Goal,List) except for its treatment of the FREE VARIABLES of Goal (those that do not occur in Term).

Whereas findall would try all possible values of all variables, bagof will pick the first set of values for the free variables that succeeds, and use only that set of values when finding the solutions in List.

Then, if you ask for an alternative solution to bagof, you'll get the results of trying another set of values for the free variables. An example:

```
parent(michael,cathy).
parent(melody,cathy).
parent(greg,stephanie).
parent(crystal,stephanie).

?- findall(Who,parent(Who,Child),L).
L = [michael,melody,greg,crystal]

?- bagof(Who,parent(Who,Child),L).    % Child is free variable
L = [michael,melody] ;                % with Child = cathy
L = [greg,crystal]                    % with Child = stephanie
```

If in place of Goal you write Term^Goal, any variables that occur in Term will not be considered free variables. Thus:

```
?- bagof(Who,Child^parent(Who,Child),L).
L = [michael,melody,greg,crystal]
```

The order of solutions obtained by bagof is up to the implementor.

setof(Term,Goal,List)

Like bagof(Term,Goal,List), but the elements of List are sorted into alphabetical order (see @< under "Comparisons" above) and duplicates are removed.

A.8.7. Terminating Execution

halt

Exits from the Prolog system (or from a compiled program).

halt(N)

Exits from the Prolog system (or from a compiled program), passing the integer N to the operating system as a return code. (The significance of the return code depends on the operating system. For example, in MS-DOS and UNIX, return code 0 is the usual way of indicating normal termination.)

A.9. MODULES

A.9.1. Preventing Name Conflicts

Ordinarily, in a Prolog program, there cannot be two different predicates with the same name and arity. This can pose a problem when two programmers, writing different parts of the same program, inadvertently choose the same name and arity for different predicates.

The solution is to divide large programs into MODULES, or sections, each of which has its own namespace. Names defined in one module are not recognized in other modules unless explicitly made visible there. Thus, like-named predicates in different modules do not conflict.

A.9.2. Example of a Module

Some Prolog vendors have had module systems for several years, but as this is written, the proposed ISO system has not fully taken shape. What follows is a sketch of the proposal made in the August 1995 working draft (WG17 N142, Hodgson 1995).

In the proposed system, there are, by default, two modules, `system` (for built-in predicates) and `user` (for user-defined predicates). The predicates in `system` are visible in `user` and in all other modules.

The user can create more modules ad libitum; Figure A.1 shows an example. The module consists of two parts: an INTERFACE, specifying what is to be made callable from other modules, and a BODY, giving the actual predicate definitions.

This module is named `my_list_stuff` and, crucially, `last/2` and `reverse/2` are callable from other modules but `reverse_aux/3` is not. Thus, `reverse_aux` will not conflict with anything that happens to have the same name elsewhere.

To use a predicate in one module which is defined in another, the defining module must EXPORT it and the calling module must IMPORT it. Thus, any module that wants to call `reverse` (as defined here) must import `my_list_stuff`.

Note that importing a module is not the same thing as loading it into memory (using `compile`, `consult`, or the like). In order to have access to a module, you must do both.

A.9.3. Module Syntax

Basically, exporting is done in the module interface, while defining and importing are done in the module body. The syntax is:

```
:- module( name , export-list , metapredicate-list , accessible-list ).
```
Some `import`, `metapredicate`, and other directives
The predicates themselves
```
:- end_module( name ).
```

The four arguments of `module` are:

- The name of the module.

```
:- module(my_list_stuff,[last/2,reverse/2],[],all).

:- begin_module(my_list_stuff).

last([E],E).
last([_|E],Last) :- last(E,Last).

reverse(List1,List2) :- reverse_aux(List1,[],List2).

reverse_aux([H|T],Stack,Result) :-  reverse_aux(T,[H|Stack],Result).
reverse_aux([],Result,Result).

:- end_module(my_list_stuff).
```

Figure A.1 Example of a module.

- A list of ordinary predicates to be EXPORTED (made callable from other modules that import this one).

- A list of metapredicates to be exported (we'll return to this point shortly).

- A list of predicates to be made ACCESSIBLE from other modules (i.e., callable only by prefixing the name of this module and a colon to their names).

If you write **module_part** instead of **module**, you can give just part of the definition of a module; later you can add to it with another **module_part** with the same module name.

In a module, **op** and **dynamic** work the same way as if you aren't using the module system, except that they have scope only over one module. The other declarations work as follows:

```
:- import(Module).
```
   All the predicates that are exported by **Module** are to be imported into (and hence usable in) the current module. (Used in module body.)

```
:- import(Module,[Pred/Arity,Pred/Arity...]).
```
   Same, but only the specified predicates are imported.

```
:- metapredicate(Functor(Mode1,Mode2,Mode3...)).
```
   The specified predicate is declared to be a METAPREDICATE (see next section).

A.9.4. Metapredicates

A METAPREDICATE is a predicate that needs to know what module it is called from. Examples include **abolish**, **asserta**, **assertz**, **clause**, **current_predicate**, and **retract**, all of which manipulate the predicates in the module that they are called from (not the module they are defined in); and **bagof**, **setof**, **findall**, **catch**, **call**, and once, all of which take goals as arguments and need to be able to execute them in the module they are called from.

A metapredicate declaration looks like this:

```
:- metapredicate(xyz(+,?,-,:)).
```

That is: xyz has four arguments. The first will always be instantiated, the second may or may not be instantiated, the third will always be uninstantiated, and the fourth needs the calling module's name prefixed to it when it is called. Thus, if module mymod calls predicate xyz, the fourth argument of xyz will arrive with mymod: prefixed to it. Recall that : is an infix operator.

A.9.5. Explicit Module Qualifiers

If, instead of Goal, you write Module:Goal, you gain the ability to call any ACCESSIBLE predicate of Module, whether or not that module has exported it or the current module has imported it. In the example in Figure A.1, the query

```
?- my_list_stuff:reverse_aux([a,b,c],X,Y).
```

would work from any module, even though reverse_aux is not exported by the module that defines it.

A.9.6. Additional Built-In Predicates

calling_context(Module)
> Unifies Module with the name of the module from which this predicate was called. Used in metapredicates.

current_module(Module)
> Succeeds if its argument is the name of any currently existing module. Arguments need not be instantiated.

current_visible(Module,Pred/Arity)
> Succeeds if Pred/Arity describes a predicate that is defined in Module and is visible (callable) from the module in which this query is taking place. Arguments need not be instantiated.

current_accessible(Module,Pred/Arity)
> Same as current_visible except that it picks up predicates that are accessible but not exported, i.e., predicates that can only be called by prefixing them with the module name and a colon.

abolish_module(Module)
> Like abolish but unloads a complete module in a single step.

A.9.7. A Word of Caution

The module system is not yet part of the official ISO standard. Substantial changes are still quite possible.

Appendix B

Some Differences Between Prolog Implementations

B.1. INTRODUCTION

In this appendix, we briefly note some differences between implementations that affect portability of Prolog programs. We make no attempt to be complete; all we want to do is alert you to some sources of difficulty that you might otherwise overlook.[1]

We deal only with implementations that are, at least at first sight, compatible with Edinburgh Prolog. There are many other Prolog-like languages (some of them even called "Prolog") that are outside our purview.

All the discrepancies noted here will diminish or disappear as implementors adopt the emerging ISO standard.

Much of the information in this appendix is based on tests performed with ALS Prolog 1.2, Arity Prolog versions 4.0 and 6.1.9, Cogent Prolog 2.0, LPA Prolog 3.1, and Expert Systems Ltd. (ESL) Public Domain Prolog-2 version 2.35 (all for MS-DOS); LPA Prolog 2.3 for Windows (considerably newer than 3.1 for DOS); and Quintus Prolog 2.5.1 and 3.1.4 and SWI Prolog 1.6.14 (for UNIX). These are intended only as samples, to give you some idea of the diversity that exists. We deliberately chose older versions of these products, rather than the latest, because the oldest versions are the least compatible with each other.[2]

---

[1] We thank Fergus Henderson for his comments on a draft of this appendix.

[2] Dennis Merritt advises us that the data on Cogent Prolog here also apply to later versions of Amzi Prolog.

B.2. WHICH PREDICATES ARE BUILT-IN?

B.2.1. Failure as the Symptom

Notoriously, in most implementations, Prolog queries simply fail if they involve a call to a nonexistent predicate, or a predicate with an argument of the wrong type. Quintus Prolog complains about nonexistent predicates, but most other Prologs do not.

Normally, then, you will attack portability problems by using the debugger to find out which query is failing that ought to be succeeding. When porting a program, be sure to test it thoroughly so that all the calls to built-in predicates are exercised.

B.2.2. Minimum Set of Built-In Predicates

The built-in predicates that are available in almost every Prolog include: `<`, `=`, `==`, `\==`, `<=`, `>=`, `=..`, `\+` (written not in older Prologs), `arg`, `asserta`, `assertz`, `atom`, `atomic`, `call`, `clause`, `display`, `fail`, `functor`, `get0`, `get`, `integer`, `is`, `listing`, `name`, `nl`, `nonvar`, `op`, `put`, `read`, `repeat`, `retract`, `see`, `seeing`, `seen`, `tell`, `telling`, `told`, `true`, `var`, `write`. These are the built-in predicates of Clocksin and Mellish (1984) minus some predicates that we have found to be poorly standardized (e.g., Quintus Prolog lacks `\=`). Any built-in predicate not on this list is likely to be missing from some implementation somewhere.

B.2.3. The Quintus Library

Besides its built-in predicates, Quintus Prolog has a large library of predicates that can be loaded as needed. See the manual or type "`?- help(library).`" for details. For example, here is how to compute a square root (in versions that do not yet have the ISO standard `sqrt()` evaluable functor):

```
:- ensure_loaded(library(math)).

test :- sqrt(2,What),
        write(What), nl.
```

Many of the library predicates are worth studying as examples of good (and sometimes remarkably creative) Prolog code.

B.3. VARIATION IN BEHAVIOR OF BUILT-IN PREDICATES

B.3.1. `abolish` **and** `retractall`

To retract all the clauses of `f/2`, use `abolish(f/2)` in Arity, LPA, ESL, Quintus, and the ISO standard, but `abolish(f,2)` in ALS and SWI, and either one in Cogent Prolog.

Note that `retractall` is not part of the ISO standard and is not supported by Arity or ALS. Further, `abolish` and `retractall` are not equivalent: `abolish` wipes out all memory of a predicate (including its dynamic declaration if any), while `retractall` merely removes all the clauses.

B.3.2. `name`: Numeric Arguments

The first argument of `name` can be a number, as in `name(2.5,"2.5")`, in Arity, LPA, and Quintus Prolog, but not in Cogent, ALS, or ESL (which give `name('2.5',"2.5")`). In SWI-Prolog, the first argument can be an integer but not a floating-point number. The ISO standard does not include `name`.

B.3.3. `functor`: Numeric Arguments

The behavior of `functor/3` differs among implementations in the following way: the first two arguments can be a number, as in `functor(2.3,2.3,0)`, in Arity, LPA, Quintus, and ISO Prolog, but not in Cogent, ALS, ESL, or SWI Prolog.

B.3.4. `op`, Operators, and `current_op`

Most Prologs today use the operator priorities specified by the ISO standard (e.g., ':-' is 1200), but older Prologs used a different set in which the highest priority was 256. Before declaring operators, check the actual priorities of the operators in the implementation that you are using.

Not all Prologs support `current_op` (ALS and Cogent don't), and in those that have it, its behavior is not well standardized (for example, in ESL Prolog-2, it retrieves not only the operators, but also all the other atoms in the symbol table, giving them priority 0).

The ISO standard says that there cannot be an infix operator and a postfix operator with the same name — so that the Prolog reader will not have to backtrack — but not all Prologs enforce this restriction.

B.3.5. `findall`, `setof`, and `bagof`

We found some variation in the semantics of `findall`, `setof`, and `bagof`. Specifically:

- `findall` is not implemented in ALS Prolog or ESL Prolog-2.

- ALS Prolog 1.2 crashes (!) if the goal argument of `bagof` or `setof` contains a cut. In the other Prologs, cuts in this position are permitted and `bagof` and `setof` are opaque to cuts.

- In Cogent Prolog and older versions of LPA Prolog, if you use ^ to indicate a free variable in the goal, the left-hand argument of ^ must be the variable itself. The other Prologs accept any term there and recognize as free all of the variables that occur in it.

B.3.6. `listing`

In many Prologs, `listing` (with no arguments) dumps more information than just the knowledge base loaded from your program. For example, in Quintus Prolog, it also dumps some facts about file paths, and in ESL Prolog-2, it dumps a number of built-in predicates.

B.4. CONTROL CONSTRUCTS

B.4.1. Negation

The negation operator is written `not` in earlier Prologs, but `\+` in virtually all Prologs today, including the ISO standard.

B.4.2. Scope of Cuts

Cuts in the following environments are problematic:

- The argument of `\+` (`not`, `fail_if`);

- A goal that is an argument of `call`, `findall`, `setof`, or `bagof`;

- A variable goal not written with `call`;

- The left-hand argument of `->`;

- Goals that are separated by `;` (disjunction).

The question is whether the cut is allowed at all, and if so, whether its effect extends to the whole clause or just the specified environment.

The ISO standard says that cuts are allowed in all these places, and that each of these environments except disjunction is OPAQUE TO CUTS (i.e., the effect of a cut is confined to the environment). Disjunction is TRANSPARENT TO CUTS (just like conjunction).

Actual usage varies widely; here's what we found:

- Negation is opaque to cuts in ALS, Cogent, and LPA, but transparent in Arity, ESL, and SWI. Quintus Prolog does not allow cuts within a negation.

- `call` is transparent to cuts in ALS and opaque in all the others that we tried.

- `findall`, `setof`, and `bagof` are opaque to cuts (but see Section B.3.5 above).

- Variable goals written without `call` are transparent to cuts in ALS, LPA, and Cogent Prolog and opaque in the others.

- The left-hand argument of `->` is opaque to cuts in ALS, LPA, and Cogent, and transparent in the others; Quintus Prolog does not allow cuts there at all.

- Disjunction is transparent to cuts in all the Prologs that we tried (thank goodness), but O'Keefe (1990:277) indicates that there may be Prologs in which it is not.

B.4.3. If-Then-Else

The "if-then-else" construct (`Goal1 -> Goal2 ; Goal3`) is completely absent from Arity Prolog through version 6, which uses `ifthenelse(Goal1,Goal2,Goal3)` instead (and likewise `ifthen(Goal1,Goal2)` in place of `Goal1 -> Goal2`).

Among Prologs that have "if-then-else," there is considerable variation in semantics. The main differences are in the effect of cuts (see previous subsection) and whether the whole structure fails if all the goals in it fail. Rather surprisingly, in Arity Prolog, `ifthen(fail,fail)` succeeds (although `ifthenelse(fail,fail,fail)` fails), and in ESL Prolog-2, `fail -> fail` succeeds (although `fail -> fail ; fail` fails). In all the other examples that we tried, if-then-else structures composed entirely of failing goals will fail (as the ISO standard says they should).

B.4.4. Tail Recursion and Backtrack Points

In almost all Prologs, the following predicates are tail recursive because of the cut and because of first-argument indexing respectively (along with appropriate garbage collection):

```
test1 :- write('I run forever'), !, test1.
test1 :- write('This clause never executes').

test2(1) :- write('I run forever'), test2(1).
test2(0) :- write('This clause never executes').
```

However, *the ISO standard says nothing about tail recursion* (nor indexing nor any other memory management issue), and, indeed, in our tests, neither of these examples was tail recursive in ESL Public Domain Prolog-2 (which admittedly was designed for free distribution to students and made no pretensions to be an optimizing implementation).

In several implementations that include both an interpreter and a compiler, the compiler performs more thorough tail-recursion optimization than does the interpreter.

B.4.5. Alternatives Created by Asserting

Suppose a query, in the process of being executed, asserts a new clause for itself, or for one of its subgoals. Does this create a new alternative solution for the query?

In almost all Prologs, no, because the set of clauses that will be searched is determined at the beginning of the execution of the query. But a few Prologs (notably LPA) do consider the new clause to be a genuine alternative for the query that is already in progress.

The predicate `count/1` in Chapter 3 illustrated this problem.

B.5. SYNTAX AND PROGRAM LAYOUT

B.5.1. Syntax Selection

Expert Systems Ltd. (ESL) Public Domain Prolog-2 version 2.35, widely used by students, requires the directive

```
:- state(token_class,_,dec10).
```

at the beginning of the program in order to select DEC-10-compatible syntax. Otherwise the syntax is slightly different: % does not introduce comments, and strings delimited by double quotes (`"like this"`) are not equivalent to lists of codes.

Because ESL is no longer in business, updates are not immediately forthcoming, but the implementor (Tony Dodd) hopes to be able to release updates later.

B.5.2. Comments

Some early Prologs did not recognize % as a comment delimiter, but we know of no present-day implementations with this limitation.

Some Prologs allow nesting of /*...*/ comments, but most do not. SWI and ALS Prolog allow nesting and take /* /* */ */ to be a valid comment with another comment inside it. But in the other Prologs that we tried, and in the ISO standard, the comment begins with the first /* and ends with the first */, regardless of what has intervened. This means you cannot use /* */ to comment out any Prolog code that has comments delimited with /* */ within it.

B.5.3. Whitespace

Arity Prolog 4.0 does not allow an operator to appear immediately before a left parenthesis; if it does, it loses its operator status. For example, if you write 2+(3-4), Arity Prolog will think the first + is an ordinary functor with the left parenthesis introducing its argument list, and will report a syntax error; you should write 2 + (3 + 4) instead.

As far as we know, no Prolog allows whitespace between an ordinary functor and its argument list; f(a) cannot be written f (a).

The ISO standard and all the Prologs that we have tested allow whitespace to appear within an empty list (e.g., [ ] in place of []), but discussions on Usenet indicate that there may be Prologs that do not do so.

B.5.4. Backslashes

The ISO standard gives backslashes a special meaning, so that if you want backslashes in file names (e.g., `'c:\prolog\myfile'`) you have to write them double (`'c:\\prolog\\myfile'`). The Prologs that we have worked with, however, treat backslashes as ordinary characters.

B.5.5. Directives

Quintus Prolog and the ISO standard require `dynamic` and `multifile` declarations (see Chapter 2). SWI Prolog requires `multifile` and accepts `dynamic` but does not require it. Other Prologs reject these declarations as syntax errors.

In Quintus and SWI Prolog, `dynamic` and `multifile` are prefix operators, so that you can write

```
:- dynamic mypred/2.
```

But the ISO standard does not specify this; instead, ISO Prolog will require (and Quintus and SWI already accept) ordinary functor notation:

```
:- dynamic(mypred/2).
```

B.5.6. `consult` and `reconsult`

The behavior of `consult` and `reconsult` varies quite a bit between implementations, and these predicates are not included in the ISO standard; the method for loading a program is left up to the implementor. We have not attempted to track down all the variation.

In older Prologs, `consult`ing a file twice will result in two copies of it in memory, while `reconsult`ing will throw away the previous copy when loading the new one. In Quintus Prolog, however, `consult` is equivalent to `reconsult`, and `compile` causes the program to be compiled rather than interpreted.

B.5.7. Embedded Queries

All the Prologs that we tried allow you to put arbitrary queries into the program file at any point by preceding them with ':-'. (All but Arity allow ?- as an alternative.) The ISO standard does not require implementations to permit this.

Some Prologs `consult` by redirecting standard input to the program file. This means that a query embedded in the program cannot perform keyboard input. Thus it is a bad idea to start an interactive program by executing an embedded query at the end.

B.6. ARITHMETIC

B.6.1. Evaluable Functors

The set of functors that can appear in expressions is subject to great variation. The original set from Clocksin and Mellish (1984) comprises only +, -, *, /, and `mod` (modulo; an infix operator).

Quintus Prolog adds // (integer division), prefix - (for sign reversal), `integer()` and `float()` (for type conversion), and some operations on the individual bits of integers.

Other Prologs, including the ISO standard, have added other functions such as `sqrt()` and `sin()`.

B.6.2. Where Expressions are Evaluated

In Clocksin and Mellish (1984), <, =<, >, and >= do not evaluate arithmetic expressions. In all the Prologs that we tried, they do (and =:= tests for arithmetic equality), but you have been forewarned.

B.6.3. Expressions Created at Runtime in Quintus Prolog

Quintus-Prolog compiles arithmetic queries into efficient machine code where possible. This led to an unusual quirk in earlier versions:

```
?- X = 2+3, Y is X.
[ERROR: invalid arithmetic expression: 2+3 (error 302)]
```

But the query should succeed, because Y is X = Y is 2+3, and indeed it does in Quintus Prolog 3.1.

The problem in Quintus Prolog 2.5 was that before looking at the instantiation of X, the-Prolog-system has already converted Y is X into an operation that simply copies a number. What you had to do instead is this:

```
?- X = 2+3, call(Y is X).
X = 2+3
Y = 5
```

That way, the Prolog system does not try to do anything with is until the entire argument of call has been constructed.

B.7. INPUT AND OUTPUT

B.7.1. Keyboard Buffering

It is up to the implementor whether keyboard input is buffered, i.e., whether keystrokes are available for reading immediately, or only after the user presses Return. Keyboard input is buffered in all the Prologs that we tried except Arity Prolog.

B.7.2. Flushing Output

In Quintus Prolog, output that is sent to the screen does not actually appear there until a complete line has been sent, or input is requested from the keyboard, or ttyflush/0 is executed.

For example, if you want to write a row of dots (.........) to the screen, with each dot indicating a successful step in a long computation, then you must ttyflush after writing each dot so that the operating system will go ahead and send it to the user. Otherwise the user will get the whole row of dots all at once at the end of the process.

```
% Quintus Prolog

test :- open('myfile1.txt',read,File1),
        read(File1,Term),
        close(File1),

        open('myfile2.txt',write,File2),
        write(File2,Term),
        close(File2).


% Arity Prolog

test :- open(File1,'myfile1.txt',r),
        read(File1,Term),
        close(File1),

        create(File2,'myfile2.txt'),
        write(File2,Term),
        close(File2).
```

Figure B.1   Examples of file input and output.

B.7.3. get and get0

In most Prologs, get and get0 return −1 at end of file. In Arity Prolog, they simply fail at end of file.

In most Prologs, get0 reads every byte of the input file. In ALS Prolog, get0 skips all bytes that contain code 0, and converts the sequence 13, 10 (Return, Linefeed) to simply 10. See the discussion of get_byte in Chapter 5.

B.7.4. File Handling

As an alternative to see, seen, tell, and told, most if not all Prologs let you access files without redirecting standard input and output. However, the method for doing this is entirely up to the implementor. Figure B.1 shows examples in Quintus Prolog and Arity Prolog. Note that the concepts are the same but the syntax is different. See your manual for further guidance.

B.7.5. Formatted Output

Quintus Prolog and SWI Prolog offer a powerful format predicate that is similar to the printf statement in C:

```
?- format('The answers are ~D, ~4f, ~s.',[1234567,1.3,"abc"]).
The answers are 1,234,567, 1.3000, abc.
```

TABLE B.1   SOME `format` SPECIFIERS IN QUINTUS PROLOG.

~a Print an atom (without quotes).

~nc Print an integer by taking it as an ASCII code and printing the corresponding character n times. If omitted, $n = 1$.

~ne Print a floating-point number in E format with n digits after the point (e.g., 125.6 = 1.256000e+02). If omitted, $n = 6$.

~nE Same, with capital E (1.25600E+02).

~nf Print a floating-point number in ordinary format with n digits after the point (e.g., 125.600000). If omitted, $n = 6$. If $n = 0$, no point is printed.

~ng Print a floating-point number in either E format or ordinary format, as appropriate, with at most n significant digits. If omitted, $n = 6$.

~nG Same, but if E format is chosen, capital E is used.

~nd Print an integer as if it were floating-point by shifting it to the right n decimal places. For example, ~2d prints 1234 as 12.34. If n is omitted, the integer is printed as an integer in the ordinary manner.

~nD Same as ~nd, but commas are used to separate groups of three digits to the left of the point. For example, ~2D prints 12345678 as 123,456.78.

~i Ignore an argument in the list.

~nr Print an integer in base n (for example, ~16r prints an integer in hex). If omitted, $n = 8$.

~nR Same, but uses capital A, B, C... for digits greater than 9.

~ns Print an (Edinburgh-style) string as a series of characters. Only the first n characters are printed. If n is omitted, the whole string is printed.
NOTE: `format('~s',["abcde"])` is correct; `format('~s',"abcde")` is incorrect syntax (because `"abcde"` is a list of integers and is taken to be the whole list of arguments to be printed).

Here n stands for any integer and is optional. If you write * in place of n, the next element in the list of values will be used as n. See the manual for further details.

The first argument is either an atom or a string; the second argument is a list of values to be printed. Table B.1 lists some of the format specifiers that you can use in Quintus Prolog 2.5.1.

B.8. DEFINITE-CLAUSE GRAMMARS

B.8.1. Terminal Symbols

Traditionally, a rule that introduces a terminal symbol, such as

```
noun --> [dog].
```

is translated as `noun([dog|X],X)`. However, this raises a problem if there is something in the rule with a side effect, such as a cut:

```
noun --> !, [dog].
```

As written, this rule should perform the cut before looking for dog, but its usual translation is

```
noun([dog|X],X) :- !.
```

which does these two things in the wrong order.

Of the Prologs that we tried, only Arity and Cogent make no attempt to solve this problem. The translations of noun --> !, [dog] in the other Prologs are:

```
noun(X,Y) :- !, 'C'(dog,X,Y).        (Quintus, ESL, newer LPA)
noun(X,Y) :- !, '$C'(dog,X,Y).       (older LPA)
noun(X,Y) :- !, '$char'(dog,X,Y).    (SWI)
noun(X,Y) :- !, X = [dog|Y].         (ALS)
```

The ALS solution is the most elegant. The others rely on a built-in predicate 'C'/3 or equivalent, defined as:

```
'C'([X|Y],X,Y).
```

Quintus uses 'C' to deal with all terminal symbols, but SWI uses '$char' only where the rule introduces both terminal symbols and nonterminals or Prolog goals.

B.8.2. Commas on the Left

In the Quintus implementation of DCG, the rule

```
verbaux, [not] --> [hasnt].
```

means "Parse *hasnt* as a *verbaux*, and put *not* at the beginning of the input string," and translates to:

```
verbaux(A,B) :- 'C'(A,hasnt,B), 'C'(B,not,C).
```

Of the Prologs we tried, only Quintus, SWI, and the freeware DCG translator written by R. A. O'Keefe handled this rule correctly.

B.8.3. phrase

To parse a sentence in Clocksin and Mellish (1984) Prolog, you'd use a query like this:

```
?- phrase(s,[the,dog,barks],[]).
```

Nowadays the preferred form is:

```
?- s([the,dog,barks],[]).
```

Of the Prologs that we tested, only Quintus and LPA still support phrase.

Bibliography

Abelson, H., and Sussman, G. J. (1985) *Structure and interpretation of computer programs.* Cambridge, Massachusetts: MIT Press.

Abramowitz, M., and Stegun, I. A. (1964) *Handbook of mathematical functions with formulas, graphs, and mathematical tables.* (National Bureau of Standards Applied Mathematics Series, 55.) Washington: U.S. Government Printing Office.

Adams, J. B. (1976) A probability model of medical reasoning and the MYCIN model. *Mathematical Biosciences* 32:177–186.

Aikins, J. S.; Kunz, J. C.; and Shortliffe, E. H. (1983) PUFF: an expert system for interpretation of pulmonary function data. *Computers and Biomedical Research* 16:199–208.

Aït-Kaci, H. (1991) *Warren's abstract machine: a tutorial reconstruction.* Cambridge, Massachusetts: MIT Press.

Allen, J. F. (1987) *Natural language understanding.* Menlo Park, California: Benjamin-Cummings.

Boizumault, P. (1993) *The implementation of Prolog.* Princeton, New Jersey: Princeton University Press.

Bol, R. H. (1991) An analysis of loop checking mechanisms for logic programs. *Theoretical computer science* 86:35–79.

Bowen, K. A. (1991) *Prolog and expert systems.* New York: McGraw-Hill.

Buchanan, B. G. (1986) Expert systems: working systems and the research literature. *Expert Systems* 3.32–51.

Campbell, J. A., ed. (1984) *Implementations of Prolog.* Chichester: Ellis Horwood.

Charniak, E., and McDermott, D. (1985) *Introduction to artificial intelligence.* Reading, Massachusetts: Addison-Wesley.

Chomsky, N. (1957) *Syntactic structures.* The Hague: Mouton.

Clocksin, W. F., and Mellish, C. S. (1984) *Programming in Prolog.* 2nd edition. Berlin: Springer-Verlag.

Covington, M. A. (1989) A numerical equation solver in Prolog. *Computer Language* 6.10 (October), 45–51.

Covington, M. A. (1994) *Natural language processing for Prolog programmers.* Englewood Cliffs, New Jersey: Prentice-Hall.

Dahl, V., and Saint-Dizier, P., eds. (1985) *Natural language understanding and Prolog programming.* Amsterdam: North-Holland.

Dahl, V., and Saint-Dizier, P., eds. (1988) *Natural language understanding and Prolog programming, II.* Amsterdam: North-Holland.

Dahl, V., and McCord, M. C. (1983) Treating coordination in logic grammars. *American Journal of Computational Linguistics* 9:69–91.

Duda, R.; Hart, P. E.; Nilsson, N. J.; Barrett, P.; Gaschnig, J. G.; Konolige, K.; Reboh, R.; and Slocum, J. (1978) Development of the PROSPECTOR consultation system for mineral exploration. Research report, Stanford Research Institute.

Fromkin, V., and Rodman, R. (1993) *An introduction to language.* 5th edition. Ft. Worth, Texas: Harcourt Brace Jovanovich.

Gabbay, D.; Hogger, C.; and Robinson, A., eds. (1994) *Handbook of logic for artificial intelligence and logic programming,* vol. 3. Oxford: Oxford University Press.

Ginsberg, M. L. (1987) *Readings in nonmonotonic reasoning.* Los Altos, California: Morgan Kaufmann.

Grishman, R. (1986) *Computational linguistics: an introduction.* Cambridge: Cambridge University Press.

Grosz, B. J.; Sparck Jones, K.; and Webber, B. L., eds. (1986) *Readings in natural language processing.* Los Altos, California: Morgan Kaufmann.

Hamming, R. W. (1971) *Introduction to applied numerical analysis.* New York: McGraw-Hill.

Hanks, S., and McDermott, D. (1987) Nonmonotonic logic and temporal projection. *Artificial intelligence* 33:379–412.

Hoare, C. A. R. (1962) Quicksort. *Computer Journal* 5:10–15.

Hodgson, J. P. E., ed. (1995) *Prolog: part 2, modules — working draft 8.1.* (ISO/IEC JTC1 SC22 WG17 N142.) Teddington, England: National Physical Laboratory (for ISO).

Hogger, C. J. (1984) *Introduction to logic programming.* London: Academic Press.

Jackson, P. (1986) *Introduction to expert systems.* Reading, Massachusetts: Addison-Wesley.

Kain, Richard Y. (1989) *Computer architecture,* vol. 1. Englewood Cliffs, New Jersey: Prentice-Hall.

Karickhoff, S. W.; Carreira, L. A.; Vellino, A. N.; Nute, D. E.; and McDaniel, V. K. (1991) Predicting chemical reactivity by computer. *Environmental Toxicology and Chemistry* 10:1405–1416.

Kluzniak, F., and Szpakowicz, S. (1985) *Prolog for programmers.* London: Academic Press.

Knuth, D. E. (1973) *The art of computer programming,* vol. 3: *Sorting and searching.* Reading, Massachusetts: Addison-Wesley.

Lindsay, R. K.; Buchanan, B. G.; Feigenbaum, E. A.; and Lederberg, J. (1980) *Applications of artificial intelligence for organic chemistry: the DENDRAL project.* New York: McGraw-Hill.

Luger, G. F. (1989) *Artificial intelligence and the design of expert systems.* Redwood City, California: Benjamin-Cummings.

Maier, D., and Warren, D. S. (1988) *Computing with logic: logic programming with Prolog.* Menlo Park, California: Benjamin-Cummings.

Mamdani, E. H., and Gaines, B. R., eds. (1981) *Fuzzy reasoning and its applications.* London: Academic Press.

Marcus, C. (1986) *Prolog programming.* Reading, Massachusetts: Addison-Wesley.

Matsumoto, Y.; Tanaka, H.; and Kiyono, M. (1986) BUP: a bottom-up parsing system for natural languages. In van Caneghem and Warren (1986), 262–275.

McCarthy, J., and Hayes, P. J. (1969) Some philosophical problems from the standpoint of artificial intelligence. In B. Meltzer and D. Michie, eds., *Machine intelligence 4,* 463–502. New York: American Elsevier.

McDermott, D. (1982) A temporal logic for reasoning about processes and plans. *Cognitive Science* 6:101–155.

McDermott, D. (1987) We've been framed: or why AI is innocent of the frame problem. In Z. Pylyshyn, ed., *The robot's dilemma: the frame problem in artificial intelligence,* 113–122. Norwood, New Jersey: Ablex.

Merritt, D. (1989) *Building expert systems in Prolog.* New York: Springer-Verlag.

Newmeyer, F. J. (1983) *Grammatical theory: its limits and its possibilities.* Chicago: University of Chicago Press.

Newmeyer, F. J. (1986) *Linguistic theory in America.* 2nd edition. Orlando: Academic Press.

Nute, D. (1992) Basic defeasible logic. In L. Fariñas del Cerro and M. Penttonen, eds., *Intensional logics for programming,* 125–154. Oxford: Oxford University Press.

Nute, D. (1994) A decidable quantified defeasible logic. In D. Prawitz, B. Skyrms, and D. Westerstahl, eds., *Logic, methodology and philosophy of science IX,* 263–284. New York: Elsevier.

O'Connor, D. E. (1984) Using expert systems to manage change and complexity in manufacturing. In W. Reitman, ed., *Artificial intelligence applications for business: proceedings of the NPU Symposium, May, 1983,* 149–157. Norwood, New Jersey: Ablex.

O'Keefe, R. A. (1990) *The craft of Prolog.* Cambridge, Massachusetts: MIT Press.

Parkinson, R. C.; Colby, K. M.; and Faught, W. S. (1977) Conversational language comprehension using integrated pattern-matching and parsing. *Artificial Intelligence* 9:111–134. Reprinted in Grosz et al. (1986), 551–562.

Patil, R. S.; Szolovits, P.; and Schwartz, W. B. (1981) Modeling knowledge of the patient in acid-base and electrolyte disorders. In P. Szolovits, ed., *Artificial intelligence in medicine,* 191–226. (AAAS Selected Symposium 51.) Boulder, Colorado: Westview Press.

Pereira, F. C. N. (1981) Extraposition grammars. *American Journal of Computational Linguistics* 7:243–256.

Pereira, F. C. N., and Shieber, S. M. (1987) *Prolog and natural-language analysis.* (CSLI Lecture Notes, 10.) Stanford: Center for the Study of Language and Information (distributed by University of Chicago Press).

Pereira, F. C. N., and Warren, D. H. D. (1980) Definite clause grammars for language analysis — a survey of the formalism and a comparison with augmented transition networks. *Artificial Intelligence* 13:231–278. Reprinted in Grosz et al. (1986), 101–124.

Press, W. H.; Flannery, B. P.; Teukolsky, S. A.; and Vetterling, W. T. (1986) *Numerical recipes: the art of scientific computing.* Cambridge: Cambridge University Press.

Richer, M. H. (1986) An evaluation of expert system development tools. *Expert Systems* 3:167–183.

Scowen, R., ed. (1995) *Prolog — part 1, general core.* (ISO/IEC 13211-1:1995.) Geneva: International Organization for Standardization (ISO).

Sells, P. (1985) *Lectures on contemporary grammatical theories.* (CSLI Lecture Notes, 3.) Stanford: Center for the Study of Language and Information (distributed by University of Chicago Press).

Shieber, S. M. (1986) *An introduction to unification-based approaches to grammar.* (CSLI Lecture Notes, 4.) Stanford: Center for the Study of Language and Information (distributed by University of Chicago Press).

Shoham, Y. (1994) *Artificial intelligence techniques in Prolog.* San Francisco: Morgan Kaufmann.

Shortliffe, E. H. (1976) *Computer-based medical consultation: MYCIN.* New York: Elsevier.

Slocum, J. (1985) A survey of machine translation: its history, current status, and future prospects. *Computational Linguistics* 11:1–17.

Smith, D. E.; Genesereth, M. R.; and Ginsberg, M. L. (1986) Controlling recursive inference. *Artificial Intelligence* 30:343–389.

Steele, G. L. (1978) *RABBIT: a compiler for SCHEME*. Artificial Intelligence Technical Report 474, Massachusetts Institute of Technology.

Sterling, L., and Shapiro, E. (1994) *The art of Prolog*. 2nd edition. Cambridge, Massachusetts: MIT Press.

van Caneghem, M., and Warren, D. H. D., eds. (1986) *Logic programming and its applications*. Norwood, New Jersey: Ablex.

Walden, J. (1986) *File formats for popular PC software: a programmer's reference*. New York: Wiley.

Warren, D. H. D. (1986) Optimizing tail recursion in Prolog. In van Caneghem and Warren (1986), 77–90.

Warren, D. H. D., and Pereira, F. C. N. (1982) An efficient easily adaptable system for interpreting natural language queries. *American Journal of Computational Linguistics* 8:110–122.

Wirth, N. (1986) *Algorithms and data structures*. Englewood Cliffs, New Jersey: Prentice-Hall.

Index